D1465824

The Oxford & Cambridge Boat Race

By the same author

Henley Royal Regatta
Boating

THE
OXFORD & CAMBRIDGE
BOAT RACE

Christopher Dodd

STANLEY PAUL
London Melbourne Sydney Auckland Johannesburg

Stanley Paul & Co. Ltd

An imprint of the Hutchinson Publishing Group

17–21 Conway Street, London W1P 6JD

Hutchinson Group (Australia) Pty Ltd
30–32 Cremorne Street, Richmond South, Victoria 3121
PO Box 151, Broadway, New South Wales 2007

Hutchinson Group (NZ) Ltd
32–34 View Road, PO Box 40-086, Glenfield, Auckland 10

Hutchinson Group (SA) Pty Ltd
PO Box 337, Bergvlei 2012, South Africa

First published 1983
© Christopher Dodd 1983

Set in Linotron Sabon by
Rowland Phototypesetting Ltd
Bury St Edmunds, Suffolk

Printed in Great Britain by The Anchor Press Ltd
and bound by Wm Brendon & Son Ltd,
both of Tiptree, Essex

British Library Cataloguing in Publication Data
Dodd, Christopher
The Oxford and Cambridge boat race.
1. Oxford and Cambridge Boat Race – History
I. Title
797.1'4   GV799

ISBN 0 09 151340 5

Photographic acknowledgements

For permission to use photographs reproduced in this
book, the author and publisher would like to thank All
Sport, Martin Argles, the BBC, the British Museum, the
British Tourist Authority, *Cambridge Evening News*,
Central Press Photos, Athar Chaudhry, Fleet Fotos,
Fox, Goldie Boat Club, the *Guardian*, Tommy Hindley,
Hulton Picture Library, Tom Jedrej, Jesus College, Cam-
bridge, Keystone, Eamonn McCabe, Percy Macquoid,
Don Morley, *Le Figaro*, *Illustrated London News*, the
Observer, the *Oxford Mail*, the *Radio Times*, Kenneth
Saunders, Sport and General, John Swaebe, Garry
Weaser and E. Hamilton West.

Contents

Preface

Since 1829 the rowing blues have scripted and acted out the Boat Race. They are an exclusive group engaged in a perpetual private match which comes to public exhibition once a year, and it is to them, the light and dark blues, that this book is dedicated. It is a celebration of their efforts to give the sport of rowing its most popular annual showing.

If at the end of it readers feel that one shade of blue has received more attention than the other, I make no apology. I was fortunate to attend neither of the universities engaged in the aquatic Battle of the Blues, so I declare no-interest. My intention was to relate the history of the Boat Race by telling its best stories. If more of them turn out to be of one colour than the other, so be it. However, the details of selection, preparation and practice, fitness and psychology entailed in producing a crew to get from Putney to Mortlake in the shortest possible time apply equally to Oxford and Cambridge, and so in most cases both places can draw on the morals of the tales. The book, then, is selective of incidents, dates and people, but they are chosen to contribute to an overall picture of the Boat Race. Surprisingly, perhaps, there are few absolutes in this kind of history. They are outweighed by a multiplicity of viewpoints, and I have tried to be fair to these.

I am particularly grateful to the coaches and crews from both Oxford and Cambridge for 1981–82. Both presidents, Roger Stephens (Cambridge) and Nick Conington (Oxford), allowed me to keep much closer to their crews than is customary for correspondents. Both of them trusted me with information before their race which they would normally withhold. Their crews put up cheerfully with my invasions of their privacy, and their chief coaches, Graeme Hall (Cambridge) and

Daniel Topolski (Oxford), cooperated to an equal degree, giving me access to classified information before the race and amplifying and clarifying afterwards. Thanks, then, to both crews for their tolerance and for making such a fine build-up to a Boat Race.

There are several people closely involved with one or other club to whom I owe special thanks. They have gone to great lengths to find information and pictures, to verify queries and check facts. In the Cambridge camp are Douglas Calder, Alec Clark-Kennedy, James Crowden, David Jennens, the 1982 coaches Mark Bathurst, Donald Leggett and Bob Winckless, the 1982 trials coaches Alan Inns and John Pritchard, the non-rowing secretary for that year, Malcolm Harrison, and Alf Twinn the boatman.

From the Oxford camp are the past and present coaches Michael Barry, George Harris, Ronnie Howard and Hugh Matheson, the boatman Albert Andrews, and the Blues Colin Moynihan, Jim Rogers Jr and Reed Rubin.

I received invaluable help from colleagues at the *Guardian* and among rowing correspondents and broadcasters, particularly Harry Carpenter, Jim Railton, John Snagge and John Vernon. Others have provided specialist knowledge and research, notably Harry Boggis-Rolfe, Tom Mendenhall, John McKeown and Dick Phelps. I would also like to pay tribute to some of the press photographers whose work appears in the book, for the Boat Race is notoriously difficult to photograph. In recent years the efforts of, among others, Martin Argles, Tommy Hindley, Eamonn McCabe and Kenneth Saunders have added considerably to our understanding of the race.

I am indebted to many librarians who have put their fingers on what I have wanted, particularly those at Balliol College, Oxford, the British Museum Newspaper Library, the *Guardian*, the London Library, Queen's College, Oxford, Richmond, St Andrews University, St John's College, Cambridge, and the London Borough of Wandsworth.

Roderick Bloomfield of Stanley Paul and Sue Hogg, managing editor at Hutchinson, have coached and coxed me with maximum support and encouragement. I would like to thank the Estate of the late P. G. Wodehouse for permission to reproduce a verse of P. G. Wodehouse's song about Grassy Corner, and Putnam & Co. Ltd for permission to reproduce David Haig-Thomas's account of a Boat Race from *I Leap Before I Look*.

Selected Chronology

1828   Cambridge University Boat Club founded, 9 December

1829   First Boat Race at Henley-upon-Thames

1836   Second race, Westminster to Putney

1837   Head of River crews race at Henley (Queen's, Oxford *v.* Lady Margaret (St John's), Cambridge)

1839   Third race, Westminster to Putney, after which Oxford college captains found Oxford University Boat Club. Henley Regatta founded

1840–42 Races Westminster to Putney

1845   Seventh race, Putney to Mortlake church

1846   Eighth race, Mortlake church to Putney; outriggers first used in match

1847   Oxford condition that neither side should employ watermen as coaches. Cambridge disagree. No race, nor in 1848

1849   Two races, in second of which Oxford win on foul. Putney to Mortlake, the course used ever since

1852   Eleventh race. Cambridge take inside span of Hammersmith Bridge on advice of professional coach, and lose

1853   No Boat Race. Crews meet at Henley Regatta by mutual agreement

1854   Twelfth race

1855   Isis and Cam frozen. Agree to meet at Henley

1856   Thirteenth race. Boat Race becomes annual fixture

1857   Oxford win in Taylor's keelless boat. Trial eights
          established at Oxford. Round oars first used
1859   Cambridge sink at White Hart, Mortlake
1861–69   Oxford win
1862   Trial eights established at Cambridge
1869   Oxford win four-oared race with Harvard
1870–74   Cambridge win
1873   Both crews use sliding seats for first time
1877   Dead heat. Last occasion when professional waterman acts
          as judge
1880–83   Oxford win
1881   Dinner to mark fiftieth anniversary which was two years
          earlier
1882   Goldie boathouse completed in Cambridge
1884   Umpire takes on starter's duties
1886–89   Cambridge win
1886   First time crew behind at Barnes Bridge (Cambridge) win
1887   Oxford break oar after Barnes Bridge
1888–89   Cambridge boat same crew except for change of cox
1890–98   Oxford win
1893   Oxford first crew to get under nineteen minutes
1897   Oxford boat seven Etonians
1898   Cambridge waterlogged, but finish course
1900   Cambridge's twenty-length win
1902–4   Cambridge win
1902   Oxford use swivels for first time
1906–8   Cambridge win
1906   Cambridge beat Harvard
1909–13   Oxford win
1912   Cambridge sink at Harrods; Oxford waterlogged; rerow
1915–19   No Boat Races during First World War
1919   Both universities attend Peace Regatta at Henley.
          Cambridge win Allied Peace Regatta in Paris
1920–22   Cambridge win

1924–36 Cambridge win
1925 Oxford sink at the Doves
1926 H. R. A. Edwards blacks out in Oxford boat
1927 Running commentary broadcast for first time
1929 Centenary: score – 40 wins each with one dead heat
1934 Oxford boat built in seventy-two hours
1935 Cambridge use swivels and coaches revolt
1936 Oxford president resigns over argument with coaches
1937 Oxford president stands down against advice of coaches, and crew win
1938 First televised Boat Race
1940–45 No Putney–Mortlake races during Second World War. Half-blues awarded to oarsmen for races in 1940 at Henley (1½ miles), 1943 at Sandford, 1944 at Ely, 1945 over Henley Regatta course
1946 Oxford win first post-war race
1946–49 Cambridge use fixed pins again
1947–51 Cambridge win
1947 Cambridge president M. A. Nicholson stands down and never gets his blue
1948 Cambridge first crew to get under eighteen minutes
1949 Cambridge win round the outside of bend after Barnes Bridge, never accomplished before. First end-to-end television commentary
1951 Oxford sink in two minutes. Rerow. Cambridge beat Yale and three other US universities, Harvard, MIT and Boston, on victors' American tour
1952 Oxford win by a canvas, first time in history of race
1954 Oxford win the hundredth race
1955–58 Cambridge win
1955 Oxford's J. G. McLeod blacks out off Duke's Meadows
1957 Oxford's P. F. Barnard 'dies' by Duke's Meadows
1959 Oxford's rebel crew beaten off the water
1960 Oxford first use spade blades
1965–67 Oxford win

1966   Both crews use 'German' rig, i.e. Nos. 4 and 5 both row on
            bow side

1968–73   Cambridge win

1976–82   Oxford win

1976   Oxford first crew to get under seventeen minutes.
            Ladbrokes begin sponsorship of OUBC and CUBC

1978   Cambridge sink at Barnes Bridge

1979   Cambridge stroke J. W. Woodhouse substituted on
            morning of race because of illness. Hundred and fiftieth
            anniversary, 125th race

1980   Oxford's bow S. R. W. Francis 'dies' at the bandstand.
            Canvas verdict, second time in history

1981   Susan Brown steers Oxford, first woman to take part in
            the Boat Race

1982   Oxford's N. B. Rankov becomes first oarsman to win five
            consecutive races

1983   129th race, Cambridge's challenge

PART ONE
Birth

I

Toogood defies his Master's voice
1829: The first university Boat Race

Jenkyns, Master of Balliol, sent for J. J. Toogood and told him that if he did not attend the logic lecture at one o'clock the next day he could not continue a member of the college. Toogood said certainly he would attend the lecture, for the race was not until the evening. The Master was not pleased: he strongly disapproved of the projected boating match between Oxford and Cambridge arranged for Henley-upon-Thames and he hoped that by preventing Toogood, the number five man in the Oxford crew, from going, he would put an end to the folly.

Jenkyns was a small, round, cantankerous man who was leading a successful attempt to restore the academic side of Balliol's life, with a sharp mistrust of, if not opposition to, sportsmen. At 14 stone 8 pounds, then, Jonathan James Toogood was unlikely to be intimidated by his Master, though maybe by his voice. He attended his lecture and was taken down to Henley by Lord Ossulston where he found the rest of the crew quietly waiting. It was Wednesday, 10 June, in 1829. Carter was in the bow, Arbuthnot, another Balliol man, at two, Bates at three, Charles Wordsworth, who had had a hand in setting the venture up, at four, Toogood himself at five, Garnier at six, Moore at seven, and Staniforth of Christ Church at stroke.

Wordsworth wrote to his old Harrovian contact Charles Merivale at Cambridge with some information about the crew, naming four days of practice at Henley after a considerable pickle over selection and progress, and giving some details of the men. 'Staniforth, four foot across the shoulders and as many through the chest; Moore, six foot one inch, in all probability a relation of the giant whom the "three rosy cheeked schoolboys built up on top of Helm Crag" so renowned for length and strength of limb; Arbuthnot, strong as Bliss's Harrow best bitter; Toogood – for you, etc.' Because Bates, Wordsworth, Moore, and captain Staniforth and the coxswain Fremantle were all from Christ Church, and because it was through that college's boat club that the match had been made, they were wearing the college colours. Their boat was built by Stephen Davis of Oxford and lent to them by Balliol. Oxford had been training at Henley, being taken there in a drag by a coachman known to them as Bottle Brand. Their boat was a real boat with a keel; she would not upset if you stepped on her side to get into her. They had oars long and strong, according to Toogood, who almost fifty years later remembered the boat as being about ninety feet long. She wasn't. She was 45 feet 4 inches, widest of beam where Toogood sat at 4 feet 3⅞ inches, 2 feet 5½ inches deep in the bows, 1 foot 7½ inches amidships, and 2 feet 6 inches in the stern. The boat and the oars weighed six hundredweight, and the oars varied in length from 13 feet 6 inches to 15 feet 3½ inches.

The crew were not allowed to eat puddings or fruit. They lived chiefly on beef. And their stroke Staniforth knew exactly what he was going to do in the race, which was to be over two and a quarter miles upstream between Hambleden Lock near Medmenham and Henley Bridge, because he and the boatbuilder Davis had studied the course together and determined that Oxford would take the Berkshire side of the little island in the river, which was just round the bend after leaving Hambleden. This narrow channel they reckoned to be a farther distance than the main course on the Buckinghamshire side of the island, but it avoided the stream which would be against the crews in the race.

From the middle of the appointed day when Toogood was still struggling with his logic at Oxford, Henley was filling up with spectators. The newspapers' estimates of the turnout reached twenty thousand. A general meeting at the town hall had raised money for fireworks for the occasion and the town was going to have a fête; every road was thronged with pedestrians, horsemen and vehicles. By two o'clock there were bands playing along the banks and a race between two wherries for a prize offered by the town took place. All of Oxford (except presumably Master Jenkyns) seemed to be present, sporting dark blue favours.

The whole university turned itself out [said *London Society*]. The gravest and most unexpected men were to be seen riding or even driving on some part or other of that three-and-twenty miles between Oxford and Henley. There were gigs, tandems, pairs; and one party of friends actually approached the scene, and I believe returned in safety, in a four-horse drag driven by themselves. At least I saw them safe baiting at Benson on the way back.

There was a sizable turnout from the other place as well, which was a lot farther away. The river was crowded with cutters from London, Eton and Oxford, and the newspapermen present reached for their superlatives and their credibility in describing the scene.

> A very faint idea may be formed of the triumphant scene from what our readers have often seen on the Isis [said *Jackson's Oxford Journal* after the race]. Amongst the assembled multitude were to be seen the very flower of the kingdom, for such surely may be called the fine high-spirited young men of the universities of Oxford and Cambridge, of Eton and Westminster. The splendid scenery, the beautiful river, on which were boats of every description, and the immense company, made a picture of so superb, of so unique a nature that none but those who saw it can form an adequate idea of its richness and variety.

Bell's Life in London records that the town was filling up several days in advance of the race, that there was scarcely a bed to be found, that six guineas was offered and refused for an apartment facing the water. A traveller from Oxford recalled later in *London Society* that he and three friends drove over with a hamper of provisions. They and a few more secured a room at an inn and added slightly to their stock of food from the host's larder in the shape of a shoulder of mutton and some cheese. For these they found themselves charged at ten shillings per head, and on remonstrating were silenced by the host telling them with an air of injured integrity that they might consider themselves generously treated in not being charged corkage for their own wine. *London Society*'s correspondent watched from the roof of the little bridge house on the Berkshire side of Henley's elegant bridge. The bells at St Mary's opposite had been ringing all day. From his perch, even using a good eyeglass, he couldn't see the start.

The Oxford and Cambridge crews embarked and made their way downstream to the start, Oxford wearing black straw hats with broad

blue ribbons, jerseys with large dark blue stripes, horizontal in the
Christ Church colours, and canvas trousers, Cambridge wearing white
with pink neckties, which some of them wore as sashes or waistbands,
in honour of their stroke Snow of St John's. Merivale, the Cambridge
number four man, whose friendship with Wordsworth at Harrow had
resulted in the first idea of setting up this inter-university match, was
also from St John's, as was the number seven, Selwyn. Holdsworth at
bow, Warren at three, and the coxswain Heath were from Trinity,
Bayford at two and Entwisle at five from Trinity Hall, and Thompson
at six from Jesus.

The accounts of the betting vary. *Bell's Life* said that:

> the betting for some time was in favour of the Cambridge gentlemen,
> but it being ascertained that their opponents were using every precau-
> tion and leaving nothing untried in the way of training beforehand,
> added to which it was said that they were all good men, the betting
> materially veered round to their favour, and it subsequently became
> scarcely possible for anyone to get a bet that Cambridge did not
> come off the victors.

The event had been widely publicized in the sporting press and there
was a strong rumour that there were 500 guineas at stake on the result,
rumour so strong that Charles Merivale had written to his mother on
29 May: 'I hardly know whether it is necessary to caution you not to
believe an advertisement which is to be seen in some of the papers
about the match being for £500. It is not an exaggeration even, but a
lie. In fact, I have not a sixpence staked thereon.' *Jackson's Oxford
Journal* said: 'It was reported that the match was for a very large sum;
but we have authority for stating that it was by no means a gambling
match, but a trial of strength and skill.'

Intelligence reaching the roof of the bridge house indicated Cambridge as favourites, and they became hotter favourites when they won
the toss and chose the Berkshire station, with its bend of ninety degrees
in its favour in the first threequarters of a mile and another considerable one near the finish at the bridge. This did not help the well-laid
plans of Staniforth. Soon after the start there was a clash and the race
stopped. One version had it that Cambridge ran into weeds and halted
to complain, and that after the second start Oxford went through the
same water with the coxswain calling out, 'Weeds! Weeds!' to the

Cambridge crew. But this is not what happened. After the first start Cambridge intended to steer out from Berkshire towards Bucks to take the outside of Temple Island, while Oxford intended to hug the Berkshire bank from the Bucks station and take the inside of the island. Neither boat was clear at the crucial moment and so they clashed. According to Staniforth's diary, Oxford's umpire Cyril Page declared that both boats could row on the Berkshire side as there was plenty of water, and the Cambridge umpire J. Stuart Roupell declined to answer because he was not appealed to by his captain. The name of the referee between the umpires is not recorded.

A restart was ordered. It is not known from where this occurred, but it is likely that the crews returned to the original start or somewhere near it, for on the second occasion Oxford were able to take enough clear water to cross over in front of Cambridge and pass the island on the Berkshire side. Cambridge passed on the Bucks side, and Oxford won by several lengths. One newspaper had reported that Cambridge's boat built by Searle and Co., Lambeth, was for lightness and scientific construction perhaps never surpassed; another that: 'The Cambridge boat was far inferior in the water, dipping to the oar, while the other rose to every stroke in fine style.' The time is variously given at ten minutes, eleven minutes, fourteen minutes, and fourteen and a half minutes. Opinion seems to favour the longest time and the confusion is probably down to the restart.

The Oxford boat shot the bridge and came into the landing place, and a tumultuous din greeted them. 'Never shall I forget the shout that rose among the hills,' said the man on the bridge-house roof. He found that the valley at Henley lay well for reverberating sound. 'Certainly the echo, image of the Berkshire hills, made itself heard. Men who loved Horace must have thought of his lines to Maecenas . . .', and as the reporter was carried away into the hills, the massive frame of Toogood was hoisted off the ground and transported in triumph to the inn as the Oxford supporters shouted, 'Somersetshire for ever,' a cry that was lost on him, and to the mysteries of time. The roof squatter came down but always remembered the noise. 'There was fierce applause at the installation of the Duke of Wellington a few years after, and there has been applause under a hundred roofs since; but applause that fills a valley is a different thing,' he reflected.

The very flower of the kingdom then set about celebrating victory and defeat. After sacrifices at the shrine of Bacchus, as *Bell's Life* soberly reported more than a week later, they set out among the fireworks and general revelry to see if they could achieve as great a feat on land as they had on water.

They sailed out just at the moment the Stroud Mail, driven by the veteran Hampton, came up. No sooner were the horses taken out than they found substitutes in the tits of Alma Mater, who, about forty in number, seizing the pole and splinter bars, set off with the mail at full speed, and in the twinkling of an eye, and to no small astonishment of the passengers, conveyed it about a mile and a quarter on its journey. The coachman and guard soon followed with the quadrupeds, but had some difficulty in rescuing the coach from the bipeds, who, jealous of their new functions, belaboured them with their white castors with as much vigour as they had been themselves tickled by Dr Birch in the earlier period of their probation. Nothing but the good humour and forebearance of the legitimate guardians of His Majesty's letter bags could have saved these marauders from a severe castigation.

2

Isis, goddess of fertility
The dark blues' silver chalice

A glance at a map shows the importance of water to Oxford. The city is encircled by it, held within a silver chalice by its rivers, as F. V. Morley put it when he voyaged past to write his *River Thames from Source to Mouth*. Only the way north towards Banbury does not cross running water, and even that has to bridge the Oxford Canal which links Isis to Cherwell. The dreaming spires, the lost causes, rise up from water-meadows which, until the proper management of the silvery Isis by lasher and lock, were frequently converted to a lake which lapped at the streets and the quadrangles. In winter it can still become obvious why the city was built where it is.

The Thames in this part is usually known as the Isis, the Egyptian goddess of fertility, sister and wife of the chief god Osiris. She is the mother of Horus, the sun god; she has nurtured the muse in Oxford, and given Oxford people an enchanting playground for their leisure and their sport. John Masefield used to show his visitors the view from his little red house up on Boars Hill, a dream eternally renewed, grey spires and glittering panes above a mist, or sparkling and dappled with yellow shadows, or a vision of Arabian nights by moonlight. Beautiful city, said Matthew Arnold in the essay where he penned the 'home of lost causes', 'so venerable, so lovely, so unravaged by the fierce intellectual life of our century, so serene! There are your young barbarians, all at play!' The poet Robert Southey:

> So on thy banks, too, Isis, have I strayed
> A tasselled student, witness you who shared
> My morning walk, my ramble at high noon,
> My evening voyage, an unskilful sail

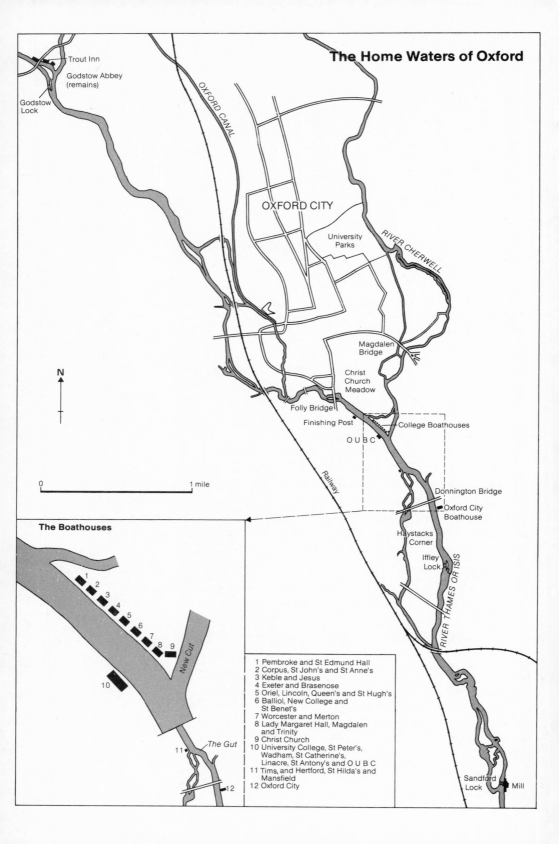

The Home Waters of Oxford

Trout Inn
Godstow Abbey (remains)
Godstow Lock

OXFORD CANAL

OXFORD CITY

University Parks

RIVER CHERWELL

N

Magdalen Bridge

Christ Church Meadow

Folly Bridge

Finishing Post

College Boathouses

O U B C

0   1 mile

Railway

Donnington Bridge

Oxford City Boathouse

Haystacks Corner

The Boathouses

Iffley Lock

RIVER THAMES OR ISIS

New Cut

The Gut

10

11

12

1 Pembroke and St Edmund Hall
2 Corpus, St John's and St Anne's
3 Keble and Jesus
4 Exeter and Brasenose
5 Oriel, Lincoln, Queen's and St Hugh's
6 Balliol, New College and
  St Benet's
7 Worcester and Merton
8 Lady Margaret Hall, Magdalen
  and Trinity
9 Christ Church
10 University College, St Peter's,
   Wadham, St Catherine's,
   Linacre, St Antony's and O U B C
11 Tims, and Hertford, St Hilda's and
   Mansfield
12 Oxford City

Sandford Lock
Mill

To Godstow bound, or some inferior port,
For strawberries and cream. What have we found
In life's austerer hours delectable
As the long day so loitered?

Lewis Farnell found a paradise for an explorer in a cause:

Also in those undeveloped days there was much primeval waterway of Upper Thames and Cherwell unknown to all save a few adventurers. The old Thames from its source in the Cotswolds was left happily unregulated down to King's Weir: there were no locks and the river flowed free and fast with swirling little rapids; and in summer-time the banks and margins of the stream were full of lovely water-growths, white water-lilies, flowering rushes (noblest of all our river-flowers), lithrums, willow-herb, meadow-sweet, and moon-daisy. Therefore the voyage from Oxford to Lechlade, which tempted Shelley, drew many of us lovers of water-travel. But it could not be wholly delightful until the introduction of the 'Canadian' canoe, for it alone glides lightly and accommodatingly up and down rapids, and the rhythmic movement of its paddle can be an all-day pleasure to the hardened expert. The upper Thames valley was then the land of deep peace; so also was the upper Cherwell. In those days when one was two miles above 'Parson's Pleasure', one might think oneself on Alph, the sacred river of Kubla Khan's dream. For only a few enthusiasts in canoes struggled past that bathing-place, where the park curators had not yet installed the easy rollers and thereby betrayed to the many what had been the privilege of the few. Nor were there any boat-houses or women-students, and very few North Oxford residents. And where now on a fine summer morning the Cherwell is almost solid with boats, in old days I have pursued the otter and studied the heron; and now the true magic of the water, of which perfect solitude is an ingredient, can only be found in the haunts above Islip.

But it still survives up and down the numerous small branches of the Thames between Folly Bridge and Wytham, which even now are very rarely explored, and where the ardent adventurers who can push a canoe through obstacles may leave part of their skin hanging on the thorns, but will find much that savours of Paradise.

Oxford's river begins upstream at Godstow, or, if you go along with Morley, farther up still, where the Windrush joins in above Newbridge. From there round a huge bend to Abingdon are the undergraduates' temptations, the Cumnor Hills, Bablock Hythe, Godstow Bridge and the Trout, Hinksey Hill, Bagley Wood. Take any generation and read its thoughts on Oxford, says Morley, and you will learn to appreciate how each yard of smiling angle of high ground makes the river swerve, and the reason for Oxford men being proud and lazy. It was here that Charles Dodgson rowed with Alice Liddell and her sisters, the children of the Master of Christ Church, and began a fairy tale for her which he published under the name Lewis Carroll. It was this bend in the Isis which inspired Arnold's *Thyrsis* and *The Scholar-Gipsy*; it was at Bablock Hythe that Shelley heard his skylarks and Keats mapped out *Endymion*; and nearby at Stanton Harcourt Alexander Pope worked on his translation of the *Iliad*. A tower at the house contained a boarded-up room known as the adultery chamber, where a freak of Lady Frances was once taken in the act with a neighbouring prior. When Pope was there he wished to engage a servant, but the mothers of the village refused to allow their girls to wait upon the Pope.

The Evenlode joins Isis by Cassington, a tributary nursed on the Cotswolds, fed by the lake in Blenheim Park, and once by fair Rosamond's tears in olden times. It was at Godstow Nunnery, now a ruin near the Trout Inn, that Henry II spied her while riding by and persuaded her, despite his old queen, to flee the nunnery and go to his bower in Woodstock, where, according to legend, she was protected by a labyrinth whose mazes no stranger could unthread. Except, that is, the queen, who got through with a cup of poison and Rosamond returned to Godstow in a lead box. From the King's Weir the river ambles to the Trout and Godstow lock and through the Port Meadow past Binsey and Fiddler's Island to join the canal and wind through the west end of the city, almost unnoticed, to emerge at rowing man's Isis at Folly Bridge.

In the clutter of boatyards and beside the canal upstream of the bridge is the legacy of another side of Oxford's water connection. Before it was a university city, before the holy men and the scholars and the pedants and the clergy moved in in great numbers and formed their cosy quadrangles, their buttery bars and rising spires of dreams, the city was a fishing and crossing place. The fishermen's era was pre-railway and bolstered by Lent, which if it had not existed would have to have been invented to maintain the balance of economy between agricultural produce and fish. Pike, perch, eels, crayfish contributed to the diet of the town and later the colleges. When the river was opened up for commercial traffic the boatmen spread far, and when the canal age arrived the carriage trade spread farther and wider until there was a thriving community of water people, fishermen and bargees on Thames and canal, whose families can be traced over four hundred years and whose linear connections spread wherever waters are navigable.

Folly Bridge is just below the bend which bargees used to find troublesome, so troublesome that the author Richard Burton used to get relief from *Anatomy of Melancholy* by splitting his sides watching them scold and storm and swear at one another. The older bridge had a three-storeyed tower on it which Friar Bacon used as his study. Eventually the university authorities considered it unsafe and took it down. That bend saw bad times for other reasons, explaining why much of the best fishing was upstream. John Taylor was a river inspector who described his function in verse:

> I was commanded with the Water Baylie
> To see the Rivers clensed, both night and dayly.
> Dead Hogges, Dogges, Cats, and well flayed Carryon Horses,
> Their noysom Corpses soyld the Water Courses;
> Both swines and Stable dunge, Beasts guts and Garbage,
> Street durt, with Gardners weeds and Rotten Herbage.
> And from those Waters filthy putrifaction,
> Our meate and drinke were made, which bred Infection.
> My self and partner, with cost paines and Travell,
> Saw all made clean, from Carryon, Mud, and Gravell:
> And now and then was punisht a Delinquent,
> By which good meanes away the filth and stink went.

Happily, the waters of the Isis are no longer a place where members of the Charon Club – those who have unwillingly entered the river fully clothed from a punt – or the novice sculler who has lost his balance need resort to a stomach pump. Organized pleasure boating came on to this scene comparatively late, organized by the community of fishermen and watermen who also branched into boatbuilding and serviced the colleges when they began to develop facilities of their own. In the eighteenth century Skinner of Trinity wrote home in verse,

telling of how he hired 'the gay yacht the Hobby Horse' from Mrs
Hooper at Folly Bridge:

> Where a Dame,
> Hooper ycelpt, at station waits
> For gownsmen, whom she aptly freights
> In various vessels moored in view,
> Skiff, gig, and cutter, or canoe.
> Election made, each in a trice
> Becomes transformed with trousers nice,
> Jacket and catskin cap supplied,
> Black gowns and trenchers laid aside.

You can still get a skiff from Salters or a camping punt from
Hubbocks under the bridge. The Cherwell is the punters' stream,
sneaking off through Christ Church Meadows to the botanical garden,
once known as the Physic, through Magdalen Bridge, where the old
watering place for the tram horses is a punt-hiring station run by
Charles Howard. From here the lower Cherwell can be explored,
along St Hilda's college garden or northwards to Mesopotamia Island.
From the Cherwell boathouse in Bardwell Road, originally built by the
Oxford University Boat Club boatman Tom Tims in 1901, carving his
initials over the centre of it, it is possible to go upstream past Wolfson
College with its own punt harbour to the Victoria Arms and the old
Marston punt ferry. The Cherwell continues from here through
Summertown, past the island of Cromwell's Meadow, under the city's
bypass and on for several miles to Water Eaton and Islip, a charming
village which is about the farthest range of the punt, the place where
Edward the Confessor was born and where once, again according to
the foraging of Morley, a bear got loose and played havoc with the
village sweetshop. Downstream from the Cherwell boathouse and its
restaurant are the playing field of the Dragon School and the gardens
of Lady Margaret Hall and then the university parks. Farther below
the river divides, the New College backwater leading an overgrown
way to St Catherine's College punthouse and a weir, the main stream
to Parson's Pleasure, where the river since 1832 has been paled off for
men's nude bathing, but where punts can get through the palings to the
rollers which lead to the Mesopotamia ('between two rivers') Island
level.

This is the place to play truant in May or June with a much-enduring book, says Morley, to serve as pillow, backrest, missile, fan, anything save reading matter. This is the place to feel the ripple of the water and watch the sunlight dancing in the branches overhead. Or farther down the Isis. There is a danger here of getting mixed up in the business end of things, of sport interrupting the sojourn of the muse, but for the moment we will stay with the aesthetes and the plain idle. From Folly Bridge to the New Cut, which is now the main Cherwell channel, are the college boathouses on the Christ Church or Oxfordshire bank. They are less picturesque than the barges which used to serve as boathouses, elaborate ornate craft which started life as the floating staterooms of City livery companies or were constructed in their image. By 1982 there was none left in position along this Isis reach, which is the parade ground of Oxford college crews, but a few remain in backwaters awaiting the careful reconstruction of the preservers. On the Berkshire bank is the OUBC boathouse and college cricket and athletics grounds. The Green Bank on the other side is wild but the willows have been drastically pruned. Before Long Bridges is the Tims boathouse, now occupied by several college boat-clubs, and the stream turns sharply into the Gut which has been the undoing of novice scullers and novice coxswains over the years. After Freshman's River joins the Isis on the Oxford side, the modern Donnington Bridge crosses, Oxford City boathouse close by it on the downstream bank. Meadows continue on the Berkshire bank and rising wooded ground on the Oxfordshire, the back garden of the village of Iffley, barely visible from the river which is banked with greenery. The towpath and the starting posts for the bumping races, 130 feet apart, are on the Berkshire side. Before Iffley lock and lasher is George Harris the boatbuilder, Isis Cottage, two paddles standing in the porch and a model junk peeping from the window, and then the Isis tavern, a Morrells house with a beer garden. A rectangular stone stands between them, placed here by the friends of Gilbert Charles Bourne FRS, 1861–1933, a devoted friend of Oxford rowing.

Then comes the lock. It is immaculate, lined with flower beds in white, yellow, lilac colours, freshly painted wooden bollards, rose bushes standing guard, the little bridge near the rollers arched with a stone balustrade. The keeper's house is early twentieth century, Cotswold stone, with central door and flanking windows, a greenhouse and orchard at the side guarded by a neat privet hedge. There are rollers for skiffs and punts on the Berkshire bank, and a wooden bridge leads from the hut where the immaculate Mr Sargent sees to the day's shipping across the lasher and round a quiet deep green pool to the back lane of Iffley. To the neighbouring village of Littlemore came Cardinal Newman in 1842 when his position at the university became intolerable, where he converted some cottages into a semimonastic recluse and lived there with a few disciples.

The stretch below Iffley lock has long been a popular destination of picnic parties. The Isis continues to Sandford where George Napier's body is supposed to have been made whole by the waters of the goddess of fertility after he was denounced as a Jesuit in 1568 and hanged, drawn and quartered. His quarters were hung at the four gates of the city and his head in front of Christ Church. The authorities eventually cast the bits into the river and the Knights Templar, who at that time owned Sandford Mill and chapel, fished the whole-again corpse and gave Napier a fitting burial under their altar. Expeditions in more recent times are much more likely to stop at the King's Arms and its garden hard by the mill, which has made a lot of parchment and exam paper in its time, and the lock, which rivals Iffley for its immaculate appearance. Or they may head for Sandford pool below the huge lasher, round which the anglers fish and which is Oxford's best bathing place, when the stream permits. When, however, there is a lot of current flowing, its undercut bank becomes a dangerous death trap, as witness the little stone obelisk in the middle of the weir in memory of five Christ Church men: Richard Phillimore and William Gaisford drowned there in 1843, George Dasent in 1872, Rupert Buxton and Michael Llewelyn Davies, the fourth of J. M. Barrie's 'boys' on whom he modelled Peter Pan meeting their fate in 1921. There have been others, and the public is no longer allowed on the top of the weir where the Isis crashes through to provide a good head of water for the mill.

On from the mill past Radley College's boathouses, the nursery of thousands of oarsmen and hundreds of blues, to Nuneham, a house built early in the eighteenth century by the Harcourt family, who impatiently used Stanton Harcourt as a quarry, knocking down all of it except parts of the kitchen and Pope's tower to create a new seat. They moved the village of Nuneham Courtney, too, so that it was not too near the house. They sheltered it with groves of birches and fronted it with peacocked terraces and green slopes to the water, flanked it with garden walks. This was a destination for a muse or a resting place after a decent row, a bit far for a skiff, and just before the Isis turns southwest. Morley found it placid between flat meadows of deep green spotted with buttercups and hawksbit, on his voyage of discovery, with the pure Jersey cows of Nuneham giving way to just ordinary common cows before Abingdon's trim lock is reached. Then public bathing place, tea garden, low bridge with dangerous eddies and hidden stones under it, red town with high grey church marking the end of Oxford's river. Here the stream is apprenticed to pleasure, Morley senses; one expects steamers, boys cadging pennies, noisy songs straight from London. We will return to the stretch between Folly Bridge and Iffley lock, in the company of Miss Guiney:

> Furrow to furrow, oar to oar succeeds,
> Each length away, more bright, more exquisite;
> The sister shells that hither, thither flit,
> Strew the long stream like dropping maple-seeds.
> A comrade on the marge now lags, now leads,
> Who with short calls his pace doth intermit:
> An angry Pan, afoot; but if he sit,
> Auspicious Pan among the river reeds.
> West of the glowing hay-ricks (tawny-black,
> Where waters by their warm escarpments run),
> Two lovers, slowly crossed from Kennington,
> Print in the early dew a married track,
> And drain the aroma's eve, and spend the sun,
> Ere, in laborious health, the crews come back.

Writing home to tell the folks what getting his rowing blue was all about an American student began by announcing that, like Gaul, Oxford rowing was divided into three parts. There the resemblance to Caesar's politics is promptly concluded, but he was right about the division, in more than one way. Rowing is a question of levels. The stream of the Isis and her tributaries which we have slid along thus far from a large and diffuse playground for the boating man, secluded, lazy, sunlit or moonlit. He can just as easily be a boating woman. He or she is in the land of the muses, exploring nooks and creeks, alone or in pleasant company, with book or tranny, with beer or plonk. Then there are the college people, pulling for the college, intent on keeping the standard up or raising it higher in Torpids, Eights, or even downriver at Henley. Most of their activity is between the bumps start at the lock and the finishing post near the bridge, where the Salters steamers and hire cruisers nestle in their off season. Then there is the highest form of lunacy for the fit and strong-willed, the pursuit of a blue and winning against what the Summer Eights programme in 1982 called the 'Filth from the Fens' from Putney to Mortlake. They are actually never seen on Oxford's course except in their college boats or in smaller craft, all their training nowadays taking place on wider, longer reaches below Sandford from the Radley boathouse, or at Cleve near Wallingford, or at Pangbourne or Marlow or Henley.

Thousands upon thousands have learned to row or carried on doing so for one or all of these three levels. University oarsmen are banned from the Torpids in the Hilary term; the Summer Eights are the height of Oxford's rowing year and sweep the exams away before multitudes of bankside revellers, a very private affair well worth crashing; the blues are a select few who give London and a worldwide television audience an annual water Derby. Isis draws them all down to her boathouses. Tom Brown, when he escaped the rigours of Thomas Arnold's Rugby, went to St Ambrose College in the sequel to *Tom Brown's Schooldays* and started behind Oriel on the final day:

> Miller [the cox] is twirling the tassel of his right-hand tiller-rope round his head, like a wiry little lunatic; from the towing path, from Christ Church meadow, from the row of punts, from the clustered tops of the barges, comes a roar of encouragement and applause, and the band, unable to resist the impulse, breaks with a crash into the 'Jolly Young Watermen', playing two bars to the second. . . . Tom had an atom of go still left in the back of his head . . . in another six strokes the gap is lessened and St Ambrose has crept up to ten feet, and now to five from the stern of Oriel. . . . 'A bump, a bump,' shout the St Ambrosians on shore. 'Row on, row on,' screams Miller. He has not yet felt the electric shock, and knows he will miss his bump if the young ones slacken for a moment. A young coxswain would have gone on making shots at the stern of the Oriel boat, and so have lost. . . . A bump now and no mistake; the bow of the St Ambrose boat jams the oar of the Oriel stroke, and the two boats pass the winning post with the way that was on them when the bump was made. So near a shave was it.

That was 1842. Oriel were really Trinity, St Ambrose were really Oriel, and the stroke Jervis of Tom's crew was really the blue George Hughes, brother of the author Tom Hughes.

Sometimes life has been stranger than fiction, in the bumps as elsewhere. In 1867 the Head crew Brasenose faced a crisis on the last day. Their coach Guts Woodgate had to get into the boat at the last minute because one man was seedy. Corpus, coached by the poet Robert Bridges, gave them a run night after night. On one of them Brasenose were in the Gut moving downstream to the start when Rumsey's oar snapped like a carrot just as the five-minute gun went off. The captain of Lincoln, who was on the bank as a coach, immediately sent sprinters to the barges on behalf of BNC while Woodgate's men got on the start. Woodgate hailed another friend who was in a gig with ladies and borrowed the best stick on board to make up the full complement of weapons; but it was of little use, he said, beyond that of a lady's fan. Bow took the fan, the second gun fired and they waited for the worst. Then Bullock raised a shout and the Brasenose men saw their spare oar coming down the bank at twenty miles an hour. They got it twenty-five seconds before the starting gun, and kept the headship. There was an almighty big drink in the college afterwards, with the Corpus and Lincoln eights as guests.

The bumping races are run in much the same way now as they were then. The boats are arranged in divisions, beginning the series in the order they finished on the final day of the year before and beginning each day in the order in which they finished on the previous day. The cox holds a fifty-foot rope attached to his post, while somebody on the bank with a pole keeps the bows out in the stream. A gun is fired for the division to get on station, a second gun is fired four minutes later to give warning of the start, and one minute after that the starting gun is fired. The OUBC rulebook says: 'When a boat touches any part of the boat in front of it, or its oars or rudder, it shall be considered a bump, and also if a boat rows clean by another it shall be equivalent to a bump. After every bump the boat.bumping shall change places with the boat bumped whatever be their order before starting.' A coxswain must raise his hand to acknowledge a bump and give way to the bumping crew. The division-one crews are the best that the colleges can put on, but towards the lower divisions, each of which has twelve crews, are the scratch boats, rugby clubs, graduates and jokers. In 1982 there were 109 men's and forty-nine women's crews in the Summer Eights, the last division of each having thirteen boats.

Judas was another fictitious college who had a go at getting to the Head. They met the *femme fatale* Zuleika by the barges, as all of

Oxford did in Max Beerbohm's story. Zuleika Dobson had arrived off the London train to be met by her grandpa, the Warden of Judas, 'in a white travelling dress, in a toque a-twinkle with fine diamonds, a lithe and radiant creature,' after which she put Oxford off its pleasure, let alone its work. The Judas men had already achieved two bumps and were on their way to the starting post, yet 'for the moment, these eight young men seemed to have forgotten the awful responsibility that rested on their over-developed shoulders. Their hearts, already strained by rowing, had been transfixed by Eros' darts. All of them had seen Zuleika as she came down to the river; and now they sat gaping up at her, fumbling with their oars. . . .' All was not quite lost because the magic of the bumps fought back. From the barges puntloads of young men, all suffering the same affliction, were nevertheless ferried across to the towing path, 'naked of knee, armed with rattles, post-horns, motor-hooters, gongs, and other instruments of clangour,' and hurried along as if by custom to the starting point. The rest we leave with Beerbohm, but there are hints of the consequences in a series of paintings in the public rooms of the Randolph Hotel.

The Rev. Edward Bradley in his guise of Cuthbert Bede introduced another hero to the Isis, Mr Verdant Green, in the *Adventures of an Oxford Freshman* in 1853. The tender Green hired the *Sylph* from Folly Bridge and ventured forth to teach himself to catch crabs. He succeeded several times, on one occasion netting a very large one, after which there was a loud cry of 'Boat ahead!' which rang in his ears as the university eight passed over the place where he and the *Sylph* had so lately disported themselves. Perhaps a more usual and less alarming introduction to the river would be that experienced by the actor Raymond Massey at Balliol in the twenties. His first days of tubbing in a heavy clapboard four-oared contraption with fixed seats were 'directed by an antique don who apparently had come out of the woodwork. . . . His instruction was, I gathered, faithful to the ortho-doxy of Oxford and Cambridge rowing as developed at Eton. . . . Rowing, he explained, was an art in which the oar was moved through the water by the legs and the swing of the back. . . .' This sort of instruction may have had something to do with Cambridge's long run of Boat Race victories between the wars, for the oar moves the boat through the water, not the water past the boat. Nevertheless, it is easy to mock the coaches, but the fact is that Oxford, and Cambridge for that matter, by and large teach their own, giving many men and women pleasure in aquatic activity at several levels of competence, and that is borne out by the latest phenomenon at both places, namely the women's crews queuing up for boats at half past seven on a winter's morning. Time was when nothing save the watermen moved until after lunch.

The traditions of rowing started before the foundation of OUBC in 1839. The first record of boating activities comes from T. F. Dibden in 1793 who lists 'rowing, hunting, shooting, and fishing' as the chief amusements of the Oxford scholar: 'The lecture is over, and half the college is abroad, some few to bend their steps "where harebells and violets do blow", and to return upon the bosom of Isis beneath the trembling radiance of the moon, after having visited the ruins of Godstow, or entered the sacred antiquity of Iffley.' Or Thackeray in *Vanity Fair* in the 1840s, describing the Rev. Bute Crawley as stroking the Christ Church boat and taking ten years to pay off his college debts. He anticipates by twenty-five years or so the first records of races, G. V. Cox recollecting in 1860 that, in 1805, 'Boating had not yet become a systematic pursuit. . . . Men went down to Nuneham for occasional parties in six-oared boats but these boats belonged to the boat people; the crew were a mixed crew got up for the day.' The first record of eight-oared racing is in 1815 when Brasenose were Head. Much of the influence of competitive rowing was probably introduced by students from Eton and Westminster schools, who would be familiar with the activity of wet-bobs. An old Westminster, Gresley, took his degree in 1823 and described the start of the races as seen from Iffley churchyard in his *Portrait of an English Churchman*:

> Presently a gallant eight oar appeared in the bend of the river, and then another boat succeeded, and then another. They entered the lock together, and for a short time all was hushed in silence. Soon the creaking of the opening gate was heard, and the boats sprang forth one by one; the sky was rent by the mingled shouts of the friends of each party. . . .

The boat at that time had a centre plank, the men sitting either side of it without outriggers. While in the lock the oars would be raised to the vertical. As the gate opened the stroke man would be standing in the bows pushing the boat into the river with a pole and running down the centreboard or the gunwale until he took his place.

King, the boatbuilders, had a barge a little downstream from Folly Bridge on the Oxfordshire bank which was much used by the boaters and where the new order of college colours was run up the flagpole, which also served as winning post. There was also much boating activity at the Boat House Tavern, sandwiched between the old Folly Bridge lock on the Berkshire side and the bridge itself, where Messrs Salters' offices now are. The lock was taken out in 1886.

Disputes developed about watermen sitting in the college crews for races, and from 1824 they were no longer allowed, although there is an entry in the Exeter records for 1849 reading, 'Tims, to row bow of the Torpid, 2s 6d.' Torpids as a term applied to college second boats comes into use in the mid-1820s. They rowed after the Eights, but in 1852 their races were moved to the Lent term and thereafter second boats became recognized as feeders for first boats. Why such a term is used for them is obscure. Dormant, dull, sluggish, apathetic or numb they may be, but not all of them all of the time. Some lack torpidness, some move torpidly, some demonstrate torpidity, some torpify the torporific; the term is a mystery, but in 1873 they almost ran the whole gamut:

> A fearful scrimmage occurred among the upper crafts. Balliol had bumped Trinity, and failed to get out of the way of Lincoln, who were driven against the wall by Queen's. Wadham, in hot pursuit, cut right into Queen's, and were themselves upset by Oriel. Into the midst of this mass of confusion came the luckless Exeter; Pembroke were upon them in an instant, and Magdalen rushed into Pembroke, followed by Corpus, who managed to paddle past the debris and reach the winning post. Exeter and Balliol were each fined £5.

In 1824 Exeter took delivery of a white boat built in Plymouth, sailed to Portsmouth, and brought by road from there. At around this time the wearing of tall hats was giving way to tam o'shanters. In 1828 Christ Church ventured to the Tideway to race Leander and were badly defeated; in the following year was the first race with Cambridge at Henley. Twenty-five years after eight-oared racing began, the OUBC was formed. Hitherto the stroke man of the Head crew had been omnipotent. In 1839 the colleges got together, worried that they had won the first Boat Race but lost the second and third, and appointed the strokes, i.e. the captains, as the legislators on boating matters but with the stroke of the university boat as president. The original rule 18 says: 'That the president, or a majority of the committee, have the power to call a meeting of strokes and representatives of other colleges at any time, but that he be bound to do so previous to every public race.' The earliest record of a college club is Exeter's treasurer's book of 1831, although several clubs probably pre-dated this. Exeter's rule 20 said: 'That anyone who swears or uses other bad language, either in or out of the boat, during the time he may be down the river, shall be fined not exceeding 5s.'

With OUBC in existence – a decade after its opposite number in Cambridge but with longer experience of eight-oared racing among its constituent parts – there were several rapid developments. Races for pairs were started in 1839, for fours in 1840, for sculls in 1841. Scratch fours were started in 1846, the year when the club bought a barge from the Merchant Taylors' Co. The most significant development as far as the Boat Race is concerned, though, was the beginning of trial eights in 1858, when Edmond Warre was president. At the end of the Michaelmas term, after the fours, the president and secretary 'are to choose two crews, and train them for not less than twelve days and the race is to be rowed either on the Iffley course or at Nuneham, as the committee may decide. The object of this is to get sixteen of the best oars in the University, with a view to having a fit and proper crew going at the very beginning of the term ensuing for Putney.' A nursery for the eight had begun. In the same year Salters took over from King, and King's last account to OUBC, not so far renowned for having its accounts in order or in the black, was closely written but was 5 feet 2 inches long.

In 1862 the club built a boathouse in Isis Street above Folly Bridge. In 1863 the Prince and Princess of Wales were rowed from the bridge to the university barge by the OUBC committee in a special boat with two pilot fours and the Trinity eight as escort. The procession had been deferred to allow the royal visitors to witness it. The eights and torpids and fours paraded along the Iffley course, their colours flying on their standards in the stern, tossing their oars at the barges. In 1839 the *Black Prince* had been among them, a foreigner from First Trinity, Cambridge, on its way to Henley-on-Thames for the first Grand Challenge Cup. The last procession was held in 1893, the custom having got tacky and undisciplined. But in 1870 the first aquatic sports were held, the events including running headers, distance dive, 350 yards, and a hurdle race. Watermen were allowed to coach from this year, on the grounds that the smaller colleges found it difficult to find enough people good enough to teach. Four years earlier the university presented a lifeboat to the Royal Lifeboat Institute, which was demonstrated at Folly Bridge before being sent to Hayle in Cornwall. In 1867 Christ Church recognized the attractions of their meadows by erecting railings along them and charging rent for gates for access to the river.

Coxless fours were instituted in 1873, and both Eights and Torpids split into two divisions in 1874. In 1881 a new boathouse, started the previous year and almost completed, was destroyed by fire, and the CUBC sent 100 guineas as against Oxford University's £100 towards the subscription fund set up to replace it. In 1888 clinker fours were established and a new rule required a rubber ball on the bows of every boat after a fatal accident in Cambridge. In the following year Inman of Magdalen became the first coach to use a bicycle on the towpath, horses being the common aid until then, and by 1896 regulations about bicycles had to be made to avoid collisions. In that year also new and stricter rules were made about swimming certificates – four lengths of the Merton baths – after two men who had provided certificates with false information had to be rescued from very near the bank when a torpid crew were wrecked in the Gut, the rescuers receiving rewards from the Royal Humane Society. In 1890 the club joined with CUBC in giving a cup for a new inter-university race in Australia.

By now OUBC were installed in their new boathouse on the Berkshire bank, which still houses their boats and their workshop, but they have no clubroom. The land is owned by University College, and the two clubs share the building with Wadham, St Peter's, St Catherine's, St Antony's and Linacre colleges. There are still a few of OUBC's relics of the past in the University College clubroom. The seat made out of the famous seven-oar Henley boat of 1843, the back made of seven oars, is there. So is a model of the boat. There is an example of the oval brass badge which the club issued to licensed ferrymen back in 1843 to deal with the excess of men with boats plying for trade to take the rowers to the barges: 'In consequence of the inconvenience occasioned by incivility of some of the puntmen who ply from Christ Church meadow on Boat Race nights,' said President Fletcher Menzies's notice, 'the committee of the Oxford Boat Club particularly request all members of the university to employ those puntsmen only who wear the University Badge, viz. a brass plate on the arm.' The bows of the boat which beat Cambridge by two fifths of a length in 1901 are there, with the proud plate of the Brocas Boat House Ltd, of Eton, who are still building boats. At one time the words of King Alcinous in welcoming his guest were on the wall: 'Thou shalt know for thyself how far my ships are the best, and how my young men excel at tossing the salt water with the oarblade.'

There, then, are the nineteenth-century mileposts and folklore of the dark blues. The rules have altered a bit since; custom and practice have changed; the methods of training, which were set down as early as 1868 by Archibald Maclaren, the keeper of the university's gymnasium, have developed; the boats and oars have improved. But basically this is the place and this is the foundation on which blues are bred. Their heavy work is done in the winter, which can still be extremely tough, can still turn the watermeadows into a sea, although the excesses and extremities seem to have been worse during the decades of development of the last century. In 1891 a coach and four was driven down the ice to Iffley; in 1894 the old lock there was entirely submerged. Theodore Cook remembers catching his scull on a small ice pancake below Folly Bridge in the 1880s, pitching himself into a swirling stream of ice packs ranging in size from tea trays to a 10-foot table, and coming up under a large one which felt like the polar ice field. He was pulled out and rushed to a public house for hot whisky and water. Lewis Farnell remembers skating to Abingdon and up the Cherwell to Kidlington, and over Port Meadow in the hazardous dark. 'Returning alone from Abingdon on long skates up the dark, lonely river . . . I could see my own shadow on the blue ice and the glint of my blades under the moon that glowered over Nuneham Woods, where the boughs were cracking in the frost.'

But Farnell's best memory is of flood, not ice. Here are some of his adventures from his college magazine:

In the autumn of 1875 and the Lent Term of 1876 the adventurous who did not wish to be imprisoned in Oxford had two courses open to them. They could sally forth on foot for water-steeplechases: this form of sport was partly suggested by the Hare and Hounds Club, which was then newly instituted and which felt obliged to take to the water as the land had disappeared. We followed the hares waist-deep through the flood: what was chiefly wanted was good swimming and the power of enduring cold water: for those who possessed these it was a very rational and refreshing afternoon's enjoyment. But the boating-men had on the whole the better time; and scores of them put forth in fours and pairs and canoes to enjoy the scenery down to Sandford and back. The wiser went in a four, for they alone had a reasonable prospect of return. The first difficulty was to settle who should row bow, as that place was most important; for naturally our course lay through the hedges, and it was obviously desirable to charge them at full speed; so that bow was our buffer whose patient back tore a way through the brambles that would take their tribute of his raiment and skin, while the rest of us glided pleasurably through the breach he had made. We rowed easily over five-barred gates, and passed Iffley Lock without payment, either going past on the right, or through the lock itself down the water-shoot, as both gates were left open. The appearance of Iffley church rising as on an islet above this inland sea was a sight not easily forgotten: even so Ely Minster might have appeared 'when Canute the King rowed by'. Far on the right was the submerged railway, which had not then banked itself up above the highest water-level. And on one afternoon we were pleased to find a train water-logged and the passengers nervous and excited but refusing our well-intentioned offers to take them off in canoes. Perhaps they were right.

So Oxford took to the Isis and her tributaries like ducks to water for sport as well as recreation. There were always dons who did not see the enlightenment of this, as there are today. Woodgate, who was a great oarsman, a great coach, and a great chronicler of rowing and its affairs, mentions several tussles with authority during his time at Brasenose. He got Claude Holland, a superb Eton oar, into his college by persuading the 'Chief', Dr Cradock, to allow him to matriculate and take residence at the same time, in January. Dr Warren of Magdalen, on the other hand, insisted on the letter of Responsions before admitting the Eton captain of boats, John Edwards-Moss Jr. Magdalen gathered no Moss because the poor boy would not swot for the long vac, which would have entailed abandoning the season at his sire's Scottish shooting box. He threw in his lot with the Third Trinity club in Cambridge. Result, says Woodgate, a high-class oar lost to Oxford and undeniably an important factor in the defeats from Putney to Mortlake that befell Oxford in the years immediately following. Dr Symonds, Warden of Wadham, was of the school who thought rowing men on the high road to Hades, and caused the university eight to

spend a week longer on home waters than they intended by refusing to
allow his scholar Charles R. Carr to take off even one day of term in
1863, even though Carr had meticulously done his statutory forty-two
days on 'batels', the requirements of residence. And the proctors had
to be sweetened on occasions, for the eight seldom got back to their
barge in time to tramp home for cap and gown before meeting in a
convenient college for dinner, creeping home in mufti later.

Of course there were some frightful snobberies, too, concerning the
rowing men who were the early blues, the founders of Vincents through
Woodgate, and who, some of them, considered that they were superior
beings among, until well into the twentieth century, a very privileged
and mostly moneyed community. 'Bloody hell, man, I *am* president of
OUBC' is a cry which rang across a junior commonroom on some
point of non-rowing issue in the 1960s, not the 1860s, and is the sort of
stance that gives a clean sport a bad name. Bump suppers, too, have
become legendary:

> You shall hear how once our college,
> When our boat had done great wonders,
> And had bumped all boats before it,
> Gave a great and grand bump-supper.
> First the scouts, the sherry-swiggers,
> And the scouts' boys, beer imbibers,
> Spread the things upon the table.
> All of glass were made the tumblers,
> All the spoons were made of silver,
> All the forks were made of silver,
> All except the two-pronged carvers,
> Which were made of steel well-tempered. . . .

The grand meal in the grand setting drank itself to song, waking the
dons in their rooms and old ladies in houses round about, disquieting
the thirsty bobby on his beat in the street.

Oranges, watermelons, filberts, chairs, glass flew, and, like the
burning of boats, the bump supper is best left to the private myth-
ologies of the colleges. They still continue, along with the races. The
course and the rivers have changed little since racing first became
formal, and the reason that no mention has been made of the industrial
aspect of Oxford is that, apart from a highway bridge here and there,
little of the twentieth-century city can be witnessed from a boat. It is

still a spire or a college tower which appears through the trees as a corner is turned.

The blues about whom we will learn more, particularly of their twentieth-century activities and their adventures outside the silver chalice which cradles them to alma mater, have become as enduring as Mrs Frank Cooper's Oxford Marmalade whose tonic and digestive properties often contribute to their training. The interest in the water sports waxes and wanes with fashion, like the Oxford accent and Oxford bags, presided over in all its quirkiness by OUBC, who look after the domestic affairs of Oxford rowing as well as the blues and, nowadays, the lightweight crews. They have thrown successive heroes into the public limelight, inspiring fiction and even a movie or two, such as MGM British's first production in 1937, Maureen O'Sullivan and Lionel Barrymore in *A Yank at Oxford*, which has a touch of the Zuleikas about it, a slice of feminine interest. They are not a lost cause, these men who borrowed their colours from Christ Church. Some say the colours came from Trinity, Cambridge, but there seems no evidence that OUBC at one time had to ask permission from that cornerstone of the other place to wear the dark blue with the purple tinge. But by 1982 they were losing the perennial battle, being a few wins behind Cambridge. Sir Walter Raleigh once said that there are two things scarce matched in the universe – the sun in heaven and the Thames on earth. It is fitting that Isis, goddess of the Thames and fertility, mother of the sun god, should trade in her ancient Egyptian symbol of the cow's horns for the crossed oars. Ladies and gentlemen, rowers and philistines, aesthetes and others: the dark blues.

3

The Cam and the Great Ouse way
Fenland playground of the light blues

' "Oxford" . . . it's so indigo . . . and leaden – like an Arctic sea. But
"Cambridge" . . . Ah, *there's* a word – the colour of a peach!' Alison
Waley to Arthur Waley. In a sense she was right. So often the two
places are lumped together, even in conflict, as standing out against
other universities or other places. They ape and jape each other, they
are full of different names for similar things. But they are different
colours, and not just by the happenstance of adopting dark and light
blue. They have a different feel. Cambridge is a peach formed to
flowering perfection in the flat Fens. It is somehow more coherent, its
parts making a more complete whole in its less industrial isolation in
East Anglia. In the sun it is somehow lighter, sparkling to the glittering
pinnacles of King's College chapel, its grand and solid collegiate
buildings lining its promenade from Trumpington Street past Caius to
Trinity and St John's. At the same time it has a cosiness which offsets
the biting winds from Russia that whistle round its alleyways and shut
the college gates. It has a river too, though hardly a silvery stream. The
pleasure part is much more accessible to the visitor than Oxford's, the
rowing end even more cut off from the gaze of the casual wanderer,
although paradoxically its boathouses are if anything more easily
approached by foot and bicycle. By foundation it is much more regal,
more aristocratic, more Establishment, maybe more righteous and
more Right. It has fewer colleges but they are larger, grander in size
and maybe in aspiration.

The Granta branch of the Cam meanders in from the south from
beyond Audley End and Saffron Walden, past hamlets of old England –
Littlebury, Little and Great Chesterford, Ickleton, Hinxton, Duxford,
Whittlesford, Sawston, Little and Great Shelford, Hauxton – to

The Home Waters of Cambridge

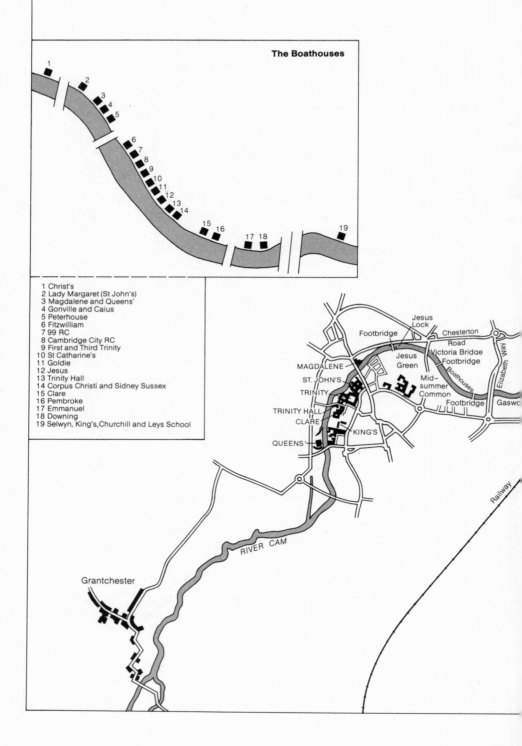

The Boathouses

1 Christ's
2 Lady Margaret (St John's)
3 Magdalene and Queens'
4 Gonville and Caius
5 Peterhouse
6 Fitzwilliam
7 99 RC
8 Cambridge City RC
9 First and Third Trinity
10 St Catharine's
11 Goldie
12 Jesus
13 Trinity Hall
14 Corpus Christi and Sidney Sussex
15 Clare
16 Pembroke
17 Emmanuel
18 Downing
19 Selwyn, King's, Churchill and Leys School

Jesus Lock
Footbridge
Chesterton Road
Victoria Bridge
Elizabeth Way
MAGDALENE
Jesus Green
ST. JOHN'S
TRINITY
Mid-summer Common
Boathouses
Footbridge
Gaswo
TRINITY HALL
CLARE
KING'S
QUEENS'
Railway
RIVER CAM
Grantchester

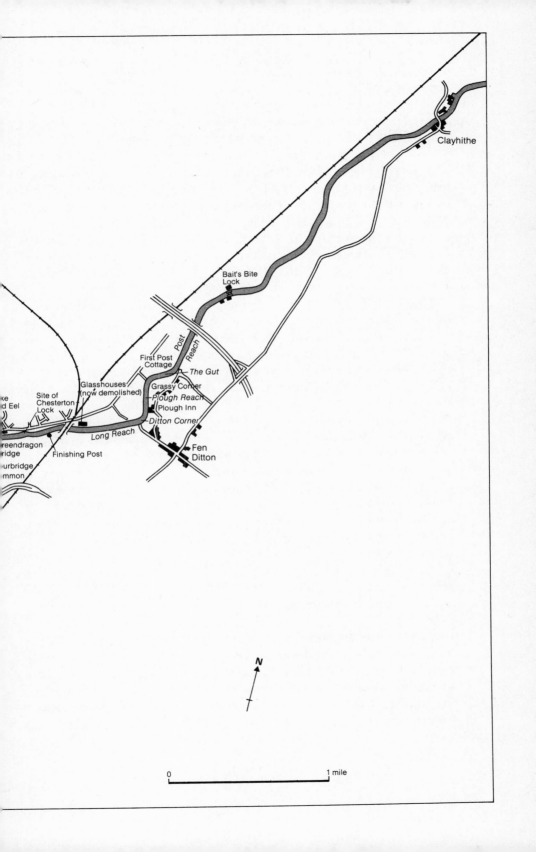

Clayhithe

Bait's Bite
Lock

Post
Reach

First Post
Cottage
The Gut

Grassy Corner
Glasshouses
(now demolished)
Plough Reach

ke
d Eel

Site of
Chesterton
Lock

Plough Inn

Ditton Corner

Long Reach

Fen
Ditton

reendragon
ridge

Finishing Post

urbridge
mmon

N

0   1 mile

Trumpington and Grantchester. Just above here is a weir and a pool named after Byron, although there is no evidence that he swam there. But generations of Cambridge undergraduates have walked and cycled and punted to Grantchester for tea. From the village are glimpses of the colleges and King's chapel a mile away, peaking through the trees and over the fields. The Rhee branch of the Cam joins the Granta a little upstream of the weir and the Bourn Brook joins it there, the limit of navigation for punts. The river continues to the city, a cut to Newnham Mill going off to the left and Vicar's Brook coming in on the right, past Sheep's Green, under the Fen Causeway and the Robinson Crusoe footbridge to a weir at the end of Mill Lane near Silver Street Bridge, the sentinel to the Backs, designed by Lutyens in 1959 to replace an old iron one leading towards Selwyn and Newnham.

This place used to be a commercial centre. From at least the time of the Norman Conquest there were two mills here, one built by William I's sheriff and the other belonging to the Abbot of Ely. There were wharves and boatyards and a granary, and Charles Darwin's son lived in Newnham Grange which, with the Hermitage and the house called the Hermitage Granary, has become Darwin College. There are two riverside public houses, the Granta and the Jolly Miller, close to the Newnham mill pool, which is along a backwater past the college. Above the weir are the Garden House Hotel, Scudamore's boatyard, punts for the hiring thereof, rollers to the lower level. Across the weir from the Mill public house is Laundress Green, otherwise known as the Apron, a traditional spot for washing clothes; below the weir is a lower level landing stage for Scudamore's, the Anchor Hotel where chauffeur punts are available, and on the other side of the pool is a landing stage for picnic punts. This is the end of the Granta, which is called after Cambridge's old name of Grantebryce. After here, we are on the Cam in its isolated glory, through Silver Street Bridge, close to which A. C. Benson, who wrote the words for 'Land of Hope and Glory', lived for a short while.

For a back door into a city this is a sensational entrance. Queens' College stands on both banks, the left court built in 1935 and the buildings on the right dating from the fifteenth century, with others from the eighteenth. Queen Margaret, wife of Henry VI, and Queen Elizabeth Woodville, wife of Edward IV, assisted in the founding of the college, which was set up by Andrew Dockett, and from them it gets its name. The two Queens are connected by a bridge sometimes known as the Mathematical Bridge, a 1902 replica of a wooden structure designed by a young man called Etheridge who had been influenced by a visit to China. The bridge was constructed using only pegs. Queens' has much to answer for, because Erasmus lived there and was the first man to teach Greek in the university. Daffodils bloom in the spring in their thousands in the grove beyond the bridge.

The next bridge is that of King's, through which the vista of the chapel and Clare College opens up on the right, offset by sheep grazing in the meadow on the left. Henry VI began King's in 1441 and cleared a large area of the medieval town to do it, and ninety years later the chapel was complete with 1200 square yards of coloured glass. The Cam continues under the oldest Backs bridge, the three almost semi-circular spans of Clare, and past the fellows' garden on the left, then reaches Trinity Hall's terrace before arriving at Garret Hostel Lane Bridge, built in 1960. Trinity's bridge, completed in 1765, links its property on the left bank with its great courts, including the magnificent library designed by Wren. Weeping willows border the river here, which turns right and then left to the balustraded parapet and carved panels of Wren's old St John's Bridge (1712) and the Bridge of Sighs, in the slight image of Venice's, which from 1831 has linked the college's New Court with its older parts. Rising above the buildings is the tower of St John's chapel, designed by Sir George G. Scott and completed by 1869, where a service is held at the summit on Ascension Day. St John's was founded by Lady Margaret Beaufort, mother of Henry VII, in 1511 on the site of the Hospital of St John. Its New Court, completed in 1831, stands where once there were nineteen fishponds belonging to the hospital. It is Lady Margaret whose name appeared on the early boats of St John's, and her name has endured for the boat club ever since. Past the newer buildings of Cripps Court is a punt lake bordered by Lutyens's building for Magdalene College, and then the river reaches Magdalene Bridge, through which are rafts for the punt-hire businesses of Tyrrell's and Scudamore's. Magdalene College is opposite on the left with gardens along Chesterton Road beyond it, and after some way Jesus Green opens out on the right before Jesus lock and weir.

On this stretch from Silver Street to Jesus lock, punts rule where eights used to roam. Before 1834 there was no lock at Jesus, the first lock below the mill pool being farther downstream on Midsummer Common where the college boathouses begin. Before 1835, when this lock and the next at Chesterton, near the Pike and Eel public house, were demolished, the rowing crews raced between these two locks but also ventured up to the mill pool, and until 1892 a procession from the pool to King's brought the Mays races to a grand and colourful conclusion. The Backs are spectacular at the worst of times to take a walk in, and at best they are hard to better for their extensive canvas of foliage and stone bisected by the lazy stream of the Cam, where in commercial days a causeway was maintained down the middle for the horses which, shoulder deep in the water, pulled barges, there being no towpath on the bank here.

The procession of boats took the form of thirty or so eights bedecked with flowers, with crews in blazers and straw hats. The boats were ranged side by side opposite King's and the crews stood with oars vertical in the boats and toasted each other in turn, portrayed splendidly in a lithograph by J. M. Ince, and again by an *Illustrated London News* artist for the visit of the Prince and Princess of Wales in 1864. The custom has been replaced by a concert of madrigals during a May Week evening, the singers sitting in punts, although there was a brief revival for the jubilee year of Queen Elizabeth II in 1977. Very occasionally a crew pays a visit to their old haunts, such as when Lord Adrian, the Master of Trinity, was elected Vice-Chancellor of the university. The world-famous physiologist who could quote Greek plays by the ream was introduced to a third culture by steering the college eight along the Backs to deliver himself to a dinner at the University Centre in Mill Lane. He took the very middle of the centre arch of Clare Bridge at full speed, and it was the first time he had ever coxed a boat.

While dawdling in this exquisite back garden of England, sheltered, it seems, from the flatlands which stretch inexorably away from the town, a word about punts at Cambridge. The pleasure variety arrived as imports from the Thames very early in the twentieth century, and during the 1960s local boatbuilders developed a shorter version which has a strong identical deck at both ends, having a higher centre of gravity than those prevalent at Oxford. Cambridge punters prefer to stand on the deck while Oxford punters tend to stand in the boat. The risk in Cam punting is falling victim to pole pickers, students who await the unsuspecting punter on low bridges and grab the top of the pole as the punt passes underneath. There is also a club for the clothed who unwillingly fall in the drink, similar to the Charon at Oxford, known as the Dampers. Before the Thames punt arrived on the Cam there were three other types of boat propelled by poles in use. The fen punt was double-ended and low in the water to avoid the winds. The garden punt was a small box-framed work boat, a floating wheelbarrow. The Great Ouse work punt was used for river maintenance, built strong with a double bottom, one cross-planked and the other fore-and-aft. Square-ended Thames-type barges were also seen on the river.

Through Jesus lock is the lowest level of the river in the Cambridge environs. It lives up to the Celtic derivation of its name, crooked, as it runs along the edge of Jesus Green and Midsummer Common until it reaches the Malodours, as the map in the Jesus College rowing history so neatly describes the gasworks. From the town the river is not visible over the green as the pedestrians and cyclists crisscross their ways to and from the boathouses which are all on the far bank. They are much more spread out than their counterparts in Oxford, accessible from the Victoria Road Bridge or the footbridge near the Fort St George public house on the common, or another footbridge which links the eastern end of the common with Manhattan Drive, or in a roundabout way from the Elizabeth Way highway bridge. In a mile from Magdalene Bridge to the Elizabeth Bridge, the Cam has swept round a huge bend which has held in the green and the common and wriggled back to the left a bit, turning right again at the gasworks for a short distance, with the towpath on the southern bank as far as another footbridge threequarters of a mile farther on. Here the river turns right, heading northeast into one mile of Long Reach to Fen Ditton, past the Pike and Eel on the north bank and the site of old Chesterton lock. This footbridge replaced a horse grind, a ferry punt large enough to take the Cam coaches on horseback, worked by winding the craft across the river on a rope. The footbridges along the boathouse reaches also replaced grinds. At one time several colleges had their own, and there are accounts of creeps who were always at the grind when the captain or the president of CUBC turned up for his outing, to wind him across. The boathouses are rich in variety and the bridges in the 1980s are much graffitied by the student supporters of the bump crews. Returning to Jesus lock and moving swiftly along the reach again, we come first to Christ's on the western side of the Victoria Bridge, then between the bridge and the Fort St George footbridge are Lady Margaret with resplendent scarlet doors, then Magdalene and

Queens', then Gonville and Caius, then Peterhouse. From the foot-bridge they are bunched, edging the stream too narrow to turn an eight. The town's 99 Rowing Club follows Fitzwilliam, then come Cambridge City RC, First and Third Trinity, St Catharine's, CUBC's magnificent Goldie boathouse, a benefaction of the blue J. H. D. Goldie, Jesus, Trinity Hall, Corpus Christi and Sidney Sussex, Clare and Pembroke. After the next footbridge are Emmanuel and Downing, and after the Elizabeth Bridge are Selwyn, King's, and Churchill sharing with the Leys School, near Banham's boatyard and marina.

The finish of the Lents and the Mays bumping races is at the up-stream end on Long Reach. The Cam flows on through a railway bridge carrying the Ely line, past the Glasshouses, which have been de-molished but which remain a landmark of the course, with Chesterton Fields on the north bank, and Stourbridge Common, venue of a famous fair and place where horses graze, and Ditton meadows on the south. Turning Ditton Corner the river arrives in Plough Reach, with Fen Ditton church snug on a green hillock on the south side and poplars lining the towpath on the north bank. Lawns run down to the water from Ditton homes and the Plough is set well back from the river but has a meadow which serves as a well-patronized beer garden from which form can be studied. Between there and Grassy Corner the Pitt Club used to have a lawn, and at Grassy the Cam turns sharply east into the Gut, like its Isis counterpart a graveyard for coxes, and then less sharply northeast again round First Post Corner into Post Reach, where the boats are started by gun. The huge bridge carrying the A45 road crosses here and the river continues to the turning point at Bait's Bite lock, built at the same time as the present Jesus lock.

As will be deduced from the layout at Cambridge, the water sport is divided into three parts, just like on the Isis. The upper and middle levels of the Granta/Cam are the province of the pleasure seekers, drinkers and idlers. From Jesus to Bait's Bite locks the college crews roam, slipping out from their homely boathouses past the Malodours and the Pye factories to the exposed wilds of the Fens, moving up and down in beautiful isolation, sheltered a little by the high towpath and foliage along much of the way but nevertheless exposed to the wind. And the blues are never seen on this 3 mile, 3 furlong, 110 yard stretch except – as on the Isis – in small boats or college boats, or in summer training. They drive off to the Great Ouse at Ely, where they share a boathouse with the King's School and can row for miles and miles into the teeth of the Fen gales, breaking the ice or disturbing the profusion of bird life with seldom another boat in sight. They can row down to Ely as well, dropping through Bait's Bite, which has an Anglian wildness quite unlike the pristine locks of the Thames, to Clayhithe and beyond. The organization of the rowing is also broadly similar to that found in Oxford, bumping races being held in the Lent and the summer terms, known as the Lents and the Mays. There are other events supervised by CUBC also, such as the Colquhoun Sculls and the Forster–Fairbairn Pairs and the Light Fours:

> Down the river the light fours roll
>> Like a tramp in the trough of a heavy sea,
> Like a rakish elephant on a spree,
>> Striking despair to the inmost soul
> Of the coach on his towpath bike or gee,
>> Watching their plunging, staggering motion,
> (As though they were not on the Cam, but the ocean).

Cambridge University Boat Club first met on 9 December 1828 in Mr Smith's room in Caius, and it almost certainly resulted in the decision to send a challenge to Oxford, which eventually occurred on 20 February in 1829. Thus the establishment of Cambridge's governing body of rowing predates Oxford's by a decade, although organized rowing on the Cam was younger than the Isis activities. Races were first held on 26 February 1827 when there was only a handful of boats on the river – a ten-oar and an eight-oar from Trinity, an eight from John's and a six-oar from Jesus, with some claims that Emmanuel and Caius had sixes. The races lasted for thirty-two days, an early indication of the time devoted to the 'new sport'. Bumps were introduced casually according to some accounts, early boats carrying bugles with them to give warning of their approach at bends or to announce they were issuing a challenge, and another boat would give chase. Some also carried picnicking equipment, like the Panthermanticon possessed by the Johnians. However, there was clearly influence both from the men who had learned their rowing at schools on the Thames and from the methods already adopted on the Isis where the river was much too narrow to race boats alongside one another. In the 1982 Mays there were 114 men's crews and fifty-eight women's.

Jesus College claims to have been Head of the River from Queen

Elizabeth's reign until 1827 on the grounds that John Alcock, twenty-eighth Bishop of Ely, started something by rowing up to Cambridge when he was supervising the conversion of St Radegund's Priory into a college. This was in the fifteenth century, but the Jesus boat club history says:

> . . . we find documentary evidence of the existence of a Jesus boat in the year 1594. . . . There is no evidence that this boat was used for recreation. On the other hand there is no evidence that it was not used for rowing, and until it is shown that any other college possessed a boat to challenge a Jesus crew during the period in question, we may regard the headship of the river as an appanage of Jesus College from the reign of Queen Elizabeth at latest until that of George IV.

The growth of the clubs was haphazard but fairly rapid. By 1830 Magdalene, Christ's and Peterhouse had joined in on the river and shortly after that King's, Pembroke, Trinity Hall, Downing, Sidney Sussex, Corpus and St Catharine's were in evidence, leasing space from the boatbuilders and yards which were clustered on the north bank where the college boathouses are today. It was in the last quarter of the nineteenth century that the colleges built clubhouses; they bought out several of the yards and constructed their own elegant headquarters. The Goldie, completed in 1882, is the best remaining example. Its original balcony has been replaced and the staircase at the side was demolished in the fifties, and the Japanese lantern light was removed in 1950. But the changing rooms and the elegant blues room remain the same, the walls of the latter panelled, with the names of the university eights gold-leafed on them, and an octagonal table in the centre for the president and committee to use while addressing the college captains who are seated on benches round the perimeter.

During the early days there were controversies and confusions. It was the custom in some places, notably among the oarsmen of London, to name clubs after the boats which the crews borrowed or hired from boatmen or publicans, and a similar practice seems to have occurred at St John's, founded by the Hon. Richard Le Poer Trench in the October term of 1825. The first minute book has 'Johnian Boat Club' embossed on the cover. The early records of races refer to the Johnian BC, although the club's first eight-oar, bought by Trench from Eton in 1826, was named Lady Margaret after the college's benefactrice. The rules of the Colquhoun Sculls, first published in

1836, clearly refer to Lady Margaret. This piece of detective work was carried out by James Douglas in *Rowing on the Cam*, published in 1977. He found other early references to both names, but what is difficult to discern is whether the writers were assuming that students from St John's would shout 'John's' in support of their crews instead of 'Maggie', or whether they applied the name Lady Margaret retrospectively after it became clear that the college's club was known by that name. It does not matter much, except that for years there have been persistent rumours about the reason for the use of the name Lady Margaret. These remain undocumented, although it is quite usual to be told that the Johnian club was banned from the river by the college authorities because of some frightful overindulgence, so re-forming itself with a new name to defy the authorities. Overindulgence there has certainly been at St John's: in 1892, for example, at that last great parade and toast before King's, the Lady Maggie boat turned up dressed overall but with only two oarsmen and a cox, the empty seats having poles with placards reading 'Sent down'. On the stern was another placard reading 'For further particulars apply to Messrs Cox and Caldecote', the respective senior and junior deans of the college who were responsible for the disciplinary measures. The story of the ban on St John's is usually linked to one of a fatal accident during the bumps in which someone met his fate on a Johnian prow. However, the fatal accident on the third day of the Lent races of 1888 did not involve a Lady Margaret crew. Clare College were lying at the far side of the river near the First Post after making a bump, when Trinity Hall's cox, 'apparently owing to a defect in the rudder', was not able to get his boat round the corner. E. S. Campbell, number four in the Clare boat, was killed in the ensuing collision, and the Lents were cancelled. It was this incident which caused OUBC to make it a rule that all boats on the Isis carry rubber balls on their bows.

The rumours about St John's have also been gruesomely linked with the scarlet blazer which has been part of the club's uniform since at least 1852, namely, that the adoption of scarlet had something to do with a blood feud or vengeance over an accident. There seems no evidence of this either, but what is pretty certain is that Lady Margaret BC gave the word 'blazer' to the language, or at least gave it its accepted meaning. According to diligent research by Hugh Stewart into the club's history, most dictionaries agree that the term was applied exclusively to the bright scarlet jackets worn by the Johnians from 1852 until about 1870, after which the inverted commas were dropped and the term began to be applied to other colleges' jackets which were in bright colours – Corpus, for example, having cherry blazers trimmed with white silk. The Royal Navy had ships called *Blazer* from time to time, notably fire ships in the late seventeenth century, but the evidence from naval historians which Stewart found did not confirm that the term was applied to uniforms which captains sometimes imposed upon their men.

Several other clubs from St John's have put boats on the river from time to time. There was a Lady Somerset BC from 1856 to 1862, later revived as a flag of convenience for summer regattas in the 1950s, though as a part of LMBC. There was St John's Corsair, who used the boat which lost to Oxford in 1829, St John's Tallyho, St John's Argo, Second St John's, and St John's College BC, the latter during the 1860s. Several of the clubs presumably followed the custom of naming themselves after the boats that they were able to put on the river, or perhaps naming the boats after themselves. The reason for their appearance is more obscure than for their disappearance. The latter was due to lack of support, the former maybe to ginger groups of dissatisfaction within the LMBC, pressure for more rowing facilities or, as the club history hints, a class division exercised by the blackball system of election in its early years. Careful examination of the rules shows that it was easy to discriminate against those who had not attended rowing schools. Evidence is cited from the Salopian who coxed the Lents and Mays Head of River boats in 1857, one Samuel Butler, who wrote of a Johnian acquaintance: '. . . and so, I suppose, considering me "a bloated aristocrat", in company with all the rest of the Lady Margaret Boat Club, he has determined to have none of us.'

Happily, this attitude has been largely dispelled, even at Trinity, by far the largest college, which at one time had three boat clubs. First Trinity distinguished themselves by winning the Grand Challenge Cup at Henley in 1839, the first year in which it was offered. Second Trinity were often known as Reading Trinity or the Hallelujahs, their original name being Nautilus, with a change to the Queen Bess after the first boat used, before Second Trinity was adopted. They were largely drawn from the Simeonites or low churchmen and evangelicals. Their various incarnations and crews were withdrawn finally in 1876 by absorption into First Trinity, although there was a one-season revival in 1895. Third Trinity, however, lasted until the Second World War and were a club drawn almost exclusively from Etonians and West-minsters, mostly the former. They merged with First Trinity by 1946 and the club is now known as First and Third.

Individually and collectively, then, the Cambridge men developed a private playground, hard to find for the casual visitor to their alma mater, where the boats slip home from Bait's Bite in the gloaming and hardly notice that they are approaching an ancient and beautiful city until they are moving up to a landing stage off Midsummer Common or Jesus Green, a private place of usually placid water hidden from what was then a private university in a pretty private corner of England. Even the races, which were split into Lents and Mays in 1887, when the college second boats became the first Lent boats and so on, take place a long way from the boathouses, passing meadows where the spectators congregate at Ditton Corner and the Plough and Grassy Corner in the hope of spectacular bumps or spectacular chaos. The races were stopped by the Vice-Chancellor in 1831 because of an outbreak of cholera in Sunderland, a tangential excuse for tackling debauchery, according to the then secretary of CUBC. His minute states 'that the man, Dr Haviland, who prompted the vice-chancellor to cancel the race, had confused rowing (rowdyness) with rowing (oarsmanship) and was anxious to stop any debauchery.' James Douglas in his *Rowing on the Cam* suggests that the connection may have been with a phenomenon seen in much more recent times, prostitutes waiting at the ferries and in the shady lanes behind the boathouses for their friends in the eights. Certainly this was a problem brushed upon in Shane Leslie's heavy novel of religion and rowing in 1926, *The Cantab*. His hero Edward, a Kingsman, took cold showers for his three years to keep his back turned towards the temptations of Veronica, and by the end of the book lay awake wondering: 'Was nothing certain in heaven or earth, no Absolute in religion or in rowing?'

Here by this gentle brown river in the 1840s Frederick Furnivall spent a long vac building an outrigger sculling boat, the earliest seen on the Cam, when he was a student at the Hall. Of here in 1828 *Sporting Magazine* said:

The boating at Cambridge was miserable work. The boats were well-manned, of course, as they had the flower of Westminster and Eton to pick from; but the farce of a boat race upon a river which will not in

most places permit of two boats abreast is too absurd. . . . Would
anybody go to see two fellows run a race in a narrow passage, where the
only proof of superior speed would be the hindmost now and then
giving his leader an application with his toe *a posteriori*? I humbly
conceive – No.

In 1840 the captain of Caius asked the other captains to exert their
influence to prevail upon their crews to limit themselves to taking half
a dozen of champagne to the procession to prevent the indecorous
scenes that had generally taken place. On this water the second boats
were called Cannibals after Cannibal Carlton, stroke of the first
second boat to appear, although Armytage's *Cam and Cambridge
Rowing* attributes the term to a popular song of about 1837 called
'The King of the Cannibal Isles', the term being applied to any
rough-and-ready ill-disciplined crew. The boats used to wear emblems
like the skull and crossbones and sharks' teeth. Boats which were not
on the river, that is not in the bumping divisions, were called Sloggers,
the winner of the Sloggers 'getting on' to the races. In more recent
times the qualifying races are called Getting On races. Now that there
are many divisions in the Lents and Mays, the leading boat of a
division must row again behind the division above on the final day of a
series to try and 'bump on'.

In 1849 four-oared races were introduced on the Cam. In 1865 the
Eastern Counties Railway refused a request from CUBC to widen the
bridge, but four years later the river was widened and deepened and a
new bridge was constructed. In 1872 the fours went coxless. Varsity
trials were established in 1861 and moved to Ely in 1863, and twenty
years later trial eight caps were awarded. By the turn of the century it
was customary for many of the college crews to row down there to
watch the final race of the Ely week in December, lunching at the
Cutter or the Lamb. In 1910 the Forster–Fairbairn Trial Pairs were
started by R. H. Forster, a past captain of LMBC, and Steve Fairbairn,
blue and Jesus coach.

By this time Fairbairn, an Australian from a family of whom several
became blues, had started a revolution on the Cam whose supporters
and opponents were to be locked in controversy for many years and in
many places. He had challenged the accepted English orthodox style,
the methods of the swing and the straight back, the long lay-back and
the eyes in the boat, by evolving a philosophy of rowing which his

enemies summarized as sloppiness and easiness. He realized that in a small college like Jesus there were limits to the number of ideally shaped men available and limits to the discomforts which a coach could expect to put them to, so he set out to ensure more enjoyment of high-level rowing. His teachings spread by pamphlet, disciples and results, Jesus moving to the Head for several years, and then the metropolitan and Oxford clubs adopting the 'endless chain' movement and other such catchphrases. They took Henley by storm one after another, and the style influenced Boat Race crews also. Fairbairn became known throughout the rowing world as Steve, and he was a great supporter of rowing for women on the Cam, encouraging Jesus coaches in the twenties and thirties to help out at Newnham, where the boat club began as the Newnham Rowing Society in 1896. Shorts replaced gym tunics in 1919 and Cambridge University Women's Boat Club emerged from a Second World War link-up between Newnham and Girton. But the first women's side-by-side race against Oxford took place in 1930 and there have been several series since, the present one being held at Henley in an atmosphere of rampaging partisanship which must resemble the experiences of racegoers in 1829.

It was to see the work of men like Steve, and a host of other coaches who became famous and famous dons who became coaches, that people like the Master of Trinity Hall, Henry Roy Dean, propelled by a leg drive that would do credit to any oarsman, cycled well over twenty thousand miles in support of his crews. It was along the Cam that Sir Henry Howard, bursar of St John's, made full use of his bike for the job in hand:

> Observe how with a *rapid* poke
> I keep this bike-wheel spinning;
> That's what I mean, my worthy stroke,
> By getting the beginning.

It was here, according to Leslie Stephen, that a man in the fever of his youth spent 790 of his estimated 800 days in Cambridge, nine of the remainder being spent recovering from the exertions thereon, and the tenth wasted in lionizing his mother and sisters, regretted as long as he lives. History for him will be measured in races, his library consisting chiefly of the *Boating Almanack* and old copies of *Bell's Life*, his cramming only partially pacified by mathematical examples taken from the mechanics of the river, his seasons the sculls, the pairs, the fours and the eights. On the other hand, Stephen said, in partial answer to another don who claimed that every visit to the river drops a man down a place in the tripos, the captain of a boat club may receive a better intellectual training from his position as captain than he does from studying for the ordinary degree. 'Anyone who has tried the experiment will admit that it is a severe trial of judgement to keep eight oarsmen in due subjection.'

Stephen's remarks were made in a series of essays in the *Pall Mall Gazette* in the 1860s when he was taking a hard look at his university where he tutored at Trinity Hall. He was about to renounce cloth and gown and go to London to try his hand at journalism, eventually becoming the founding editor of the *Dictionary of National Biography* as well as fathering Virginia Woolf. His acute and fresh mind never lost faith with rowing. He recognized that it fulfils all the requisite conditions by which an undergraduate's amusements must be fitted to his liking.

> It goes on all the year round, and interferes with his studies; it requires a great deal of very hard and disagreeable work; it rubs holes in his skin, raises blisters on his hands, and gives him a chance of an occasional ducking; when pursued to excess, it may even injure his health for life; and it gives him an excuse for periodical outbursts of hilarity, which, if skilfully managed, may lead into scrapes with the authorities.

His other observation, that the propensity for rowing depends much upon the tribute derived from the town drains, was also echoed, or was an echo of, anonymous lines which borrowed their metre from Robert Browning:

> Barnwell Pool is dreary and dank,
>   The birthplace of smells and the grave of hope;
> Would his death be swift if a man once drank
>   This oozy mixture of slime and soap?

The Browningesque lament ends with a growl which contains the Absolute that the luckless Edward of Shane Leslie's infamous book was hunting:

> So these are our joys, and this our toil;
>   And this is truth that I now record;

Rowing is – what with blister and boil,
  And the rain and the sewers – its own reward.

Yet every day it is just the same
  Though my nose be red and my fingers blue,
I visit the river and sink my name
  And become one-eighth of an eight-oared crew.

No crewman ever won by himself. The muse of the Camus is not the muse of the Isis. Fewer heavies of poetry queue for inspiration from the Fens, notwithstanding Rupert Brooke's discovery of the church clock in Grantchester and the enthusiasm of Charles Kingsley. But the rowers of the Cam have received plenty of support from rhymesters and versifiers, the journeymen and satirists of the undergraduate press. It is fortunate for them that Rudie Lehmann, founder of *Granta* magazine (1889) and for years a staff man on *Punch*, was a Trinity oarsman, and the magazine produced a huge centenary number for the Mays in 1927, reprinting many of its old contributors and contributions. It included Lehmann's multi-stanzaed account of the Incident In 1890, when the respective presidents Muttlebury and Guy Nickalls had an argument because in the correspondence arranging the date of the Boat Race Nickalls wrote bluntly that Cambridge were 'a poorer lot than usual'. Nickalls and Reggie Rowe eventually visited Cambridge to make amends and reconciliation was celebrated at a banquet. But this is heavy stuff; we will take a few tasters from other hands, first from Sir Owen Seaman, aping advice from Horace, to coxes in the bumps. He would have to watch his language this century but has the ignorance of 1894 as his excuse:

> Round serried Ditton's sinuous bay.
>   Till up the Reach with dancing riggers
> They feel the wash and pound away
>   Like niggers;
>
> Then, even as the crafty cub
>   Closes upon his evening mutton,
> Swiftly apply your indiarub-
>   ber button.

The magazine has a page of corn, samples being: 'Enthusiast (clapping pillar box on the back): "Well rowed, Lady Maggie!" ' Or:

'We are asked to deny the rumour that several Lent Boats have been equipped with those little signs – "If you can read this you are too d—n close".'

Then there are the limerick specialists:

> There was a superb rowing fella
> Whose socks were all ebon and yella;
>   When they cried, 'Look how four sits!'
>   He said, 'It's my corsets,
> The *dernier cri* from Spirella.'

> At Clayhithe an oarsman of First
> Developed a terrible thirst;
>   To quench it, I hear,
>   He drank nine quarts of beer,
> But on the way homeward he burst.

And there are 'Lines on a Last Century Beauty', written in 1901:

> She was neat and she was slender,
>   Wondrous light and fair to see;
> Countless men would oft defend her
>   Merits o'er their dish of tea.

> See her meet inferior lasses,
>   Bashfully they draw aside,
> With a graceful bow she passes
>   Full of beauty, full of pride.

> Jealous critics, vain and tainted,
>   Vulgar-born and vulgar-bred,
> Said that she was 'fast' and painted,
>   And declared her nose was red.

> Once in London she'd a rival
>   For a gallant judge's hand;
> But she won – so could deprive all
>   Challengers of hope so grand.

> She is now a by-gone glory,
>   Old and battered, once so fine;
> She, the subject of my story,
>   The Varsity boat of '99

It was that boat, or rather the victory of the light blues that year, that the Cambridge 99 Rowing Club was named after.

The Cambridge men have shown great propensity for seeing the funny side of rowing as they tore off adventuring in the floods to Clayhithe, imagining that the Wash came right past King's Lynn to their own city like it did centuries before; or embarked on long expeditions, rowing down the Great Ouse way, past Ely's cathedral tower, a lighthouse in a sea of corn, to King's Lynn and across the Wash to Lincoln and Boston. Or picnicking on their more familiar stretches, at the perennially popular Grassy for instance, of where that cricket and rugby fan P. G. Wodehouse made his first attempt at lyric writing:

> She's my Grassy Corner girl,
>   Shy and sweet,
> And my heart is in a whirl
>   When we meet,
> Just we two in my canoe,
> With none to come between;
> But we're never quite alone,
> We've Cupid for our chaperone.
> She's my little Grassy Corner Queen.

The young Wodehouse was visiting Kenneth Duffield in Trinity, Duffield being the melody writer who was composing for the May Week Footlights' production. Duffield himself caught a crab at Grassy while trying to impress three pretty girls, Madge Titheradge, Beatrice Terry and Kidlette Howard, whom he had invited to spectate with his parents. As Trinity were about to bump Caius, Duffield sneaked a look at Zuleika Madge and caught a whopper, rocking the eight so much that it filled up and sank.

The Cam's answer to Tom Hughes and his superb description of the Oxford bumps in *Tom Brown at Oxford* is Ian Hay's *A Man's Man*. Hay was the pen-name of J. H. Beith who was captain of LMBC in 1899, and here St Benedict's are hell-bent on bumping All Saints to go head:

Hughie, who was keeping to a steady 32, felt with satisfaction that the men behind him were well together. Number Seven, small but plucky, was setting bow-side a beautiful example in steady swing and smart finish. Six – Mr Puffin – was rowing a great blade. To look at him now you would ask why he had not been included in the university crew. If you saw him trying to row forty to the minute you would marvel that he should be included in any crew at all.

Five was not looking happy. He was lying too far back at the finish. To him the boat seemed heavier than usual, for he was just beginning to realise the difference between seconding the efforts of Hughie Marrable and those of Mr Duncombe. Still, he was plugging gamely. Four, a painstaking person, was encouraging himself in a fashion entirely his own. After every stroke, as he sat up and swung forward, he gasped out some little *sotto voce* remark to himself, such as 'Oh, well *rowed*, Four! . . . Stick to it, Four! . . . Use your *legs*, old man! . . . That's better! . . . That's a *beauty*! . . . Oh, well *rowed*, Four!' And so on. Where he got the necessary breath for these exercises nobody knew; but some folk possess these little peculiarities, and row none the worse for them.

Bow was another instance. He was a chirpy but eccentric individual, and used to sing to himself some little ditty of the moment – or possibly a hymn – all through a race, beginning with the first stroke and ending exactly, if possible, with the last. He had been known, when stroking a boat, to quicken up to a perfectly incredible rate simply because he feared that the song would end before he completed the course, a contingency which he regarded as unlucky in the extreme. On the other hand, he would become quite depressed if he had to stop in the middle of a verse, and he was quite capable of rowing *rallentando* if he desired to synchronise his two conclusions.

But few people have the time or the inclination for these diversions while oscillating upon a sixteen-inch slide, and the rest of the crew were swinging out and plugging in grim silence. The two boats swept into the roaring medley of Ditton Corner. They flashed past the row of piles and tethered punts amid a hurricane of shouts and waving handkerchiefs. Hughie, wrongfully exercising his privilege as stroke, allowed his eyes to slide to the right for a moment. He had a fleeting glimpse of the crimson and excited countenance of Miss Gaymer, as some man held her aloft in the crowd. . . .

Eventually two revolver shots from the bank told Hughie when to go for the All Saints, let off by pre-arrangement by a stout clergyman whooping like a Choctaw, tearing along the bank with his weapon smoking in his hand, and of course, the Benedictines went Head, the bowman croaking, 'Two bars too soon, Hughie! Oh my aunt, we've gone Head! Two bars too soon!'

In real life Jesus once had a feud with Clare because according to

Jesus gospels, Clare coxes developed the habit of not raising an arm to acknowledge a bump. In 1869 this led to this minuted entry: 'The Clare cox as usual neglected to hold up his hand in acknowledgement of a bump – an omission on his part which resulted in the Clare boat becoming simultaneously a wreck and an example.'

And the serious side of the bumps is well put by an anonymous Cambridge poet:

> I met a solid rowing friend, and asked about the race,
> 'How fared it with your wind,' I said, 'when stroke increased the pace?
> You swung it forward mightily, you heaved it greatly back;
> Your muscles rose in knotted lumps, I almost heard them crack.
> And while we roared and rattled too, your eyes were fixed like glue,
> What thoughts were flying through your mind, how fared it, Five, with you?'
> But Five made answer solemnly, 'I heard them fire a gun,
> No other mortal thing I knew until the race was done.'

Five is the sort of lad who may have done his tubbing on the Cam, and who may get a trial for the Varsity boat come the autumn. He's been out where the light fours roll and where the Fen winds blow, and the president may have spotted him. He may join the ranks of the blues from his peach-coloured, serene, sometimes slightly superior university. His college may measure its status on the place of its boats on the river and the fact that number five has got a trial or a blue. In the 1980s this is much less likely to be the case than it was before the Second World War. But interest is still shown by many, even though – this another observation from Stephen in times past – a good many men have succeeded in living fullish lives in Cambridge without being contaminated by rowing and the river or even by cricket. The dons and the coaches and the captains report that the sport is keeping its numbers up remarkably, is the most widely participated in, among men and women alike. And one reason for this must be that the facilities are there. Students at plenty of other universities row, but they usually lack the widespread tradition of rivalry among themselves, and often lack water and boathouse on their doorstep.

If Five heads for a blue he will be looked after by the CUBC boatman Alf Twinn. An American who rowed for the light blues in the 1970s said of Alf: 'I was flattered that he called everybody else Sir and me Dick, and then looked as if he'd blasphemed when he'd said it.' Alf sorts the men from boys if he gets half the chance and has been at it since the early thirties, and we will take our leave of him at the Goldie boathouse, watching the embryo blues and the bumpers and the pleasure seekers go by, with the peach tones and glittering fruitfulness of the city lying over Jesus Green, the ornamental Backs hidden but welcoming, the mellow willow-lined drain that is the Cam and the past training ground of the light blues behind us to the east. We will visit Putney-on-Tideway, where lightness meets darkness. Men's water, Alf calls it.

4

Tideway, men's water
Putney to Mortlake, the championship course

'There is a zest about the Tideway which smoother and more sluggish courses cannot excite, which is more subtle than the attraction of more picturesque reaches.' Robert Forster first summarized the lower part of the Thames thus in the late nineteenth century, and Martin Cobbett, aquatic and horse-racing scribe of the *Sportsman* and later the *Sporting Life*, took him up on it specifically with the novice in mind. 'He ought to find out the first time he comes over the rollers at Teddington from the stream water,' wrote Cobbett, 'catches the ebb, and finds his ship, whatever it may be, change from a dead to a live thing.'

It is a very different place from the waters on which the blues are nurtured, this waterway which takes in the great S bend from Putney to Mortlake with a mean high-water spring tide of almost eighteen feet, muddy beaches, wide open spaces, and currents and stream which are alternately at one with the ebb and at odds with the flood. The particular four and a quarter miles from Putney Bridge to Chiswick Bridge has become the most famous rowing course in the world, not only because the University Boat Race settled upon it in 1845 but because it was, and is, the championship course for other contests of oar. The Boat Race has now been running there for longer than any other current fixture. Many contests took place there for the professional sculling championship of England and of the world before the professional side of the sport died out. The Amateur Sculling Championship of Great Britain is still held there, a title combined with the Wingfield Sculls.

In the middle of the last century the river above old Putney Bridge became the most popular venue for London amateurs, a quiet village not too far from the city where some of the largest clubs, notably

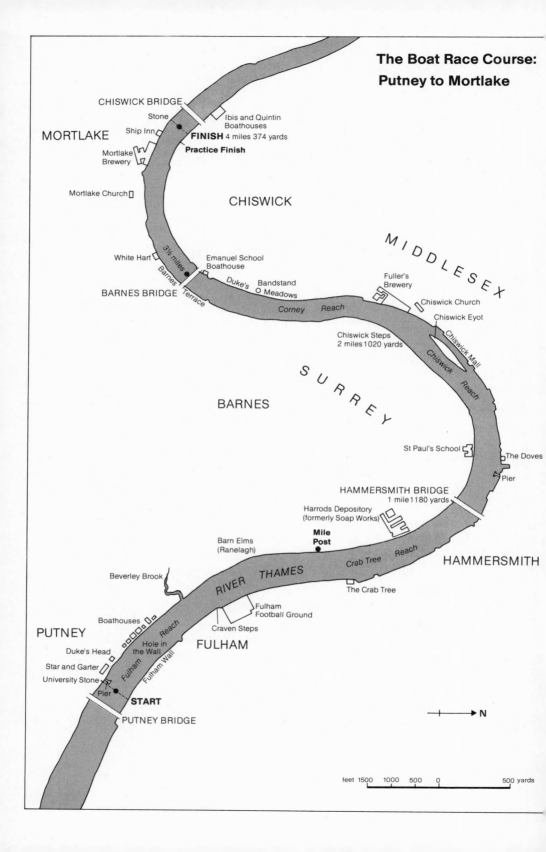

Leander, London and Thames, set up shop. They went there because
the river farther east became too crowded. And now, in an age when
Putney is swallowed into the suburbia of London, it remains one of the
most important places in the rowing man's atlas. The Head of the
River race attracts more than four hundred eights each year and the
Scullers Head more than five hundred scullers.

The use of the Tideway for rowing long predates the Boat Race. The
Romans probably introduced the oar to the Thames in place of the
paddle when they found the British crossing point at Westminster.
Rowing became part of the fabric of commercial London, and some of
its pageantry and sporting attributes may be gleaned from the diaries
of Pepys, the plays of Shakespeare, and the novels of Dickens. Sail was
little threat to the oar in such a place, but steam power was a rival to
them both. This, and the growth of trade, traffic and the city itself, plus
the building of bridges, forced the professionals into other livelihoods,
increased the commercial use of the Tideway, and drove the amateurs
west. Not for long into the latter half of the nineteenth century was it
viable for Messrs Godfrey and Searle to keep their boathouses opposite the Palace of Westminster or for the State Barge House to remain
there, and the construction of the Embankment changed the relationship of the city to its river.

What the early blues and the mid-century clubmen found west of
Putney's wooden bridge, designed by the surgeon Cheselden and built
by George III's carpenter Thomas Phillips for £23,084 14s 1d in 1727,
was a stretch of beach on the Surrey bank leading down to the river
from houses both private and public. The church with its Gothic tower
stood at the end of the bridge with the Putney Hotel opposite, then the
Eight Bells, an elegant row of Georgian houses, the Star and Garter
and the Duke's Head, a house on the present site of the Putney
Constitutional Club, a field leading to the White House, and tree-lined
meadows to Beverley Brook, beyond which was the political writer
and MP William Cobbett's house, named after its majestic trees, Barn
Elms. Cobbett was of the same family as the aforementioned Martin,
and before his time at Barn Elms the house had been occupied by Jacob
Tonson of the Kit-Cat Club, Cowley the poet, and Heidigger, Master
of the Revels to George II.

The earliest Putney was a fringe of marsh backed by a long slope of
forest or open moor, but centuries since, the village, a fishery and ferry
point, had pushed its way back from the river and achieved a notable

list of worthies among its inhabitants, including Oliver Cromwell, who set up his army headquarters there to keep an eye on the King at Hampton Court. The political philosopher Thomas Hobbes had lived there, and Edward Gibbon, whom Carlyle called 'the splendid bridge from the Old World to the New' when Gibbon produced his *Decline and Fall of the Roman Empire*, was born there, and one James Belcher gave his name to the blue and white spotted handkerchief which he wore when prizefighting.

Opposite Putney was the village of Fulham, a fruit and vegetable garden for London, sometimes visited by Putney lads, who would knock up a log raft and sail over to raid the orchards. The places were connected by the old bridge which was at an angle across the river, ending at a point near the present District Line station of Putney Bridge. There was a toll house spanning the Fulham end of the bridge, and between there and the parish church sporting a simple pointed tower were the Swan public house and a malt house. Then came Bishop's Walk and the Bishop of London's Palace, erected in Henry VII's time by Bishop Fitzjames. Most of London's bishops since the Restoration are buried in the churchyard. The garden for exotics was started by Bishop Grindall and Bishop Compton extended its curiosities as long ago as 1560. The Middlesex bank was wooded as far as Craven Cottage, built by Margravine of Auspach when she was Lady Craven. Then came Lord Londonderry's The Old Crab Tree, opposite Barn Elms, and a malt house and a cottage and the site of demolished Brandenburgh House where Margravine also lived and where Queen Caroline died in 1821. This was roughly opposite the present Harrods depository. The City Arms tavern acted as downstream sentinel of Hammersmith.

Hammersmith itself is a comparatively recent place in terms of local government, having been part of the parish of Fulham until 1834. But the dwelling on the creek appears as Hermodewode in the Domesday Book and there is a legendary tale of how it gets its modern name. The story goes that the churches of Fulham and Putney were built by two sisters of gigantic proportions who had only one hammer between them which they bandied across the river to each other. One day the hammer throwers were foiled because the tool landed on its claws and broke, but a smith who lived in west Fulham repaired it, hence the etymology of Hammersmith!

From Barn Elms on the Surrey bank there was no development until

Miss Ibbett's house was reached coming into Barnes. Marshy meadows leaked streams into the Thames and the towing path crossed them on little wooden bridges. Old Hammersmith Bridge was built in 1827 for £40,000, the first suspension bridge to be erected in the south of England. It had a twenty-foot roadway suspended sixteen feet above the waterway, plus a footpath, and gave a clear waterway span of 688 feet. There were octagonal toll houses at each end, the suspension towers having archways of the Tuscan order. On the Middlesex side was a boatbuilder's on the upstream side of the bridge, some houses, and a nunnery inland in King Street for the English Benedictine Dames. A rude wooden bridge over a creek, built by Bishop Sherlock in 1751, divides the Lower Mall from the Upper Mall, and there is the Doves public house, which was a coffee house until 1860. The Old Ship, farther upstream, is also on the waterfront.

Then came West Middlesex water works, built in 1806, the new church of St Nicholas set back from the river, and Hammersmith Terrace where the dramatic writer Murphy and the landscape painter Loutherbourg had lived. Between there and the west end of Chiswick Eyot where there was a ferry were a malt house, a marine store, Whittingham's printing office and the Red Lion. After the ferry came Parsonage House and Chiswick church which has a host of famous graves, including those of Kent the gardener who built the Duke of Devonshire's house close by, Loutherbourg, Ralph the historian, Cromwell's daughter Mary Countess of Falconberg, and Hogarth with its famous epitaph by Garrick.

After the church came a timber wharf and then the aforementioned Devonshire, or Chiswick, House where Fox died in 1806 and Canning in 1827, and the Duke's meadows and marsh stretched westwards round a huge bend with Chiswick and Turnham Green glimpsed occasionally behind their screen of trees from a passing boat at high tide. Opposite the meadows was the Surrey village of Barnes, a terrace of houses interrupted by a malt house and ending at the White Hart, followed by two more houses, another malt house, the church, the Queen's Head, the pottery, and yet more malt houses. Barnes Terrace was notorious because the Count and Countess d'Antraigues were murdered in their home there by their Italian footman. Cromwell had lived at the manor house, and after him the benefactor of Bristol, Edward Colston, but it has also been occupied by several archbishops of Canterbury. A long wall flanked the towpath to the Ship, where the championship course ends. There was a large house, probably part of the brewery, behind the pub. Just beyond the finish was Mr Searle's house, and then Sir W. Kay's and Lady Best's.

Between these banks the Thames ebbed and flowed. There have been changes alongside the course and several new landmarks have been added to the panorama, such as the soap works which were then superseded by Harrods depository on the Surrey bank east of Hammersmith Bridge, and the bandstand in Duke's Meadows. In 1884 a new bridge between Putney and Fulham was opened. It was designed by Sir Joseph Bazalgette who as the chief engineer of the Metropolitan Board of Works designed the Thames Embankment which prevented floods in Westminster and the City. The toll was abolished and the new bridge met Fulham in a different place, closer to Bishop's Park, and incorporating under its roadway the aqueduct which had been constructed apart from the old bridge. At some time, too, the District Railway pushed across the river towards Putney and Wimbledon on its own span east of the road bridge. In 1887 the Putney embankment was built, replacing the path and presumably as an appendage to the new bridge, for Bazalgette was into embankments. It went as far as Beverley Brook but has never been extended, as many hoped, to Hammersmith Bridge.

It was in 1887 that the present Hammersmith Bridge was built. The old one, which had a mid-channel steamboat pier which narrowed the navigation, was a light and inexpensive structure and some of its problems were caused by the 11,000–12,000 people who gathered on it to watch the Boat Race. The new bridge was designed by Tierney Clarke and opened by the Duke of Clarence, and the designer earned criticism at the time. 'It speaks very little for the judgement of our municipal authorities,' said one critic, 'that they failed to realize that a much wider structure would later become quite imperative.' He was certainly to be proved right in the case of the roadway users.

The third bridge on the course, Barnes railway bridge, has been dubbed the ugliest crossing of the Tideway. The original design was by Joseph Locke for the London and South Western's loop line to Richmond and Hounslow. It was opened in 1849, additions being made in the 1890s. The opening was delayed for a month when an expectant mother could not be moved from a house in Malthouse Lane which had to be demolished to make way for the iron road. Chiswick Bridge does not actually span the course, but it is the landmark of the finish. Designed by Sir Herbert Baker, it is the largest concrete archway across the Tideway and was opened in 1933, a joint enterprise of the counties of Surrey and Middlesex.

Now, the Middlesex bank is fleshed out from Fulham football ground at the end of Bishop's Park near the site of Craven Cottage to the wharfs before the Duke's meadows. The Civil Service sports club occupies his fields, and the boathouses of Emanuel School and the Civil Service are just downstream of Barnes Bridge. On the other side of the bridge is the site of Green's boathouse, the last place in the area which rented out skiffs and racing boats, burned down in the late 1970s. Then comes a new municipal boathouse shared by a number of clubs, and just through Chiswick Bridge, which marks the end of Duke's Meadows, are the adjacent clubs of Quintin and Ibis (the Prudential), who host Oxford and Cambridge respectively at the end of the race. A little way upstream from here is the University of London's large slipway and boathouse, and almost opposite Ibis are Mortlake Anglian and Chiswick and the much more famous Thames Tradesmen.

The nature of development has changed much in recent years, too. Once industry reigned from the Fulham FC to Hammersmith. Now more and more housing is replacing wharfs and warehouses, giving Fulham folk a back window onto a none-too-friendly reach of the river. Close to Hammersmith Bridge the Riverside Studios have sprung among industrial property. Hammersmith itself has attracted a number of notable innovators who have enjoyed the noble sweep of the Thames past their front doors or rear windows. A house in the Upper Mall once occupied by the novelist Dr George Macdonald was taken by William Morris in 1878. He changed its name from The Retreat to Kelmscott House after his other house on the upper Thames, and sometimes a party of summer voyagers would row from his front door at Hammersmith to his upper Thames meadow. Morris had a tapestry loom at the house and he converted the coach house into a weaving room where Hammersmith carpets and rugs were made, and which later became the meeting place of the local socialists. He also started the Kelmscott Press in a cottage close by, designing his famous typefaces and typographical ornaments for it. He died in 1896. Next door, Sir Francis Ronalds FRS made the first electric telegraph, eight miles long. Catharine of Braganza lived on the Upper Mall during her widowhood; Dr Radcliffe, the court physician who founded the library at Oxford, lived here, and Turner the painter at West End from 1808 to 1814. Beavor Lodge became the residence of Sir William Richmond RA, and the great Thamesophile Sir Alan Herbert lived in Hammersmith Terrace. All sorts of people boat from the area now, among them the boys of Latymer Upper School, Sons of the Thames, Auriol Kensington Rowing Club, the London Corinthian Sailing Club, and the renowned Tideway Scullers' School squatting with Furnivall Sculling Club. The latter was started by Dr Frederick Furnivall to teach sculling to girls he recruited locally and from among his English students and academic friends, and from the waitresses in an ABC café which he frequented. Come hell or high water, great picnicking expeditions set forth each summer Sunday bound for Richmond with the doctor in command, often with a boatload of Britain's best academic brains among the company. He also coached his girls in an eight rigged for eight scullers, himself steering the octuple. In Hammersmith also is now the headquarters of the Amateur Rowing Association, formed from the Putney-based Metropolitan Rowing Association in 1882 and occupying a splendid boathouse on the Lower Mall acquired from the National Provincial Bank. And Bill Colley makes fine wooden sculling boats there, in a workshop tucked round the back of the Rutland Arms.

The Surrey bank has changed much less, although Putney has little trace of the grand houses – Fairfax, Essex, Grove, Lime Grove – which used to be in easy reach of the High Street, where the painter Leigh Hunt, on a visit from faraway Hammersmith, dropped dead, or of Putney Hill, where Cardinal Wolsey is said to have given his fool to be escorted by a chamberlain to his King by way of thanking him for a kindness after he was kicked out of Whitehall Palace. 'I assure you,' Wolsey told the chamberlain to tell the King, 'for any nobleman's pleasure he is worth a thousand pounds.'

The rowing clubs spread along the Putney embankment, London first using the Star and Garter, now rebuilt, before they erected their own premises next door to Leander, who moved to Henley in 1898. The cricket field behind these boathouses gave way to housing long ago; Aylings the oar makers and Phelps the boatbuilder and Matt Wood's outrigging company were nearby, but all have now moved from Putney. George Sims and Sons still build boats there. The line of clubs includes several banks, Westminster School, Ranelagh Sailing Club, Vesta and Thames rowing clubs, Imperial College boathouse,

Jack Holt's chandlers, and a few terraced houses to Leaders Gardens which extend almost to Beverley Brook. Barn Elms is now an Inner London Education Authority sports centre with a boathouse on the river. The reservoirs on the west side of Hammersmith Bridge have been filled in to accommodate a new campus for St Paul's School, which also has a boathouse. The profile of Barnes and Mortlake is hardly changed except that there is now only one brewery, Watneys, much larger than before, and flats lining the river west of the railway bridge.

Here, then, is the place where time and tide stay for no man, as the legend on the sundial on Putney church puts it. It is the place where a ship is a live thing, particularly a thin-skinned, open boat which can pick up any tremor on the water and easily fracture its skin on floating debris. At low tide the Thames is a quiet stream, the rowing men deep below the towpath level, taking the bends wide to avoid the shallows along the Fulham wall and round Craven Cottage and the Crab Tree on the Middlesex side, then shooting Hammersmith Bridge close to the central-span side of the Surrey pillar to stay with the dredged channel, then keeping out a bit to avoid St Paul's slipway. Hammersmith Mall is high up, with a long gentle beach in the foreground leading to a massive escarpment of embankment which has flood gates let into it for access to the rowing clubs' pontoons, now low and dry. Chiswick Eyot stands ridiculous and top heavy, and at the crossing where what is left of the stream switches from Surrey to Middlesex, ripples reveal the rocks and the shallows, gentle sandbanks appear, and the floating police launch base above Barnes Bridge is aground. It never feels like a great highway in these circumstances, almost drained, nautical miles from both the placidity of its non-tidal upper self and the grand visions of Canaletto or Whistler downstream, from where it pours into the North Sea and Channel, taking great ships with it.

A few hours later it is utterly transformed. In the spring it spills over Putney embankment until the railings and trees are freestanding moorings and the riverside buildings isolated floating homes for the boat people. The tide deposits its driftwood in a ragged line along the banks, and on the broad sweep of Hammersmith one feels balanced on the very curvature of the earth as the setting sun burnishes the Mall fronts in copper and gold, their image cascading from a thousand windowpanes into bottleglass water which, but for the embankment battlements, would link their first floors with the dark shadows of

Castelnau and St Paul's School's studies. One can see why Turner lived in Hammersmith. He may not have painted it as such, but he caught and borrowed its every mood, its pale dawns when the bridge is merely a suggestion suspended in air, its hazy blue-rinse breakfasts, its sparkling fresh elevenses, its warm lazy lunches, its sluggish oppressive teatime, its opening-time slide into an inky trickle beneath the orange-hued night sky of London, or suppertime charcoal blackness pricked here and there by a light. At Hammersmith at high tide, and farther upstream where the Eyot is now a minor unkempt verge, and round the bends past Barnes where the waterway is above the road and the railway bridge looks almost graceful when not showing its legs, the Tideway displays all its power and its romance, pushing up to Teddington Lock and gathering itself for its salty charge to the sea, to the lure of London and more exotic distant places. The airliners hang over it like great preying gulls, almost silent, on their glide in to Heathrow Airport. This is not the sparkling water of an Isis sonnet or a lazy Granta verse, not Vivaldi and bubbly in a punt. This is Elgar's tide, pomping and circumstancing to the sea.

And it can lose its beat, displaying a contrapuntal anger by a cauldron of white caps and bitter gusts, battering the buoyed boats along Putney Reach. It exposes the man in the open boat to snow, sleet, hail, horizontal rain like flying bolts, and winds which sear the face or the back and which quickly teach the novice, and the novice coxswain, that there is a lot more to moving a boat than dipping oars in the water or occasionally pulling a rudder string. Watermanship takes on wholly new proportions here, quite unlike non-tidal work. Here he will meet the weather of bleak marshes and electric storms as well as wind-shadow, fog, and the barge traffic of London's salmon-stocked river.

The adoption of Putney to Mortlake as the championship course brought people in their thousands to watch boat races, particularly the Oxford and Cambridge. It became a water Derby Day, with all manner of sickly things to eat offered by vendors, with entertainers and buskers performing along the embankments and on the bridge at Hammersmith. Dick Phelps of the renowned Putney watermen's family remembers pushing his nose through the railings first in 1906. There was the man who escaped from chains, the woman who swallowed a needle and thread and regurgitated a threaded needle, as well as the blue needlers to watch. Forty years before that time, when the river and race authorities had not got a grip on controlling boating, there was often a dreadful mêlée both along the course and following the crews. Then, the best way to see the start on land was to station yourself on the high ground around the Duke's Head. When the race passed and the accompanying flotilla screened the contestants, you made over the market garden by the Half Moon field, at the risk of being tomahawked by a gardener's spade or lanced by a pitchfork. Next came a rush of cabs and traps across Barnes Common to the waterside near the White Hart. Martin Cobbett reckoned that you saw more racing this way than on a steamer, but were less liberally provided with excitement. This was because your ship would be one of twenty or thirty paddle boats,

all bumping and jostling and fouling each other in frantic style, sufficiently exciting to make a nervous passenger jump overboard for fear of being knocked into the water or blown up. Most of the fleet would be shut out all the way by the leaders, some be hung up when they should be starting, and others fail to stay. The only thing really certain was a collection being made by the crew for the crew and skipper. . . .

How was it that most of them escaped shipwrecks and burstings and blowings up, and we who took our chances abroad were not drowned, smashed, burnt, boiled, or converted into sausage-meat among the machinery, like the poor chap who went to a down-river fight, and was taken out of the engineroom a spoonful at a time? There they were, the passenger boats, whose captains did their steering by wireless telegraphy, a sort of deaf and dumb finger talk, to a watchful nipper, who translated orders, signalled from the bridge, to the engineer; such despatches as 'back her', 'stop her', 'half a tarn a-starn', 'go on a-'ed'. There they were, each doing its best pretty much regardless of the other or consequences, charging and fouling, and ramming into the rest, and being done to likewise. I have been one of a crowd conveyed on a solid wall of, say, eight or nine steamers jammed sponson to sponson, going straight full speed at a buttress of Hammersmith Bridge with a certainty thrown in of the funnels being smashed off before they could be lowered on top of the wedged-in passengers. If you or your ship got in front you might see some of the rowing. Most likely all you did see was the mob of boats ahead, and at that were thankful indeed when the expected arrived in the shape of an easy, and the time came for the devoted crew to go round collecting in spare moments afforded through something's going wrong with the works. In those days the captain appointed himself official stakeholder, and charged a shilling in the pound for acting as such. You could get your pocket picked on most reasonable

terms, and probably did if you displayed money, or looked like being
worth 'going over', and had had a good day if you didn't stop a live
spark or some sort of grit with your eye before the voyage was over.

Cobbett concluded his reminiscence with a frontal attack on sirens,
advanced navigational aids which he hated.

By the 1880s Londoners had adopted the race as their own,
enveloping what the university clubs envisaged as a private match.
Charles Dickens Jr, in his *Dictionary of the Thames*, took a wistful
look at what it used to be, and recorded the change:

> The comparatively few people who watched the practice of the crews
> all seemed to know each other. It was a wonderful week for parsons.
> Past University oarsmen, their jerseys exchanged for the decorous high
> waistcoat, the white choker taking the place of the rowing man's
> muffler, were to be met all over Putney, and about Searle's yard and the
> London Boat-house. The towing-path was a sort of Rialto or High
> 'Change, on which old friends met and renewed their youth as they
> talked over old times and criticised their successors. There were but few
> rowing-clubs then; the river had not become the fashion; the pro-
> fessional touts and tipsters had not fastened on the boat-race; the
> graphic reporter as yet was not. There was betting, of course, but it was
> of a modest kind, and was unaccompanied by publicity. The whole had
> the ring of true sport about it. It seemed indeed to be the only event that
> kept alive that idea of sport for its own sake which was fast fading out, if
> it was not already extinct in most other contests.
>
> Of course it was all too good to last. The popularising process was
> not likely to spare the boat-race. First all aquatics generally grew more
> in favour, and so a larger public was attracted to take an interest in the
> battle of the blues. Then the newspapers took the subject up, and the
> graphic reporter worked his will with the race and its surroundings, and
> the extraordinary multiplication of sporting newspapers and sporting
> articles in papers of all sorts let loose any number of touts on to the
> towing-path. Finally the ominous announcement of 'Boat-race 5 to 4 on
> Oxford (taken in hundreds)' and the like began to appear in the price
> current of Tattersall's; and the whole character of the race was changed.
> What the blue fever is now, and has been for some years, every
> Londoner knows well. . . .
>
> It is certain, at all events, that for some time before the race there is
> taken in it – or affected to be taken, which does just as well – an interest
> which has about it even something ludicrous. Every scrap of gossip

about the men and their boats, their trials and their coaches, is greedily devoured. Year by year, to gratify the public taste in that direction, has the language of the industrious gentlemen who describe the practice become more and more candid, not to say personal. . . . The gushing reporter not only attends the race itself, but disports himself on the towing-path after his peculiar and diverting fashion on practice days, and daily develops the strangest conglomeration of views on matters-aquatic in the greatest possible number of words. . . . Cabmen, butcher boys, and omnibus drivers sport the colours of the Universities in all directions: the dark blue of Oxford and the light blue of Cambridge fill all the hosiers' shops, and are flaunted in all sorts of indescribable company. Every publican who has a flag-staff hoists a flag to mark his preference and to show which way his crown or so has gone – unless, as is sometimes the case, he be a dispassionate person with no pecuniary interest involved, in which case he impartially displays the banners of both crews. Everybody talks about the race, and it generally happens that the more ignorant of the matter is the company the more heated the discussion, and the more confident and dogmatic the opinions expressed.

That thousands and thousands of people go down to the river on the important day who do not know one end of a boat from the other, who have no prospect of seeing anything at all, and no particular care whether they do see anything or not, is not surprising. That other thousands go, knowing perfectly well that all they are likely to see is a mere glimpse of the two crews as they dash by, perhaps separated by some boats' lengths after the real struggle is over, is equally natural. Thousands and thousands of people go to the Derby on exactly the same principles. That 'Arry has claimed the boat-race for his own is only to say that he is there as he is everywhere, and that circumstance is not perhaps to be laid to the charge of the boat-race. But the fact is, and becomes more and more plain every year, that the boat-race is becoming vulgarised – not in the sense that it is patronised and in favour with what are called 'the common people', but in the sense that it has got to be the centre of the most undesirable surroundings – and that its removal from metropolitan waters would not be lamented by the real friends of the Universities, or lovers of genuine sport. . . .

The crowding of spectators to see the practice – and as many people go nowadays to Putney on a Saturday afternoon, if there be a good tide, as used to go to the race itself twenty years ago – has been complained of. The general exhibition of interest has been deprecated. It has been intimated that all this newspaper publicity is distasteful and undesirable. In some strange way the boat devoted to the service of the general body of the press on the day of the race is always either so slow a tub as to be of little use, or else meets with some mysterious accident which deprives its occupants of any but a very distant view of the proceedings, while their more fortunate brethren, who happen to have been educated at Oxford or Cambridge, are careering gaily after the racing boats on board one of the University steamers. The independent sporting papers say that accurate information has become more and more difficult to get, and newspaper reports – except in special quarters – are, following out the private-match theory, discouraged as much as possible. But it is all to no purpose. The boat-race can never shake off its surroundings so long as it continues to be rowed at Putney. Change of air will, in all probability, shortly be found necessary to restore it to a healthy condition – a condition in which it certainly is not now.

The tide has changed again since the days of Cobbett and Dickens, although Putney is still very much the boating man's headquarters. The coming of soccer and rugby, athletics and indoor tennis has given the populace other heroes to watch and other interests on which to bet, and the coming of radio and particularly television has given them new ways of tracking the Battle of the Blues. But if the weather is crisp they still turn out to watch in their thousands, some still have a flutter, and most importantly for the boat clubs involved, they still identify with the colours. The simple unreasonableness of supporting light or dark blues gives the annual battle a nationwide, and through broadcasting, a worldwide appeal. There is nothing so widely followed as a Putney-to-Mortlake, a straightforward two-horse race on the championship course, where time and tide stay for no man.

PART TWO
History

5
Pilgrims' progress
The story of the Boat Race

The preacher was speaking, he told his congregation, among old friends; his experience had been gained under the auspicious radiance of these stars in our firmament, between these four walls, but he came now amongst them as a pilgrim to offer 'what poor tribute he can bring of Christian advice and exhortation'. He avowed that he was no friend of athletic sports such as 'running and leaping' for the same reason for which St Paul looked with disfavour on the contests of the pagans at Corinth. They are, he said, essentially selfish.

The chaplain to the Speaker of the House of Commons and rector of Lawford in Essex was giving the commemoration sermon in the chapel of St John's College, Cambridge, in 1868.

I need not refrain from using a tone which might be thought hardly congruous with a pulpit elsewhere; and I will go on to point out the essential difference between the old English, the old university sports of cricket and boating, and the reckless and thoughtless amusements, and *selfish* – such they are in my view – that distinguish collegiate society at the present day.

The games of an earlier generation were *social* combinations; several individuals joining together, to assist one another in a common object; to merge their own individuality in the common weal; to institute for the time a commonwealth, in which each member should work together with a common sympathy for a general effect. The effort was corporate – and so was the honour – no single man need be too proud of being the eighth part, or the eleventh part of such a triumphant confederation. No one need arrogate to himself even his own due proportion of the glory; it might be an exercise of kindliness and humility to prefer his comrades before himself, to think himself the least of the eight or the eleven, not

worthy to be called one of them at all. And when he reflected that what
was his own side's victory and triumph, was the defeat and humiliation
of his opponents – he might, if he were a kindly and a Christian
gentleman, console himself with the thought that each individual on the
other side, some of them perhaps among the dearest of his own friends,
felt only an eighth or an eleventh part of the disappointment and
chagrin.

As he laboured his point few of his congregation would have been
aware of his double distinction; for the Rev. Charles Merivale had
played for Harrow in the first cricket match against Eton in 1824 and
had rowed for Cambridge in the first Boat Race against Oxford. Since
that occasion in 1829, a year in which he also won the Browne Medal
for a Greek epigram and an Alcaic ode, his life seemed to be devoted to
more sedentary pursuits. He became Dean of Ely in 1869, succeeding
Harvey Goodwin, who had been his active predecessor, and the joke
that went about was that the first sermon that he preached was on the
text 'From henceforth let no man trouble me' and that from henceforth
he personally applied it to himself. His friend Christopher Wordsworth, Bishop of Lincoln, took up the theme in his obituary in the
Cambridge Review after Merivale's death in 1893.

> There can be no doubt that he was happiest as he sat, slightly reclining
> his head backwards, in his library chair, with his eyes upon the book
> held well before them. Twenty-two years at St John's College Cam-
> bridge, where he was Fellow and Tutor (1833–48); twenty-two years
> more at a college rectory (Lawford in Essex, pop. 700); and a third
> period of like length spent as the dean of a noble cathedral in a small
> provincial city, apart from the last few years of his life when his physical
> powers were much diminished – with such a history, it certainly cannot
> be said that Charles Merivale's lot was cast amid stirring scenes.

Yet, the Bishop of Lincoln pointed out, Merivale's early life had
almost sent him in another direction entirely. Born in 1808, son of
John Herman Merivale, a Devonshire lawyer, and Louisa Heath *née*
Drury, daughter of the headmaster of Harrow, he was sent to his
grandfather's school where he met the Wordsworth brothers and
where his uncle, the Rev. Henry Joseph Thomas Drury, was a distinguished classical scholar and an assistant master with a reputation of
classical scholarship. Old Harry, as he was known at Harrow, once

said the whole of Lucan's *Pharsalia* to himself while walking from Harrow to Eton. From Harrow Charles Merivale went to the East India College at Haileybury and won a prize for Persian, but resisted the idea of going off to Bengal, and entered St John's in 1826, a year after the boat club there was started. He joined it. In 1830 he came fourth in the classical tripos, the future Bishop of Lincoln being first, and came out as a senior optime in the mathematical tripos in the same year. He became a Fellow of the college in 1833, was an admirer of Gibbon and found fame in the world of letters for his *History of the Romans under the Empire*.

His most important claim to a place in history was made at the commemoration dinner of the inter-university crews in 1881 at the Freemasons' Tavern in Great Queen Street. Two hundred men who had represented the university boat clubs against each other sat down on Thursday, 7 April, the day before that year's race, in a hall bedecked with the flags of college boat clubs and of the schools who had contributed most to the Boat Race, such as Eton, Westminster, Harrow, Winchester, Marlborough and Repton. Two hundred was a sizable total: the organizers calculated that 370 survivors were resident in Great Britain (thirty-seven Oxonians and forty-four Cantabs were dead, and a total of thirty-four were abroad or in the colonies). Among the absentees were forty clergymen detained by the duties of Lent, and the flag of Rugby School which was bespoken that evening for a lecture given to the boys by the Rev. Tom Hughes. At least one man from every representative university crew to date was at the Freemasons' Tavern. The Hon. Sir Joseph W. Chitty, justice of the Chancery Division of the High Court, took the chair, seated at a high table at the side of the room. On his right was the Rev. T. Staniforth, stroke of the victorious Oxford crew in the 1829 race, and on his left was Merivale, Dean of Ely, who addressed the company, which included Mr Edward Searle who had started every Putney race to date, thus:

'It has been said that the Bishop of St Andrews was the first to suggest the race. I don't think I can quite admit that. He and I were old school friends, and had often competed in contests both grave and gay, and I should rather say that the original idea was common to us both.' The Bishop of St Andrews was not present personally, but had sent his shirt. Over the back of Chitty's high-pitched chair was hung the jersey worn by Charles Wordsworth in the 1829 race, *suspendisse potenti*

vestimenta maris Deo. The only other attendant representative of
those original crews was wearing his jersey – Toogood, still the
heaviest man from either place ever to row.

Charles Wordsworth had stayed with his father and his brother Kit
at Trinity Lodge when home from Oxford in those undergraduate
days. He thus saw much of his old Harrow friend Merivale nearby
at St John's. He would sit in the Johnian boat occasionally when they
were short of a man. He had founded and played in the first university
cricket match in 1827, and he and Merivale dreamed up the idea of a
boat race together, almost certainly while they were messing about on
the Cam. Wordsworth returned to Christ Church and planted the idea
with his captain, Staniforth, while Merivale talked to Snow, his
captain at St John's. Staniforth and Snow knew each other at Eton.
Thus the idea came from a connection at landlocked Harrow; the
practical steps were taken by Etonians. On 20 February 1829 a
resolution was passed by the University Boat Club at Cambridge that
'Mr Snow, St John's, be requested to write immediately to Mr
Staniforth, Christ Church, Oxford, proposing to make up a University
Match.'

That is how the first Boat Race came about. Wordsworth took a first
in Greats, became a tutor at Christ Church, was ordained and spent
ten years as an assistant master at Winchester before becoming
Warden of Trinity College, Glenalmond, from 1847 to 1853. Then he
became Bishop of St Andrews. He worked on the revision of the New
Testament, and at one time was private tutor at Oxford to Cardinal
Manning and to William Gladstone, the Lancastrian aspiring PM,
who once said: 'I don't believe there's a single spot on the Thames
where I couldn't tell you, in calm weather, the power of the current and
the depth of the water.' And Wordsworth retained his interest in sport,
combining it with his love of and facility in classical scholarship, well
past the passing of his competitive days. On 21 January 1888 he
addressed the students of St Andrews on the subject of Pindar and
Athletics, Ancient and Modern, with the following introductory
remark:

> In an age where athletic exercises of all kinds are so much in vogue that
> the result of an Inter-University boat-race or cricket-match is tele-
> graphed to Calcutta, to New York, to Australia, with no less speed, and
> received with no less eagerness, than if it were intelligence of a change of

Ministry, or of the issue of a great battle, we may well feel surprise . . . that no poet has arisen to do for our modern victorious gymnasts what Pindar did for the conquerors in the four Athletic Festivals of ancient Greece. [These were at Olympia, Delphi, Nemea and the Corinthian Isthmus.]

In his odes, says Wordsworth, Pindar nowhere appears to regard athleticism as sufficient in itself. 'It is evident that he looked upon the games as an instrument for the development not of the bodily powers only, but of the whole man. He never praises an athlete merely as such, without reference to his mental and moral qualities.' Two other Pindaric lessons are, says Wordsworth, to be generous towards your opponents and never to be envious of their success. Turning to modern athletics, Wordsworth lists a half dozen sporting songs, including those produced at the jubilee celebrations of the inter-university cricket match and the first Boat Race, admitting that he is mentioned in both. They constitute almost the sum total of what 'we have done to encourage our athletes poetically or artistically. . . . Taken together they would scarcely outweigh a single ode of Pindar.'

He points out that although in his own estimation national character and position in the annals of athleticism are not to be despised, and that astonishing progress has been made during his memory, Professor Jowett nevertheless found it necessary to complain in his introduction to Plato's *Republic* that 'any improvements that have been made during the last 2000 years have been more than counterbalanced by the disuse of gymnastics.' And Wordsworth warns that 'we have not yet sufficiently made up our minds as to the place which athleticism ought to hold in our system of education.' That it already holds a prominent place, no one can doubt, he says. Many masters in public schools and colleges appear to think that as much credit is gained to their respective institutions by a pupil being chosen to pull stroke in a boat race as by his becoming Senior Wrangler at Cambridge. . . . 'That under such circumstances the young men themselves should be only too ready to think the same is not to be wondered at.' And hence, says Wordsworth, we have had censors such as the late Justice Coleridge, whose *Memoirs of Keble* complained of 'the insane and excessive passion for athletics indulged in our universities and great schools'. That was eighteen years before Wordsworth's address to the St Andrews students, and during that time he thinks he can detect a sort of conspiracy between boys and masters to 'perpetrate in practice a monstrous double false quantity, that is, to make schooling short which ought to be long and to make play long, which ought to be short.'

Later he quotes Dr John Morgan, the Manchester physician, whose book *University Oars*, published in 1873, was the result of quizzing every traceable blue to date about his health in order to assuage popular notions that rowing damages it. A friend of the oar, then, Dr Morgan wrote:

> The young generation are not satisfied with expending a large portion of their nervous energy on the contraction of their muscles in propelling boats, but when they are out of those boats, even at times when *their books lie open before them*, their thoughts and their conversation are directed rather to the chances of making another bump, than to mastering the difficulties of Aeschylus or Thucydides; indeed, the minds of young men at the present day seem to be alive to no other questions than those which relate to the cultivation of their muscles.

Wordsworth even throws Xenophon into the argument, quoting the philosopher–soldier–sportsman's words 'which deserve to be printed in letters of gold: "In proportion as the mind is something better than the body, in the same proportion are the contests of our minds to be pursued more zealously than those of our bodies." '

Morgan tells us, Wordsworth says, that there are now champions of the oar and of the cricket field whose achievements are more familiar to the rising generation than those of any general, statesman, or poet. Wordsworth hopes Morgan is exaggerating, although he testifies that 'I have never since been nearly so great a man, or perhaps so happy, as I was when in my boyhood I was captain of the eleven at Harrow. But the greatness, such as it was, has left no record. And so of Dr Morgan's champions. In another generation they will be all unknown.'

Faced a hundred years later with the alternatives for youthful enthusiasm presented by Dr Morgan, the choice for most would not be difficult, but later generations can see the drift of his argument, and of Wordsworth's pleas to keep matters in proportion.

Snow, the stroke of the Cambridge crew of 1829, wrote to Morgan: 'Reading men will always beat non-reading men.' Talk to the coaches more than a hundred years later and they will tell you that not only is a lot of academic effort required of everyone, which was certainly not the case until some time after the Second World War, but that the best crews, the fastest crews, have the best academic records. Furthermore, at Oxford or Cambridge a convincing case can be made to show that the standard of oarsmanship has risen in general in the 1970s and 1980s, not in proportion to the national rise at the top end of the sport, but enough to assert rowing as the major sport at both universities. In 1888, Wordsworth warned the students of St Andrews of the evils of material prizes for athletics, and imagined a day to come when

> athletes and their friends from all quarters of the globe shall be gathered together upon the banks of the Thames in a more glorious Olympia, which, while ministering to the game-loving propensities of our race, shall have an eye to nobler and more enduring ends; a day when, under influence of the large-heartedness and brotherly affection which all innocent social enjoyment on a grand scale tends to inspire, Evangelical associations and Pan-Anglican and Pan-Presbyterian Conferences may be merged into one.

He was connecting the sports with religious ceremonies, a long custom of the English, and he extended his hand to followers of Buddha and Islam as well. Did he know that the young Baron de Coubertin had had a vision in Rugby School chapel that the slab on which Thomas Arnold's name is inscribed was the cornerstone of the British Empire? That the French aristocrat had fallen in love with the Rugby of *Tom Brown's Schooldays*, and was about to embark on a crusade to convert the *lycées* to adopt the sporting ideas of English public schools?

Wordsworth was probably unaware of this, but his message was indicative of the mess that sport had got itself into over the definition of the amateur at a time when more games and activities were catching on. The Amateur Rowing Association, which had developed in 1882 out of the Metropolitan Rowing Association, was getting itself in a frightful mess over its rule which barred mechanics, artisans, labourers, or anyone engaged in menial duties from being designated amateurs. By 1890 several clubs broke to form the National Amateur Rowing Association, which had similar rules without the pejorative clauses referred to above. Henley was to follow the ARA line, and the NARA did not see its view vindicated until 1938, when the ARA changed its definition and talks began towards a merger which took place in 1956.

Meanwhile, Coubertin made one of his many visits to Britain in 1893 with the Société Nautique de la Basse Seine, who sent a crew to the Grand Challenge Cup at Henley. They were beaten by Thames RC and were not happy about their treatment by the regatta stewards, but Coubertin himself urged caution and was much impressed by the way the regatta was run. Just as Thames RC's pioneering of 'hare and hounds' as a winter activity could well have influenced the Amateur Athletic Association (founded 1881) in forming its definition of an amateur, so Coubertin's experience at Henley could well have coloured his view of how his modern Olympic Games should be run when he eventually got them on the road in Athens in 1896. At a distance, the International Olympic Committee looks very similar to the Stewards of Henley regatta.

Several men who have rowed in the Boat Race have been embroiled in such world-wide sporting activities, but for the most part such arguments have passed by the race itself. In having a hand in starting it the Dean of Ely and the Bishop of St Andrews were involved in something which has remained private in eligibility and performance, though it has become public in spectacle and support. It is time to trace the course of its development.

After the first race in 1829 several attempts were made to arrange another match, and Cambridge sent challenges in 1831 and 1834. The first failed because of an outbreak of cholera in London, and the second because Oxford countered the Cambridge offer to race on 'any day between 4 and 21 June, on any part of the river between Westminster and Richmond, either against or with the tide, in slack water, and at high or low water, whichever suits the Oxford crew' by insisting that the contest should be at Henley or Maidenhead. In 1836 the second race was held at 4.20 p.m. on Friday, 17 June, on what was then the championship course for professional scullers, Westminster to Putney, a distance of approximately five and threequarter miles. Cambridge pulled away on the flood and won by nearly a minute, and they adopted light blue as their colour when Mr Phillips of Christ's, not a member of the crew, tied a piece of Eton ribbon to the bows of the boat for luck. Cambridge wore white jerseys, Oxford white jerseys with dark blue stripes. There was an argument about the course to be used for this race, Oxford suggesting Putney to Hammersmith against the tide, Cambridge objecting to rowing against the tide and predicting fouls on such a short course, and Oxford countering by proposing Putney to Hammersmith and back, thus giving the crews the chance of showing their paces both with and against the tide. They also demanded that university men should steer the boats and not professionals, and to this Cambridge agreed.

The Head of the River crews of the two universities met at Henley in 1837, Queen's College, Oxford, beating St John's by about 150 yards over about two and a half miles. To mark the victory the other boat clubs at Oxford presented Queen's with a handsome flag depicting a boar's head. The Queen's captain's book says in 1866 that in honour of the win two blue stripes were added to the college's ribbon of white by the university as a mark of admiration. If this is true, and if the reference to 'university' referred to the OUBC, then it must have happened retrospectively, because OUBC was not founded until two years later. Or, records of an earlier university club have been lost. Strictly speaking, too, Queen's were not Head, but rose to the occasion when the dean of Christ Church refused permission for his charges, who were Head, to row at Henley.

In 1837 Cambridge beat the London club Leander from Westminster to Putney, and in 1838 the return fixture was abandoned by the umpire because of a series of fouls caused by the professional watermen who steered both crews and regarded fouling as part of the game. In the Easter vacation of 1839 the universities met for the third time, Cambridge adding the light blue stripes to their jerseys and winning by upwards of a minute and a half in thirty-one minutes from Westminster to Putney. Both crews were steered by university men, which has been the custom since. Thus the Boat Race has never had professional coxswains, although it was soon to have disputes about professional coaches.

The first Henley Regatta was held later that year, set up by the townspeople to boost their trade and inspired by the turnout at the first Boat Race ten years previously, and repeated in 1831 when Leander beat Oxford for £200, Oxford using a professional cox, George West. W. W. Smyth and Charles Penrose from the Cambridge boat rowed for Trinity and won the Grand Challenge Cup at the regatta.

There were Boat Races again in 1840, 1841 and 1842. The brothers the Hon. G. and the Hon. L. W. Denman rowed for Cambridge in 1841 and 1842, winning the former and losing the latter. The Hon. G., who later became a judge, left an interesting account of training and preparing to race with CUBC:

The Oxford and Cambridge Boatrace was to come off on Easter Tuesday, and during the whole of the Lent Term a crew, of which I was seven, was in practice. The race in 1840 had been a very close affair, won by Cambridge after an apparently losing race up to Battersea Reach. Several old oars remained in each boat. The new ones in ours were W. Croker, Caius, bow (9th Wrangler in 1839), my brother Lewis, Magdalene (two), Ritchie, Trinity (three), Cobbold, Peterhouse (five), and myself (seven); our steerer, too, was new, J. Croker, brother of our bow and 8th Wrangler in 1840. Vialls, our stroke, and Somers-Cocks of Brasenose, the Oxford stroke, both Westminster men, had each rowed stroke in 1840. The coxswains were new to the river and it seemed a very open affair. The race in those days was from Westminster Bridge to Putney Bridge, 5¾ miles; about half an hour's work with an average tide. There were no police arrangements for keeping the course clear and it was often ticklish work for the coxswains to decide whether to go ahead or astern of a train of barges catering across the river. There was no practising at Ely in those days, nor any coaching from the banks, but, before coming to town, the crew used to row at its best pace from the town lock to Baitsbite, coached by the steerer, and the time occupied was, on an average, from nineteen to twenty-one minutes, according to the wind and stream prevailing at the time.

When the time came for moving to London, our captain, C. M. Vialls, the old Westminster, determined to drive us up to London. He was a capital whip who often drove the mail. A good drag was hired and we had a fine day and enjoyed the drive immensely. Arrived in London, the majority of the crew took up its quarters at Ginger's Hotel (which stood about where the booking office of the District Railway for the Westminster Bridge station now stands), but I and my brother 'trained' at home at my father's house in Portland Place. Our training was probably less rigid than that of the present day; but it was pretty strict, and our kind mother made no difficulty about it as far as diet was concerned. The Broad Walk which runs across the Regent's Park above Portland Place towards the Zoological Gardens was then just being made, and a part of our training was to run to the end of that walk and back before breakfast. Then, in the course of the day, sooner or later, according to the tide, we walked to Searle's Boathouse (where St Thomas's Hospital now stands) and prepared to race to Putney against a crew of Cambridge Subscription Rooms (sometimes supplemented by a waterman or two), and this we did daily, with two days' exception, until the day before the race, giving the other crew a long start of 200 or 300 yards and judging of our performance by the distance we had covered before we passed them, which generally occurred before half the course had been chased.

The race, as I have said, was to be rowed on Easter Tuesday, 13 April. [The race was actually rowed on 14 April.]

On the Good Friday the crew did not row together; but my brother Lewis and I took a wherry and paddled up the river with the intention of rowing to Richmond and back for exercise. About 300 yards below Kew Bridge I, rowing bow and steering, or rather directing the steering (for we had no rudder), saw a boat ahead with a man's face towards me about 100 yards off. I took this to be a boat rowing in the same direction as we were; but in a few seconds I was undeceived by a tremendous blow on the shoulder, and the sight of a wherry's sharp-pointed bow appearing close to my left ear. The wherry was full of rough holiday-makers who rowed on triumphantly as our boat filled with water and gradually sank to the bottom not far from the shore, so that my brother got hold of the painter and pulled me and the boat to the towing-path, and after he had bestowed his benediction on the enemy and emptied the boat, we again embarked and I tried to row. It was in vain. The pain was too great, and I felt quite sick from the attempt. Happily at that moment we spied a four-oar, manned by some others of our crew, and it was arranged that I should go back as steerer of that boat and one of them take my place; and so I got back in time to Portland Place. But what was to be done? We did not dare to send for the doctor for fear that he might forbid me to row on the Tuesday. It was necessary to keep my mother and sisters in the dark for the same reason. Happily the junior footman (George Pearman) was a man who seemed to know every-thing. So we took him into counsel. He had been a barber, and we had a notion that he might therefore possess some knowledge of surgery. After gravely considering the case and inspecting the bruised shoulder, he advised us to allow him to fetch just one leech, which he very skilfully applied. It was about the size of the two lower joints of the little finger when it began its meal, and nearly as large as a lemon when it rolled off satisfied. George's prescription was a complete success; for, though I was obliged to abstain from rowing and could not have practised on the following day, even if it had not been a Sunday, I took my oar again on the Monday, when we practised starts and had a few short rows, and on the following day was in my place and felt no inconvenience from the accident, and we won the race by the unusually long interval of 1 minute and 5 seconds (about 360 yards).

I may as well add that in the following year (1842) after a hard race and with a decidedly inferior stroke and three changes, all for the worse, in the crew, we were beaten by 13 seconds. So that my career was a fair sample of the general result of the University match (six of one and half a dozen of the other).

After 1841 the score was 4–1 to Cambridge, and there were some real stirrings on the Isis. The latest beating had been by more than a minute, in spite of Denman's threatened incapacity in the Cambridge boat, and the first incidence took place of a rebel crew. Fletcher Menzies and his brother Sir Robert first came to prominence in Oxford rowing in 1839 when they won the University Pairs, Fletcher in his freshman year. In October 1840 he was apparently elected president of OUBC, but J. J. T. Somers-Cocks of Brasenose, who had been president for the 1840 race, was back in the chair in March 1841 to supervise disaster for that year. Menzies stroked University College to the Head of the River in 1841, and in March 1842 George Hughes of Oriel became president. But in October 1841 Menzies formed a crew who were far better than the official one, according to contemporaries, and before Christmas he was regarded as the 'captain'. At any rate, Hughes's crew won, with Menzies at stroke, his brother Sir Robert at two, Gilbert Bourne – who was to become a famous name in coaching the orthodox English style of rowing – at five, and Arthur Thomas Whitmore Shadwell steering. Hughes, brother of Thomas Hughes who would later write *Tom Brown at Oxford*, began to flag during the race and was revived when he was reminded to suck the piece of lemon under his seat.

There was no Boat Race the next year, but the crew with only two changes, R. Lowndes replacing F. T. M. M'Dougall at bow and E. Royds replacing E. A. Breedon at three, won the Grand at Henley with only seven men. Fletcher Menzies was too ill to race in the final and the rule at the time allowed no substitutes once the regatta had started, a rule encouraged by Oxford the previous year to foil a Cambridge plan to shuffle men between the Cambridge crew and their 'old boys', the Cambridge Subscription Rooms, according to progress in the draw. Cambridge, the seven-oars' opponents in this 1843 final, objected to rowing against only seven men, but the acting steward Lord Camoys ruled that there was nothing to prevent an eight rowing with seven men.

The coxswain Shadwell published *A Treatise on Steering* in 1844, and the principles of rowing and steering which he preached held good until the introduction of the sliding seat in the 1870s, an invention which Shadwell attributed to the devil. He learned his coxing at Eton and St John's College, Cambridge. His elder brother, Alfred Hudson Shadwell, rowed for St John's and for Cambridge in 1839 and 1840, but Arthur moved to Balliol and became an Oxford man. While at Cambridge, though, he came across Tom Egan of Caius, to whom is attributed more than to anyone else the introduction of the amateur style of rowing. Egan steered Cambridge in 1836 and from 1839 to 1844 in various regattas and races, and was president in 1853. He coached eight Cambridge crews including the 1836 boat. He also became a barrister and a major in the 3rd London Rifle Volunteers, and editor of *Bell's Life*, the weekly newspaper whose interests were mainly sporting. It was fortunate for rowing that Egan steered the nearest thing England had to a national sporting newspaper, because the coverage of the sport under him was as diligent as the attention paid to the principles of amateurism on the Cam.

George Drinkwater, a compiler of the Boat Race's official centenary history, reckons that Egan had a hand in Shadwell's steering pamphlet, a publication followed in 1846 by *Principles of Rowing* by 'Oarsmen'. Freddie Brittain's bibliography of rowing attributes this book to Shadwell alone. *Principles of Rowing and Steering* followed in 1857, again attributed to Shadwell. Whether or not Egan applied his pen to Shadwell's early work, there are indications that the two thought on similar lines, that coxswains at that time often assumed the role of coach, and that their position was very influential. As early as 1839, C. J. Selwyn of Leander said in his Boat Race speech: 'The true way to make my office unnecessary is to allow no waterman to have anything to do with the matches, but to leave it all to gentlemen. I do not wish to say a word against watermen, but watermen's ways are not our ways, or watermen's notions our notions.' After the 1840 race he set out the Boat Race principles: 'First, gentlemen should steer; second, that fouling should be abolished; and last, not least, that victory should be its own reward.' The 1840 race, he said, had been conducted in gentlemanly and generous spirit.

After Shadwell's steering pamphlet appeared, Oxford fought for the principle of amateur coaching. There was a race against Cambridge in 1845 from Putney aqueduct to Mortlake church, that course being chosen because of the density of river traffic nearer Westminster. Two

of Oxford's men were teetotal, and a lot of good it did them:
Cambridge won. The next year Oxford banned the use of professional
coaches for the college crews within three weeks of the Torpids or the
Summer Eights. Professional coaches continued on the Cam, however,
Robert Coombes helping them for the first race in 1849 and again in
1852. In 1847 Cambridge would not agree to Oxford's proposal that
neither side should employ watermen as coaches, and eventually
Oxford withdrew because of illness and opposition from dons. Unusually, there were two races in 1849 and Cambridge picked a
seven-man crew for the second one on 26 November, the number
seven seat being left blank and filled by whoever would row. J. C.
Wray became available after a week. The race took place on 15
December with Cambridge on the Surrey station taking an early lead
and advantage of the strong tail wind to cross to Middlesex and use
Oxford's bend. Oxford then came up and Cambridge tried to get back
towards Surrey and were bumped. The rules at that time said that
when one crew has taken the other's water and the boats afterwards
come into contact, the boat whose water has been taken shall be
deemed to have committed a foul if the leading boat stays on station;
but if the leading boat departs from the water so taken, then the
leading boat has committed a foul. Oxford stopped, restarted, and
were moving up again at the finish, and umpire Fellowes of Leander
awarded them the race. It is the only occasion on which the Boat Race
has been decided on a foul, and because Coombes had again had a
hand in coaching Cambridge, he got the blame from some quarters.

For the next two years there was no race. Then in 1852 Cambridge
engaged Coombes again and Tom Egan offered his services to Oxford.
The loss of the race by Cambridge for taking the inside arch of
Hammersmith Bridge was again blamed on the advice of Coombes,
but Egan had had quite a hand in coaching Cambridge as well. In fact
he coached both crews in alternate weeks, and wrote his apologia in
Bell's Life:

> I am a Cambridge man, and have trained a victorious Oxford crew.
> Those arts which once led Cambridge to victory have now contributed
> to the success of Oxford, and to Cambridge men should be made known
> the cause of this apparent change of allegiance. . . . Our favourite
> science, rowing, ought to be the first object of our love. . . . The chief end
> of these great contests is to exhibit to the world rowing in perfection;

whatever, therefore, tended to lower style in rowing, or to diminish aught of the beauty and polish of the perfect eight-oar, was to be resisted and condemned. . . . The Universities did neither wisely nor well in ever allowing watermen to touch the yolk-lines of their match-boats.

We ought to be able, Egan said, to point to our match crews and challenge the world to produce anything so uniform in motion, so polished in form, at once so speedy and so graceful, as one of those picked eights of the gentleblood of England. Professionals were apparently incapable of doing this, and Cambridge's clinging conviction that their influence was useful because of their knowledge of the Tideway, where the Putney-to-Mortlake course was now the favoured venue of the Boat Race as well as the professionals' champion track, was wearing a bit thin. 'I have not been contending for Oxford, but for Rowing,' Egan continued, '. . . not with Oxford against Cambridge, but with the spirit and genius of the victorious past against the poorer inventions of later years.'

Egan's plea for pride and gentleblood got him back in favour on the Cam, notwithstanding the victory of Oxford's 'Chitty's crew' whom he had helped, for in November 1853 he became president although he had taken his degree in 1839. There had been no race in 1853 and in 1854 Oxford won by 'eleven strokes'. No more professionals were seen coaching except when Oxford used Matt Taylor of Newcastle in 1857. There was a special reason for that, though: they used a keelless boat built by Taylor and paid for by Lonsdale, the president, because he encountered so much opposition to the idea that nobody would put their money where their mouth wasn't. The boat was 55 feet long and Oxford won by more than half a minute, and Taylor's services were engaged 'not to instruct us in the art of rowing, but to show us the proper way to send his boat along as quickly as possible.' The boat was of carvel construction, stroked on the bow side, and one of those who benefited by Taylor's demonstration was Edmond Warre, who was to acquire great influence on rowing at Eton, Oxford and beyond. Some coaches now get expenses, and the argument concerning professionalism is dissipated beyond recognition.

In 1853 and 1855 the universities met at Henley Regatta 'by agreement', the latter occasion caused by the hard winter in which the Cam and the Isis froze up and put a stop to training. After the 1854 race the score was Cambridge 7, Oxford 5. 1856 was notable because the race was run on the ebb from Barker's Rails, upstream about three minutes from the usual finishing point at Mortlake, to Putney. M'Cormick, one of three double blues in the race – he and Wingfield representing Cambridge and Bennett Oxford in the university cricket match – crabbed off his seat before Cambridge scrambled home half a length in front; and henceforth, apart from the two world wars, the Boat Race has been an annual event.

When the First World War interrupted, the score stood at Oxford 39, Cambridge 31, and one dead heat. The latter occurred in 1877 and was the last occasion on which a professional waterman officiated as a judge because of the controversy surrounding the decision (see chapter 8). In 1859 conditions were so rough that Cambridge requested a postponement. Oxford refused and Cambridge then kept them waiting on their stakeboat for half an hour. After the race got started, Cambridge sank at the White Hart, Mortlake. During the 1860s the popularity of the race reached boiling point and threatened the event itself. Steamers not only followed the race but lay in wait along the course, and they got in the way of the crews as well as each other. In 1864 the presidents warned that if there were any steamers ahead of the crews at the start, they would race on the ebb. A delay of the start would have left the steamers grounded. However, because of the presence of royalty in the person of the Prince of Wales, they could not use their threatened tactic. But the next year the boats returned to the boathouses to force the steamer captains to get behind them at the start. Cambridge led at Hammersmith but Oxford won the race, the first time in which a crew came from behind while still trailing at the long Surrey bend. The CUBC records say: 'The Prince of Wales for the first time in aquatic annals honoured the race with his presence though from the collisions that occurred among the steamboats he saw little of the race.'

An argument about status developed in 1865, Cambridge proposing that no men should row in the university race more than four years from the time of commencing residence. Oxford disagreed, 'admitting that they have an advantage which they are not willing to give up,' say the Cambridge minutes.

There was almost no Boat Race in 1868 when the Hon. J. H. Gordon shot himself accidentally, and died on 17 February. He rowed in the previous year and, incidentally, had canoed from Dover to

Rotterdam via Cape Gris-Nez, the Saône, the Rhône, and the Mediterranean to Genoa, thence to Switzerland and on to the Reuss, the Dar, and the Rhine. Cambridge asked to withdraw their challenge, but the meeting did take place.

In 1869 the Oxford coach George Morrison was invited to coach Cambridge and five men refused to row. Oxford won their ninth consecutive race in spite of Morrison's efforts, but Cambridge found a brilliant stroke in J. H. D. Goldie of Eton and Lady Margaret. Later a four made up of Oxford blues beat Harvard on the Putney-to-Mortlake course, one of the earliest examples of sports meetings between teams from different sides of the Atlantic. By 1870, when Goldie was in his first of three years as president and led Cambridge to victory, the steamer problem appears to have been sorted out. The *Graphic* reported, 'Only two steamers followed the race, one for the press and one for the umpire; the Prince of Wales, Prince of Teck, and other notables being in the latter.' Goldie and his victory were commemorated in song:

> For thrice three years dark blue had won
> Hurrah! They're best at last!
> Twas said that Cambridge rowing was
> A Phantom of the past.
> Yet here's a song to celebrate
> The 1870 crew
> Who turned the tide of victory
> In favour of Light Blue!
>
> Our stroke was worth his weight i'gold,
> And well did Granta's sons
> Take up the time they'd given them
> By Goldie of St John's!

. . . and so on, words by S. H. Catty of New College, Oxford, music by A. Christian of Cambridge.

Goldie was to follow this up with two more victories. Before he got as far as the soap works, now Harrods, in 1872, a bolt in his rigger broke and he could only sit there setting the rate without doing any work – or conduct, as one account had it. The conditions were absolutely foul. He told James B. Close, the bow man, that he had considered jumping overboard if Oxford got dangerously close to them. That was the nearest thing Cambridge have had to a seven-oar crew, and they got home by two lengths.

Goldie was also a pioneer in the use of the new-fangled invention of the sliding seat at this time. Clasper, the Tyneside boatbuilder, received an order for a ship 'smaller than last year as the crew promised to be somewhat lighter. He was anxious to fit it with sliding seats, but the President thought it would be a great risk to make an experiment with a Varsity crew,' say the CUBC minutes. Both crews used slides in the following year, Cambridge winning their fourth successive race and reducing the P–M record by a massive twenty-nine seconds to 19 minutes 35 seconds. Oxford kicked their slides away before they had rowed the stroke, reported one paper, so their motion was more visible, leading the papers, except the *Field*, to tip them. The watermen did so also, but bet the other way, and when Cambridge won with ease, their oars seen from the steamers were 'like a pianist's fingers'. Goldie was out of things by this year, but the influence of his efforts and those of the Oxford coach Morrison were being felt on the Cam. He also struck a blow against coxswains, for in 1872, the same year in which he broke First Trinity's six-year run as Head of the River by stroking Lady Margaret to the top, Goldie proposed that fours went coxless on the Cam. Four years before, a Brasenose cox had jumped overboard at Henley to give his college a runaway victory and a disqualification in the Henley Stewards'.

In 1875 E. A. Phillips's slide broke in the Cambridge boat when they were leading before the Crab Tree, and from then on he was practically a passenger, seeing Oxford move past by the time Hammersmith was reached. The dead heat came in 1877; the fiftieth anniversary, which fell in 1879, was celebrated by a blues dinner in 1881. In 1880 the fog was too thick on the appointed day and nobody thought fit to tell the finishing judge, E. H. Fairrie. He sat in his punt fogbound at Mortlake until the ebbing tide told him it was useless to stop any longer. The race was held on the following Monday. The Goldie boathouse was completed at Cambridge in 1882, a capital headquarters for CUBC; and there was a kerfuffle over the starting arrangements in 1883 when Edward Searle, starter for forty years, apparently dropped his handkerchief before giving the word go. It was snowing and almost dark, and some of the Oxford men started, then stopped, and then the whole crew took off at 42. Cambridge followed but were out of the race. After that the starting was done by the umpire.

Cambridge follow Oxford at the crossing, where the going in 1978 was roughest

Oxford after winning by a canvas in 1980

The Oxford crew of 1829

The Cambridge crew of 1829

Paddle steamers jostle for the best view

The original Oxford boat alongside a fixed-pin outrigger

The Varsity eight returning from Abingdon, passing homeward-bound picnic parties

The procession at Commem, 1863

The first two boats ready for the start of a bumping race

Folly Bridge and lock, about 1830

Goldie Boathouse in 1888

Coaching from the bank

A bump in the Gut during the Lents

Bump supper, Jesus College, 1927

Left: The Backs at Cambridge

Below: The Isis in the 1950s, with college barges

Cambridge were entering a strong period. Frederick Islay Pitman was stroke in 1884, and his crew won the race. Oxford won in the next year, and in 1886 Cambridge struggled home by two thirds of a length after being behind at Barnes Bridge, the first time a crew had come through to win when losing at such a late stage. Next year Ducker McLean, Oxford's number seven, broke his oar at the button just after Barnes Bridge and Cambridge won again. The light blues took the next two years with the same crew except for a change of cox, a unique occurrence in the Boat Race. S. D. Muttlebury was the president responsible for this. By now he had won four consecutive races, but he has been described as the personification of matter over mind, and in 1890 he rowed again to face the consequences of running the same crew twice. Everyone save himself had gone down, and his new crew lost in a race which was to begin Oxford's second run of nine consecutive wins. It was also said that Muttlebury lost this race because he was suffering from the clap. Whatever the truth of that, he and his crew put up a tremendous fight and the freshman W. A. L. Fletcher drove Oxford home by only a length. Oxford's president was Guy Nickalls, who was in his fourth race and first victory. He went on to have one of the finest rowing records of all time.

The 1891 race was a struggle for Oxford, under the presidency of Lord Ampthill. Frederick Wilkinson at number five was suffering from the after effects of influenza, returning to the boat before he was fully fit. 'He couldn't pull a sprat off a plate,' said Nickalls, the number four man. Fletcher was moved to number seven, which was a bad place for him, and the new stroke, C. W. Kent of Brasenose, rowed a superbly tactical race, always mindful of the weakness of Wilkinson. There was never clear water between the crews for the whole four and a quarter miles, and Oxford arrived first by half a length. They were coached by Rudie Lehmann who, although not a blue, was a Cambridge man. In 1892 he coached both crews, then Cambridge in 1893, Oxford from 1894 to 1896, and Cambridge again in 1899. His Oxford crew lowered the record in 1892 to 19 minutes 11 seconds, but when Lehmann coached Cambridge in the next year Oxford won again, this time setting the record at 18 minutes 45 seconds, thus breaking the nineteen-minute barrier. When Oxford's run of victories was under way, not broken until 1899, heart-searching began on the Cam. A letter to the *Field*, signed 'Eton Cantab', in 1893 said that Oxford had two permanent advantages, namely twice as many Etonians rowing for them and a home on the Thames, 'similar water' to Eton and the teaching of Dr Warre. 'All honour then to the pluck of the Cantabs who year by year continue the struggle with, under the circumstances, such success, but let not the public suppose that the great rivals meet on equal terms.'

Whatever the difference in the properties of Thames water and Cam water, it is certainly true that Oxford were dominated by Eton oarsmen at the time. None of their crews of the nineties had fewer than five Etonians and several of them had seven. In 1897 they had seven Eton oarsmen and a cox and set a record in practice on the ebb to Putney Bridge of 18 minutes 27 seconds, which stood for fifty years. They were coached at Henley by Ducker McLean and finished at Putney by Dr Bourne, and were helped to their record by enormous quantities of land water coming down the river. Etonians achieved the same statistical dominance in the Oxford boat in the next two years. But in 1898 Cambridge had imported W. A. L. Fletcher to coach, and he produced a good crew through a torrent of troubles. The president responsible was Dudley Ward, who encountered great opposition, several men refusing to row. He was kept out of the boat himself by his doctors, the stroke, C. M. Steele, became ill at Bourne End and had to drop out, and A. S. Bell took the seat although he didn't want it. When the crew was at Putney, Bell broke his slide on every outing until Fletcher had C. W. Atkinson, an Oxford science don, design one with wheels which would take any possible strain. On the day the weather was foul. Oxford won the toss and took Middlesex where the shelter was, and by the time Hawkins steered Cambridge across, their boat was full of water. Waterlogged, they lost. Claude John Dashwood, son of their benefactor and old blue John Haviland Dashwood Goldie, was on board.

Fletcher coached Cambridge again in 1899 under the presidency of R. B. Etherington-Smith, with Dudley Ward fit again and Goldie making another appearance. Fletcher 'finally imparted the lightning entry into the water and instantaneous drive from the stretcher', according to *Battles of the Blues*, and they won, breaking Oxford's nine-year run, in spite of the fact that J. E. Payne in the Cambridge boat had influenza and in spite of Oxford's now customary line-up of eight Etonians (to Cambridge's five), including Felix Warre, son and maybe heir to the formidable high priest of Eton and orthodoxy. Fletcher's Cambridge crew did it again in 1900, by twenty lengths in a time which equalled Oxford's record of 18 minutes 45 seconds in 1893. Warre was president at Oxford but went down with scarlet fever and did not row.

Warre was president again in 1901 and, in a southwest gale accompanied by heavy rain, Oxford, who had Middlesex, tucked in behind Cambridge and slowed to a paddle to avoid bumping them as both crews hugged the Surrey bank as far as Barnes Terrace. Maclagan took Oxford out nearing the bridge and they began to race, drawing level at the brewery and winning by two fifths of a length. In 1902 Oxford experimented with swivels for a year. In 1903 the starting pistol jammed and Cambridge were dragged off their stakeboat with squared blades. The umpire, Fred Pitman, did not notice as he was wrestling with the gun. After Cambridge won in 1906 they took on Harvard in September and beat them by two lengths over the Putney-to-Mortlake course. In 1908 the light blues were much criticized for their style, variously described as the 'Douggie Stuart style' and the 'Stuart sculling style' after their stroke, D. C. R. Stuart. Oxford caused controversy also because their chief coach, Harcourt Gold, arranged a secret trial on the Tideway just before the race, eluding the press and annoying both them and Cambridge. Cambridge won the race whatever their style, and were invited to be one of Britain's representatives in the Olympic regatta at Henley. In a different order and with H. M. Goldsmith replacing G. E. Fairbairn, they were badly beaten by the Belgians. The Belgians were regarded as enemy number one in those days because they had lifted the Grand Challenge Cup at Henley in 1906 and 1907, the first foreigners to do so. But they were beaten in the Olympic final by a Leander crew made up of the grand old men of English rowing, and, what is more, of orthodox English university rowing. The Henley Olympics witnessed zenith.

The Leander crew was A. C. Gladstone (OUBC, 1906–9), F. S. Kelly (OUBC, 1903), B. C. Johnstone (CUBC, 1904–7), G. Nickalls (OUBC, 1887–91), C. D. Burnell (OUBC, 1895–98), R. H. Sanderson (CUBC, 1899–1900), R. B. Etherington-Smith (CUBC, 1898–1900), H. C. Bucknall (OUBC, 1905–7), cox G. S. Maclagan (OUBC, 1899–1902).

Oxford began another run in 1909 when Robert Croft Bourne stroked them to the first of five wins and the first of four with himself in the key seat. He was son of Gilbert Bourne, now professor of comparative anatomy and Fellow of Merton, who rejoined the coaching team and, with W. F. C. Holland and Harcourt Gold, produced a fine crew. The achievements of the Leander Olympic crew had re-emphasized orthodoxy on the Isis and the Cam, and experimentation was eschewed first by Oxford. In 1911 the princes Edward and George followed the race, rowed out to the launch by the Putney waterman 'Doggett' Cobb, who is supposed to have greeted them with 'Hallo, my little princes! How's yer farver an' yer muvver?' For the first time aeroplanes flew overhead. In 1912 there were two races because Cambridge filled with water as they crabbed their way past London RC and eventually foundered near Harrods. Oxford stopped opposite the oil mills, just past the Doves and before Chiswick Eyot is reached, to empty their boat, and umpire Fred Pitman declared the race off. Oxford won the rerow on the following Monday in rough conditions, both boats having splash boards and inflatable bladders under the seats. The Australian blue, Stanley Melbourne Bruce, who later became Prime Minister there, coached Cambridge in 1914 and produced a four-and-a-half-length win. As the crews shot Hammersmith Bridge, a wooden grandstand erected on a barge creaked and groaned and then collapsed into the hold, dropping a hundred spectators with it, ten of whom were injured.

By this time it is possible to detect a pattern emerging in the Boat Race. Crews and coaches had learned to deal with a variety of conditions on the Tideway, and with a variety of situations which affected their selection. From the contemporary accounts emerges a long trail of illness, particularly outbreaks of influenza and various fevers, which quite often played havoc with the best-laid plans of a president. There had also been, since the race became an annual affair in 1856, several technical developments which affected rowing. The keelless boat, or more precisely the boat with a carvel skin outside the keel, was beginning to make its mark. Outriggers were already used, but the major change was to be the introduction of sliding seats, used by both universities in 1873. By the turn of the century Steve Fairbairn was beginning the coaching with Jesus College, Cambridge, which was to overthrow orthodoxy, but as we have seen it had hardly touched the Boat Race by the time of the First World War, although the experiments of Stuart and others may well have been a breeze from Steve.

The most noticeable theme, though, is the needle. By and large the advantage in the race swung from one university to the other in runs of a few years at a time, and to Oxford's advantage during this period.

Winning coaches, winning presidents, winning styles produced winning systems, and in the inevitable dialectical nature of an event which is competitive and annual, losers made war and revolution, evolved other methods to redress their sense of shame. In 1869 Cambridge imported George Morrison from Oxford and broke Oxford's nine wins with five of their own. Oxford's second run of nine wins from 1890 to 1898 was broken by another importation of an Oxford coach, W. A. L. Fletcher, to Cambridge. And in 1909 Oxford went back to their textbook of Warre and Bourne to set up another run. Runs of success, even if they do not breed complacency, which they well might, place the winning crew in the vulnerable position of having faith in a well-tried procedure while not knowing exactly how the next attack will be mounted.

Forty-two blues died in action in the First World War. With the outbreak of peace in 1919, hostilities re-opened between the universities. When the Second World War started the score had a different ring: Cambridge 48, Oxford 42, and one dead heat.

There was a Peace Regatta at Henley in 1919, hastily arranged, in which Cambridge beat the New Zealand Army and lost their semifinal to the Australian Army, who went on to beat Oxford in the final. Oxford had beaten the Canadian and United States armies on the way. Cambridge also went to the Allied Peace Regatta in Paris and won against New Zealand and Australia. Cambridge won the first three races after the war, and the official records have it that Steve Fairbairn was one of their coaches in 1920, the only time which he coached a blue boat. In 1923 Oxford won by threequarters of a length in a boat designed by Dr Bourne and with Gully Nickalls, son of Guy, as president. Then Peter Haig-Thomas, who rowed for Cambridge in 1902–5 and who had coached a succession of Third Trinity fours to victory in the Henley Stewards', was invited to coach the blue boat. He and Colonel D. A. Wauchope and F. J. Escombe produced a light crew whom they appeared to be able to shuffle into any seating order and won the race, reverting to strict orthodoxy which now had its fists up to the Fairbairn–Jesus style on the Cam. Haig-Thomas believed in the lightning beginning, and this win of 1924 was the first of a series of thirteen which reduced rowing on the Isis to despair and decline. In 1925 Pitman was once more the umpire when Oxford stopped at the Doves, waterlogged. In 1926 Hugh Robert Arthur Edwards blacked out in the Oxford boat for several strokes at Chiswick Eyot, his crew's fitness being in question. Later, he was to carry Oxford's rowing cross for many years, the beloved Jumbo Edwards possessed by needle. In 1927 a running commentary on the race was broadcast for the first time, and after the race in the centenary year 1929 the score was 40 wins each, with one dead heat.

In 1930 the Oxford president, Alastair Graham, resigned in favour of D. E. Tinné after Graham fell out with the coaches, Dr Mallam, A. F. R. Wiggins and Stanley Garton. By 1932 Cambridge were in danger of matching the runs of nine wins set up by Oxford in the last century. Oxford borrowed a Cambridge trick by importing a Cambridge coach. Colonel J. H. 'Boon' Gibbon arrived, keen, ruthless and lacking finesse. Unhappiness prevailed for Oxford, as Haig-Thomas produced his by now familiar act, shuffling the order until late in the day, and winning after his crew overhauled Oxford at the Crab Tree on a perfect day. Cambridge stayed together and, rowing as Leander, won the Grand at Henley and went to the Olympic regatta in Long Beach, California. They lost the final to the Americans from California University by threequarters of a length. Edwards was at Long Beach, too: he won two gold medals at the Olympics after warming up with three Henley medals in 1931. His Olympic medals were for coxless pairs and coxless fours.

In 1932 also, CUBC received a letter from F. M. L. Fitzwilliams of London RC offering the services of T. Puntin of Newcastle-on-Tyne as a masseur. He is a first-class masseur, said Fitzwilliams, 'and not in the least bit a tiring thumper'.

Through this period fresh controversy was brewing at Cambridge, where more and more colleges were turning to the use of swivel rowlocks instead of fixed tholes or pins. Apart from anything else, swivels made a boat sound different. No longer at dusk could you hear an eight from miles away as the thump, thump . . . thump, thump . . . of the tholes echoed into the gloamin'. Swivels found a welcome place in the creed of Fairbairnism, and in the Mays of 1932, Pembroke, Selwyn and Jesus were first, second and third, all of them Fairbairn colleges. The incoming president, C. J. S. Sergel, was asked at a meeting in December 1932 whether he preferred the use of swivel or fixed-pin rowlocks. He refused to commit himself and was anxious to avoid a split in the CUBC which could have had dire consequences. After ascertaining that the swingers would accept his presidency even if the decision went for pins, he took a vote and the meeting gave fixed pins a two to one advantage. The debate was also going on in Oxford, where Edwards, who had been sent down for failing to pass Mods after his 1926 collapse, returned to try for a degree in 1930, complete with a private aeroplane which he licensed with the proctors. He had spent much time rowing with London RC in the intervening period of schoolmastering, and he had rowed for Oxford again in 1930 using a swivel, while the rest of the crew used fixed pins. Cambridge stuck with pins until 1935, and set a record in 1934 of 18 minutes 3 seconds. Oxford also set a record of sorts when the coach Gibbon, at his own expense, had a new boat built by George Sims in seventy-two working hours, for cash and a barrel of beer. Fairbairn crews from London RC were generally getting the upper hand of orthodox clubs like Leander, and in 1935 the Cambridge president, N. J. Bradley of Pembroke, looked to Archie Nisbet, coach of Pembroke. He was the man who, as captain of London, had invited Fairbairn to coach there when he became available from Thames.

It was now that CUBC broke faith with orthodoxy. The voice of the colleges was coming through, and it did not speak kindly of Haig-Thomas. Only First Trinity, Third Trinity and Lady Margaret were enjoying success while rowing the orthodox way. George Drinkwater described what happened in his book *The Boat Race*: 'To a man like Haig-Thomas orthodoxy was a matter of faith far transcending allegiance to his old university, though while he was wanted on the Cam he did not, apart from sporadic help to college boat clubs, accept Oxford's invitations. Now, however, he gave his services willingly and completely.' He took two other Cambridge coaches with him, Kenneth Payne and Jerram Escombe. Oxford started with swivels but Escombe reverted to fixed pins. Nisbet, meanwhile, enlisted D. H. M. McCowen and the London RC coach Charles Rew, and they found an admirable stern pair in Ran Laurie at stroke and J. H. T. Wilson at seven. Cambridge won with ease, and later that year Pembroke won the Henley Grand with their Mays crew.

When Wilson was secretary he wrote after Nisbet's win:

The old Cambridge coaches P. Haig-Thomas and Escombe coached Oxford on orthodox lines so that the race . . . was a battle of styles. Although the change over to swivels had been resisted so long by CUBC it was inevitable that it should come with the great preponderance of swivel rowing in the Cambridge colleges. Whether Cambridge can maintain their superiority with the new style against such hardened old stagers as Mr Haig-Thomas and Mr Escombe remains to be seen. I personally think they can and will, for the swivel is in my mind a better mechanical instrument and the style that goes with it a pleasanter form of sport.

Oxford were in trouble again in 1936 when their president, R. Hope, resigned after disagreements with the coaches, and B. S. Sciortino was elected in the autumn term. Haig-Thomas and Brigadier Boon Gibbon fell out over who should stroke, and the crew got precious little peace. They won the toss and chose Surrey, the wrong station in the bad conditions, and were taken by Cambridge after Hammersmith with Laurie and Wilson once more in the stern. They broke the run in 1937 when the president, Jock Lewes, reverted to Oxford coaches and trained his trial eights well, so well that he never obtained a blue, taking himself out of the boat. This he did against the advice of his own coaches. It was the first time, too, that an Isis or reserve crew was kept in training after the trials. In the following year Oxford showed that their revival of fortune was not merely a flash in the pan. They won again, and Isis went to the Head of the River race where they came second. Three seconds faster and winners were Goldie, the Cambridge reserves. In 1939, Cambridge took the honours in the Boat Race.

The two decades between the wars were fascinating from the point of view of style-watchers. They also reflected something of the differences in the influence of college rowing. Cambridge has fewer but larger colleges than Oxford, so the prestige of the college clubs is greater in the land of the light blues, and their voices were ignored at peril as far as CUBC was concerned. That CUBC managed to maintain a run of thirteen wins while its constituent members fought the battle of the styles is remarkable. In 1929 all blues except for a Selwyn cox and a Trinity Hall oarsman were from Trinity clubs, but over the period a considerable number of Jesus and Pembroke men found their way into the Boat Race crews.

Life was not all a serious debate about styles between outings, either. In 1933 the Master of Clare had to sort out a problem about the residence qualifications and the date of the race, because the terms were different, the calendar was awkward, and Oxford refused to row in Holy Week. The Cambridge correspondence and accounts for 1934 are interesting for the life style which they reveal. Thurston and Co., billiard table makers, installed a table at Hurlingham for the use of the crew. Muller and Sons of Cambridge lent them a new HMV radio-gramophone and records in return for a photograph of the crew with the machine. John Snagge, by this time the BBC's regular wireless commentator on the race, invited the crew to visit Broadcasting House when he wrote requesting the times of practice outings. The general manager of the Southern Railway wrote to point out that if 17 March was to be the day, then he could not close Barnes Bridge to trains, allowing spectators to line it as was the custom, because the England versus Scotland rugby match was on the same day. Messrs Block, Grey and Block wrote to the president, Kenneth Payne, touting a wine order: 'I have known your father for a great number of years,' crept G. A. H. Robinson, the manager, 'and so I am writing to you a personal letter.' He suggested an order which Payne eventually sent in. It was for two Lanson 1921 vintage, six bottles of Speaker scotch, three of Exhibition brandy, two dozen of Graham late bottled port, two dozen of claret. Then he couldn't supply the Lanson '21 so they had to make do with '26. Dale's Brewery were asked for a kilderkin each of Champion and Audit ale. Hurlingham Club were asked once more to supply staff – 'Mrs Gibson and three maids' – for Haig-Thomas's house in Goring, where the crew were put up for part of their training. A bus was hired from London Transport to get them from there to Hurlingham for £7. The price of the steamer tickets was set at twenty-five shillings, and the Oxford president, Gerald Ellison, later to become Bishop of London, strongly objected to Movietone's request to put a cameraman aboard the *Valiant*, the old blues launch. 'I think you would agree,' he wrote to Payne, 'that it would be a bad show that an old Blue should have to go on a steamer to make room for the film-man.'

From 1940 to 1945 there were no Boat Races as such, but a few fixtures took place between OUBC and CUBC. Cambridge won at Henley over one and a half miles in 1940, Oxford won at Sandford in 1943, again at Ely in 1944, and Cambridge over the Henley Regatta course in 1945. A letter arrived at CUBC on 16 July 1941 to the treasurer enclosing a minute book which Jack Wilson, president in 1936 and secretary before that, had borrowed in 1935. It said: 'I am afraid Henley Regatta 1934 is still blank as I have no records. Will you please bring the book to Henley next year and I will try to finish it off.' The book had not reached Henley from the Goldie boathouse by May 1982, but Wilson had. He and Ran Laurie won the Goblets in 1938, spent nearly ten years in the Sudan, and returned to win again in 1948, and then got the Olympic team nomination for coxless pairs and won the gold medal.

Hostilities resumed for the second time in 1946, though sadly not for George Drinkwater or several others. He had concluded his book on the Boat Race with the 1938 race and the sentiment 'so we leave the race, which it may be hoped will never again be interrupted as it was from 1914–18'. He was killed in an air raid, having rowed in the race for Oxford in 1902–3, and having executed a bust of Steve Fairbairn which forms the trophy for the Head of the River race which Steve founded.

Oxford won in 1946, and Cambridge in the next year after their president, M. A. Nicholson, stood down, never getting a blue. Cambridge had reverted to fixed pins in 1946 and stayed with them for four years. They broke the eighteen-minute barrier for the first time in 1948 in a race in which they started in front, dropped behind, and came through to retake the lead and build a five-length advantage. At one point they stopped completely to recover from a whopping crab caught by E. A. P. Bircher. In the next year they won again by taking the lead on the outside of the bend after Barnes Bridge, which had never been done before. The fact that CUBC had purchased a cow that year to beat milk rationing may have had something to do with it. Christopher Davidge was in the Oxford boat for the first time then, and in 1950 he was president but did not row, under doctor's orders. It was another Cambridge victory, and they were steered by Antony Armstrong-Jones of Jesus in a boat nicknamed the 'Banham Bombshell' which didn't hold in the water all that well. They were frightened of going up Beverley Brook. In 1951 Davidge stroked Oxford when they chose Surrey and disaster. While Cambridge tucked under Fulham wall, Oxford were waterlogged after a minute and sank after two, plunging headlong into freezing grey gloom. The umpire was Gerald Ellison, by this time Bishop of Willesden, and he declared a rerow, contrary to the rules but on the grounds that neither crew had reached the end of the Fulham wall. Cambridge won the rerow on the following Monday by twelve lengths (see chapter 9).

So Cambridge had had another run, this time of five, but Davidge in his last attempt made amends for the sinking when he stroked Oxford home by a canvas in a ding-dong battle in a blizzard in 1952. Oxford started as clear favourites and lost in 1953 but won the hundredth Boat Race in 1954 with four Australians on board. Then they hit all kinds of trouble in 1956 with an experienced crew which was some-how stroked from the number six seat by the American R. A. G. Monks. In Corney Reach Cambridge had a slight lead when Oxford's Australian Pain and president McLeod were seen to be in trouble. McLeod eventually blacked out, and Cambridge were showing them a cruel wake; sixteen lengths of it.

In 1957 Rod Carnegie was president at Oxford. He planned a revival carefully, introducing land training and American rig. Two coaches resigned in the face of his severe training standards. In the race P. F. Barnard collapsed at the Duke's Meadows crossing, and although Carnegie's men had done a practice course threequarters of a minute faster than Cambridge, they lost again. But the seeds had been sown, at least as far as a new look at training was concerned. Nineteen fifty-eight passed in miserable fog with another Cambridge win, and then in 1959 came Ronnie Howard's year as Oxford's president. He had a mutiny on his hands as soon as he got going, but received a vote of confidence from the college captains and won the race (see chapter 10). In 1960 Jumbo Edwards produced the first 'spade' blade for Oxford, an oar the standard length of 12 feet 2 inches but with a blade 8 inches by 20 inches instead of 6½ inches by 32 inches. They also used interval training for the first time for the Boat Race. After a par-ticularly bizarre course steered by the Cambridge cox R. T. Weston, whereby from the Surrey station he followed Oxford on the Middlesex side, Oxford won by one and a quarter lengths. Before doing so though, P. J. Reynolds took them straight on at the crossing to take the bend to Barnes on the Surrey side, so that Cambridge were inside the dark blues. Later, G. V. Cooper substituted for Oxford's president, D. C. Rutherford, in this crew after they lost the Grand at Henley to Molesey and went to the Olympic Games.

Jumbo produced a longer spade oar for Oxford in 1961, Cooper was in trouble in the boat, and Cambridge won. They did so again the next year when Oxford relied very heavily on interval training. The winter of 1963 was extreme, and Oxford moved to Henley for training and Cambridge to Earith. Oxford had a good Isis crew to sharpen them and won the race with Cambridge, who turned the tables in the next year. Oxford won in 1965 with four Yale men in the stern and

Ronnie Howard coaching for almost the whole training period (chapter 11). In 1966 Oxford substituted C. H. Freeman for the American C. E. Albert four days before the race, and Cambridge broke their boat on the Black Buoy two days later. Oxford won a close match. And in 1967 they won again, in spite of Cambridge at an average of 13 stone 11 pounds being the heaviest crew to date. Daniel Topolski was in the number seven seat for Oxford, and the story from his first year is taken up in chapter 15, where Cambridge are about to establish another run of wins. But the story since the Second World War has been very different from that between the wars. Oxford, by innovating, probing, testing, and fighting their bad morale, had brought the ratio of wins back to two out of five, not satisfactory for them, but at least not leaving their needle wallowing in the slough of despair. Cambridge were to give them such a pummelling that by 1971 they had only twenty-four trialists. But Topolski and others with Oxford needle were preparing to reverse the trend.

6

Rhapsody in blue
Episodes and amazing facts

Pray, Cyril, do not read the *Field*,
  Nor seek for any detailed knowledge
Concerning those great louts who wield
  An oar for 'Varsity or College;
I don't know why my breast should swell
  With pride of those whose only function
Is to defeat the men who dwell
  On t'other side of Bletchley Junction.

The *Granta* poet R. E. Swartwout was a coxswain, so he was in a good if dangerous position to hurl brickbats. The Boat Race is belaboured by statistics, enough of them to turn the aesthete off before he could even contemplate raising a cheer. The latest official history, *One Hundred and Fifty Years of the Oxford and Cambridge Boat Race*, published in 1979 is stacked to the gunwales with them, painstakingly researched and updated by Richard Burnell. He gets among his own calculations under 'Heredity: Four members of a family: Three generations: P. C. D. Burnell (OUBC 1962); his father R. D. Burnell (OUBC 1939); and two grandfathers, C. D. Burnell (OUBC 1895–98) and A. S. Garton (OUBC 1909–11).' The blues are distributed by schools and colleges, there is an enormous heredity chart, graphs of times and weights, a chart of overseas blues, and so on. There are pages of records recording 'bridgers' (courses from one bridge to another), mile posts to practice finish, full-course trials and actual races, on ebb and flood. This is the stuff for Gallup and institutes of economic forecasting; it is harder to assemble than it is to row in the race, and a good deal less rewarding, and for that Burnell deserves to be the first blue to be canonized.

The blues are a motley lot. The early years produced a fantastic number of muscular gentlemen of the cloth, but taking orders was a very popular career in the nineteenth century for the sort of sons who could afford to go to Oxbridge. The first two crews in 1829 set the tone: from Oxford Wordsworth became Bishop of St Andrews, Toogood a prebendary of York, Garnier became Dean of Lincoln and coxswain Fremantle became Dean of Ripon; Carter became rector of Frenchay, Somerset; Bates, rector of Stratton Audley, St Brides, Liverpool; Moore, rector of Tunstall, Kent; Staniforth, rector of Bolton-by-Bolland, Lancs., and a noted breeder of shorthorns. The odd man out, Arbuthnot, joined the East Indian Army and retired to become a sugar planter in Mauritius. For Cambridge Merivale became Dean of Ely, Selwyn, Bishop of New Zealand and later of Lichfield; Holdsworth became lay rector of Okehampton and Stokenham Priory, took a commission in the 4th Royal Irish Dragoon Guards and became a JP for Devon; Warren became rector of Farnborough, Banbury; Thompson, curate of Ridley and Ash, Kent; Snow changed his name to Strahan and was a London banker who later moved to Italy; Bayford and Entwisle went to the bar; and Heath became a captain in the East Sussex Militia. With so many priests about, it is bad news for Burnell that Britain is no longer in the See of Rome.

Quite a number of blues have changed their names for one reason or another. Snow seems unpopular: Snow W., became Strahan; Snow, H., (Cambridge, 1856–57) became Kynaston, headmaster of Cheltenham and a canon of Durham and professor of Greek at the university there; and even Snow, R. Ebsworth, (Oxford, 1946) preferred to be known as Ebsworth-Snow. R. Lybbe-Powys (Oxford, 1839) became Lybbe-Powys-Lybbe; W. S. Lockhart (Cambridge, 1845) became Lockhart-Scott; R. J. Buller (Oxford, 1852–53) became Manningham-Buller; A. P. Lonsdale (Oxford, 1889–92) became Heywood-Lonsdale; P. P. Pearson (Cambridge, 1857) became Pearson-Pennant; G. G. T. Thomas (Oxford, 1859) became Trehearne; W. C. Lecky-Browne (Cambridge, 1973–74) became Lecky-Browne-Lecky; and E. A. Szilagyi (Cambridge, 1935) became Seeley.

The University Boat Race Official Centenary History by George Drinkwater and Terence Sanders, another scholastic statistical work, contains a succinct chapter on old blues and their careers, supplemented by J. D. Betham's biographies of nineteenth-century blues, which are a mine of information for people who like compiling lists. This present chapter is of necessity a meal from a Chinese takeaway, a random choice of dishes, unwrapped to be tasted in any order and spiced with what you will. Staying close to godliness for starters, by 1929 the blues had produced very nearly a crew of bishops. M'Dougall (Oxford, 1842) became Labuan (Malaysia), J. R. Selwyn (Cambridge, 1864–66 and son of New Zealand) became Melanesia (Pacific Ocean); Edwin Hoskyns (Cambridge, 1873) became South-well. His younger brother B. G. Hoskyns (Cambridge, 1877) became archdeacon of Chichester; Houblon (Oxford, 1872) became Archer-Houblon, T. H., and archdeacon of Oxford; and Ernald Lane (Oxford, 1858) Dean of Rochester. In more recent times A. S. Reeve (Cambridge, 1930) became Bishop of Lichfield and J. P. Burrough (Oxford, 1937–38) became Bishop of Mashonaland. Gerald Ellison (Oxford, 1932–33) became Bishop of Willesden, then Bishop of Chester, and then Bishop of London. He also held a parish which the church does not recognize, for he became the embodiment of Trinity Hall rowing when he moved to Cambridge after New College, Oxford. He coached on the Cam like a shepherd, with a whistle in his pocket, which pierced the air to produce a spurt of half a length's advantage for any Hall crew within hearing. For the good of the ecumenical movement, W. T. Heard (Oxford, 1907) must be included. He was a Vatican lawyer who became the first Scotsman to be made a cardinal since the Reformation.

The only thing that all these people have in common, we should remind ourselves, is that they have all done a Putney-to-Mortlake for and against OUBC and CUBC or vice versa. A few of them did it at Henley or from Westminster to Putney, but for the great majority Putney to Mortlake has been the venue. For the first main course we join Martin Cobbett down there. He is not a blue, but a prominent sporting scribe of his era. He relished Boat Race day.

> In the old days, before everything was quite so superfine, we used to have a set feast on the Monday before the Boat Race. The company varied, but for years two of us, generally three, were what you might call regulars, the foundation of the feast, with power to add to their number. The menu never varied, and it consisted of three courses, the last being bread and cheese. On the Thursday, after all the work had been done, my business was to slip up to London and see that good British yeoman cricketer and business man, Mr Maxted, of Spiers and Pond, who would, with his own hands – a great condescension for the manager of

several departments of the great going concern – cut the steak. Not *a* steak, please understand, but *the* steak. Beginning from the point, and so on till a perfectly equally thick all the way through – say two and a half inches – slab of meat was laid out. What weight I do not know. Whatever the weight was we never left any, and however many came in, it made plenty for all. Then my good friend had a quantity of scallops ready to be opened, which were duly seen to and sealed over in a trustworthy jar. Not one fishmonger in a hundred knows how to treat scallops properly, nor one cook in a thousand how to begin to cook them. I had someone at home who could do it, with just enough calculated margin of underdoneness to finish them properly while being made thoroughly hot for dinner next day. Then at midday we would repair – F. S. Gulston, old Harry Kelley, always a gentleman; perhaps G. D. Lister, remembered by many still; myself; and likely some more, to the White Lion, a very humble public-house indeed, where I was allowed, as a favoured customer of many years' standing, to do my own cooking. Never have I dined better than at these times. What can you have better of itself? We had good ale, and ale, and ale, the best old red Cheshire cheese, whereof I knew a fount, a constant supply, and so we ran; puffing the pipe of contentment, afterwards, ere taking to the foreshore again to watch the tide, and perhaps some professionals training; then make for the London Rowing Club, to foregather with old friends – among them E. D. and L. P. Brickwood. Perhaps the late Mr Walsh of the *Field* – oh! such an editor in wrestling with a case or a proposition, and getting its true inwardness and value out in less than no time. Often that magnificent oarsman the late Mr William Stout of Gloucester would be with us; mayhap he had helped us out with the scallop feast – anyway, we had jolly companions every one, and being on good terms with ourselves felt that no matter whether they did race the next day or not, we had done our duty in carrying out the most important preliminaries.

No matter that the race has never taken place on a Tuesday. After a feast like that they would have needed time for digestion. Presently they will see a race which we will join, but first the politicians. The blues have produced two prime ministers, one of Australia in S. M. Bruce (Cambridge, 1904) and one of France, William Henri Waddington (Cambridge, 1849, first race), the more remarkable because he was an Englishman. He was born in France, though, and became a naturalized Frenchman, holding various ministerial posts while he was first Deputy for the Department de l'Aisne and then a senator. He was

Minister for Foreign Affairs in 1877–79 and Prime Minister for a period in 1879 when the republicans, who drew their support from the upper bourgeoisie, had the electoral whip hand over the petit bourgeois radicals under Clemenceau. Waddington became ambassador to the Court of St James's in 1883 and died the following year. W. H. Grenfell (Oxford, 1877–78) sat in Parliament for both Salisbury and Hereford, though at different times and for different parties. He became Lord Desborough and was a prodigious sportsman: amateur punting champion three times, épée champion three times, stroked an eight across the Channel, swam the pool beneath Niagara twice, the second time before witnesses because nobody would believe he had done it the first time, and wreaked terrible carnage on anything with horns or wings which moved between Scotland and the Rockies. Lord Ampthill (Oxford, 1889–91), first lord to get a blue, became private secretary to Joseph Chamberlain and Governor of Madras, and for a short time Viceroy and Governor-General of India. The Hon. Valentine Frederick Lawless (Oxford, 1859), became Lord Cloncurry. The Rt Hon. W. Dudley Ward (Cambridge, 1897, 1899–1900) was the elected Member for Southampton and a prominent Liberal. R. C. Bourne (Oxford, 1909–12), who won four successive races as stroke, became MP for Oxford City. The Rt Hon. Reginald McKenna (Cambridge, 1887) became MP for North Monmouthshire, Home Secretary and then Chancellor of the Exchequer. A. H. D. R. Steel (Oxford, 1899) became the Rt Hon. Sir A. H. D. R. Steel-Maitland, MP for East Birmingham and Baldwin's Minister of Labour from 1924 to 1929, during which time striking meant something more sinister than a rate of strokes, poor fellow. A. T. Herbert (Oxford, 1898–99) became Lord Lucas and Dingwall, South African war correspondent for *The Times*, held various ministerial offices and became a skilful pilot, reported missing 4 November 1916. G. A. Lloyd (Cambridge, 1899–1900) followed the governorship of Bombay with the post as High Commissioner for Egypt and Sudan.

After that gallery of worthies, a glimpse at what some of them may have gone through on the morning of the race. David Haig-Thomas won with Cambridge from 1930 to 1932, part of their run of thirteen, when his father was coach and the controversy over fixed pins versus swivels was in full cry. He was not an undergraduate who stood out in the academic records of St John's. He said in his autobiography: 'I, like my father and my grandfather before me, would go down without a degree. Grandfather never looked like passing an exam. Father passed one and I had passed two, and I thought it would spoil the family tradition if I did any more, as well as being impertinent to my elders and betters!' He was, though, an expert night climber, once putting umbrellas on the pinnacles of King's College chapel. He knew Cambridge from the rooftops to the troughs of the Tideway, and he woke up one morning in a trough of despond. Something was the matter. It was Boat Race day!

This would definitely be the last time he would row, he vowed. He remembered making this excellent resolution many times before.

The morning dragged on. We all tried to be cheerful and look unconcerned. Some people skimmed through the papers and read out what were thought to be foolish remarks made by old Blues writing to the press. . . . We had early lunch at eleven o'clock. The authorities thought it was a bad thing to row on a full stomach, but it is certainly worse to row on an empty one. We ate sparingly and drank little. Then, putting on our pale blue caps, which thank goodness we would be wearing for the last time, we walked off down to the boathouse. Usually, we came down in a car, but now we wanted to kill time. . . . The usual Boat Race crowd was already beginning to collect. There were men with ridiculous dolls dressed up in pale blue and dark ribbon. Little groups of schoolboys collected behind us as if we were some strange animals from the zoo, and bands of flappers, armed with autograph books, besieged us from all sides.

In the changing-room little piles of clean clothes lay along the benches. Languidly I undressed and put on my shorts. Damn! the top button had gone, and the next one to it was sure to come off. How annoying! These were the most comfortable shorts I had, and I should not feel at home in any others. I searched in the pile of dirty clothes in the corner. I would be comfortable and at my ease even if I did not look my best.

In the sitting room piles of open telegrams lay on the table. No one bothered to look at them. Who cared a damn whether some old fellow of whom we had never heard wished us luck or not? . . . Once in the boat, things felt better, but the first few strokes felt unrhythmical and awkward. . . . We paddled up to the mile post, easied, and lay drifting on the tide. Nobody talked, because nobody wanted to. A little party of ducks swam past. How I envied them! Though why the devil they wanted to come to this stinking place, Putney, when they could be splashing about on the Wash I could not imagine.

We had another hour to wait before the tide would be at its best, and with our blanket trousers pulled over our shorts and our scarves round our necks, we waited in the sitting room. We shivered and shook, though the room was, if anything, too warm. First we felt full and then we felt empty, and however we sat we could never feel right. Slowly the clock ticked round. Dozens of old Blues came in and tried to be cheery. It was all right for them to be feeling happy, but why the devil couldn't they leave us in peace and let us be miserable if we wanted to?

A loud speaker began to blare and shout from the Star and Garter Hotel. We could hear our names being read out, coupled with remarks both complimentary and uncomplimentary. . . . The boat felt like lead as we carried it down to the water. . . . How slow everyone was! Why couldn't they buck up and let us get away from this loathsome crowd! Now Lu [Luxton, stroke] was taking his place. With a final 'Good Luck' Cooie Phillips, the boatman, pushed us off. Nearly thirty years before he had pushed my father off in the same way. A dead dog floated down under my oar; of all the things people might do to help, why couldn't they keep the dead dogs away? We easied below Putney Bridge, and Oxford paddled past. How sure they looked! They didn't care a damn for anyone. They would just row better than they had ever rowed before, and would be a length ahead at the end of the mile. . . . Once more a tide of panic swept over me.

Haig-Thomas was in the bow. Cambridge squared their blades in the water as the umpire Harcourt Gold held up his flag, letting the tide pull them out to their full reach. If the umpire didn't say 'Go' at the right moment, no one knew what would happen, but he always did, said Haig-Thomas. Oxford kept their blades on the feather on top of the water, and on the word squared them and drove them back. Every year Cambridge got a fifth of a second's advantage by starting with squared blades, by the bow man's reckoning. The first stroke seemed unending. The second was short, and they swung out to the third and fourth. Haig-Thomas watched Oxford from the corner of his eye. They were bouncing their boat and lifting their bodies over without driving from the stretcher with their legs. A thrill of excitement ran through him. They would settle down and go right through the dark blues. After the mile they did a burst of ten and shot right past, becoming short and ragged, and then, seeing Oxford's discomfiture, grew longer and steadier. They were ahead by Hammersmith.

At Barnes Haig-Thomas began to think of the bread and cheese and beer awaiting him at the Ibis Boat Club and the dinner and theatre that they would enjoy afterwards.

I felt the shadow of Barnes Bridge above us; in a few moments I should be able to smell the smell of the brewery. Surely the smell of malt and of tar and of the tang of seaweed on the marshes are the best three smells in the world. Out of the corner of my eye I saw the practice finishing post. Only ten more strokes, and we would easy. I counted them, and found there were thirteen. We easied, and watched those poor perspiring wretches in the crew behind, who individually had expended much more energy than ourselves. Every one of them was so tired that he could hardly swing forward for another stroke.... We paddled into the boathouse and put our boat away for the last time. Forgotten were my thoughts of half an hour ago that I would never row again. Surely, rowing was the best sport in the world! As we washed and dressed we discussed plans for winning the Grand and going to the Olympic Games.

Cambridge went to Henley and won the Grand, rowing as Leander, and they went to the Games in Los Angeles and finished fourth.

Cooie Phillips's presence to see the crew off from one generation of blues to another is about par for the course. He had a young apprentice that day, Alf Twinn, although Twinn did not attend the crew at Putney until 1934, when they had a record win. The boat in which they did it hangs in the Science Museum in South Kensington. Twinn has been down every year since. Oxford have had only four boatmen: Tom Tims, Walt Taylor, Dick Tallboys and Albert Andrews. Tims worked out a patent plan for winning the toss and put it to every president. 'Don't let him toss, sir, because if he does and you say Heads and it's Tails, well, there you are, but if you toss he may say Heads or Tails so you stand two chances to one.' He was impressed with the belief according to Rudie Lehmann that the fact of calling halves a man's power of choice, and thus places him in an inferior position in respect of the coin. Tims could be seen in his day laboriously blowing air through an india-rubber tube into the canvased bows of the boat before launching, blowing for buoyancy.

In the lifetime of Andrews and Twinn, boats have changed greatly. With longer slides, longer runners, riggers adjusted outwards, up-wards, this way and that, says Andrews, 'You've got it all. Mind you, with so much adjustment, there's so much that can go wrong.'

Longevity and plenty of wind is naturally not confined to boatmen connected with the race. The histories provide abundant evidence that blue-blooded oarsmen survive in droves into their seventies, boatloads into their eighties, and push on in sculling boats into their nineties. Dr Morgan's exhaustive inquiries into the health of blues began in 1869 as a contribution to the debate on public health and the craze for athleticism which were thought by some to be mutually exclusive. His researches showed that a surprisingly large number of blues had time to fill in questionnaires and that the general state of their health was good. He concluded that rowing is good for you. He also produced figures from a Fellow of his college, St John's, Oxford, to show that the rowers were academically more distinguished than the non-rowers. The rueful may reflect that this says more about academic teaching than brainpower of oarsmen, who until considerably after the Second World War seemed to fall into the two categories of those who read and those who did not. In the 1980s they all have to read, and there is evidence that fast crews get high degrees. A David Haig-Thomas would not now survive for more than one Boat Race if he had been skilful enough to gain admission to a college in the first place. But Morgan's figures and thesis, based on blues before 1869, are vigorous. He quotes R. F. Clarke, the aforementioned Fellow of St John's:

> The gladiatorial feats of Cowley Marsh may be a very lamentable result of Oxford culture . . . but so far from hindering mental energy, may be shown by the clearest proof to encourage and develop it; for while the average of class men in the university generally is 30 per cent, among cricketers it rises to 42, and among rowing men to 45 per cent; nay, the very elite of the university, the men who subsequently obtain open fellowships, are more often found in their college eights or eleven than any other section of the community.

Morgan's report includes 'life-tables' and honours tables. Charles Merivale and Charles Wordsworth started the things off right by getting firsts, as Selwyn did from the first Cambridge crew.

Blues are also good at keeping it in the family, and not bad at breeding more blues. Burnell's book has three pages of relatives who have chased each other over the P–M, including the Raikes family, who have had five blues over three generations. Then there are the brothers Raymond Broadley (First Trinity) and Thomas Basil Etherington-Smith (Oriel), who raced against each other in 1900, the elder brother Raymond helping Cambridge to a famous victory of twenty lengths. There is a great blue dynasty which reads like the ultimate firm of solicitors: Bourne, Graham, Graham, Crum, Bourne, Ellison, Erskine-Crum, Graham, Gladstone, and Tinné, Tinné, Tinné, Tinné. And then there are the great individualists like C. R. W. Tottenham, who steered five winning Oxford crews from 1864 to 1868, and J. A. Brown who steered Cambridge in four winning crews. The Oxonian hall of fame for four wins reads R. Willan, W. A. L. Fletcher, H. B. Cotton, C. M. Pitman, W. E. Crum, C. K. Philips, C. D. Burnell, and R. C. Bourne. Plus Boris Rankov who has joined Tottenham in the five-win category. Cambridge has not done so well, though the excuse given is that it takes blues longer to get out of Oxford. Their only four-win oarsmen are the Hon. Treasurer of the Islington War Pensions and stockbroker Stanley Duff Muttlebury OBE, and Christopher L. Baillieu (1970–73), MBE with six bars for international sculling and still in his single when last heard of in 1982.

One little dynasty with a formidable rowing record was that of Nickalls. The brothers Guy (1887–91) and Vivian (1891–93) rowed for Oxford, and Guy's son G. O. 'Gully' rowed in 1921–23. Gully was greatly loved among rowing men, and in the dispassionate observer John Snagge's opinion a great man because he was an eternal optimist.

Gully once told James Crowden (Cambridge, 1951–52) that when he was rowing at seven behind the American Mellen, 'All I said behind him was "Steady, Pussy" and we won.' In his autobiography he recorded a lunch at Fulham Palace in 1921, where it was customary for the then Bishop of London, Dr Arthur Foley Winnington Ingram, to entertain the crews. The Oxford crew were ushered towards the presence and 'suddenly there he was, standing with what I believe in ecclesiastical circles is known as a Canterbury cap on his head, in a sort of somewhat claustrophobic cul-de-sac'. He advanced with outstretched arms and bonhomie, saying, 'Boys, boys, welcome to Fulham Palace. I had better tell you right away that I have a number of curates and their wives to meet you. So you'll have a lady and a curate each. Next week I have the Cambridge crew coming. I have five bishops for them. I should think they'll have a fit.' Pat Mallam said, 'Please, Bishop, do you think I could dispense with my curate and have two ladies?'

Gully Nickalls had a broadcasting adventure in the Boat Race (see chapter 14) but we will join his father Guy for his race in 1889. He had already been beaten twice, the second time after the tragic circumstance of the death in January of the president, Hector McLean. Guy was taking his time at Oxford even if he was fast in a boat, viz. this letter sent to him at his home in Redhill from McLean a week before he died:

> My dear Guy, I hope what Ducker [McLean's brother] tells me is not true. He met Tooley Holland in town last week and he told the Ducker that you had been ploughed again for Mods. If this is the case I am awfully sorry for you. I hope whatever has happened in that way won't have any effect on your rowing in the Varsity as that could be a great catastrafy (catastraphy) (I don't know how to spell it) . . . I have been beastly seedy for the last week and still am very bad. Got a chill on my liver. . . . I am staying with my sister and Colonel Lynch for some balls, none of which I have been able to go to. . . . My brother-in-law has been offered a brigade or a division which ever is the biggest (I don't know) in India. . . . Yours ever, Hector McLean. Sorry I can't remember your address but I expect they know you in Redhill.

McLean died of chilly liver, not dyslexia or amnesia.

Guy carried on pulling. For the 1889 race he stood for president and was beaten by his friend Tooley by one vote. Nickalls voted for Tooley and Tooley voted for Tooley, so Nickalls defeated himself. Anyway, they were both in the crew which did their downriver spell at Llewellyn's at Cookham and were chiefly noted for a vast number of positional changes to get three and four right. These were Cook and Drake and in Nickall's estimation were by no means flyers. Also noteworthy was the memorable concert they gave for the Cookham charities.

'The race was only what we had expected, and we were glad when it was over and forgotten. I was made president for the next season,' was all Guy put down about it afterwards. Muttlebury had made it four in a row for Cambridge – and with the same crew as the year before. But for Theodore Andreas Cook of Wadham in the three seat it was the experience of a lifetime. The town and he mutually lit each other up. He joined the blue boat early one morning in his room at Wadham when, after receiving a message from the president and stroke Claude

Holland, Tom Tims the boatman roused him from his bed to run round Oxford University's cricket ground, the Parks.

> Waiting had not helped to keep me fit, but I managed to last out as far as Nuneham and back on my first attempt. The next day was a real twister. We went from the Varsity Barge, without stopping anywhere except at the locks, to Abingdon lasher; and when we got there number seven [Nickalls], with his usual sympathetic courtesy, asked in a loud voice whether three was sick yet. The question unluckily postponed a natural reaction which might have done me the deal of good. . . . It was fortunately almost dark when we got in. Tom Tims, who saw fast enough what was the matter, stood right in front of me 'til the president and secretary had disappeared. Then I was lifted over the side of the boat into a punt, landed at Folly Bridge, and driven to Wadham as swiftly as a handsome cab could gallop. After dinner that night we had port in Ampthill's rooms [Lord Ampthill, number five] at New College, and I could barely keep my eyes open. But I was running round the Parks next morning with the rest of them before breakfast. . . .

At Cookham they were coached by T. C. 'Cottie' Edwards-Moss and Willy Grenfell, who gave them Sunday lunch at his magnificent house, Taplow Court, where they draped themselves round the classical statue before his front door. At Putney they galloped over Richmond Park and had good dinners, the best fish followed by the best joint of beef or mutton procurable, stewed fruit, oranges and a biscuit, two glasses of beer and a brimming glass of port. Lemon-flavoured gruel followed later as a signal for an early bed. Absolutely no liquid was allowed between meals, and no smoking. They led for the first two minutes but were well adrift by Hammersmith. Cook, who became a journalist and eventually a renowned editor of the *Field*, assembled a painstaking account of the race for his memoirs, but at the time he said: 'Beyond Ampthill's back I can fairly say I saw nothing, and apart from occasional bursts of cheering at the bridges I heard nothing except laboured breathing, the crash of the blades at the beginning, and the rattle in the rowlocks as our hands came away together.' He couldn't have seen much of Ampthill's back either, because Drake's was in the way. Puxley, the bow man, was known as Lot's Wife because he looked round several times during the race and cheered them up by telling them that they were gaining.

'The welcome spirit of hospitality and admiration which begins at dawn on Saturday of the race continues throughout London until midnight. . . . The number of invitations to theatres, music halls, and other entertainments received by both crews is incredible.' During an extraordinary week they went to a concert at the Lyric, a prize fight at the Pelican, a dance at the Gardenia, a gala at the Empire. On the night after the race young Theodore took Lot's Wife in a hansom to Bailey's Hotel to tell his mother that he was still alive. They continued to the Westminster Aquarium where they saw the first flickering cinematograph of the fight between Corbett and Fitzsimmons. They reached a hotel in Jermyn Street to deck themselves out for the banquet at the Holborn Restaurant. They enjoyed the dinner, and the next evening each crew had been given a huge box in the first tier at Drury Lane, where a variety bill was playing. Puxley and Cook decorously applauded for the first half hour and then went exploring, through the door outside their box marked 'No Admission'. They found themselves on stage, hidden by brilliant birds of large and tropical variety. The bow man advanced to assist a bird who was trying to move her splendid tail feathers by means of a tape which extended down her tights towards her ankle. Puxley was relieving her of this strenuous task when an enormous flower in front of them fell suddenly through a slot prepared for the purpose into the recesses underneath the stage. The impromptu group instantly became visible to the whole Cambridge crew in the box on the other side, and loud shouts of 'Well rowed bow' rang through the house. They escaped up a ladder and found themselves in the limelight loft, and next thing Harriet Vernon was tripping through a delicate romance in song while bathed in green, purple, and of course blue, shade unspecified. Before fleeing the theatre Puxley was seen in the wings instructing the wee *danseuses* of the children's ballet to lift a leg a little or bend a little, Nelly. In short, Lot's Wife turned the blues and the audience ruddy with mirth.

Each year a little extra is added to the obscure league tables charting the battles of the blues. Schools and colleges are listed after the participants, the general rule being that the last place of education and the college represented is entered in the records. This is simple enough, but leads to all kinds of difficulties. If the place of education does not have to be the rowing place of education, then presumably the college name refers to the college and not to the boat club. In that case Lady Margaret BC should be referred to as St John's. Several of the earliest entries say 'Private' before the name of the college. This means that they had the benefit of a private tutor, not a one-to-one military experience. Further difficulties have arisen with foreigners over the designation of the place of education because foreigners educated at British or Irish schools do not appear as overseas blues, and British or Irish blues educated abroad appear as foreigners, so not all foreigners are foreign and not all British blues are British. Irishmen educated in Ireland are British, Irishmen educated in Britain are British; Irishmen or Welshmen or Siamese educated in Tasmania are foreign, but not Australian according to the Boat Race records. Then there are complications about colleges where blues move from one to another, as they do occasionally when they take up junior teaching posts, like Rankov from Corpus moving to the women's college St Hugh's in 1981.

Then there are differences of opinion about how many years a member of the university should be allowed to row, further complicated by the question: 'When does a don who is carrying out research for a degree cease to be a student but a paid member of the academic community?' This is further complicated by the small number of graduate students who arrive from overseas and the occasional phalanx of Harvard or Yale or Sydney or Melbourne men who threaten to take over like a rentacrew. After all, the Boat Race is a free show put on by the students of two English universities each year, isn't it? Somebody bright should be able to get a substantial research grant from the Social Science Research Council to sort all this out with questionnaires and so forth. But would he be eligible to try for a seat in the boat?

As far as the league tables are concerned, things are clear-cut at the top. Eton are streets ahead among the schools, their total being more than 650, with the next two, Shrewsbury and Radley, struggling with less than 150 each. The old public schools had the field almost to themselves until well into the latter half of the twentieth century, and some of the schools which have made a rowing reputation since the Second World War such as Hampton and Emanuel are still way down the table, behind Geelong which is the top overseas institution to figure. Harvard is the top university. On the college side, it is Trinity, Cambridge's largest college, which in its various guises is in a clear lead, with nearly 400 blues against approximately 150 each for the leading Oxford colleges Magdalen and Christ Church, and the closest Cambridge colleges Jesus, Trinity Hall and St John's (Lady Margaret BC). Counting Tasmania and Australia as the same country, eight countries can claim representation: Australia, Canada, Denmark, New Zealand, Pakistan, South Africa, Siam, and the United States. The favours of the overseas blues have been divided more or less evenly. They have won slightly more than they have lost, although Cambridge's foreigners have been more successful than Oxford's. The aforementioned SSRC-funded researcher may care to plot a computerized graph relating foreigners' wins to Oxford and Cambridge wins, admissions policy and academic records. But we will spend a Boat Race day with the Rt Hon. Harold Macmillan.

He addressed the dinner to celebrate the 150th race held at the Savoy on 17 March 1979. Oxford, by the way, won the race after the Cambridge president, John Woodhouse, was ill on the morning and Graham Phillips stepped in from Goldie. Macmillan, Chancellor of the University of Oxford, and former Prime Minister, said: 'How well I remember the Boat Race as it was in that Victorian world which I suppose it would be reactionary to call agreeable. But it was agreeable, it *was* very agreeable, in my own childhood when London was a country town, with carriages and carts and horse, smelling not of oil and carbohydrates, but of horse dung and straw in the streets. . . .' Boat Race day, he told the 199 assembled blues and their few chosen guests,

meant something quite extraordinary to London. Not just you chaps who care about rowing – why you care about rowing, God knows – but the whole of London. Of course it was before – can you imagine it, some of you – the days of the halfpenny press. No Harmsworths, no radio, of course no television, no institutionalized and professionalized sport, no international sport, which is chiefly now, so far as I can see, a reason for international dispute, when one could go into some sports without having first to go through a long test to discover whether you are a man or a woman, and then to see whether you have been submitted to a variety of different drugs. When games were games and sport was sport, I took a great interest in cricket, knew all the batting averages, and all the great players of the day, Hobbs and Hayward – terrible degenerate days, when you could still play a match between the Gentlemen and Players, reactionary, regressive, awful.

Still, it was a happy world. And everyone, the whole of London, the costermongers, the drivers of four-wheelers, those delicious Hansom cabs – the gondolas of London as Disraeli called them – everyone cared about the Boat Race. All wore the colours, light blue or dark blue. In the household everyone, the housemaid, the butler, there were great divisions. My father was at Cambridge, so as a child we were Cambridge. Nannie was violently for Oxford. And on the day, on that great day, the whole of London, people in offices, streets and homes, cared only for this great event.

He recognized that the race was not destroyed by professionalism, not ruined by the machinery of 1980s sport, even though it is shadowed by one of the largest television outside-broadcasting operations and involves Ladbrokes the bookmakers to fund the larger part of the year's work by OUBC and CUBC. 'It is a true test of young men from our two great universities who train and work for their teams and now, after 150 years, dine together,' said Macmillan.

If anything, the Boat Race is at least maintaining the standard of its athletes in a competitive world. In spite of the demands on students' time it continues to produce at least one high-level crew each year, and usually a handful of men who go on to compete internationally for their countries. There are few university sports which do that. Rowing has asserted itself as the first sport at both universities, refusing to let its standards slip, apart from seasonal waverings, and attracting more and more participants, particularly among women who have their own Oxford versus Cambridge match. The proportion of medals taken in world, European and Olympic regattas by blues used to be two out of three and has declined in recent years to nearer two out of five, but the standard of rowing both internationally and outside the universities in Britain has risen more steeply than it is possible to achieve in the context of an all-round educational establishment. The blues' influence was disproportionate in the past and is now more realistic, but it is immense. The event itself has also contributed significantly to the technical developments and the physical and psychological aspects of training for sport, as well as to the technical developments in communications and broadcasting. And the secret of its success is that, even if it no longer dresses the villages of London in shades of blue on the great day, it is a simple two-horse race, easy to understand, in which millions of people identify with one side or the other. Its result each year is as clear as a bell, except in the confusion of 1877 (see chapter 8).

Yards of newsprint have been expended arguing about weight. In some circumstances and in some seats heavy men are at an advantage, in others not. How much difference does an extra pound of cox make? Or boat? Or an extra inch of oar? These are other questions to be fielded to the SSRC or the Science Research Council or the Medical Research Council. The official history can supply them with the statistics; if you can believe the measurements, that is. Roughly, heavier crews win two times out of three. The first time crews averaged 11½ stone or over was in 1836, 13 stone or over 1936, 14 stone or over 1976. The heaviest ever Oxford crew averaged 14 stone 0⅝ pound in 1976, Cambridge 13 stone 11⅛ pound in 1972. The lightest ever Oxford crew averaged 11 stone in 1854, Cambridge 10 stone 10¼ pounds in the same year. Oxford's heaviest and lightest oarsmen were respectively S. G. H. Plunkett, 16 stone 5 pounds in 1976, and A. H. Higgins, 9 stone 6½ pounds in 1854. Cambridge's heaviest and lightest are D. L. Cruttenden, 16 stone in 1970, and R. C. Galton, 9 stone 10 pounds in 1854. The heaviest coxes are F. J. Richards at 10 stone 10 pounds in 1845 for Oxford and J. M. Crocker at 10 stone 8 pounds for Cambridge in 1841. The lightest coxes are H. P. V. Massey at 5 stone 2 pounds for Oxford in 1939 and F. H. Archer at the same weight for Cambridge in 1862.

> Thinner and thinner grows each tiny coxswain.
> Fed upon husks, but ever uncomplaining,
> He fades and fades, and thus fulfils his training.

Rudie Lehmann wrote the rhyme in 1900 and Ian Bernstein was the latest person to try it, in 1982 (see chapter 16). Lehmann coached Oxford, Cambridge and Harvard, with mixed results. Those coaches who stand out in the early days for Cambridge are Egan, Lord Macnaghten, the Eton coach J. G. Chambers, and George Morrison, who came over from Oxford. He coached Guts Woodgate in the 1862 Oxford boat in floods on the Isis. He would scull a dinghy to the Freewater Stone, the only object on the bank above the water from Iffley to the barges. Sitting on this with his legs tucked under him out of the swirling flood, he would shout an abusive epithet at Poole of Trinity, whom he had his knife into, as the eight shot by. Then he would paddle to the Abingdon road, mount a horse and gallop to the railway near Nuneham and mount the wooden bridge and shout his opprobrious epithet again. In five seconds the stream had swept the eight out of hearing. He once had to stop the eight, while coxing it himself, for a freshman in a becalmed sailing dinghy. 'Look ahead,' he roared, and the eight shaved the dinghy. Morrison let fly his best vocabulary in his deep, penetrating voice and the man was so impressed by his lungs that he replied, 'Why don't you blow, then?' 'I'll show you how I blow; hold her stroke side – let me get at him. I'll blow him out of the water.' The freshman was off with a scull to the bank, and ran like a rabbit across the fields.

J. H. D. Goldie, James B. Close, Steve Fairbairn and Muttlebury married legwork to the sliding seat, and Oxford, whose chief seers of fixed-seat days were Shadwell, Fletcher Menzies, Chitty and Warre, did not catch on to the proper use of the legs until Ducker McLean, Gully Nickalls and Claude Holland rowed behind Muttle in a Leander crew in 1888. Then they caught on fast. Oxford also had W. A. L. Fletcher, who, like Morrison, moved to Cambridge. They both reversed Oxford's nine-year runs at their second attempt, and each time there was a Goldie in the Cambridge crew who lost his first Boat Race and then won.

It was during this period that Guts Woodgate coached both crews. In 1883:

> I coached both crews an equal number of days, and one day took Cambridge on a morning tideway course, and caught the train to Taplow in time for Oxford's afternoon show. Of course one is glad to see one's own colour win, where it merits victory: but the chief sentiment that grows upon us is a desire to see the standard of UBC oarsmanship maintained high. It is small satisfaction to see Oxford win with a bad crew, beating a still-worse Cantab team. Far more satisfactory to see a tiptop crew win, even though it be from the rival club.

Gilbert Bourne had much to do with grounding the four Oxford crews stroked by his son from 1909. At the time he had the chair of comparative anatomy, foreshadowed during his school days at Eton by experiments he conducted to determine the muscular action in rowing. He was impressed by arguments in the *Field* whereby the laying down of the law by people ignorant of human anatomy was refuted by a surgeon. The young Bourne got possession of a defunct monkey during the school holidays and worked out the musculature of its back, legs, shoulders and arms with the aid of Quain's *Treatise on Human Anatomy*. He submitted his drawings and diagrams to Dr

Warre, suggesting that a straight back has no value per se, but if it is the result of the vertebral column with the pelvis being swung forward from the thigh joints in the proper manner, then the oarsman is swinging correctly. Warre accepted his propositions as agreeing with his own views. In 1925 Bourne published his masterful *Textbook of Oarsmanship* with his well-executed drawings.

Harcourt Gold was coaching Oxford at around the same time; the difficulty with tracing coaches is that styles and fads and coaches change and change about, overlap one another, merge their differences, disappear and return, and, in the case of styles, are relabelled. Some were innovators, some were the right men at the right time, some turned indifferent ore to gold. Cambridge had Bruce on his way back to Australia in 1914, and their golden age of wins between the wars was not always a golden age of coaching, but it cashed several cheques from Muttle, Dudley Ward and Boon Gibbon, the latter from the crew who set up the twenty-length win in 1900. At the 1979 dinner James Crowden remembered him from 1951 when the contemporary Cambridge crew were moving so far ahead that Gibbon saw his record margin in danger. 'We all thought he should have worn his mackintosh trousers under his blanket bags because he had such a needle that his 20 lengths was going to be beaten.' He needn't have worried, for the margin was twelve. Between the wars the light blue mentors were Steve Fairbairn (briefly), the Rev. R. E. Swann, Colonel Wauchope, Peter Haig-Thomas, the father of David, and Escombe. The last three helped Oxford out as well in the great swivel-rowlock argument. F. E. 'Two-legs' Hellyer was there too, so-called because he lost them in the war. He taught Fairbairnism tempered with a bit of orthodoxy, which made his crews whistle. Harcourt Gold and later P. C. Mallam continued at Oxford.

After the Second World War Jumbo Edwards came onto Oxford's scene, prying and trying, and Freddie Page, and then Ronnie Howard. J. B. Rosher, Blackheath rugby player who claimed to have been the heaviest man to have lost three Boat Races (1909–11), used to attempt analyses of the 'Mumbo-Jumbo phenomenon' at CUBC dinners. Jumbo would fly in from Germany to coach, being whisked from airfield to river by his wife, and piloting himself back to his German mess after the outing. He once experimented with wiring the seats of an eight together, a better theory than practice. At Cambridge it was the turn of Derek Mays-Smith and Harold Rickett to assert their ideas.

Steve Fairbairn came to the old blues dinner when Rickett was president in 1931 and said, 'Our Father which art in Heaven, Harold be thy name,' and walked out again. Roy Meldrum and R. H. H. Symonds introduced the long lay-back style known as the Meldrumatic or Lady Margaret from 1950 to 1953, successful three out of four times. They had great successes with Lady Margaret, one of their crews winning the Henley Grand in 1951, the last college club to do so.

Meldrum was very shrewd, a talented painter, who set down his rowing ideas in *Coach and Eight* and was ahead of his time. After Lady Margaret won the Grand he lunched with Amy Gentry, chairman of the Women's Amateur Rowing Council, who suddenly said to him: 'The more I looked at your crew, Mr Meldrum, the more I realized they're trying to row like my girls.' 'Oh, really?' he said. He is dead now, but his overcoat still attends the Boat Race annually on the back of Dr Edward Bevan, who was for many years the CUBC's treasurer, a rare case of a man who got an Olympic gold medal but missed a blue in his Cambridge student days. Meldrum's widow gave him the Meldrumatic overcoat.

While Oxford were under the mixed fortunes of Jumbo and the Radley coaches, Cambridge had Crowden and Dr David Jennens, veterans of the Meldrum- and Rickett-coached crews, and Donald Legget and the inspirator of Tideway Scullers' School, Lou Barry, as a finisher. Dan Topolski picked up Oxford from where they had fallen by the early 1970s with the aid of fellow young bloods like Hugh Matheson and old sages like George Harris, until he overturned Cambridge's winning streak and orchestrated a longer one for Oxford, being called by the *Guardian* the university mastermind. Oxford-watchers now hang more success round Topolski's neck than Jumbo achieved. Cambridge, meanwhile, tried Bob Janousek, formerly Britain's principal national coach, for the 150th anniversary year, and Graeme Hall has been moving farther and farther to the forefront.

More than two hundred men have been involved in coaching blue boats. They have woven the tapestry of the Putney–Mortlake race. What none of them has taught, and what no coaching manual has suggested, is the startling method by which one recent blue has tested his mental application. This man is an exceptionally strong oarsman who, as is sometimes the case, worries that his brain-power may not match his brawn-power. To get himself into mental condition to race he has been witnessed to take a car up to eighty miles an hour on a motorway in the overtaking lane and then shut his eyes for as long as he dare.

Before this takeaway is completely consumed there are some little sweets with contrasting tastes. Guts Woodgate again:

> Our 1862 race did something to cement *entente cordiale*: in that the two crews, the night before the race, entered into partnership for a cat hunt. Oxford were to find the cat, and the dog, my terrier Jenny. Cambridge's share was to supply the room for the sport. The cat, tortoise-shell, cost one shilling. She was given sanctuary in a big zinc bucket, used for holding dirty plates, and placed in the Cantab sitting room in the old Star and Garter. Then Jenny was turned in, to draw and chase her. The cat was as big as Jenny, but in due time, with a badly clawed nose, Jenny got her fangs into puss's windpipe, and hung on. It was then only a matter of time. Oxford had 6 to 4 the best of the partnership, for the Cantab room was so odiferous next morning that they had to seek another apartment for breakfast! . . . I'm afraid we one and all had no qualms of conscience as to the hunt. The cat was under sentence of drowning when we bought her; so she was, *mutatis mutandis*, only out of the frying-pan into fire when we gave her a run for life.

They gave puss a watery tomb that night. 'As a fact, she actually came back, on the morning flood, to reproach our cruelty, just as we were launching. We could identify her beyond doubt, as she floated by.'

Ernest Balfour (Oxford, 1896–97) found more congenial and less bloodthirsty celebrants after his winning race in 1896. He wrote home five days after the race:

> I was not able to stay another night at Oxford House as I had to go to Blue Monday dinner. I was very much honoured in being asked. It is held every year on the Monday after the Boat Race; and when once you have been invited, you may always go again, never waiting to be asked. You call everyone at table by their nicknames, and after dinner you play all sorts of games like 'cockfighting', holding a lighted candle in one hand, while you sit on a champagne bottle with just one heel on the ground, and try to light another candle with the first one without tumbling over onto the floor. It was great fun. The guests are all old Blues, and only about one from Oxford and Cambridge crews is asked. . . .

One last, but not least, list for the honours board. The lines of lawyers, bankers, dons and city gents will have to go unsung, a smattering of Lords of Appeal, viscounts, and several boatloads of schoolmasters, headed by J. J. Hornby (Oxford, 1849, second race), who was an undergraduate at Balliol but is recorded at Brasenose because he had been elected a Fellow there, the future headmaster and provost of Eton. There were double blues and rugby players and jumpers and rifle shots of distinction, too. There were runners and cyclists and sculptors like George Drinkwater (Oxford, 1902–3), and C. B. Lawes (Cambridge, 1865), later Sir Charles Lawes-Wittewronge, Bart; and composers like F. S. Kelly (Oxford, 1903); and the printer to the Queen, W. Spottiswoode, who rowed for Oxford in 1844 at the Henley and Thames regattas in a year in which there was not a Boat Race as such, and therefore is not strictly a blue. There are the unlucky men like A. C. Gladstone, who lost his place through sickness for three years in succession. There are several others who have dropped out a few days before, and A. H. Franklin whom Burnell thinks to be the only man to get a blue without ever rowing over the course. He was brought in very late, after the full-course trial, and Oxford sank with him on board in 1925.

Cambridge have fared much better than Oxford with presidents who have missed the race, usually because of illness but in a few cases because they have de-selected themselves. Light blue stand-down presidents are: N. J. Bradley (1935), J. G. Chambers (1865), C. R. Le Blanc-Smith (1913), and M. A. Nicholson (1947), who never got his blue. Oxford's are: W. D. Benson (1871), E. A. Berrisford (1920), C. R. Carr (1864), C. G. V. Davidge (1950), R. S. de Haviland (1884), G. A. Ellison (1934), W. H. Grenfell (1879), R. Lesley (1973), J. S. Lewes (1937), A. Morrison (1864), G. Morrison (1862), W. Pinckney (1856), T. W. Tennant (1963), F. W. Warre (1901) and C. A. Willis (1903).

Oarsmen and their friends are much too sensible to indulge in hooliganism. They only blow off their high spirits in a manner befitting gentlemen, when the music halls close round Piccadilly. How typical things were in 1898 when Cambridge sank, who knows? 'St James's Restaurant Besieged' ran the headline in the *Sunday Times*. Slight collisions with the police in the vicinity of Piccadilly and Leicester Square have become customary, said the paper.

Last night proved no exception to the rule. Shortly before closing time a number of young men who had been visiting one of the music halls in the vicinity paid a visit en masse to the St James's Restaurant. It is said that they attacked the place both from the Regent Street and Piccadilly entrances. But the police at Vine Street are used to these raids. They were on duty in force last night, and the would-be raiders, whom it was feared would cause a disturbance, were driven back when they attempted to force their way through St James's doors. A mild form of mêlée followed. Constables were mixed up with civilians and for a few moments a riotous scene was witnessed; the raiders were driven back and punctually on the stroke of midnight the entrances to the restaurant were closed. This proved distasteful to the marauders and repeated endeavours were made to effect an entry – all to no avail.

Constables lined the pavements and the unruly were severely moved on. The more daring were removed to Vine Street Station where they were charged with disorderly conduct or some similar offence. In due course the miscreants would appear before the magistrate at Marlborough Street Police Station. The names of the persons charged were not divulged.

Harold Macmillan may not care passionately about rowing, but on the day when he addressed the assembly at the Savoy his university had narrowed the scoreline to Cambridge 68, Oxford 56, with one dead heat, by their three-and-a-half-length win in the 125th race. 'I hope,' he concluded, '– but of course as chancellor of the University of Oxford I have to be careful – you will go out and generally break up the town. If Piccadilly Circus stands tomorrow I shall be disappointed. If Eros has not been moved, or draped with suitable decorations, it will not be a good night.' It must have been the first time that a premier, albeit an ex-premier, has incited the mob to violence. Harold Macmillan was converted. For him P–M no longer means Prime Minister, but is the toast for Putney to Mortlake.

As for the weak-hearted, they may defy the warnings of Dr Morgan and stay with coxswain Swartwout's aesthete to pity, not despise, the vulgar men of brawn and sinew:

> Nay, Cyril! Let us shun brute strife
>   And turn our thoughts in the direction
> Of things that *matter* in our life –
>   The taper waist, the fair complexion.

7

The ninth men, and Miss Brown
The coxswains' casebook

So heed, O coxswains, and take heart!
The royal founder of your art
Should teach you how to play your part
    On reedy Camus.
And if his style you imitate
Some fine day it may be your fate
To get a Blue; at any rate
    To be quite famous!

The royal founder of the art of steering referred to in the stanza from
R. E. Swartwout's poem was Edgar the Peaceable, who had the good
sense, according to legend, to organize the eight kings at his command
into a crew and seize the rudder lines himself. Swartwout was from
Middlesex in Concord, USA, and Trinity, and he steered Cambridge
to victory in 1930, fifty years or so before one with taper waist and fair
complexion took the ninth seat for the first time. Another early
rhymster from his college was Rudie Lehmann, who put his finger on
the essential qualities. Just as it has been said that a tenor is not a man
but a disease, so he pointed out that coxswains are not so much
individuals as members of a secret society, small men meeting to devise
torments for other mortals, and like white cats with blue eyes they are
always deaf. Sometimes they remain deaf to the end of their careers,
content to concentrate on not being jerked out of the boat, an
occurrence which all oarsmen should aim at, according to Fairbairn.
The aural powers of Lionel Portman who steered Oxford to victory in
1893 are not known, but he weighed 7 stone 7 pounds then and later
grew up to 6 feet 2 inches, 13 stone in weight, and became both a
writer and a baritone.

Sir George Trevelyan also captured their essence in *Macmillan's Magazine* in about 1860:

You may search the whole coast from Land's End to North Foreland,
But where will you find such a steersman as Morland?
Just look at him peering, as sharp as a rat,
From under his rum little shaggy black hat.
Let all honest Cambridge men fervently pray
That our pet Harrow coxswain, for once in a way,
Though as valiant a sergeant as any we know,
On Saturday next may show back to the foe.

Coxswains are essential to steering racing eights. They also played a key role in the coaching of early Boat Race crews in the days of Tom Egan and Arthur Shadwell, when these two in particular took major parts in doing away with professional coaches and steerers for the university match. The Rev. Shadwell's *Principles of Rowing and Steering*, published in approximately 1857, remains a masterpiece of exposition of the coxswain's office. Everyone but sensitive crews take coxes for granted, but a cox who knows what he is doing is worth a couple of oarsmen in the Boat Race. There have been a few cases where good steering has probably won the race, and there have been more where bad steering has been the principal factor in losing it. Shadwell steered Oxford six times in various regattas and races during the 1840s after migrating there from Cambridge, where he had come into contact with the legendary Egan of Caius. Here is his view from the ninth seat, after many miles of steering and coaching. The cox, Shadwell wrote, is regarded as the maker of the crew and the presiding spirit of its work. He is indeed a steerer, but also more, a Master and Governor, a Palinurus and Mentor in one:

The best stamp of man combines a scientific well-digested knowledge of rowing, with acute wits, and lightness of weight. There is an acquired knowledge necessary, which is gained by study: hence the best man for this place is one who is himself a real rowing man, gradually educated for his high post by actual use of the oar, and the observation of others' work. It has been usually found that there can be no better introduction to the mechanical art of steering proper, than frequent sculling in narrow waters. His eye is then well initiated to judge of the distance of an oar's end from banks, of the most advantageous manner of meeting currents, and of keeping close round corners: in fact, it more than anything else makes him a waterman. His height had better not exceed 5 feet 8 inches, and his weight 9½ stone. But his wits are of far more importance than his weight. So much depends on his penetration, judgment and coolness, that you may well be content to carry a few pounds more in the stern, if you can secure a steady hand, an unerring eye, fixedness of purpose, and self-possession. Choose no man because he is light, nor even on the higher qualification of steering tidily through College races: he will never rise to the level of an efficient coxswain, unless he is practically acquainted with rowing on a system, and is also a reflecting, observant, and an undaunted man. The fact is that crews are either to be made or marred by him who handles their yolk-lines in training. Consider what he has to do for them, and what is involved in his functions. Let alone the thorough knowledge required for selecting the members, and accompanying them separately in pair oars, to pick out their ever varying, subtle, and inveterate faults: he has, after the crew is fairly formed and set to row, to attend to the whole boat itself from stem to stern, and overlook everything belonging to it: to see that each man is properly placed for his work, and none injured in efficiency by the carelessness of the boatbuilder, or by the inattention of the man in the yard in tying on seats, or allowing thowls to be loose, leathers torn away, handles badly rasped, stretchers shifted, irons bent out of form, sprung or twisted oars to remain in use.

Besides this he has to watch the peculiar motions of each man, to teach diligently and temperately, to trim the boat when lurching under uneven rowing, to calculate the advances made in speed as the rowing improves, to time accurately, and remember the difference between one day's work and another's, to keep up his heart and nerve in trying circumstances, to keep in good humour with all his crew, and to keep them in good humour. This is a small list of accomplishments beseeming the coxswain, who is also the boatswain of a match crew. And after all comes the day that decides all, when he must steer a true course on a broad river without any deviation. How often must he have studied that course, and made sure of his points, and have marked the shoals, and the sets of tideway, and how well have educated his eyes to keep parallel with the banks though doing violence to his senses; but doing this to avoid the greater violence of jamming the tide, or travelling needlessly athwart a wide stream in obedience to some traditional practice of crossing over, or cutting off corners only to steer out again in order to clear them. Then he may neither foul his adversary, nor yet suffer himself to be shoved out of his true course by the other's ignorance of it: and he is conscious that after the start the eyes of all the rowing men in

England are on him, and that a turn of his wrist on either side of a lazy obstructive lighter may win or lose the day, which shall award the highest of aquatic honours to the light or dark blue flag.

Supposing a fit man to have been placed upon the honourable thwart abaft the stroke oar of a university crew, Shadwell goes on, 'henceforth he is their waterman, and on what he does and says, all their comforts, and a great part of their efficiency, depends.' He must look after the equipment, for it cannot be calculated how many good men's work is marred, and how many beginners precluded from forming into oarsmen by the overlooking of very small matters in the paraphernalia of boats.

The Hon. Colin Moynihan steered Oxford to their seven-length win in 1977, but in some ways his race in the cox's seat of Isis in 1975 was much more interesting. It would have reduced the Rev. Shadwell to apoplexy before he knew the result. Isis were a very strong crew who took an early lead on the Surrey station and immediately crossed to Middlesex for some corner-cutting and shelter from the rough conditions. Goldie saw their chance and went for the bump, and somebody in the Isis boat asked Moynihan if he realized that they were only a few feet behind. He put his rudder on hard and went almost at right angles for the Black Buoy and the Surrey shore, and by the time he had straightened up Goldie were two to three lengths ahead in the centre of the stream. They were seven seconds ahead at the mile. And Isis had shipped a lot of water. Moynihan removed the cap which the coach Chris Blackwall had lent him, and while yelling his men onwards with the help of the tide, he let go of the strings and baled with the cap. Approaching Hammersmith he was still close to the Surrey bank and asked if it was all right to take the inside span of the bridge. 'No,' screamed Boris Rankov, 'it has to be the centre,' and Moynihan was heaving at his strings again. But they reached the bridge an incredible seventeen seconds ahead of Goldie and eventually beat them by nine and a half lengths in a time eleven seconds faster than Cambridge's win in the Boat Race half an hour later.

Shadwell's concluding word to the coxswain is to 'study well your course, I should say, your own course as intended to be taken: study it in the eight and out of it: row, scull over it, contemplate it; resolve upon every point to be steered for in each reach, and map them all on your memory.'

Nowadays the umpire takes the coxes over the course together on the Thursday before the race, each cox driving a launch while the umpire tells them where he considers the stream, and therefore the centre of the course, which could become a matter of controversy, is to be found. On that interpretation he will judge them.

Moynihan was lucky: he made several mistakes and still came out on top, and his Boat Race course two years later was superb. He is just the sort of character that Shadwell had in mind when he said that the duties were 'maker of the crew and the presiding spirit of its work'. Moynihan knows when to cajole and when to sympathize, when to instruct and when to advise, when to joke and when to keep quiet, and how to encourage. He can play the dominant role or keep in the background, knows his rowing thoroughly, and can be a leader on the bank as well as in the boat. He can weave and duck and parry, light of tongue and on his feet, as befits a man with a boxing blue. He has put his talents of leadership to good use for Oxford and for Britain, for whose teams he has steered eights to a gold medal and twice to silver medals in lightweight, Olympic and world championships respectively. On the water he knows all the tricks. Always have the shell pointed the way you wish it to point; never given an opponent an advantage of position or start if you can possibly avoid it; have the measure of your own men as well as of the course, being aware who can take insults and who cannot; and do not be averse to speaking just loud enough for the other crew to hear if you want them to. Know how to wind your own crew up and wind them down, and sometimes wind some up and some down simultaneously; know exactly how the boat will turn and how it will react to wind and water; be decisive, quick-witted, and have a light touch on the rudder strings. It is a lot to ask. These qualities, or a good dollop of most of them, are worth much more than being a few pounds lighter than your opponent in the race. The fate of the crew is in the cox's hands and, as Lehmann says in his *Complete Oarsman*, a little movement or a mere twitch of hand, a failure of judgement or a momentary aberration, may win or lose a race.

An example of aberration was provided by W. E. Maynard for Oxford in 1886. That was the year in which the centre span of Hammersmith Bridge was narrowed by repair men's scaffolding so that there was barely room for two boats to get through abreast. With the dark blues on the Surrey station, the crews arrived at the bridge together and shot it dead level, virtually knitting their oars but not touching, and shortly afterwards they hit a full head wind. Cambridge got the worst of the water and it was breaking over their bow man, and at Barnes Oxford were nearly two lengths up. Maynard took Cambridge's water and Pitman, the Cantab stroke, took his men up to 40 and threatened a bump. Maynard, instead of edging outwards, put the rudder hard on, moving athwart the tide, and by the time he had straightened up in his own water Cambridge had harnessed their second wind and won by two thirds of a length. That was also the first time that a crew won from behind at Barnes Bridge.

In 1901 there was intelligent steering in another race won from behind after Barnes Bridge. Cambridge won the toss and got the Surrey station, which afforded shelter before the storm awaiting at Hammersmith. Oxford could not build a good enough lead to take Cambridge's water so Maclagan took them in behind Cambridge. The light blues were over-rating Oxford and built a lead at Hammersmith but the dark blues crept up to within half a length of them along Corney Reach. It was unwise to move out and they were fearful of bumping the Cantabs, for the foul would be theirs, so Maclagan dropped the crew to a paddle until smooth water was reached. They were overlapping again at Barnes Bridge with the advantage of being on the inside of the bend, and they went on to win by two fifths of a length.

G. L. Davis, who coxed Cambridge from 1875 to 1879 and Leander from 1880 to 1885 contributed a piece to R. C. Lehmann's *Rowing* in which he said that one coxswain should not bore the other. Boring is when one cox steers close to another so that he gradually pushes him out of his own water. It is impossible, wrote Davis, when both are skilful and equally acquainted with the course. It is trickery and not sportsmanlike, he said, but it is difficult to believe that a man who won two, lost two, and dead heated was not a bore sometimes during his twenty-one and a quarter miles of boat racing. He quotes an Oxford opponent who was pressed out of his course by the light blues in the fog at the beginning of the race as opening his remarks at the Boat Race dinner thus: 'I have been very much interested in this race, but I have also been very much bored.'

Charles Robert Worsley Tottenham of Eton and Christ Church steered Oxford from 1864 to 1869 and was the most successful blue until his record was equalled by an oarsman in 1982. He had a different sort of brush with boredom in 1865, at which time the Boat

Race was like an obstacle course. In 1868 the Thames Conservancy obtained statutory powers to clear the course for racing, but before then anything that could move was permitted to do so. Just below Barnes Bridge Tottenham was confronted by a sailing barge which was tacking across his course. It looked as if there was room to pass in front of the barge but Tottenham did not alter course. He was in the lead and he was damned if he was going to lose ground. He made his calculations of speed, movement and parallax and continued towards what the spectators on the steamers thought was going to be a spectacular smash. Both ships maintained course and the barge passed clear just before Oxford came up under her stern, requiring not even a trifling deflectional twinge of the strings.

The Boat Race has had its share of the good, the bad and the indifferent when it comes to coxing, and played an important role in the development of the art of steering in two-boat races generally. The most recent, most notable coxswain to meet fate on a fine day and 'to get a blue; at any rate to be quite famous' is Miss Susan Brown of Honiton in Devon and Wadham College, Oxford. This slight, dark-haired, mellow-complexioned student of biochemistry became the first woman to steer in the men's Boat Race in 1981, at the invitation of the president, Chris Mahoney. She learned to cox at Wadham and became a member of the British women's training team, eventually going to the Moscow Olympic Games. They were coached by Oxford's coach Dan Topolski, so he spotted her talents early in her steering career, much of it spent with the women on the Tideway. She was twenty-two, very softly spoken, purposeful, yet slipping about on the bank almost unseen. She was a nightmare for the reporters because she had very little to say to their repetitive trite questions about women's lib, diet, making history, had she got a boyfriend in the crew, and so on. She was a nightmare for the broadcasters for similar reasons, and when she did say something they couldn't hear her. She was a dream for the photographers because, without resorting to the gimmickry of showing her legs or wearing tight singlets, she looked like a revelation in every picture taken. For the first three months of 1981 Sue Brown must have passed before more shutters than anyone except for Lady Diana Spencer. Miss Brown was the tousled girl next door enjoying the fresh air and the good fortune to be engaged by the blues; Lady Diana was the enchanting salon smasher, engaged to the heir to the throne. They could never have swopped places, but for a while they both filled the papers. The crew got angry at times. Soon after Brown's blue boat seat was announced one of the oarsmen at a Radley practice session yelled, 'Go back to Lady Diana, you vultures.' But she was the toast of Honiton, which dressed the High Street and had the town crier in full spate of anticipatory praise.

She took on personality in the boat. In the trial eights for 1981 she bored with Steve Higgins past the Putney boathouses and sheered him towards the Surrey shore. Eventually he had to make hell for leather for the beach, waterlogged and with a very unhappy crew. The press and coach's launches rescued the men and Miss Brown's trialists were cruising towards Hammersmith. This was after Adrian Rossiter had retired from the race for the smallest blue, deciding to go and work for the new Social Democratic Party instead. He chose the Gang of Four instead of the gang of eight, and Miss Brown beat Higgins for the nomination. Mahoney was very kind to her, she said. He said, 'Well done,' to her three times during the year. Mahoney was a very powerful oar who didn't waste energy talking. In her crew's win by eight lengths, the largest margin for Oxford in the twentieth century, she was hardly troubled by the steering because they went immediately into a lead and she was able to take whatever water she liked. But she steered a good course, to the relief and the chagrin, one feels, of some old heavies. She appeared reluctantly on the steps of Quintin for pictures with the magnum and the boys for a great crush of photographers. She's a damn good cox, said John Snagge, 'tough with them but a quiet and gentle person'. By 1982, when she was chosen for her second Boat Race, again beating Higgins for the selection, she had done a lot of thinking about coxing. 'I had no sense of taking a step into history,' she said, amiably putting down the cliché questions. 'The race is just like any other outing. It happens all around you but you don't realize it is happening. The enjoyment is winning, not the race.'

The first time she had terrible match nerves on the start. The stroke John Bland was supposed to tell her when the umpire had his flag up, but he didn't. Or if he did, it didn't register with her. The umpire, Ronnie Howard, shouted, 'Relax, Oxford.' Someone told her that she should look behind her once during the race to see the pursuing flotilla, but she didn't.

In 1982 she was much more relaxed about going before the television cameras or opening fêtes or restaurants. She quite enjoys doing so, but in her first year was embarrassed, believing her place to be in the background. She was the newcomer; everyone else had done the Boat Race or the Isis–Goldie match before. She came to the start for the second time with a different idea of what coxing was about. 'Part of the cox's role is to look after the crew. I get them up, but I don't take them tea like I did the first year. That's really because this lot get up earlier. That's just a little thing. I realized that you don't have to be that much better to get a blue, but just a little bit. And I have realized that I have not got the personality to lift the crew both on and off the water. I just don't have the mouth to do it off the water, which I think is quite an important part of it. But it doesn't make any difference to the present blue boat because there are other personalities to do that sort of thing. Oxford have a dominant coach.' She knew the crew, too. Conington is frequently ill. Rankov is the strong man, in the head and at the oar. Kirkpatrick is tension. Rob Clay is brilliance. Yonge is comedy.

'Moynihan is the best cox I've come across because he's got absolute confidence in himself. He can pull a crew together. I have my limitations in that way, but I get a lot of help. I go over the course every day with Bert Green [the National Westminster Bank boatman] and I know a lot more about the Tideway for it.'

Sue Brown's second race proved very different from her first. She had had a tough year in trials because she always seemed to be steering the losing crew, which she didn't like, and she was led by Cambridge and bored by Bernstein. But she did her share of boring and made more music on the Tideway than Bernstein, and in better tempo. She took, if she did but know it, a leaf from the pages of E. D. Brickwood who used to write under the uncompromising nom de plume Argonaut. A cardinal point in the creed of pilots, he said, is that 'a boat should be coaxed by its rudder'. Miss Brown coaxed the dark blues to victory. She got her blue and became quite famous.

8

Oxford won, Cambridge too
1877: Honest John Phelps and the dead heat

Punch summed up the 1877 Boat Race succinctly: 'Oxford won, Cambridge too.' The impossible had happened. Two crews had raced each other over the championship course of four and a quarter miles, avoiding a number of obstacles while doing so, and arrived level. Few believed it, bad feelings were aroused, and slurs upon the finishing judge, 'Honest' John Phelps, were rife. The umpire, Joseph Chitty QC, could not find Phelps in the crush of boats at the end of the race to learn his verdict. 'When the announcement was made in our office window soon after 9 o'clock last Saturday morning that the race between Oxford and Cambridge had ended in a dead heat, the unusual circumstance was not readily believed, because most of the newspapers had recorded a victory for Oxford,' said *Bell's Life*, with the benefit of hindsight. 'Those who had been in such a hurry to be first in the field with their information were evidently engaged on a matter with which they were not thoroughly conversant, for instead of waiting to hear the decision of the judge, which is always necessary in the case of a close finish, they wired off their own version of the affair, and not only misled their readers but caused no end of confusion and suspense.'

That there was confusion there is no doubt. Lewis Farnell, an Oxford undergraduate, was watching on the towpath in a dense crowd just above Barnes Bridge.

As they came through the bridge I saw to my joy Oxford going rapidly ahead and daylight appearing for the first time between the boats; normally Oxford should have won by at least two lengths. But suddenly Oxford staggered and stood still in a mass of foam: the bow-oar, Cowles, had struck the top of a big wave in feathering and broken his blade clean off: before our boat could recover from the shock, Cambridge drew up level. Then Grenfell, now Lord Desborough, rowing four, shouted 'row on': Oxford started again with seven oars, and in the last three-quarters of a mile beat Cambridge fairly by nearly a third of a length. It was so obvious, that the Dark Blue flag was immediately hoisted on high, and the news was wired round England that Oxford had won: and every man in the Cambridge boat knew it and admitted it; and in our joy we pushed each other into the water. The only person who had not seen it was the umpire [*sic*], old John Phelps, who had never seen a near race before, and lost his head, and shut his eyes, and merely maintained that 'He could not tell who had won'. Therefore the two Presidents decided that it must be called a dead heat; and though Cambridge chivalrously offered the victory to Oxford, the latter with still greater chivalry declined to accept it. For some time after it became a joke in the music-halls, to talk of a 'dead heat by ten yards'. This was the most thrilling sporting experience of my life; and what I saw and have here narrated was confirmed by Cowles, the innocent cause of what was technically a loss but virtually a greater triumph, when I met him some thirty years afterwards.

Farnell's account suffers from his partisanship, and a somewhat optimistic opinion of his sightlines to the race finish from the towpath near Barnes Bridge. But most accounts of this race agree on one thing, and that is that Oxford were convinced they had won. The build-up to the race had been interesting because both crews were reckoned to be strong, giving the pundits a hard time in choosing between them. There had been floods on the Isis which had interrupted the training and rendered it impossible for coaching to be done from the bank, so the president, Tom Cottingham Edwards-Moss, had to coach from the stern. He also took a fairly laid-back approach to the race, not taking his place in the crew until late on in the practice. When they arrived at Putney only two weeks before the race, *Bell's Life* said that they looked the finest Oxford crew ever, and large crowds gathered to witness the outings. But they annoyed their local supporters on Saturday, 10 March, by not appearing on the Isis for a farewell row on home water. It was found that the president had taken the men on a flying excursion to Henley. Although this was doubtless intended as a 'dark visit', reported *Bell's*, 'a chield was found taking notes' who took the same train as the crew, the 12.10 from Oxford. The OUBC boatman brought the new Clasper boat there and they tested her from the bridge to the island, and then went over the course at racing pace. After twenty minutes' rest they embarked in another new boat, this one by Parkins of Eton, which had also found its way to Henley.

On the same day the Cantabs were afloat at Putney, rowing up to Barnes in their old boat and walking home, and later in the day they tried out their new boat by Swaddle and Winship. During the morning there was some delay because Mr Rhodes's launch had not got steam up and eventually Mr Close was obliged to coach from the steam yacht *Marguerite*, on which there were several visitors. Anyway, they were a fine crew also. President Lewis had five oarsmen with blues apart from himself and the coxswain Davis, including Charles Gurdon who played rugby for Cambridge in the same year and went on to become an England forward before he became a judge.

Two weeks later the race started at 8.27 a.m. with four launches in attendance, one for the umpire, one each for the clubs, and one for the fourth estate, who could get breakfast from capable hands on board. She set sail from Temple Pier at 6.35 a.m. and reached Putney at 7.15 a.m. There was brilliant sun and a chilling wind, and Oxford had won the toss and chosen Middlesex, and were on the water first. Cambridge had a last-minute panic about their Swaddle and Winship. It was a short heavily cambered craft, and according to *Battles of the Blues*, was very fast in calm water but stuck her nose into a wind if there was one, needing a great deal of rudder. The wind was from the west-northwest, the worst possible for Cambridge, and so they fixed a false keel to the boat at the last moment. They were thus late in getting out but were at the starting position by 8.12 a.m. Oxford were doffing comforters and over-jerseys. The press steamer broke away from its mooring at Putney aqueduct and had to go ahead to prevent being blown ashore. She was then warped up to a barge off Bishop's Ground and the race was started by Mr Searle.

Before half society had broke its fast, as *The Times* put it, the crews were off, Cambridge on the Surrey station. Oxford led by a few feet at first. They were level at Craven Cottage and the soap works (Harrods) and at Hammersmith Bridge, 'naked and untenanted' according to *The Times*, Oxford gave way slightly to allow room for Cambridge to pass under the centre span clear of the steamboat pier adjoining the Surrey buttress. Cambridge emerged with a lead of two or three feet, then a row boat crossed in front of the crews from the Middlesex side and almost caused calamity. Both crews altered course to avoid it, an incident best seen from the balcony of Biffen and Sons Metropolitan Boat House on the Mall, where reserved numbered seats cost 7s 6d. Oxford began to gain on the outside of the bend and both coxes steered for Middlesex on a broil of nasty surf and flowing tide. At Chiswick Eyot they were level and almost clashing, but by the end of the Eyot Oxford had taken half a length and Cambridge were rocky and suffering from Davis's free use of his rudder lines. By Chiswick church the dark blues were up by two thirds of a length. The light blues moved up again at the Bull's Head, but at Barnes Bridge Oxford had put themselves about a length in front. Opposite the White Hart, with a yard of daylight between the boats, Oxford sheered to the left to avoid a barge which projected into the course. Because of this they were close in front of Cambridge who immediately spurted. Oxford 'suddenly went all abroad and a perfect scramble ensued among the bow-side oars. During this momentary disorder the bow oar of Oxford became irretrievably damaged and the bowman was unable to do more than keep time with his crew without feathering his oar,' reported *The Times*.

Cowles's oar had broken at the button. Oxford had the advantage of the bend but Cambridge wacked their rate up to 40 and they moved up against the seven-oar. They raced past the flag alongside, and the gun fired amid a rare scene of excitement, not to say pandemonium. Somewhere in the press of small boats was Honest John Phelps the finishing judge, moored close to the Middlesex shore and with no post to assist his sight line. And he did not manage to communicate with umpire Chitty until much later in the day, when he reported to him in the robing room of the Rolls Court at Lincoln's Inn and told him that it was a dead heat. 'I couldn't separate them, sir, they were just like this,' he told Chitty, moving his hands palm to palm backwards and forwards.

Piggy Eyre was in a skiff on the Surrey side 'exactly opposite the finish' and saw quite clearly that Oxford won by a little over one foot. 'As to Honest John, whom I had known personally for many years, he *most certainly* was not able to see the boats at the distance he was from them owing to ordinary decay of eyesight,' wrote Eyre, admittedly more than thirty years later. 'He was well over seventy and probably had been so for several years previously but said nothing. He was a bit blind and had not seen the crews he judged for some years. He did not judge again.' Eyre's view was uncompromising and he took the story of Phelps's description of the finish to Chitty as further evidence. But he was not necessarily a close partisan, having rowed for neither university. 'The fact was that Oxford were leading by a few feet and Cambridge were gaining on them by inches stroke by stroke. At the finish Oxford were a trifle over one foot ahead. There could be no possible doubt about it. Every man in each crew must have known it also.'

The Oxford crew were certainly under the impression that they had won. They disembarked, changed, and took their seats in the bows of their launch to return to Putney, a pride of place reserved for winners. It was there that they learned of the verdict, which was not official until the little scene played out in the Rolls Court. Willy Grenfell, their number four, was sure that he was alongside the Cambridge number two, Lewis, and he could relive the race many years later. He recounted the race in a recording for John Snagge and is in no doubt. In the confusion there had been plenty of time for the music-hall jokes to multiply, and poor Phelps was accused of having taken a nip too many to keep out the cold, of falling asleep under a bush, and of saying, 'Dead heat to Oxford by five feet.' The truth is probably that he couldn't see. He was a long way from the crews. Posts were erected afterwards and have been used ever since.

The time for the race is officially 24 minutes 8 seconds. John Bennett wrote to *Bell's Life*:

Sir — we find today three declarations of the time of the duration of the Boat Race, viz., one, 24 mins 6½ secs; another, 24 mins 12 secs; while mine was 24 mins 5/10 sec. Permit me to assure you that the two chronographs I sent were most scrupulously prepared before starting for their duty at the race with my standard regulator. This regulator is checked by an electric current transmitted every hour in the day from the Royal Observatory. Now, I beg to state that my chronographs agreed at the start, agreed at the finish, and agreed when compared immediately afterwards.

Bell's gave the time as 24 minutes 4 seconds.

The same edition of the paper, 31 March, carried important intelligence concerning the decision on bets. 'All bets on the result are void, except such as were made after the race. In double event bets for which Oxford or Cambridge were taken in conjunction with the winner of a previous race the money must be put together and divided. In sweepstakes the holders of Oxford and Cambridge divide the money.' And information regarding Cowles's oar was passed on: 'It appears that some mis-statements have occurred with regard to the broken oar, to the effect that it was made by Ayling of Lambeth. There were, it appears, five of Ayling's oars in the boat, and three of Tozer's, and that which broke came from the workshop of the latter.' When the leather of the oar was removed, an old crack was found halfway through the back of the loom. Applied power would have compressed the crack, but it had been extended by the impact against the wave. Cowles tried to row on with his hands on the leather, which was holding the two pieces together, but found it impossible.

Far from Cambridge offering the decision to Oxford in a spirit of chivalry as Farnell would have us believe, it appears that some Cambridge men claimed the race on the grounds of a foul – which implies, as one journalist quickly pointed out, that they thought Oxford got across the line first. Umpire Chitty had to clear the matter up with a letter to *Bell's Life*:

> Dear Sir, at the end of the race, when the two boats were lying alongside, some member or members of the Cambridge crew, as I understood, claimed a foul, and I at once said there was none. There was great noise and confusion at the time. After the men had left their boats I heard nothing more about the matter. Enough certainly was said at the time to ground a more formal claim for a foul, but no more formal claim was ever made to me. I am, etc., Joseph W. Chitty.

The Oxford men were back in residence by Wednesday, 18 April, objects of sympathy and congratulation to their fellow collegians who daily became more imbued with the idea that Oxford had won. On that Wednesday there was a meeting of captains which resolved unanimously to present each of the Varsity crew with medals as if they had been declared the victors. The decision was received with much satisfaction in the university and city.

On Thursday, 26 April, the Cambridge captains met at the Hoop Hotel, in the absence of president Lewis who was not yet back in residence, and after resolving to build a boathouse for CUBC, they carried *nem. con.* a motion from Mr Rudie Lehmann of LMBC 'that oars and medals be given the University crew of 1877'. A complaint was sent to *Bell's Life* about this by someone tinted with dark blue sympathies, but by May the editor was fed up with defending Phelps and he closed the correspondence. Not before, though, he had dealt with a piece in the *Englishman* in his issue of 28 April. The rival paper carried a villainous article suggesting that a long nail had somehow found its way into Cowles's oar, with imputations against Tims, the OUBC boatman. This *Bell's Life* dismissed, and passed to glowing description of the Oxford medals, on one side the university arms with the words 'Oxford and Cambridge Putney Medal', and on the other a wreath encircling the inscription: 'Possunt quia posse videntur'. The 'orthodox' would translate this as: 'They are coming through looking like winners', while the scholars of a Fairbairn caste of mind would say: 'They are coming because they think they can'.

The absolute certainty is that Phelps lost. He was replaced as finishing judge by Fairrie, who performed with the aid of a post for the next decade or so.

9

Foul deeds and fair decisions
Sinking feelings and the umpire's dilemma

Since 1829, when the Oxford cox 'fouled Cambridge twice' according to one account, this sort of unsavoury behaviour has played very little part in the Boat Race. Considering the weather's propensity for making Putney to Mortlake into a highway of hell, sinkings have occurred infrequently; but when they have happened they have been sensational for the spectators. A study of them reveals much about watermanship if little about rowing.

Oxford won the December 1849 Boat Race after being bumped by Cambridge. The year was unique in that there were two races for no special reason. Cambridge won the first one and Oxford challenged again. The bump was a polite way of describing a foul. Oxford had won the toss, chosen Middlesex, and the light blues had edged ahead until there was daylight between the boats, and moved into Oxford's water by Craven Point. At this time the agreement between the clubs said that 'if two boats are racing and one fairly takes the other's water by a clear lead, it shall be entitled to keep the water so taken to the end of the course; and if the two boats afterwards come into contact, while the leading boat remains in the water so taken, the boat whose water has been so taken shall be deemed to have committed a foul; but if they come into contact by the leading boat's departing from the water so taken, the leading boat shall be deemed to have committed a foul.' Oxford gained on Cambridge on this occasion and the Cambridge cox could not move across towards Surrey on his approach to Hammersmith without risking a bump. He moved over anyway and forfeited his right to the water if Oxford could get close enough – which they did. One version has it that Oxford's bow eventually made contact with a rigger after striking the stern, another that after the contact the Oxford men raised their oars to the perpendicular. Cambridge were three lengths ahead by the time the dark blues recovered. The umpire, Mr Fellowes of Leander, immediately awarded the race to Oxford after both crews had reached the end of the course, causing some abusive correspondence to the newspapers, but showing no quarrel with the stated rule. So far, this is the only occasion on which the race has been decided on a foul.

The somewhat eccentric rule regarding pilot's rights on the Tideway has been changed since, and the latest revision, in the 1979 agreement, says that:

> a boat's proper course is such as will enable it to reach the winning post in the shortest possible time, provided that it allows ample water for the other crew to steer its proper course on the side on which it started, when that crew is in a position to enforce its right to that water. But both crews shall pass through the centre arches of Hammersmith and Barnes bridges. A boat failing to keep its proper course does so at its peril in the event of a foul occurring. The Umpire shall be the sole judge of a boat's proper course. . . .

The rules define a foul as occurring when, after the race has started, 'there shall be any physical contact between the boats, oars, or persons of the two crews.'

Umpiring the Boat Race is an art which can turn out to be tricky, especially at the start and during sinking conditions, which are more frequent than actual sinkings. Cambridge sank in 1859, 1912 and 1978; Oxford beached in 1912 and sank in 1925 and 1951. There were rerows after the 1912 and 1951 disasters, and on both occasions the umpire's decision was based wholly on the decision of the umpire. Like case law to the English legal system, umpires have contributed advancement to the Boat Race rules by the wide and controversial interpretation of their juridical powers.

In 1912 the crews started in 'half a gale' with a west wind with a touch of north in it, Oxford on Surrey. They both began at a high rating and were shipping spray, and then off London RC Cambridge were caught by a series of crabs which left Conrad Skinner, the cox, a bit askew on the tide, which was sluggish and rougher than it looked from the shore. They were three lengths behind and full of water at the mile and went down with all hands off Harrods, being rescued by the professional sculler Albany, who happened to be in a skiff with his wife and baby just there. The umpire's launch also stopped to lend a hand. The Oxford cox, Bensley Wells, was hugging the Surrey shore, determined on finding the calmest passage to Mortlake. He came out for the centre span of Hammersmith Bridge and realized that enough was enough when he got to the point where the embankment wall fizzled out opposite the oil mills, which is just past the Doves. Wells edged the boat into the Surrey beach, for the men could hardly take a stroke at all by now. Stroke-side disembarked first while bow-side kept the boat level. When they were all ashore they emptied the boat and refloated her, all the while persuading the spectators not to assist, because they wished to continue in the race. Bow-side boated first to keep her level again, and one by one Wells loaded his oarsmen, except that number two was missing. He'd spotted a friend and nipped off for a few words, had Tinné. Wells waded out and got aboard and they were off as the umpire's launch arrived. Fred Pitman, whose nephew was rowing bow for Oxford, shouted to Bob Bourne through his megaphone that he had decided to rule 'No race'. Wells does not record verbatim what his stroke said before he told his cox to get things moving. The launch gave chase and Pitman shouted, 'What are you doing, Oxford? Where are you going? Didn't you understand that I have declared "No race"?' Bob Bourne shouted, 'We're going to Mortlake,' and paused; 'because our clothes are there.' And to Mortlake they did go.

Cambridge proposed a rerow on the ebb that day, but Oxford demurred. The crews went back into training instead of celebrating, and started again in almost as foul conditions on the following Monday. Oxford won the toss and chose Middlesex and fitted four-inch splashboards, Cambridge having a cutwater and enormous seven-inch boards. According to the account in *Battles of the Blues* by Woodgate, the presidents made a special agreement whereby the stakeboats were moved towards the Fulham wall because there was more shelter there on this occasion, and that the crew which had the Fulham side should not attempt to keep the other out in the rough water. Oxford won by six lengths.

The sequence of events in the first race according to coxswain Wells – who must have been known as Fargo – begs another question. The official records have it that both crews sank, but it is a moot point as to what constitutes a sinking. Oxford got from Putney to Mortlake in their shortest possible time unassisted, and without impeding Cambridge's progress, though they went ashore and their passage was then interrupted by the umpire, who should probably have been up with them in the first place. If their boat was rowable when they reached the beach, then they did not technically sink. Are waterlogging and sinking the same thing? The first, according to the *Oxford English Dictionary*, is to be flooded with water so as to become impaired in buoyancy, heavy and unmanageable. The second means to become submerged in water, to go under or to the bottom; or to founder. Shells do not go to the bottom, they merely founder and take on some of the properties of a (foundered) submarine. It is a pedantic and maybe purely academic point; but umpires' courses are apt to founder on the rocks of pedantry, draughtsmanship and conflicting case law.

Fred Pitman had put a distinctive, not to say inventive, interpretation on the rules, and presumably established a precedent that a crew who stop to empty their boat, even if unassisted and in the lead, may be deemed not to be participating in the Boat Race. His interpretation seems like special pleading when examined, and it will be interesting to see what happens on the next occasion that a crew takes a tea break or stops to empty their shell on the way to Mortlake. A paragraph in *Battles of the Blues* in 1925 looking back at previous sinkings says that: 'Although the Oxford crew, after emptying their boat, finished the course, the umpire considered that by leaving their boat they had broken the rules of boatracing and so he called it "No race".' Maybe Pitman had given simply getting out of the boat as a reason to somebody. But there is as yet no reference to such an occurrence in the agreement.

The 'No race' clauses in the 1979 agreement do not cover the situation. An umpire can only declare a restart or a rerow if an outside agency interferes to such an extent as to influence the result, or if before reaching the end of the wall (i.e. the Fulham wall on the Middlesex station at Putney) either crew should suffer 'serious accident or sinking or waterlogging which is not due to the fault of any member of the crew concerned.' But it is conceivable that stopping to empty a boat could be the only way that a crew could reach the winning post in the shortest possible time.

The events of 1912 were rich pickings for reporters. On Monday, 1 April, the *Daily Mirror* devoted its front page and three inside pages to dramatic pictures of the Cambridge sinking and rescue, and revealed a remarkable prophecy that Cambridge would sink in a story published on the day before the race in the *Boy's Realm*, 'The Rival Blues, A Magnificent and Thrilling Long, Complete Tale of the Great Varsity Boatrace by a Popular Author'. The *Mirror* report reveals a few other details, chief of which being its quotation from umpire Pitman 'that it was no race on the ground that Oxford, when baling out their boat, were helped by people other than the crew.' Coxswain Wells's account does not tally with this, and has the umpire's launch arriving at a late stage in the proceedings. The *Mirror*'s race report by F. B. Wilson, who is not necessarily the same reporter who got the quote from Pitman, had Pitman bringing Oxford in to the shore, but he could have meant Wells, or the stroke Bourne, or nephew Pitman the bowman. And he muddled Barnes Bridge with Hammersmith Bridge. Still, his descriptive powers shone: Cambridge sinking 'was a most curious sight. Very quietly and deliberately the boat seemed to lie down; there is no other easy way of expressing it.' Then he expresses it another way: 'Like a portly alderman lowering himself gravely into his chair, the boat went slowly and deliberately, almost imperceptibly, down. The water races badly at that corner, and the thing looked dangerous. Some of the crew scrambled up the bank, but the rest might have been in serious trouble, but for the presence of Albany, the sculler who rowed Barry for the English championship. He was on the spot and picked up several of them.' Two weeks later the *Mirror* had another haunting front-page picture of a sinking. This time it was the *Titanic*.

The clauses in the 1979 agreement concerning rerows and the Fulham wall owe something to Gerald Ellison, Bishop of Willesden as he was in 1951 when he umpired the race. The weather was extremely rough; Oxford's president, Christopher Davidge, won the toss and chose Surrey, Oxford went for a long warm-up and had quite a lot of water in the shell when they were on the stakeboat. They were filling up rapidly as they passed London RC, were waterlogged after a minute and submerged into the flickering televised gloom of the Tideway after two. Cambridge by now had moved right across and were scudding up the Surrey bank with the bishop in hot pursuit to stop them, declaring 'No race'. His decision was based on the 1927 agreement which said that: 'If, before the crews reached the top of the wall, any serious accident should happen in either boat, which, in the opinion of the umpire, is not due to the fault of any individual member of the crew, the umpire shall have power to recall and restart the crews.' It all depended, then, on what was meant by an accident. Oxford's humiliating start was caused by wind and tide.

Conditions on the rest of the course made it doubtful whether Cambridge would have reached Mortlake, unless of course they made some stops to empty the boat. There is no doubt that the umpire's bold interpretation was a good thing for the Boat Race because the general idea is that it should be decided on skill at oarsmanship, which includes skill at watermanship but is not synonymous with it. Ellison's decision certainly caused much anger at the time, though. When the crews were back in Putney it was too late to restart there and then; conditions had not improved, and the advantage of the tide had been lost. There was a fantastic meeting in a Putney washroom between the umpire, the Oxford coach J. A. McNabb, the Cambridge coach Harold Rickett, and the two naked presidents, Davidge and Brian Lloyd. All the crews' clothes had been sent to Mortlake. Amongst the steam and hot air the presidents agreed that they would try and reach a decision on the following Monday, come what may. The importance of reaching one was that the winning boat had to be packed on the Tuesday for a trip to the United States to race Harvard and Yale separately. On Monday, 26 March 1951, Cambridge beat Oxford by twelve lengths, and the agreement under which the Boat Race took place was revised in 1952 specifically to take into account the circumstances over which umpire Ellison found himself presiding. A similar clause, quoted above, is in the 1979 agreement, its importance being the addition of the words 'waterlogging' and 'sinking' to the section concerning accidents occurring before the end of the Fulham wall.

Fred Pitman had the unique distinction of umpiring on two occasions when there were sinkings, and he got into trouble over the second one. In 1925 conditions were bad on the Surrey side when the presidents tossed and the positions of the stakeboats were fixed by Pitman, and grew considerably worse between then and the crews coming out to start. Oxford, who were on Surrey, were rowing a bath after a minute and struggled on as far as the Doves at Hammersmith before giving up, their coach Stanley Garton having attempted several times to get them to stop earlier, a move he had made with the umpire's blessing. After the race there was prolonged controversy in the press about the position of the stakeboats, for it was argued that if they had been placed nearer to the Middlesex wall, the boat on the Surrey station would have had a better chance of survival. At the request of the presidents Pitman had moved them towards Middlesex, but he argued that to have moved them farther would have taken the Middlesex crew right out of the tide and given them a disadvantage. Pitman wrote in the *Field*: 'It must be remembered that in fixing the stakeboats regard must only be had to the state of the water from the start to about the boathouses. . . . Looking back at it all, I readily admit that it would have been more satisfactory if the stakeboats had been fixed close to the Middlesex bank, even if this had involved one boat being right out of the tide, for the state of the water from the Point to the Mile was such as to render it impossible for two boats to row abreast.'

Then Dr Bourne, who was one of Oxford's coaches, wrote that the occurrences would have been avoided if the precedent of the second 1912 race had been followed, reminding his readers that conditions for the 1912 rerow were if anything worse than for the first race when both crews waterlogged. Pitman had presided over that occasion when, it will be remembered, the presidents had requested the stakeboats to be moored near to Middlesex and agreed that no boring would take place to disadvantage the Surrey boat along the Fulham wall.

Pitman's letter also stated that: 'In future I hope that the umpire may be relieved from the duty of fixing the course, or that he may have the assistance of a representative of both universities on his launch in fixing stakeboats and deciding whether the race can be rowed,' which seems to be an attempt to abrogate the umpire's responsibility. It has been generally assumed that he is in charge, and the current agreement begins by saying: 'The conduct of the race shall be the sole responsibility of the umpire, who shall be chosen by mutual consent of the Presidents of the two University Boat Clubs.'

The other sinking occasions have been more straightforward. In 1859 Cambridge on the Surrey station did not seek shelter towards the Middlesex shore and consequently took much of the tide on board. Oxford were in some trouble too, all their blue coats, which they had placed under their thwarts, being washed up to form a sodden mass under the bow canvas. At that time the boats had no bulwark between the bow man and the forward canvas, but there was a bulwark behind the cox, a design ensuring that sinking was done by nose-diving, and Cambridge dived, rowing to the last, at the White Hart. In 1898

Cambridge have been described as 'waterlogged', floating home with great difficulty and sustained by inflated bladders under their seats. There was no hope for them early on in the race, the damage being done as they made for the Fulham wall from the Surrey station, but they did row over the whole course and cross the finishing line without submerging. This feat puts a strain on the definition of water-logging.

In 1978 Cambridge had a similar experience to theirs of 1859, although they went down just through Barnes Bridge and from the stern first. That race, though, highlighted the importance of umpiring in the Boat Race. Conditions were not too bad at the start. Oxford had Surrey and led Cambridge to Hammersmith in a sprightly Easter parade, and in a record time of 6 minutes 24 seconds; but when they turned into the Surrey bend they had to seek shelter along the bank as the Tideway threw an angry fit that was to last for the rest of the race. There was a fierce head wind stonewalling the backs of the men, and horizontal rain driving into them as Guy Henderson brought Cambridge inside Oxford at some points. They had done an effective burn after Hammersmith but were now between the devil and the deep, because as they came up, John Fail, the dark blue cox, simply moved a little more inshore, more snugly into his own station. Overtaking on the outside was as impractical through the rough water as it would have been suicidal for the energy involved. There was nothing else to do than hold on until the crossing.

The crossing was dramatic, Cambridge following Oxford in line astern. The boats pitched, rolled, dipped, bucketed, covered themselves in spray, Oxford catching a wopper, and then they reached comparative calm and, if anything, Cambridge got a little closer by means of another burn. But they were beginning to feel that something was wrong. They had taken in a lot of water during the crossing. Oxford, whose Carbocraft moulded boat was absolutely identical to Cambridge's, had taken much less because they had fitted splash-boards, while the light blues had gambled on not doing so. Cambridge had been two seconds behind at the mile, four seconds behind at Hammersmith, seven seconds behind at Chiswick Steps, and when the crews ventured out into the rough once more to take the centre span at Barnes, they were ten seconds adrift. Fail came out well in time to shoot the bridge and Oxford were away as Henderson's crew, who were limping by now, just missed the pillar as he turned them

outwards, and then he could not turn the corner. Things were impossible in the stern as soon as the bridge was cleared, and they
foundered. At the end of the race Fail displayed the surety of a winner.
He told the *Guardian* that staying afloat is an attitude of mind. 'I was
surprised when I heard that Cambridge had sunk. If you keep going
steadily you forget about water and ride it out. And we've practised
handling rough water a lot.'

Oxford reckoned that they had only an inch of water on board at the
end. Even allowing for poetic licence, their experience points to the
effectiveness of splashboards, a more decisive factor than the slight
advantage they may have got by being about one and a half pounds per
man lighter. Ironically, though, the controversial start of the race may
have done the irreparable damage for Cambridge. It was about twenty
minutes behind schedule. If it had got off on time the crews – whose
race was extremely good as far as Duke's Meadows, a factor obscured
by the drama of the sinking – should have had time to get to Mortlake
before the elements which afforded records to the mile and Hammersmith changed into a grimacing gale.

James Crowden was the umpire that day, and he had a bad time.
There was a false start when, as Crowden said, 'Are you ready?'
Henderson suddenly said, 'No,' and raised his hand. Oxford had
squared their blades and left the stakeboat. As Oxford became re-
attached without displaying the attributes of alacrity, Cambridge went
adrift, so there was further delay. The second start was really by
mutual disagreement. Crowden said, 'Are you ready?' for the second
time and Cambridge started, and Oxford followed. The word 'Go' got
lost somewhere after the crews moved, more or less straight and more
or less together. After that, despite Crowden's attempts to get back on
terms with the crews on the wintry Surrey bend, he was really out of it.
This was his first Boat Race as an umpire, but he came with a
formidable reputation as a presider over races at Henley, and he went
through all the correct motions, going out with both crews and their
coxes before the race. But the elements and the cumbersome launch,
butting, like the crews, into the head wind, really combined to render
his role impotent in the latter half of the race. Fail and Henderson left
him out of it. The result was the race which never started, and never
finished for the light blues. One lesson, reinforced by clashing of the
crews in 1980, was learned. The umpire was helpless aboard the large
launch of his hosts, and in 1981, for the first time, umpire Ronnie

Howard was alone but for a pilot in his own small launch, which could thus keep closer to the crews and manoeuvre more easily.

Starting the Boat Race can be difficult, as illustrated by 1978. When the Cambridge president invited Howard to umpire in 1981, his request to the former Oxford president came with a sting in the tail. He particularly asked that the start should be fair. This led Howard to issue a useful statement explaining the different methods adopted by the universities to get their boats moving which sometimes made the start look unfair. The race starts from stakeboats anchored by 150–200 foot ropes in water more than 40 feet deep which may be moving at four knots. The stakeboats are positioned level when the crews attached to them hold their oars square in the water. Howard's explanation continued:

> The Cambridge method is that used by scullers over many years of professional races on such water and also by competitors in the Wingfield Sculls. The crew sits halfway forward with their blades feathered so that the tide can flow past them. On the words 'Are you ready?' they all square and allow themselves to be drawn fully forward so that they are fully forward on the command 'Go'. The first stroke is therefore a long one. The Oxford method was taught them by Ted Phelps, one of the last professional oarsmen, and was used in professional racing and is used throughout Europe when races are started from anchored stakeboats in a powerful current. The crew sits fully forward with their blades feathered so that the tide can flow past them. On the words 'Are you ready?' they all square and hold their strong position a little back from fully forward. On the command 'Go' they take the first stroke which is shorter than full length.
>
> The Oxford method straightens and stretches the long anchor rope more than the Cambridge method so that Oxford appear to start in front. The Oxford first stroke is shorter than the Cambridge one so that Oxford finish that stroke first. These two things make the start appear false and unfair. The only criterion for a false start must be whether the boat has been drawn out of the stakeboat man's hands or not. This is the way I intend to judge the start and the way I have judged it in the past.

The 1978 race also had something to say about television. The British Broadcasting Corporation pays between £10,000 and £20,000 per year to televise the race. As the second largest contributors to its cost, after Ladbrokes, its sponsors, they have occasionally influenced the starting time to suit their television schedules in the face of tidal considerations, and they don't like it if coxes cause delays on the start for the same reason. This is an added pressure on the umpire and on the crews to do what the *Radio Times* says they are going to do, and although it may concentrate the mind wonderfully, in the tradition of meeting deadlines, it really has no place in a sporting event which takes place on the moving Tideway. Second, the latest sinking illustrates the difficulty of television's task in following the race, and the helplessness of a commentator at the point which matters most. The commentator does his work in a hut full of monitors. When Cambridge sank the screen was showing, quite reasonably, Oxford moving away into the distance. By the time the viewers were able to see Cambridge's encounter with Father Thames, the commentator, Jim Railton, had missed many of the symptoms of waterlogging because, although they had been visible on his monitors, he was talking to the picture which was at that time being shown. He was thus unprepared for the catastrophe and found himself describing the light blues undergoing a 'dolphin effect' as they wallowed which he followed by talk of a 'rescue situation', and the sequence will become as famously well worn as John Snagge's famous radio gaffe, 'I can't see who's in the lead but it's either Oxford or Cambridge.' The dolphin effect of the rescue situation of how best to film and commentate on the Boat Race has yet to be solved. Several strong men have withered while wrestling with it. Several more, a very select band among blues, have unintentionally got a soaking in the Tideway for the troubles they have gone to in the great entertainment from Putney to Mortlake.

IO

Mutiny on the Isis
1959: A president stands alone

Ronnie Howard of Worcester College became president at Oxford in May 1958. The blues were not allowed to vote at the time. The Yale and Merton oarsman Reed Rubin stood against him, and one of the things Howard set about was to change the rules so that blues in residence had a vote as well as the college captains. The change served him well, for he was about to have a troublesome year. Howard rowed at Shrewsbury School, did his National Service, and arrived in Oxford in the autumn of 1956. He spent the later part of his childhood at Henley-on-Thames and his playground was skiffs and punts, with racing boats making their appearance at school on the Severn.

He was good, and he got his blue in his first year rowing at number three in president Carnegie's crew. Rod Carnegie went for revolution. He started 'Hot Rod's gym' in the boathouse, had everybody doing exercises, looked at the techniques used in other sports and borrowed anything he thought was useful. There was a copy of Stampfl *On Running* at the boathouse and in an interview with the Cambridge athletics blue Chris Brasher, Carnegie admitted the influence of Harry Hopman and Frank Stampfl. He was from Geelong Grammar School and Melbourne University, a physicist who had taken to politics, philosophy and economics at New College, and he attributed his ability to make changes at OUBC to being a foreigner. It didn't make it easy, but he thought that if he had been to an English rowing public school he would not have been able, or felt the desire, to do it. What Carnegie was after, having lost in 1956, was a fit and strong crew who could bat the boat along, not necessarily a pretty crew. He didn't want to overthrow college rowing, for he recognized its place and that his men must come from it, so he was not in the business of finding fifty big men like Yale would do and pulling the best eight out of them. But he wanted speed and stamina, and he set a training programme which would give them to him.

'If you have four or five men all of equivalent standards fighting for the last two seats,' he told Brasher, 'it makes flick all difference which two you pick as long as you pick them early and get rid of worry.' So each of his men must have rowed before in a fast crew, and each must have won races. And each had to prove his worth over a full twenty minutes. In the trials, two cracked.

Carnegie's crew were firm favourites, and they gave the newspapers something to write about. They were heavy and they had 'American rig' after the ideas of Hiram Conibear, who had started out as a professional cyclist, and was therefore suspect to conservative critics. They did three full-course trials and plenty of hard work in between under Freddie Page, and they once set off from Putney and rowed to Limehouse and back. This twenty-four mile trip was laboriously followed by *The Times*, working itself up with the headline 'Strenuous week for Oxford: Novel departure in Training'. The ratings were taken off all sorts of new places like Fulham power station, the Tate Gallery and Lambeth Palace. 'Many of the historic buildings were seen by the crew from the river,' said the Thunderer. Carnegie's boys were obviously not eyes-in-the-boat men. It was the first time that a university crew in training had been seen in the Pool of London, and they raised one or two eyebrows down in the busy docks. The *Manchester Guardian*'s diarist noted that there was a time when the race was held from Westminster to Putney, 'but no one living can remember that. Was the effort prompted by some strange nostalgia for the spices of the East which are apt to drift about these lower reaches? Or was it, as I like to think, out of compliment to the lightermen's eight which distinguished itself at Henley last year? The democratisation of rowing must surely work both ways.'

Carnegie had trouble with coaches. Antony Rowe resigned when he learned that American rig was to be used. Carnegie asked Jumbo Edwards to coach for six weeks in the middle period and Jumbo refused, but was eventually persuaded to help. He wanted to teach them to row, but because neither the sixteen-man Leviathan training punt nor a tub pair was made available to him, he resigned. The press all picked Oxford to win, and so did Jumbo, and they lost by two lengths. Barnard became ineffective in the number five seat at the crossing, and Carnegie's crew cracked on overconfidence. The *Manchester Guardian* made the lightest meal of eating words: 'The motor launch *Enchantress* left Mortlake for Putney on Saturday bearing as dumbfounded a load of rowing correspondents as has perhaps ever made that return voyage from the realm of speculation to the homeland of incontrovertible fact. And were our faces red? . . . One correspondent may as well reveal the full shallowness of his fallibility. . . .'

Howard did not make the blue boat in the next year. He ran Isis instead and they beat the blue boat several times in practice, and his view was that Colin Porter, the coach, drove the blue boat too hard and bullied them instead of taking them into his confidence. Reed Rubin was in that 1958 crew who lost to Cambridge by three and a half lengths, and Howard was a rebel when he stood for the presidency in May of that year. Rubin, his rival, also turned out to be a rebel, but one with a different approach to the cause.

Jumbo detected a desperation at Oxford. 'In their endeavours to find a Boat Race winning formula Oxford had tried everything in recent years,' he noted in his autobiography, *The Way of a Man with a Blade*. 'They had tried orthodoxy, they had tried Fairbairnism, and a blend of both in 1949. They had tried Cambridge coaches, they had tried Eton coaches, Australian Fairbairnism, the Metropolitan style, Americanism, Porterism, all had failed.' He concluded that they had tried everything except teaching individuals the art of rowing, then blending them into a crew, training them to give of their best, and developing the will to win. In short, said Jumbo, 'Oarsmanship, Crewmanship, Fitmanship, and Morale.'

Howard enlisted Jumbo, persuaded him to give three lectures on rowing during the Michaelmas term, which were well attended, and vested the training in him. There was an unusually large number of blues in residence – thirteen of them. By the start of the Michaelmas term it was clear that six of the 1958 crew did not want to row with Howard. On 18 October, while *The Times* published a lengthy piece about OUBC's proposal to abolish the Torpids, the *Daily Mail* broke the big story. 'Now it's MUTINY on the ISIS – Old Blues may form "Pirate" Boat Race Crew,' ran the headline. 'Six of the Oxford crew who lost the last Boat Race have threatened not to row in next year's race because they object to the present training methods.' They were joined by three other potential oarsmen and proposed to Howard that either he select them as a complete unit and allow them to use their own training methods or they would form a 'pirate' crew and train independently for the race. The mutineers included the secretary, M. J. W. Hall, and S. Douglas-Mann, who had both represented England in the Empire Games, D. C. R. Edwards, stroke of the 1958 crew and son of Jumbo, and Reed Rubin, who told the *Mail* that Oxford were trying to emulate the American style which was adapted from the pre-1914 English style and that there was too much training. The *Oxford Mail*, which also ran a large story that day, quoted Howard as saying: 'Their action is going to make it harder for Oxford to win the Boat Race next year, but if they maintain their point of view I shall do without them and carry on trial eights with the other material I have at my disposal.' He rejected the idea of a race between his crew and the pirates to decide who should represent the university.

He added: 'I have no sympathy with these people. They will certainly not get any equipment, finance, or any help from the OUBC. . . . Some of their fathers, I know, have a strong rowing tradition and their sons' refusal to row with the OUBC may well have come as a most unpleasant shock. . . . I have spoken to Group Captain Edwards and he is extremely sorry, as I am, that these people have taken this action. He supports me in the attitude I am taking.'

In its inimitable style the *Daily Express* put its finger on Rubin. Its report 'The "Pirate" Blues buy a boat' on 21 October began: 'Fourteen-stone 6 ft 4 ins Reed Rubin, the rowing Yank at Oxford, lounged back in his lodgings yesterday and talked about his plans for winning the boat race.' In ten short paragraphs readers got the message about Rubin: 'Burly, 23-year-old Merton man . . . in his room lined with inscribed oars and old rowing prints, hawk-featured Rubin announced the rebels' plans. . . . Suede shoes crossed and hands deep in whipcord slacks, he said, "We have ordered our boat. It will cost £300 to £400. The money is being provided by friends of Oxford rowing. We aim to enter the Head of the River race." . . . New Yorker Rubin. . . .' A perfect bounder, was this Rubin, a cad and a rascal. Meanwhile, the *Express* reporter spoke to Howard in a tracksuit on the Isis bank. 'There is more than just a race at stake,' said Howard. 'If I give in every president will be faced with the threat of a man who thinks he can find enough friends to make a better crew.'

On the day before this, *The Times* published the statement issued by Hall for the rebels:

There are a group of oarsmen within the University who, though very keen to win the Boat Race, are in considerable disagreement with the president about training arrangements and rowing policy for the Boat Race. We in no way question the President's authority in these matters. But since harmony in a boat is essential in a successful crew we have decided not to row under arrangements about which there is such continuing disagreement. We feel nevertheless that we can best help the interests of Oxford rowing by giving our ideas a chance and forming a crew of our own. We would like to row in the Head of the River race, and would be at the disposal of the President of the OUBC if he should want us to represent Oxford in the Boat Race. But we in no way challenge his right and duty to make this decision for himself.

The statement was signed by Hall, Rubin, Douglas-Mann, Edwards, F. D. M. Badcock, R. Barratt, C. L. Grimes, J. L. Fage, and J. G. Rowbotham.

The Times's rowing correspondent pointed out, as others began to do, that Howard was elected president after his plans and Rubin's had been aired before the captains' meeting, and that the rebels were doing exactly what their statement purported that they were not doing, i.e. challenging Howard's authority. Among all the available talent it was hard to sort out what the real difference was. Maybe it was a clash of personality between the quiet, affable, fresh-faced Worcester man who remained resolute if not quite totally uncompromising, and the 16-stone New Yorker, 'looking as if he was hewn by Henry Moore from a piece of Grand Canyon rock', as Godfrey Smith put it in the *Sunday Times*, who was the first American rowing blue to lose a Boat Race for Oxford since Kingsbury in 1927. Or maybe it was just that the rebels did not like the idea of having the crew totally in the hands of the Group Captain Jumbo.

Sympathy in the university was moving in the direction of rowers rather than shouters. Some of the pirates would not have been allowed to row anyway, because they were still at Oxford only on condition that they didn't. Rubin's aim was that Jim Rathschmidt of Yale should coach, mostly by telephone from the United States according to Howard, with Jumbo acting under him. Jumbo would certainly have picked Rathschmidt's brains but would not have coached under him. The finance of the rebels' boat was rumoured to be coming from the US Ambassador to the Court of St James's, John Hay Whitney, who had been a star athlete at Yale and had attended New College before inheriting $30 million as his portion of his father's $179 million estate in 1927.

There was a sudden reversal of the president's fortunes on 22 October at a captains' meeting called to discuss the vexed question of the future of the Torpids. Howard had intended to go there and ask for the resignation of his secretary Hall, because his patience was running out with an officer who continued to support the mutineers. On the previous day some old heavies had proposed a round-table conference in a bid for peace. Then at the captains' meeting Howard was surprised and relieved to be handed a letter expressing complete confidence in him and his actions and suggesting that the secretary resign. It was signed by all the captains but three, who had not been approached. He thanked them and, always a master tactician, asked them not to demand the resignation, for he sensed that settlement was nearer. He consulted the Provost of Worcester, J. C. Masterman, about what to do next and was advised to write something down, so he wrote to the captains restating his policy, thanked them for their expression of confidence, and offered to accept the rebels' services provided that they were wholeheartedly with the president's men, while re-iterating that there could be no compromise over the way of rowing.

A meeting was arranged at Leander with Gully Nickalls in the chair, Jumbo and Howard for the OUBC, Hall and Grimes for the mutineers, plus the Isis coaches, Richard Burnell, and Tom Durand. It was a complete failure, an argument between Jumbo and Hall and Grimes about technical points. Then Hall and Grimes came to see Howard privately and suggested that if he dropped Jumbo and accepted three Yale coaches whom they named they would cooperate. The coaches they proposed were all from the 1956 Yale crew who won the Olympic Games gold medal in eights, the crew with whom Grimes had rowed. Howard refused, and for two weeks individual rebels pestered him with their views until, without warning, Hall and Grimes went to his lodgings at 94 The High to tell him that there would be no rebel crew and that they were all available because Oxford needed them. Howard put out an agreed conciliatory statement and privately noted their conceit.

The newspapers reported the captains' letter of support and the final capitulation of the mutineers, the unavailability of Reed Rubin, and the saving of the Torpid bumping races, and then got down to watching the preparation of the crews. But they never really appreciated how much trouble Howard had been in. His battle with the rebels in fact had lasted for five months, because it started five days after his May election as president by one vote. He stood on a 'good coaching equals Jumbo Edwards' ticket as a rebel, the leader of a successful Isis crew who had embarrassed their blue boat and benefited from the Group Captain's coaching, and he knew that he could get Jumbo to take on the entire programme from trials to race. Rubin, though, was the candidate of the other eleven blues. They had met and discussed plans, and Rubin wanted to import ideas from Yale and send Jumbo, if he were to coach, to America to learn how to do so before he was let loose on Oxford. Thus Howard could accuse Rubin of wanting to adopt American ideas, and Rubin would accuse Howard of adopting them. After his slim majority, Howard asked Hall to stand as secretary, and Hall told him that he was a keen supporter of Rubin, but Howard still wanted Hall on the grounds that through him he might be able to unify the club.

Then, only five days after his election, a blue came to Howard and told him of the blues' cabal, that none of the twelve had confidence in his ability to win the race, that they couldn't row for his crew because defeat would be too humiliating, that he couldn't produce a crew without them, and that the best thing he could do would be to resign under some academic pretext. In the fourth week of the summer term he received a letter signed by the seven captains who had supported him saying that blues had persuaded them that they had voted wrongly and requesting a meeting to discuss Howard's plans for the race. He smelt a vote of no confidence and refused the meeting on the grounds that all matters concerning the race and the crew were solely the president's responsibility. He then wrote to all the captains restating his plans. After Eights Week he heard rumours of another attempt to get a captains' meeting, and then Rubin proposed a solution through an intermediary, which was that if Howard sacked Jumbo and appointed him, Rubin, as chief coach, Howard could have his pick of the blues, and as a bonus, remain president! Howard was not going to be a puppet for Rubin to pull the strings. He produced an Isis crew for Henley and then an Old Salopians crew for Maidenhead and Henley town regattas, and the rest of the summer was quiet until just before the Michaelmas term when the press reported Rubin saying that he would not row in Howard's blue boat even if asked to. This is where we came in to the public debate, at a point where the president had been under recurring pressure to lie down and die. The curious thing is that he had never had time to cause any offence since taking the office. The success of his Isis year probably holds the key. Isis is nicest only so long as blues are better.

So the rebel flag was hauled down late in the evening of Sunday, 2 November 1958. It is also worth noting that the Cambridge president, Mike Maltby, had come to Howard's aid late in October by telling the undergraduate newspaper *Varsity* that he would refuse to row against any Oxford crew who did not have the support of their president. Troubles were not yet over, but Howard had won the Battle of the Dark Blues. The blues were exempted from trials, and Grimes turned up for training and argued every point with Jumbo. He was in difficult mood and offensive clothing; offensive, that is, to Jumbo, who had years before taken a leaf from the Harold Rickett's Cambridge coaching book. Rickett never allowed his crews to be seen at a disadvantage. They were drilled, immaculate, disciplined. Jumbo liked Oxford to be like that, and he didn't like Grimes's 'engine-driver's' hat. Grimes was asked to remove this blue and white pin-striped headgear for the sake of uniformity and refused, saying that if Yale had failed to remove it, why should Oxford expect him not to wear it? Eventually Jumbo addressed both crews, telling them that in future he expected them to dress as well as row uniformly. When he said that he did not expect anyone to dress to catch the public eye, Grimes left the room and took no further part in university rowing.

Four of the former rebels rowed in the crew. Douglas-Mann was in the bow, Fage and Edwards were at five and six, and Rowbotham coxed. The last three were from the 1958 crew, and Howard himself at three was the fourth blue in the boat. A. T. Lindsay was at two, D. C. Rutherford at four, D. W. Shaw at seven and J. R. H. Lander stroked. They were a very good crew, their training under Jumbo went well, and they spent the last weekend together at Brighton, and at Brighton's expense. Just before a quarter to four on the afternoon of 28 March 1959 they arrived at Mortlake six lengths ahead of Cambridge.

Ronnie Howard paid a price for his struggle. He had to do an extra year, and his geography tutors banned 'competitive' rowing, which was hard on a keen oarsman who had Olympic ambitions, for 1960 was an Olympic year. In a sense he was beaten by the Yale Olympians of 1956. Yale, with Grimes on board, had had a fantastic season then, winning ten out of twelve races and the Olympic title on behalf of the United States. They were crew-cut world-beaters under Rathschmidt, and they believed that they could inject their spirit to make Oxford into Cambridge-beaters. Grimes was a mountain of a man who concealed his feelings with a sardonic twist of tongue, and Rubin, who was not in the 1956 Olympic crew, remembers him as one of the most powerful and effective men to pull an oar in living memory: 'If ever an individual could be credited with driving a shell to victory Charles would be given full marks for the Yale gold medal at the Olympics in Australia.' He had great intellect and sense of humour, and one can imagine the scene of the loco-driver's hat between him and Jumbo, the flying coach who believed in correctness. Charlie Grimes claimed that a British ancestor had been granted permission not to doff his hat in the presence of the king. The wearing of a favourite cap should thus be viewed with kindness was Grimes's reasoning, but the legendary coach could not take that from an Olympian asset.

The crisis on the Isis was undoubtedly precipitated by the captains favouring one candidate and the blues another. The blues thought they had Oxford's interests at heart as well as the captains'. They were disappointed at their recent defeats and wanted to know more of the successful approach to rowing developed at Yale. This is what Rubin offered them, to be done through the services of a single coach for the whole training period. In the end OUBC got Jumbo in an overseeing role, which was not what the rebels had in mind, but was not far off what would have been possible under their scheme. The close interest of the press in the argument took its toll on Rubin as well as Howard. The publicity caused considerable disruption to his studies and other student activities, so he decided to succumb to the more pleasant distractions of Oxford.

For Howard, the office of president had taken up almost all of his time. But he realized later that Rubin's rebels did a service for Oxford. They brought an intensity to loyalty by putting it in question. One of the hardest things in the president's book is to keep the motivation, the needle, right through the winter in the long weeks of training when the opposition is a remote blur the other side of Bletchley Junction, when one never gets out of the laboratory of the Isis or the Cam. Howard's trialists never had any problem with the needle, before or after they had buried their hatchets. Commenting on the end of hostilities, what

Rubin said at the time was: 'All I wish to say is that Oxford are going to beat Cambridge next year.' Ronnie Howard learned much that he would bring to bear on Oxford as a coach for many years afterwards.

A *matter of correspondence*
1965: How to lose friends and influence people

After Cambridge won the 1964 Boat Race by six and a half lengths against an Oxford crew heavily laced with Etonians, Oxford were all set to make a fairy-tale comeback in 1965. Miles Morland from Radley and Lincoln College was elected president. He had rowed in the victorious 1963 crew as well as the beaten 1964 one, and he had a straightforward, if not simple, plan. He consulted Jumbo Edwards and Ronnie Howard. Jumbo was unavailable because he was fully committed to Nautilus, a scheme designed to produce crews for Britain, but Howard, having survived the mutiny of the blues in 1958–59, was now teaching at Radley and was willing to coach. Morland's menu was to net muscle men rather than dainty stylists from the considerable pool of talent available and use two coaches only to grill them to a turn by the interval method; that is, by lots of timed pieces over regular distances in the manner made fashionable by the Ratzeburg club of Germany. They would become an exceptionally fast crew and beat the baddies Cambridge by a huge margin, in a fitting happy ending.

Morland thus assembled a crew which included another Radley man from the 1963 crew, the OUBC secretary, Sean Morris, at bow, and two first-timers at two and three, D. H. Mills and Duncan Clegg. Both, like Morris, were from St Edmund Hall. Morland himself was at four and in the stern of the boat were four Yale men: Duncan Spencer, who had stroked Oxford for the last two years, and Bill Fink, Henry Howell and Ed Trippe. For the first half of the thirteen weeks leading up to the race Ronnie Howard would supervise the intervals. For the second half Morland's magic wand would be brought into the open, namely the famous Australian Diamond sculler Stuart Mackenzie. Son of a national surfboard champion and grandson of the Test cricketer Alec 'Slasher Mac' Mackenzie, he was known as Sam from his initials – Stuart Alexander Mackenzie. He had won the Diamonds at Henley six times from 1957 to 1962, a sparkling, fire-cracking record. He was a Henley-based chicken sexer by trade, who had a reputation as a mighty sculler, a mighty charmer and a mighty competitor. An opponent had to watch his every move. He had given the run-around to a lot of them in his time, applying the professional awareness of never missing a trick to the amateur sport which he loved and excelled in, and he had given a lot of help and advice to Ronnie Howard when the latter was sculling, in a different class to Sam, on Henley reach. The two coaches were to be an ideal combination, both available for long stretches, with Sam the showman to handle all the publicity at the London end and to bring an extra dimension to Morland's heavies.

For Oxford in 1965 everything went more or less according to plan. Eight big men were found, two coaches coached, interval training was completed, they trounced everyone they met, and on 3 April beat Cambridge without much trouble by four lengths in 18 minutes 7 seconds. Richard Burnell's official history of the Boat Race in 1979 sums up Morland's year thus:

> On the day of the race odds of 7 to 2 were quoted in favour of the dark blues. One may say that in a two crew race, in which one man a little off colour, or one minor shipwreck, may tip the scales, such odds can never be justified. But, of course, bookmakers' odds are based on popular support rather than analytical judgment, and on this occasion the support for Oxford proved to be well-founded.
>
> Having said that one must add that there was not much excitement in the 1965 Boat Race. Starting at 38 to Cambridge's 36, Oxford led by half a length after a minute. The Middlesex bend helped Cambridge to close up at the mile post, but after that Oxford moved remorselessly away. Sweeney [the Cambridge stroke] launched a series of brave spurts, but quite unavailingly, and Oxford, had they wished, could no doubt have won by a larger margin than the eventual verdict of four lengths.

A tedious account of an unmemorable race thus summarizes the facts of Morland's fairy tale. Oxford and Yale had combined to beat Cambridge. The facts are indisputable; but for all that, a fairy tale it is.

It was early in January on a dark evening at Leander Club that things began to go wrong with Morland's plan. There were already differences between the president and Duncan Spencer. They had a love–hate relationship and Morland thought that Spencer thought that he, Spencer, was an English country squire adhering to the view that the way Eton rowed in the 1890s was the most gentlemanly and the best way to do it. Oxford technique, after all, had been similar at the time. Spencer was the leader of the New Haven men, and they had all been taught to row their four-mile race against Harvard at a low rating with a severe rig and a marked slow-down over the stretcher. They had little faith in the 'stop-watch rowing' which was the basis of Morland's and Howard's plan. So there was a germ of friction between the bow four and the first coach on the one hand, and the stern four on the other. Howard must have been reminded of Grimes and his engine-driver's hat which Jumbo could not stomach even though it was blue and white and pinstriped.

The crew was to assemble at Leander at 9 p.m. on an appointed day early in January to start the term's training. But there was only a coxed four until 2 a.m. on the following morning when the Americans arrived, inebriated from winter training on the piste. This caused ill feeling for days. The crew were doing land training under the Amateur Rowing Association's new director of training, Jim Railton, and Wally Holland of the British Amateur Weightlifting Association. After two weeks at Henley they moved to Radley, where David Mills replaced Hugh Thomas and positional changes were made.

Then there were two major crises. The Americans fell out with the plans of the second coach and kept Morland up to four in the morning arguing about it. A lot of energy was expended in hot air until he began coaching – in the old low-rating American style. So the crew loved it, or at least the Yale crew did. This was, however, the second crisis. The first one caused it, namely that the second coach was not Sam Mackenzie, but Lawton Fage, called up from Isis at short notice. Just before Mackenzie was due to take over the second half of the preparation period, a statement was issued by the president to the effect that for personal reasons Mackenzie was unable to coach Oxford. It was a noncommittal utterance made after a meeting somewhere near the Radley boathouse in Ronnie Howard's Volkswagen caravan, attended by Howard, Morland and Mackenzie.

Donald McLachlan of the *Daily Express* dug around a bit and found that the personal reasons were disagreement over a letter Mackenzie had written to the father of a crew 'possible'. The *Express* reported that after a meeting with members of OUBC, Mackenzie agreed that the letter might be 'misconstrued' and decided to stand down as active coach. 'Oxford coach Mackenzie quits over letter' was the headline, and the piece continued:

> Mr Miles Morland, club president, said yesterday: 'I have reluctantly accepted his resignation.' A statement from Mr Morland said Mr Mackenzie's letter to the student's father 'was in terms which were apparently interpreted as an indication that he would use his influence with other coaches to secure his son's selection'. Last night Mr Mackenzie . . . said at his home at Henley-on-Thames: 'It was a purely social letter. The boy will probably be selected anyway. But it could have been embarrassing. No one can point a bone (finger) at me. I was in at the conference we had today when it was decided to make the announcement. It was felt this kind of thing might be misconstrued.'

The *Express* report, which was on the front page of the issue of 15 February and accompanied by a picture of Sam kissing his wife after winning the Diamonds in 1962, went on to summarize his career: came from Australia in 1956, accepted invitation to coach Oxford last August, four years ago married Ann Morse, a former Reading beauty queen, for a time worked as a chicken sexer and now in insurance. 'I have not resigned as finishing coach, but I have stood down from being active coach and being involved in the selection of the crew,' he told the newspaper. 'Everything is still on a friendly relationship and I will go down to watch the crew on Wednesday.'

An argument concerning Mackenzie would come as no surprise to Sam-watchers, but this was a little peculiar. One would expect a coach taking a major part in training a Boat Race crew to be sounded by the president about the make-up of the eight and a letter of encouragement to a maybe anxious father, a maybe inquiring parent, would not be thought strange. So why was there such a fuss? And why was the *Daily Express* placing such importance on it? Was it simply a good 'people' story or did they sense a scoop or a scandal?

The *Express* got both on the next day. Its sports page announced: 'Mackenzie says "I was eased out through jealousy".' He had fallen out with Ronnie Howard, the lad he had coached and helped on Henley reach. The report said:

Stuart Mackenzie, who quit on Sunday as coach to the Oxford Boat Race crew, said last night: 'I suspect I was eased out of the job for other reasons than the boat club announced.' Mackenzie was said to have stood down because of a letter he wrote to the father of one of the oarsmen. 'But I believe the real motive was jealousy on the part of certain other coaches.' Mackenzie added: 'I was put in a position which would have made it unbearably embarrassing for me to go on.' He thought the letter a trivial reason to hang it on. Mackenzie said: 'I did write to the oarsman's father saying I would do my best to get him in, even though there might be opposition from other coaches. I stand by this because I know he should be, and almost certainly will be, in the crew. I wrote to his father as a pure gesture of friendliness to let him know how his son was getting on. It would be a pretty sorry thing if coaches went around agreeing wholeheartedly with each other like a lot of fish.'

The Oxford coaching team had been conscious for a long time that their crews go faster with Mackenzie in command. The 6 ft 4 in Australian embarrassed everyone in the first two weeks of training by causing the third crew he coached to murder the second crew in practice races. And it is known in the university that the four Americans in the Oxford boat admire his methods. Mackenzie . . . added: 'All sorts of people were talking about the letter incident before anyone told me. They seem to handle it queerly without consulting the oarsman.' He added: 'I must say I am extremely disappointed and shocked over the whole business.'

Oxford seemed in trouble with their Englishness, with four Americans with slight tendencies to dissidence almost certainly in the crew, and an Australian coach who was disaffected. It was unlike Mackenzie to be cornered in a position in which his life would be 'unbearably embarrassing'; but be that as it may, he was now out of it and Morland had to make haste with new plans. That is how Lawton Fage came to coach, and to coach in the American style, and that is why Radley College had to rally round and cover for Howard while he coached again for the last few weeks. He was annoyed about the break-up of his partnership but got down to his task with relish, planning the Tideway practice in advance. Oxford were trying to do away with pacing crews,

the seemingly endless procession of schoolboys and bank employees
and students who had a few moments of glory as they picked up the
blue boat to be left bobbing in its wake a few minutes later. Instead,
Howard wanted the crew to race, and so he announced that Oxford
would take on anyone who would give them one. Thus they were
unable to turn any challenge down, and the challenges came. They
won at Reading with Isis second. They defeated the prestigious
Tideway Scullers' over the Putney-to-Mortlake course. They an-
nihilated the University of London. They were always in front.

Meanwhile, Mackenzie was playing the jester, shadowed by a sleuth
giving information to the *Daily Express*. On 12 March the paper
reported sighting him in Cambridge's coaching launch at Henley. He
watched a 'ninety-minute haul' and chatted with coaches, clearly
guilty by association. Joe Fraser, Cambridge president, said, 'Mackenzie is not joining our coaching team. He just came along to watch my
oarsmen.' Was he spying or collaborating? That was the unasked
question in the *Express*. 'Whether Mackenzie just turned up [he lived
in Henley at the time] or came by arrangement is questionable. He was
in Oxford after lunch "to coach a college crew".' Miles Morland of
Oxford gave the classic suspicion-arousing quotation: 'I have no
comment to make.'

Oxford gave the press something to write about with their Tideway
encounters. On 19 March the *Express* said that they had moved back
into last year's boat instead of their new one. The crew were more
comfortable in it. The new one was like a barge. It was the third time in
four years that this had happened. The Isis boathouse was cluttered up
with rejects. The 1962 'Torpedo', the 1963 'Rocket', and now the
1965 'Giant' were back on the racks.

The crew stayed ahead until April Fool's day, two days before the
race. Then the rowing correspondents were treated to a rare spectacle,
something to chase their desperate takings of ratings at the Fulham
wall and the Chiswick Eyot and their monitoring of who had indiges-
tion after breakfast out of their reports. In a four-minute piece from
Hammersmith Pier, the blues of Oxford and Yale, on the outside of the
Chiswick bend, were beaten by Isis, their reserves. The *Daily Express*
again put it succinctly: 'On April 1 Rogers [the Isis cox] steered,
shoved, and almost rammed his "stiffs" to a narrow victory over
Oxford. . . . Leigh tried to overtake Isis on both sides. Morland's
brilliant eight were 20 yards from going aground on the south side of

Great Chertsey Road.' Howard had started Oxford threequarters of a length down on the outside of the bend when the tide was low and hardly running. They made up some of the deficit but finished a length behind.

Now, it is not unknown for a reserve crew to have needle against their seniors. Ronnie Howard's Isis of 1958 handed out some stick to their blue boat. And this year was to be the first time that Isis were to race Goldie, the Cambridge reserves, as a curtain-raiser to the battle of the blues and to give the up-and-coming men some experience of the Putney razzle-dazzle. The Isis coaches David Hardy, Fage and David Glynne-Jones had gone all out to secure the first win. Jim Rogers and his crew were therefore understandably aggressive in this encounter just two days before the race, but perhaps overenthusiastic, because by then both crews should have been taking their outings relatively easily, practising refinements like starts and burns rather than wearing each other out. So it was a curious thing to do, to play dodgems on the Tideway at a time when a cox ought to know where he should be going.

On 2 April, the same day as the report of the aggro, the *Express* also carried a cartoon of Morland's men comparing them with the Beatles, who had recently come to prominence. 'Down the towpath we have not seen one small boy collecting autographs, nor a teenage maiden swoon at the sight of so much manhood. Odd, because Oxford have Miles Morland who makes a Beatle look crew-cropped, Ed Trippe, more frightening to gaze on than any Stone, 6 ft 6 in of Harry Howell Jr who makes Ringo look snub-nosed. . . .'

On the Friday night before the race, which was followed by the Cambridge blue Lord Snowdon (Antony Armstrong-Jones) in the Cantab launch and his nephew Prince Charles in the BBC boat with John Snagge, another drama was played out. The *Daily Express* reported that Oxford had holed their boat on a submerged log, and the other newspapers, having seen the early edition of the *Express*, frantically rang Howard at all hours of the night at the Star and Garter in Richmond. He had to take the calls to allow Morland to get some sleep, and was furious with the *Express* for printing without checking its facts. He complained to the editor and to the Press Council, but elicited no response. In the light of that, he now thinks that the crew, or a member of it, were responsible for leading the *Express* astray, for they actively disliked one of the paper's reporters, a William Hickey man. It is conceivable that a routine inquiry after the Friday outing as Albert, the boatman, polished the shell could have extracted a story of holing from one of the men, and the sleuth rushed off with a scoop in his notebook. Anyway, the fearless seeker of the truth fell through an Oxford hole that never was.

The events leading up to 3 April, then, certainly put a livelier, more interesting layer on Miles Morland's fairy tale; gave it some wings, you might say. But shouldn't a fairy tale have a villain? With hindsight, perhaps the *Daily Express* was taking more than its usual interest in the build-up to the race. Had it missed the human drama it was after? Was there more to Roger's ramming tendencies with the rudder strings than met the public eye?

The answer to the second question is probably no. The answer to the first is yes. Or if the *Express* knew, it didn't or more likely couldn't print it. Jim Rogers Jr was a happy man at Balliol College and steering Isis until he received a letter in January which both shocked and confused him. He sat on it for several days, finding himself an innocent abroad. He then decided that because of what it said his easiest course was to resign from the whole scene. He did not want to be involved in a game where he had no idea who was playing with a full deck and who wasn't. He went to his coach David Hardy and told him that he wanted to give up his seat in the Isis crew, that he wouldn't go on. Hardy smelled a rat and followed it. He called on Rogers and tried to get out of him why he had quit. It didn't make sense to Hardy; Rogers had been doing a good job. So Rogers showed him his letter, and Hardy met Howard and Morland at Radley and a further meeting was arranged in the OUBC treasurer's rooms in Keble College. There Rogers met with Howard and Vere Davidge, keeper of OUBC's purse and bursar of Keble, whose main aim at the college was to get it from the bottom of the river to the top, and keep it there. Here, over especially good port, the letter was discussed and Davidge said to the young Yale graduate at Balliol: 'Sam was never really one of our kind.'

The letter which Mackenzie had supposedly sent to the father of an oarsman who would probably be selected for the blue boat was in fact sent to Jim Rogers Sr in Alabama, father of the Isis cox. Rogers Sr hardly knew where Oxford was or what the Boat Race was all about, but he understood the tenor of Mackenzie's remarks. The letter contained two or three paragraphs of chitchat about Oxford, the Boat Race, and how the man's son was getting on. At the bottom was a hand-written note to the effect that if there was a large increase in Mackenzie's bank account, a sum of four figures being suggested, then Rogers Jr was assured of a place in the blue boat. On the very bottom Rogers Sr had written: 'Is this man crazy, or am I?'

The meeting between Howard, Morland and Mackenzie in the Volkswagen was the first of a series of conclaves over the affair. There, out of sight of the crew, Mackenzie was confronted with the letter, and he said it was nothing but a joke. This was not difficult to believe, coming from Sam; he had played more jokes to liven up the rowing scene in his day than he had won races. The result of the second meeting, in Davidge's rooms, was confirmation that the coaching team would have to be changed. Morland felt that his only course was to dispense with Mackenzie's coaching services, which was a great blow to OUBC. To help the Australian, he was to be allowed to see the crew occasionally during the next week, but when he began to talk to the press along lines other than those agreed, he ceased to be accepted in the camp.

For Howard, jealousy of Mackenzie was just part of the fairy tale. He knew that he and Sam would have worked very well together as a Boat Race team, and he says that Mackenzie could well have become Oxford's first professional coach since the 1840s if he had not played this card. They still love Sam at OUBC.

Jim Rogers Jr stayed with Isis, steered them to a seven-length win against Goldie in 18 minutes 45 seconds, and went to Henley with them, where they won the Thames Cup. In 1966 he coxed the blue boat, winning by three and threequarters of a length in 19 minutes 12 seconds. Morland's crew did not continue after the Boat Race, partly because they were tired, and partly because the Americans wanted to race in a four at Henley. The decision was made at their Boat Race headquarters at the Star and Garter, Richmond. The English oarsmen also suspected that the Americans were scared of meeting their arch rivals Harvard, who were known to be coming to Henley. Rowing as Leander with the Hon. M. J. Leigh coxing, the Yale half of Oxford won the Prince Philip Challenge Cup. That is how Miles Morland's fairy tale won the Boat Race for Oxford and found a happy ending.

PART THREE
Connections

12

North Atlantic treatise
1869 and 1906: Harvard on tour

On 6 April 1869 William H. Simmons, captain of Harvard University Boat Club, wrote to J. C. Tinné: 'The undersigned, in behalf of the Harvard University Boat Club, hereby challenges the Oxford University Boat Club to row a race in outrigger boats from Putney to Mortlake, some time between the middle of August and the 1st of September, 1869, each boat to carry four rowers and a coxswain. The exact time to be agreed upon at a meeting of the crews. This challenge to remain open for acceptance one week after date of reception.'

The winners of the most important 'gentlemanly' athletic matches in both countries had been eyeing each other often, wrote a commentator from Harvard, and each had been hoping that the other would first throw down the gauntlet. Oxford and Cambridge had by now met twenty-six times and Oxford had won sixteen of them, while Harvard and Yale had met twelve times, with the crimson of Harvard victorious in eight of the encounters. There had been great hopes in Massachusetts that Harvard would compete in the regattas of the Paris Exposition in 1867, but the university could only muster seven men who were considered competent to represent it, and was thus forced to remain reluctantly at home.

In 1868 Harvard had a fast team and correspondence took place with Oxford about a match on the Ouse at King's Lynn. Harvard eventually declined because Oxford refused to row without a coxswain and would not allow Harvard to do so. The prospect of an eight-oar race in 1869 was declined also, because of the unknown strength of a future crew. However, Simmons, seeing the men who might be available, made another attempt at arranging a match, making several concessions. He tried for a four because he would find it easier to make one up, for his university had only about 1100 students against about 2000 at Oxford (and 2500 at Cambridge), but he proposed carrying coxes for the race, not done on the Charles River at Boston but universal and seemingly incontrovertible for the English. And he proposed the well-established championship course from Putney to Mortlake, familiar to Oxford and unknown to himself and his men. The lesson of previous negotiations had been that Oxford were fond of precedents and disliked innovations, although he was probably unaware that an Oxford blue, Guts Woodgate, had begun a significant change in English rowing scarcely a year before when his Brasenose College crew had started in the Henley Stewards' with a coxswain on board who had deliberately jumped overboard shortly after their race began. They won and were disqualified, but they proved that fours could be steered by an oarsman and needn't carry a cox. Woodgate had got the idea from the St John's of New Brunswick crew who had taken part in the Paris regatta of 1867, the one that Harvard missed. The controversy which he caused was already turning out in his favour, at least as far as the organizers of England's most prestigious regatta at Henley were concerned.

In case it was regarded as a slight to challenge Oxford alone, a like invitation was also sent to Cambridge. Oxford accepted. Cambridge, who had just suffered their ninth successive defeat at the hands of the dark blues, declined, though tardily, according to the Harvard secretary: 'Her representative was told that it seemed to us remarkably strange that a challenge arriving two months before the close of her term should be called late; and yet more so, that out of a body of 2500 men, hundreds of them more or less acquainted with rowing, four could not be found to match the representatives of an institution having hardly three score men who knew how to feather an oar.'

Directly after the challenge was accepted by Oxford came a challenge to Harvard from London Rowing Club. They asked for races in eights, fours, pairs, and singles or any of them, and said that whether or not the challenge was accepted the Americans could use their boathouses, club rooms and boats, and that forthwith the whole party were made honorary members. Harvard accepted the hospitality while declining the match: 'No Harvard crew ever yet rowed a match race with any crew except one composed of students, nor ever would,' said HUBC, 'because if they did once, a precedent was established that it would be nearly impossible not to follow, and then they would always be in danger of being called on to row in term time, which course would so interrupt their studies as to invite the interference of the college faculty.'

Oxford began training on 19 May. Harvard set about raising the money, forming a crew, and getting a boat. Private theatricals by students and subscriptions from alumni and their friends soon raised the cash, for considerable interest was already being shown in the contest both inside and outside the rowing world. Sporting matches between the gentlemen of the two countries were exceedingly rare.

Simmons was having some difficulty with crew and boat. Himself, Alden P. Loring, Rice and Bass got together in an English four-oared boat with coxswain's seat which was a dozen years old, and they had some leaky outings until a new boat, built by Elliott of Greenpoint, New York, was substituted. They defeated the Hurley crew of Boston on 15 June but were beaten by the city's best professional crew, that of George Roahr. Two days later on the Mystic near Charlestown, Massachusetts, they went coxless and beat Roahr's crew by about fourteen lengths over four miles. Some time between then and departure for England on 10 July Rice and Bass were dropped and Joseph S. Fay and E. O. Lyman were substituted, and this happened probably before they won the large prize for four-oared boats at Boston Regatta on 5 July (4 July ordinarily). They defeated the big names of American rowing, including the swiftest four west of the Alleghenies, the Hamills of Pittsburgh; the Biglins of New York; the Piscataquas of Elliot, Maine; the Unions of Worcester; and George Roahr's crew again.

By 10 July they were in New York to embark aboard the Inman steamer *City of Paris*, escorted out of harbour by crews from Nassau Boat Club of New York and others, and they were greeted in Liverpool – after an enjoyable crossing with little seasickness and obliging officers – by members of the Liverpool and Royal Chester clubs. Stanton Blake Esq. of New York City had arranged their conveyance to Putney via a special free car on the London and Northwestern and London and Southwestern railways. They put up temporarily at the Star and Garter in Putney while a house was found for them.

The fixture had aroused much press interest on both sides of the Atlantic. An American correspondent, in prophesying hollow defeat for his countrymen, said, 'Harvard must be prepared to find the contest they propose considered as an incomplete trial of strength' on the grounds that a four is not a sufficient test. 'A good eight is the culmination of all the science and art there is in rowing,' said he. Moreover, the Crimsons would have to change their whole style of rowing in order to suit the 'turbid, muddy, chemical mixture of the Thames'.

The English press welcomed the Americans and reckoned that Oxford would give the best account of themselves. So when Harvard arrived at the Star and Garter there was great curiosity shown in the riverside village just a few miles outside London. 'Every man of it was watching with most eager eyes,' wrote the Harvard secretary, William Blaikie.

> While at the Star and Garter, particularly, the door could not stand ajar but a dozen would be peeping in to see the bold strangers. George, our coloured boy, a most useful attendant, was questioned and cross-questioned on all manner of matters concerning the crew, but his wit was equal to the emergency. Mr E. Brown, of Cambridge, Massachusetts, had come along to cook, and that fact itself guaranteed all that could be desired in a culinary way.

After five days at the Star and Garter members of London RC found a house for them, large enough to accommodate the rowers, the coxswain Arthur Burnham, two gentlemen who accompanied the crew, Elliott the boatbuilder, and the servants. The White House was well worth waiting for, being comfortable, with an acre of high-walled garden, the river twenty feet from the garden gate and the boathouses not a stone's throw off.

For the first ten days the crew wrestled with the change of climate while the great boatbuilding race started. They had brought two craft with them, neither of which had they used in practice. The boat Elliott built which they used in their American races measured 52 feet 6 inches long, longer than an Elliott standard six-oar, and was only 19 inches wide. He had become much impressed with the idea of very long and narrow boats, but the crew's experience in this boat was far from happy. It sagged fearfully in the middle at every stroke. So Elliott built a second boat, 49 feet long and 18½ inches wide, which was completed on the day before the *City of Paris* sailed for Liverpool and only tried once. It was this boat which the Americans brought with them, together with another built by an Englishman recently arrived in the United States who was cracked up to be an ace builder. These two, then, were on the racks at London Rowing Club. The usual English measurements were 42 feet by 20 inches beam. Elliott, though, did not rest there. As soon as he arrived he was out and about studying the turbid, muddy, chemical mixture that was the Thames. He saw that the tide rose and fell between 18 and 20 feet, unlike the 10-foot variance on the Charles in Boston. He saw that the width from Putney to Mortlake did not exceed about 600 feet, and he calculated that a bed so narrow and deep as well as crooked must cause innumerable little swirls which could switch a long boat about much more than a short one. It took him half an hour to come to this conclusion, and a short outing in a borrowed London boat confirmed his opinion.

Elliott had taken the precaution of packing in his trunk the model and the ribs of a boat designed exactly on the lines of his most successful boat, the one in which Harvard had defeated Yale in 1867, 1868 and this year. While the English newspapers were admiring the beautiful cabinet-work of the boat launched at Putney, while rapping its design on the grounds of its length and the long since abandonment of such specimens in England, etc., Elliott hired two young fellows and, working thirteen hours a day himself, turned out a new boat by 22 August, five days before the race was to be held.

The Americans took precautions to ensure that they were not going to lose because of faulty equipment or design. They were not convinced that the fastest American boat was necessarily the fastest craft possible, and so they had also instructed Messrs J. and S. Salter of Oxford to build 'their very swiftest boat'. Salters had built Boat Race eights for both Oxford and Cambridge for years, but the London RC men said that although Salters' eights were superior, their fours were too strong and heavy and slower than those built by both Jewitt and Clasper. Arrangements were therefore made that both of the latter should, for a reasonable consideration, build his very best boat, the American crew to be the sole judges of their quality, 'adopting any plan of testing their speed that they themselves might see fit – whichever proved fastest to be paid for at the usual rates'. They said that although they would prefer to use an American-built boat, they would not do so if they could get one that was manifestly faster.

Feeling rather left out of all this, Messrs E. Searle and Sons tendered a boat free of charge, so that after a flurry of late-houred boatbuilding had taken place, quite a fleet was assembled at Putney for the young gentlemen of Harvard and the English heavies to argue about. The final tally was the two boats brought across the Atlantic, the Salter model, the best of Jewitt, Clasper, and Searle, and the kit put together by Elliott after he first set foot in Putney. The crew must have been knackered trying them all out, but the new Elliott won the nomination after going from Putney aqueduct to Bishop's Creek — presumably somewhere near Craven Cottage — seven seconds faster than any of the others. The Rev. Mr Risley, an Oxford blue, was heard to say that he hoped the Americans would abandon their boat so that his men could use it, while the Rev. 'Skum' Shadwell, the noted cox and coach and a connoisseur of shell boats in Europe, complimented the boat as one of the best he had ever seen. Elliott's masterpiece was 44 feet long, 21½ inches wide and 8 inches deep, with knees made out of light Maine hackmatack instead of heavy white oak which English boat-builders used, thus reducing weight without losing strength. She was roomy and comfortable.

The change of climate for the men, said the secretary, 'manifested itself in a looseness of joints and a lack of springiness and activity. . . . The heavy damp air of England, made more so in this instance by the river close by, would cause some of the men to hack and cough a little on rising in the morning, even though they did not feel at all cold.' It was this that had prompted Loring to rearrange the race for the 27th instead of the 16th. The comparatively small amount of work which they were seen to be doing during their first two weeks in England awoke serious apprehensions among their friends, onlookers and the pressmen. At first they were told daily in the papers how busy the Oxford men were in comparison as the latter practised in strict seclusion upriver in Pangbourne. But when the Americans found their sorts they were credited as being gluttons for work. The differences in style were discussed in great detail and *The Times*'s boating correspondent in particular, Edwin Brickwood, regularly accompanied the Harvard students.

The Harvard men sat in the middle of their fixed thwarts, had proportionately longer outriggers, rated slightly faster than Oxford, but were steady through the water. Their aim was to pull every part of the stroke equally hard. To effect this they reached farther over their toes than their antagonists and at the end of the stroke thrust their hands very quickly away from their bodies. They swung their bodies back past the perpendicular less far than Oxford, using their arms more in finishing the stroke, and the rebound from their bodies was swifter. Their dip, too, was deeper. 'The bucketful or more of water that each oar sent aft would manifestly be detrimental to a narrow boat following closely,' remarked the secretary.

Harvard aimed for continuity over the course, whereas Oxford's stately appearance, some observers noticed, was often less marked after their first mile or so. Oxford sat up straight, reached well forward, though they took their time getting there, and seemed to hang for a moment to balance their oars for a hit at the water. They then clipped their beginnings, starting to pull in the air rather than dropping their blades in vertically. The moment contact was made with the water they threw their entire weight onto the stretcher or footboard and did all the pulling they could in the first third of the arc described by the blade. They kept their arms straight until their bodies were past the perpendicular, 50 degrees with the boat's gunwale. Then they dropped their hands against their ribs and commenced another stroke. They sat up to the side of the boat farthest from the oarblade.

Two weeks before the race the Oxford crew moved down from Pangbourne. The Americans thought they had been at a disadvantage because every move they had made had been under the watchful eyes of towpath and steamers, whereas Oxford had been in much more rural retreat. Now things were more equal. *Harper's New Monthly* carried a retrospective report from the secretary Blaikie:

> On the very first day the two crews showed at Putney the people were out by hundreds attempting to judge of their respective merits. Every evening until the contest each train brought from London a generous delegation, and even in the morning row it was difficult to launch the boat, so numerous were the bystanders. Always good-natured, frequently expressing admiration at the well-developed, sun-browned arms of the strangers, they would seldom cause the latter any considerable inconvenience, and never intentionally.
>
> Daily, almost hourly, would the wish be heard expressed that the Americans might win, and if the Englishman who said so was asked why he thus opposed his countrymen he replied in terms highly flattering to the pluck and daring of their rivals. . . . Well-mounted equestrians upon the towing-path kept level with the crew and timed their every stroke.

As the race approached, the Americans were almost besieged by the press. Reporters would buttonhole them at every corner, report what they ate in more detail than they realized themselves, discover new facts every day, find varied explanations of every stop and every start. Visitors to the White House became a nuisance for the oarsmen, who had little time or disposition for meeting them. Sometimes the rest of the party would entertain forty callers, including an impressive list of celebrities. Thomas Hughes MP, Sir Charles Dilke MP, Mrs Goldschmidt (*née* Jenny Lind), Mr Moran, the Secretary of the American Legation, Mr Morse, the American consul in London, the Hon. Thomas H. Dudley, the American consul at Liverpool, prominent bankers and eminent literary men, all found their way to the White House. Plus, of course, a platoon of American tourists.

The two main concerns of the American camp were that their crew might be interfered with, either by tampering with what they ate and drank, or by something getting in the way during the race. They dealt with the former by having a double allowance of food and drink brought into the house from ten days before the race. One supply was through regular channels, while the other was by secret means through the hands of Harvard men only. They were not, of course, suspicious of their hosts in this respect. They did not think of mistrusting the Oxford crew. But they were worried about betting men, who were, they knew from experience on both sides of the Atlantic, capable of resorting to unscrupulous acts in pursuance of profit. 'Though the suspicion was day by day materially reduced, the feeling still was that we should be very much chagrined if drugging the food, or anything else in our power to foresee, was not prevented,' was how Blaikie put it.

As far as danger from interference during the race was concerned, the Conservators of the Thames, who had been given supreme control of the river during the Boat Race by Parliament in an attempt to keep the course clear, met representatives of both crews at Putney. Oxford and Harvard pointed out that, although a huge crowd was expected, this was a private match and could be held without prior notice early in the morning or evening. They wanted a clear river, and the Conservancy Board were ready to provide it.

Harvard insisted that steamers be limited to two, one for the umpires and referee, and one for the press. Even the two steam yachts being used as coaching launches were banned. Two steamers for spectators were anchored near the finish with two policemen on board each, standing over the captain 'to arrest him the moment his paddles moved'. Strings of barges and lighters were moored offshore and no small craft were allowed outside them. The river was locked up two hours before the race which was scheduled for 5 p.m. The weather was warm and it was sunny outside the White House as the Harvard men took their breakfast. By mid-morning Elliott, the boatbuilder, was dancing with delight because a strong easterly breeze had got up, which he reckoned suited his cabinet-making. His ship was full-floored and seaworthy and broader than his rival's. But at two o'clock the wind began to fade and by five it had gone. All day long Putney was lively with booths and other apparatus designed for the spasmodic gathering of small change. From early in the morning carriages had been parked in strategic viewing spots, guarded by hired hands while the owners warmed up elsewhere for the event. People poured from trains to the riverside. The Harvard secretary reported great 'buses' with three horses abreast and the ordinary kind with two, with 'ten inside and fourteen out' and a burly, dignified, weatherbeaten, grand-fatherly looking old 'whip' perched a little higher than anyone else, who stopped about every fifteen minutes for his grog or his 'arf a pint of h'olden bitters' and nodded complacently to the demure little barmaid who brought it. There were lumbering dogcarts, broughams and wagonettes, and stately four-in-hands with jaunty outriders and liveried footmen.

Every inn, dwelling house and shanty along the banks was a mine of gold to its owner. Twelve guineas were paid by one American for two small windows in the White Hart at Mortlake. The Stars and Stripes were everywhere. There was a steady stream of boats of every dimension and cut from single sculls to lumbering lighters as large as the craft that first carried Columbus to the New World. Instead of remaining unsightly old hulks, the barges became 'perfect bouquets of beauty, from the gayly-decked loads they bore', and the rowers included lovely English girls. True to their Oxford representatives, they were recovering slowly forward, catching the beginning, keeping their backs straight, and pulling a 'nipping' stroke. This indeed, marvelled Blaikie, was an everyday sight at Putney, 'and if seen oftener in our own land might make the sightly figures and the beauty of vigorous health less rare than they now are.' The London rabble also, he observed, could not all have been on the banks because so many of them were on the water. As the hour approached they all took up their positions. The southern arch of Hammersmith Bridge was by mutual agreement closed and both boats were to pass through the Middlesex span of Barnes Bridge.

Roads were blocked off, police boats were stationed at strategic points, bands played the national anthem and 'Yankee Doodle', and eight hundred policemen were deployed to control the crowds. The water was dead flat and the tide was running up sluggishly as a procession of thirty, most of them American, filed out of the White House's water gate directly on board the umpires' boat. The party included Thomas Hughes and Professor Asa Gray, the botanist; the thirty Oxford representatives whom they met on board were mostly old blues. The crews came out from London RC, Oxford first. Harvard had won the toss and chosen Middlesex because, after many trips with the cox Arthur Burnham on board the little steam yacht, they reckoned that they would get the pole position for the first half mile on Middlesex. They warmed up to cheers and attached themselves to the stout stakeboats. On Surrey, F. Willan (Eton and Exeter) in the bow, A. C. Yarborough (Eton and Lincoln) at two, J. C. Tinné (Eton and University) at three, and S. D. Darbishire (University College School and Balliol) at stroke, with F. H. Hall (Canterbury and Corpus Christi), who was not to get his blue until the following year, coxing. For Harvard, Fay was in the bow, Lyman was sitting in front of him at three, the American numbering system working in the reverse direction to the English one, Simmons was at two, and Loring stroking, with Burnham steering. Oxford were a lot heavier, their total being 790 pounds against Harvard's 731. Willan at 168 pounds was 13 pounds heavier than Fay, Yarborough was 17 pounds heavier than Lyman, Tinné was 18 pounds heavier than Simmons, and Darbishire was 14 pounds heavier than Loring. Hall of Oxford at 102 pounds was 3 pounds lighter than Harvard's Burnham.

The starter cried out, 'I shall start you by the words "Are you ready?" Then I will pause for a moment and repeat, "Are you ready?" If no response comes I will say "Go!" If either side breaks an oar in the first dozen strokes, I shall call you back by swinging my hat back vigorously. Now, then look out! Are you ready?'

'No,' says Mr Tinné.

'Again, are you ready?'

'No!' Again from Mr Tinné.

'When will you be?'

'Directly.'

Their boat was not headed just right and they were swinging it into place.

'Are you ready? Are you ready? Go!'

And both boats sprang away at fifteen minutes past five o'clock.

The Americans had made great efforts to monitor the race. One American gentleman connected with Oxford University counted and jotted down Oxford's ratings, a Harvard graduate counted Harvard's, and another American gentleman took the time using one of Benson's best chronometers, sent down by request for this purpose. In the first minute Oxford did one more stroke than they had ever done in practice, scoring 42. Loring took Harvard off at 46, dropped them to 42 in the second minute to Oxford's 40, and had stolen half a length on the dark blues. Amidst the roars of the armies on the banks, Burnham then steered a little towards Surrey and from the umpire's paddle steamer a foul looked inevitable.

'Look out, Mr Burnham!' shrieks Mr Hall in the Oxford boat, and Burnham steers the Crimsons back towards Middlesex, towards the middle of the river. At the end of three minutes Harvard are a length and a half in front, and it is here that Burnham makes a fateful mistake. Some weeks before the race the stroke man Loring had said to the Oxford crew that in his opinion the professional oarsmen's custom of steering directly in front of their opponents when leading so as to send a vigorous backwash onto the bows of the following boat was a piece of jockeyism. Gentlemen should refrain from such practice, said Loring, and the Oxford president Tinné reluctantly assented. Burnham had thus been ordered not to do it, and so instead of going for the stream towards the Surrey bank and crowding Oxford he sets off across the flats towards the Crabtree Inn.

They reach Hammersmith Bridge in 8 minutes 21 seconds, an excellent time and a length in front. Oxford have dropped to 37 and Harvard are at 39, and Loring puts in a spurt and begins to draw away again, probably wasted effort because the men cannot sustain it, and Oxford creep inexorably up on them, foot by foot, inch by inch, under-rating them, until off Chiswick Eyot Harvard hit an eddy and the two boats are level. From this point Oxford pull a steady 40 to Barnes Bridge which they reach two lengths in front, while Loring cannot get more than 39 and is himself looking distressed. Coxswain Burnham realizes that he is in trouble and vigorously dashes water over him, a novel but excellent expedient.

As Oxford lead Harvard towards the finish at Mortlake, secretary Blaikie watches the banks as well as the race:

For miles back the dense mass on shore has been swaying and struggling, and now, like a mighty river, is sweeping on over fields and fences, ditches and hedges, wild, mad with fierce excitement, yelling at every breath and with all its might. Seven hundred and fifty thousand people are said to have been there that day. Never but once in this generation has such a crowd been seen in England, and then when the Prince of Wales first brought his wife home. The Derby Day cannot compare. All previous water fêtes sink into insignificance.

Lyman in the Harvard boat has been in distress for some time because his dress has become disarranged and greatly impedes his movements. This causes the boat to roll badly and makes difficulties for the others. Oxford reach the line first, half to threequarters of a length clear according to Sir Aubrey Paul, the judge at the finish. The time was 22 minutes 20 seconds, remarkably fast for a fixed-seat four on a sluggish tide. Opinions differ about the margin, Oxford sources putting it at three to four lengths, but it is clear that Harvard faded somewhat after Barnes and that overall it was a mighty fine race. Oxford turn and paddle slowly downriver towards Putney, but the Americans are caught in the hubbub and crush of boats at the finish and eventually have to disembark onto their little steam yacht which is awaiting them. The yacht, built by John Thorneycroft and claimed by its owner Mr Blyth of Cambridge to be the fastest yacht in Europe, capable of twenty miles an hour, cannot move either, and the rowers are transferred to the umpires' steamer. Tired, hot, gloomy and depressed, they sail off down the river to the White House. Later they are dragged to a grand dinner at the house of Mr Phillips, a wealthy brewer at Mortlake. The Queen and President Grant are toasted and Tinné says that he has never been pushed so hard in a race, and he has done some hard racing in his time. Hall congratulates himself on not running into either bank or the Harvard boat. The evening breaks up late among a lot of noise and mixed feelings, mostly of bonhomie.

The English papers in general denounced Burnham's course for the Crabtree as very foolish, backed up by the opinion of respected observers both British and American. 'It is plain,' wrote the Harvard secretary, 'that had our men been directly in front of their opponents

The founders of the Boat Race

Top left: The Very Rev. Charles Merivale, Dean of Ely who was number four in the Cambridge crew.
Right: The Right Rev. Charles Wordsworth, Bishop of St Andrews, who was number four for Oxford in 1829

Postwar mentors

Below left: Group Captain 'Jumbo' Edwards coaching Oxford in 1959. *Right:* Lou Barry, Cambridge's finishing coach during their run of victories which ended in 1973

The dead heat of 1877

Oxford beating Harvard in the four-oared match of 1869

Top left: 'Honest' John Phelps, the finishing judge. *Top right:* Joseph W. Chitty, the umpire.
Below: The finish

Wiles of Tideway weather

Springlike start in 1873 and blizzard conditions in 1872

Views of Hammersmith

Top: Sketch of bridge undergoing reconstruction in 1886, when the crews passed through together. knitting their blades. *Below:* The 1866 crews clear the bridge

The Coxswains

Top left: The Hon. Colin Moynihan (Oxford 1977) shovels grain at Young's Brewery, Wandsworth, to lose weight. *Top right:* Thomas Egan (Cambridge 1836, 1839–40). *Below:* Antony Armstrong-Jones (Cambridge 1950) leads his crew out of the boathouse

Susan Brown, the first lady (Oxford 1981–82), on the bank and in the boat. *Below:* Jim Rogers Jr, whose Isis crew beat their blue boat on April Fool's Day in 1965 and who steered Oxford in 1966

Top: Cambridge embark in 1872. *Below:* Inside Oxford's boathouse in 1872. *Opposite, top:* Cambridge being coached from a steam launch in 1892. *Below:* The weigh-in in 1874

Sinking times

Top: Oxford sank at the moment of victory in 1863 and walked ashore. *Below:* Front page of the *Daily Mirror*, 1 April 1912, depicting the rescue of Cambridge

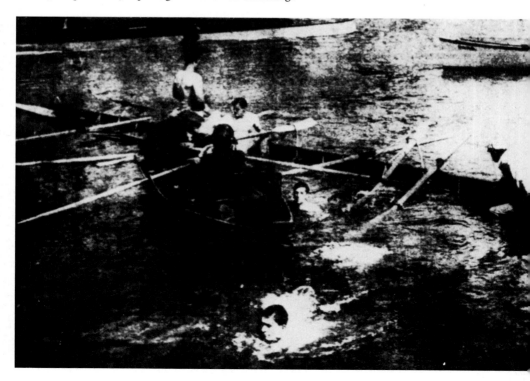

Top: Oxford sinking soon after the start in 1951. *Below:* Cambridge go down from the stern at Barnes in 1978

1965: Oxford's crew practise at Radley, with four Yale men in the stern

Lord Snowdon (Cambridge 1950) in the light blue launch

Cambridge beat milk rationing in 1949 by buying their own cow

George VI is presented to the 1951 Cambridge crew after their victorious American tour

Controversial Oxford figures

Top: Jumbo Edwards demonstrates a Moriarty to Oxford crews practising at Henley in 1959, the year of the mutiny. *Below, left:* Ronnie Howard, president in 1959. *Middle:* Reed Rubin, leader of the mutineers. *Right:* Sam Mackenzie whose 1965 coaching partnership with Howard broke up

Top: Oxford and Cambridge on the Seine in Paris

Below: On the Sumida in Tokyo and the ceremony of the oars at Luxor, preliminary to the Nile Boat Race

Top left: Tony Leadley (Cambridge 1953) explains the course for television viewers in 1962. *Right:* John Snagge, the voice of the Boat Race. *Below left:* The BBC radio launch with transmitting equipment in 1932. *Right:* The Consuta equipped to televise the race from start to finish for the first time, in 1949

all the way from the Crabtree to Chiswick Ait, the latter would not
have passed them so soon as they did, because they would have had to
row all that distance in quite lumpy water, instead of that equally good
with what the leaders had.'

Then he produced a catalogue of 'ifs' to complete his analysis.

Had the Harvard stroke been at his weight instead of nearly, if not
quite, ten pounds under it; Had Number Two been in his best condition, as he uniformly has been in all past races; had Number Three
suffered no impediment from his clothes, thus enabling Bow to lay out
all his strength effectively; and had the coxswain steered as an English
one would have done; moreover, had they all had three months of
practice together instead of three weeks, they would still have been no
better off than their rivals. Only the night before the race I asked Mr
Willan if his crew were all right, and he said they were.

Harvard received twenty invitations to dinners after the event and
accepted a couple of them. The grandest was hosted by London RC at
the Crystal Palace, the glass house that had contained all the wonders
of the Empire at the Great Exhibition of 1851 in Hyde Park, and had
been moved complete to a hill-top site near the villages of Sydenham
and Dulwich, south of London. Oxford were criticized in the press for
snubbing their visitors because only Willan of the crew attended, but
the dinner was only arranged shortly before the race and already the
Oxford students had had to build their vacation plans around the
event. One was in Switzerland, another in Scotland. Only Willan and
the Harvard boys, therefore, had the benefit of hearing the speeches,
among them those by Thomas Hughes MP and the novelist and
journalist supreme, Charles Dickens.

Examination of the race appeared in the press on both sides of the
Atlantic for about a month. The event caught the public imagination
hugely, presumably because of the novelty of a sports team coming
from so far to woo bookmakers and public to a free show, the result of
which could be known almost instantly in Harvard and New York.
From the early preparations in May, the *New York Times* gave sixteen
editorials on the race, at least fifteen American correspondents followed it, and legitimate business in Wall Street was more or less
suspended as every street-corner gathering speculated and the result
was awaited on the sidewalks and in the drugstores. More is said about

communications and this race in chapter 14, but the American press regarded the Oxford–Harvard match as an international event, and the biggest European story of the year. It pushed the negotiations between Britain and the United States over the *Alabama* claims into the background, although this was an emotive topic for both countries. The *Alabama* was a British-built ship which had inflicted great damage on Union shipping on behalf of the Confederate Government during the Civil War, and Senator Charles Sumner was now demanding compensation to the tune of $2125 million.

The London *Times* declared that the day of the race was henceforth 'ever immortal in Anglo-American annals' and concluded that the lesson of the occasion was victory for education, particularly British education:

> Thus it happened on Friday that the Oxford crew knew precisely the limits of continuous effort – they knew where to abstain as well as where to abound. The advantage is, however, perhaps, not without its drawbacks, for it may be that nations, like men, should have some reserve of natural endowments, which should be, as it were, not brought into tillage, so as to be better able to meet the days when the progress of others shall have equalized the benefits of training.

The only other occasion when a Boat Race crew have been involved in a race over the championship course against another university also involved Harvard. On Sunday, 15 July 1906, F. L. Higginson called on his former coach Rudie Lehmann at his home in Bourne End and showed him a cable which he had just received saying that the Harvard crew who had beaten Yale on 28 June were eager to row against Cambridge, winners of the Boat Race, and were ready to start for England without delay. Lehmann, who holds a probably unique distinction of having coached Oxford, Cambridge and Harvard for their respective matches, was at first sceptical. Cambridge term had already ended, Henley was over, the men were scattered. However, it was not an opportunity to be missed if it could be arranged. Higginson had first rowed in Lehmann's Harvard crew of 1898 and then as captain had turned over a run of Yale victories in the following year. Lehmann would try to arrange things for his sake.

Lehmann was rewarded by an occasion which had all the attributes which he regarded important about sport. It was 'a brilliant triumph for our English rowing men, and for the sound and ancient traditions on which their teaching had been based,' and which, incidentally, he had infiltrated into the Harvard system as coach with some success. He went on: 'It was the splendid culminating point of a genuine sporting event in which from first to last there had been neither hitch nor jar. Friendship there was and courtesy and chivalry, but of the animosity which has sometimes embittered and disfigured such contests there was never even the faintest trace.' The new president, Henry Mills Goldsmith, attended a hastily arranged meeting of old blues in London where all the details were fixed and 8 September picked as the day. Escombe and Muttlebury agreed to coach and the last man to answer, B. C. Johnstone, hurried south from a yachting trip at Portree, Skye, to attend first practice at Bourne End on Monday, 6 August. Harvard began their practice on the same water and the same day, having arrived on the previous Saturday.

Lehmann had a house called Fieldhead at Bourne End with a boathouse large enough to take eights, and both crews had a month's training in a quiet and idyllic setting, hosted by the English aquatic Edwardians. Theodore Cook wrote of Rudie: 'In his best days no one could give a better dinner or lead the conversation as a better host on multitudinous topics.' Cook found in Lehmann the striving ardour of the chase 'which Dante imagines in Odysseus', the quest which never ends until the flag falls at the finish. His stern expression was suddenly lit with laughter and his definition of sportsmanship was wider than bracing muscles and development of endurance. It took in control of anger, consideration for fellow men, suspect of trickery, cheer under disappointment. His household at Bourne End, where his American wife Alice was hostess among a small coterie of small children, reflected his notions of Rudie, the Liberal MP for Leicester, and was the base for the great Anglo-American match.

The crews moved to Putney on 23 August. Cambridge had not been able to muster their entire 1906 Boat Race crew. For A. B. Close-Brooks at bow and H. G. Baynes at five it was their first Putney-to-Mortlake, but they both did it again against Oxford in the following year. They replaced G. D. Cochrane and E. W. Powell, and the rest of the oarsmen were 1906 blues – J. H. F. Benham at two, H. M. Goldsmith at three, M. Donaldson at four, R. V. Powell at six, Johnstone at seven, and D. C. R. Stuart stroking on bow-side. They were steered by the 1903–4 cox B. G. A. Scott who replaced A. G. L.

Hunt. Harvard's line-up was R. M. Tappen, S. W. Fish, P. W. Flint, C. Morgan, J. Richardson, R. L. Bacon, D. A. Newhall, and O. D. Filley stroking, with M. B. Blagden steering. Morgan was from Harrow and Filley from Rugby.

Bob Herrick, the Harvard coach, found his men at Putney in a house littered with clothes and bags a few days before the race, bored by the waiting. The manager Emerson was wandering about with his pockets stuffed with dollars, pounds and francs, giving out change in mixtures. Speculation was as usual rife, for the Americans had a boat built by Mr Davey, an Englishman living in Cambridge, Massachusetts, which exhibited a startling bow wave to English eyes. Cambridge had a boat with a much finer entry made by the Sims brothers in five days, 15 pounds heavier than the Harvard ship. The Americans used swivel rowlocks and 21-inch slides, the Englishmen fixed pins and 16-inch slides, so the American emphasis appeared to be on legwork and the English on body swing.

On 1 September Harvard rowed a full course on a swinging spring tide in 18 minutes 50 seconds, five seconds outside the record. The day of the race itself was glorious and spectators turned out in thousands. White-gloved policemen parted the crowds for the crews' embarkation, Rudie Lehmann officiated as referee, the responsibility of restarting the race in the event of accidents being vested in him by a special agreement signed by president Goldsmith and captain Filley of Harvard, and happily there were no accidents. The Cambridge, England, crew beat the Cambridge, Massachusetts, crew by two lengths in 19 minutes 58 seconds, after taking a clear lead by Beverley Brook and keepings things in hand from there on. They dropped almost to a paddle near the end, probably out of sportsmanship rather than fatigue.

Proceedings were concluded with a dinner at Prince's restaurant in London, attended by the American ambassador, Whitelaw Reid, to which Cambridge drove in a motor omnibus greeted with spontaneous cheers in the West End. Herrick remembered it as 'about the dullest occasion I was ever present at. I have no doubt the depression caused by our defeat explains my feelings somewhat, but I still believe the dinner was a much duller affair than it would have been possible to have in this country,' he wrote in *Reminiscences of Harvard Rowing* many years later. Reid spoke of President Roosevelt's keen interest as a Harvard oarsman himself. The crew, who visited Cambridge and

Emmanuel College, from where their founder John Harvard, son of a Southwark butcher, graduated in about 1630, found difficulty in reconciling themselves to defeat, but Herrick found them delighted by their reception by the English. They remain only the second and latest American crew to race against blues from Putney to Mortlake. Later, Crimsons were to make their mark in Britain in other ways, beginning a spectacular record at Henley by winning the Grand in 1914. As far as Boat Race crews are concerned, what little subsequent transatlantic traffic has taken place has been from east to west.

I3

Images and foreign parts
Oxbridge abroad, spoils of victory, blue fiction

The dramatic sinking of Oxford in 1951 and the subsequent rerow on
Easter Monday resulting in a Cambridge victory of twelve lengths
meant that it was the light blues who made hasty preparations to travel
to the United States to race Harvard and Yale separately, at the
invitation of the English Speaking Union. Harold Rickett was in
charge and he had his time cut out making the arrangements among a
confusing series of cables. Misunderstanding arose from the use of the
word 'boat', the British applying it indiscriminately to men and craft,
the Americans to the shell. At one time it appeared that the crew were
to travel in a box on the *Queen Elizabeth*. Eventually the boat was
packed by Sims of Hammersmith with an extra fin and rudder and sent
to Southampton for the *Elizabeth*'s departure on the Thursday after
the Boat Race. Aylings of Putney made an oar crate large enough for
oars, tools and rowing clothes, and the riggers were packed separately.
The crew, meanwhile, collected their visas which had been conditional
on their possessing an international certificate of vaccination and
reaction. None of them possessed this beforehand, and the require-
ment only became known to Rickett on the day before the first Boat
Race. He dared not have his charges vaccinated for fear that positive
reactions would muck up their practice. The danger period was eight
to fourteen days after getting the needle with the difference, which
could have turned out to be five days before the scheduled Harvard
race. So he arranged with Edward Bevan, the Cambridge treasurer, to
obtain some genuine lymph which was baked in order to guarantee a
negative reaction. 'Vaccination' then took place immediately after the
Boat Race rerow.

The crew themselves had a few days off and assembled at the Bath

Club on Friday, 30 March, for two days' practice. After a long evening of delays on the following Sunday, they left at 2.15 in the morning on the BOAC Strato-Cruiser Cassiopeia, seen off by Mr and Mrs John Snagge, Harold's brother Graham and sister-in-law Pam, and newsreel cameras whirring under specially rigged arc lamps alongside the plane at Heathrow. They landed at Keflavik in Iceland and at Goose Bay in Labrador to refuel and arrived in New York at 9.30 p.m. British time to be met by representatives of the ESU and the Yale Graduates' Rowing Committee. Rickett's detailed log of the expedition, which he called Operation Cedar, gives a paddle-by-paddle and meal-by-meal account, tales of hospitality, generosity, poor college grub, excellent dinners, speeches and visits. After lunch at Avon Old Farm Schools they were presented with light blue lavatory paper; there was confusion over the length of the course against Yale; the riggers went missing on the *Queen Elizabeth* for a few hours, and the Yale trailer which collected the boat could not travel at night. Thirty-eight pressmen turned up for their press conference, which among others was addressed by the British reporters Richard Burnell, then with *The Times*, and Bush Johnstone of the *Telegraph*, who had rowed for Cambridge against Harvard in 1906.

The race was to be over one and threequarter miles of the Housatonic River at Derby, about fourteen miles from the Yale campus at New Haven. The river was very much in flood, and reminded Rickett of the Thames at Marlow, though it was two or three times wider. The men recovered well from their journey, though there were a few minor troubles. Brian Lloyd had to have a tooth extracted, Sharpley had his bottom painted with Mercurocrome solution to relieve sores, Worlidge was prescribed penicillin tablets for loss of voice and sore throat, Bill Windham and Jack King had minor tummy upsets. They behaved well, turned out smartly in Leander blazers or whites and Cambridge blazers for rowing occasions. They always dined together and met in the evenings to keep up their crew morale, and they missed their beer. Eventually beer was obtained, Rickett being careful to explain to the press the British dietary practice of taking beer with dinner in case the wrong idea got around, for the Yale crews were off alcohol completely. One evening Tom Mendenhall of Berkeley College gave them a bottle and a half of port which they added to their meal.

The race on Saturday, 14 April, was a straightforward win by Cambridge of four lengths over Yale before a crowd which seemed to support the British visitors, and the crew left for Harvard having made many friends but anxious to get to grips with the men whom they regarded as the main opposition. Their reception at Cambridge, Massachusetts, was in marked contrast to that at New Haven and was not in the tradition that Rudie Lehmann had spread as a Cambridge coach at Harvard in the late nineteenth century or when he hosted Harvard when they raced Cambridge on the Thames in 1906. They were to be billeted with students in four-man bunk rooms or in some cases given sofa space, and there was no provision for sheets and towels. On the first evening Rickett got hold of the Harvard crew manager and amidst a certain amount of ill feeling insisted that his men should be found separate rooms with the bare necessities of housekeeping provided, and after that things began to improve. They found their way to the hearts of the Harvard rowing men, to the wide course on the Charles River where they were to meet the Crimsons and the crews from MIT and Boston University, to the huge Newell boathouse from where they boated, to the radio stations and the well-attended ESU parties and a splendid evening at MIT where the tables were small and arranged by seat numbers in the boats of the four crews, so that all the number threes sat together with at least one pressman, and so on. They hoisted the CUBC flag at the Newell and on Thursday, 19 April, Patriot's Day, they won the race, over one and threequarter miles, going out in front at the start against the heavier, taller Harvard men and leaving Boston and MIT to do battle for third place. The result was Cambridge 9 minutes 38 seconds, Harvard 9 minutes 43⅗ seconds, Boston University 10 minutes 1 second, and MIT 10 minutes, 4 seconds.

Patriot's Day is a public holiday in Boston in memory of the silversmith Paul Revere, whose ride to Lexington on 19 April 1775 gave warning of the landing of British forces. A replica of Revere's celebrated rose bowl, which is preserved in Boston, was presented to the crew, a trophy donated by Union Boat Club to mark their centenary, and Oliver Filley, captain of the Harvard 1906 crew, bought their boat and oars to give to his university. On Saturday, 21 April, after flying to New York and partying at the River Club and cocktailing at the Knickerbocker Club and hitting the town, they set sail on the *Queen Elizabeth* at 5.45 in the morning.

The sun was rising over the skyscrapers as the *Queen* left the waterfront. The skyscrapers and the sun looked a lot better than the

Cambridge crew who were on deck. They began their voyage home as tourist-class passengers, four to a cabin, not very comfortable. The cabins were ventilated by an air pipe which didn't prevent them getting very hot. But they quickly established themselves as the darlings of the ship and by the time they arrived home, their trip to America had been transformed from the rowing expedition which it had remained while they were there to the triumphal return of athletic heroes who had done something special for Anglo-American relations. On the first day out from New York, Bush Johnstone requested that the first-class promenade deck and swimming pool be made available to the light blues. This was refused, but as individuals, Rickett noticed, his boys began to find their way to wherever they liked. There was a steady stream of autograph requests from passengers and Cunard crew, congratulatory telegrams from their American hosts, cocktail parties thrown by other passengers. They dined together with Johnstone with the Paul Revere bowl on the table. The commodore had them up for drinks and was admirable with his stories, and Rickett had a disturbing cable from Harcourt Gold, chairman of the Henley Stewards: 'Stewards of Regatta anxious to give you and crew dinner to celebrate great achievement.' The Stewards had never offered anyone dinner before. Rickett was troubled because there was already a glow running through his men, and he wanted them to settle down and concentrate on their examinations and the Cambridge May boats.

Then on the Wednesday of the voyage Brian Lloyd was summoned to the commodore's cabin and handed another cable. It said:

> From Cunard, Liverpool to Commodore Queen Elizabeth. Am requested by Provost, King's College, Cambridge, to pass following message through you to Mr Brian Lloyd, Captain, Cambridge crew: 'King and Queen visiting Cambridge Friday. Their Majesties wish Cambridge crew presented to them. Please parade twelve noon Friday King's Main Gate wearing blues and white flannels.' General Manager.

Lloyd returned with the cable and summoned the crew, and spontaneously they all sang 'God Save the King'. By this time, noted Rickett, their status had changed completely. Lady Astor was at a cocktail party that evening and kept pinching the crew's drinks, and Gracie Fields attended before singing in the first-class concert, which the boys attended. They were on the bridge as the ship dropped anchor in Cherbourg, though Hinde was never given a chance at coxing the *Queen*. At 3 p.m. on Friday, 27 April, they docked at Southampton to be met by Gully Nickalls, John Snagge, and a host of reporters. When Snagge asked the purser if he had seen the crew, the reply was, 'Last time I saw them they were trying to climb up the mast.' Cunard officials whisked them off the ship, they sped through customs with the minimum of fuss, signing autographs for the customs officer, and had another reception from heavies at Waterloo.

The next morning they assembled at Lloyd's rooms in Cambridge wearing white trousers and shirts, brown shoes, blue socks, Leander ties and Yale tieclips, and blue blazers, and Rickett was there with the cleaned-up cup. They walked to King's and had a warm reception from the crowd. After the royal party inspected the windows in the chapel, reinstalled after their wartime sanctuary elsewhere, the crew were presented to the King, Queen and Princess Margaret. The King told them that the presentation was his own idea. He questioned them about their training, the water they rowed on in America, the food, the courses, ratings, and congratulated them on beating Oxford and the Americans. The day went on and on. Cocktail party in King's, lunch at the Hawks Club, speech from the King who said that as an old Cambridge man he was proud of the lustre that the crew brought to CUBC and British rowing, photographs with the cup, tea with the Vice-Chancellor, the annual dinner of Rob Roy Boat Club. Exams and Mays took a back seat for a while longer.

Rickett reflected on what his crew would gain from Operation Cedar and lighted upon Bush Johnstone for the answer. For Bush the experience had been 1906 revisited, and it was a revelation to the crew to see the years roll off him. He looked twenty years younger when they returned from America.

In spite of the fact that there was much talk at New Haven and Cambridge, Mass., about repeating the fixtures and even making the Boat Race victors' transatlantic visit an annual event, nothing came of it. One reason is expense. Another is that the icier conditions in New England do not allow the rowing season to run all through the winter on the water, and it is almost impossible to find a date which suits the crews on both sides of the Atlantic. The Harvard–Yale match takes place in June. Neither Oxford nor Cambridge have ever raced Harvard or Yale over the American boat race course at New London on the river Thames (soft 'th' and rhymes with 'games') in Connecticut.

There have, however, been many other occasions on which Oxford or Cambridge crews have met Harvard or Yale crews, but mostly under different names as far as the British were concerned, often with changes of personnel from the actual blue boat, and usually at Henley Regatta. There have also been several expeditions abroad by Oxford and Cambridge crews, some of them as representative British crews, some of them as serious post-Boat Race matches, some of them as little more than jaunts. They have been on the Seine, the Nile and the Sumida, in Florida, Spain, Denmark, Oregon, in Brazil and on the Suez Canal.

Until 1860 it was usual for both universities to send representative crews to Henley Royal Regatta. Oxford won the Grand seven times and Cambridge three times during this period, and Oxford also won the Stewards' Cup for coxed fours six times and Cambridge once. Then for 101 years no Oxbridge crew entered the regatta under either flag, but of course plenty of blues and crews from OUBC and CUBC competed there under other flags. Cambridge competed in the 1908 Olympic regatta at Henley. They lost their heat to the Belgians, who were beaten by Leander in the final. Cambridge went to the Olympics again in 1932 after winning the Grand as Leander, but they didn't win in Los Angeles. Oxford were in the 1948 Olympic regatta in a coxed four, also at Henley, and lost to Hungary in the quarter final. Then in 1960 OUBC entered the Grand and lost the final to Molesey BC. With one change they represented Britain at the Olympic Games in Rome, losing to the United States in a repechage. They hadn't a hope in hell and everyone knew it, but the Jumbo men were the toast of the Italian press and were by far the most popular crew at the regatta. The blue Cardinal Heard (Oxford, 1907) gave them a party and attended Pope John on his terrace to instruct him in the details and procedures of rowing, although in spite of the Pontiff's keenness the cardinal did not succeed in getting him out in a boat. When the kayaking took place after the rowing, His Holiness was told that he couldn't watch because the women were bare-shouldered, but he wasn't having any of that. He hid behind his terrace palms and got an eyeful of biceps.

Since then OUBC have entered the Grand five times, losing on all occasions, but their Yale men won the Prince Philip for coxed fours in 1965. Then in 1981 five of the Boat Race crew won the Grand together with three Thames Tradesmen. It was a classic scrap against the

Amateur Rowing Association's national crew, fought into a brick wall of a headwind, during which the lead changed twice. The tables were reversed at the national championships a fortnight later, but three of the blues – Chris Mahoney, John Bland and Mark Andrews – were selected for the phoenix crew who arose from the ashes of the duel and they won silver medals at the world championships in Munich.

Strictly the 1981 Grand crew was not a representative OUBC crew. Nor was the Cambridge and Lady Margaret combination who won the European championships in 1951 a Cambridge crew, although five of them were from that year's blue boat and the Harvard–Yale tour. But the forays to Henley, the reshuffled Isis and Goldie crews who appear from time to time, the combinations with other clubs and representational appearances of individuals are all indicative of the contribution which the two clubs make to British rowing.

The Boat Race itself has spawned imitators. Every now and then matches are proposed and sometimes run between Glasgow and Edinburgh or Manchester and Salford. Before the Second World War there was an Italian fixture between Pisa and Milan at which the winners were presented with medals by Mussolini, which were later requisitioned for the Ethiopian war effort. The fixture between Waseda and Keio in Japan has taken place more than fifty times. The Harvard and Yale match at New London has become almost as legendary as the Oxford and Cambridge, although there is no evidence that the former was inspired by the latter. The first race at Winnipesaukee in 1852 was advertised as the 'marine drama of the age' and suggested by James N. Elkins, superintendent of the Boston, Concord and Montreal Railroad as a means of advertising the 'summer capital of the north' and promoting tourist trade.

Yale produced two crews and Harvard one, coached by their coxswains, and Harvard were victorious. Harvard's boat club had been founded in 1844, a year after Yale's, but the 1852 match was the first inter-collegiate sporting event to be held in the United States, forerunning if hardly heralding the whole shemozzle of football, baseball and athletic rivalry between American colleges.

Like the Oxford and Cambridge match, it was an intermittent fixture at first, moving venue to Springfield, Worcester and Saratoga before settling at New London in 1878, although since then it has been held at Poughkeepsie and at Derby, Connecticut, on one occasion apiece. The New London fixture also became the gathering place for

New England's socialites, particularly in the twenties and thirties when the Thames became a fantastic yacht pageant.

The programme for 1927, for example, is 168 pages, including 86 of advertisements of which 37 are to do with marine matters. The age of the motor launch is in full swing and the gasoline- and diesel-powered yachts mingle with the last of the coal burners and square riggers. It was a fantastic sight at the Harvard–Yale races to see the crews, maybe from the railroad observation train which ran along the side of the course, progress between the ranks of millionaires' craft. George W. Sutton Jr wrote in the programme: 'A glance at the big fleets of sleek, seaworthy motor craft of all types . . . will show that the day when motor boats were the playthings of wealthy and eccentric men passed some time ago.' There is a feature on Yale's new coaching launch, and the usual wag putting his finger on the lunacy of the day.

> Boat races include more pageantry and less net result athletically than any other form of insanity. Whether we journey to the Thames, the Hudson, or the Schuylkill it is, more often than not, *some* journey and after you have arrived you are not there by any means, if you get what I mean. There is still the observation train to be suffered with its long wait while you sit weeping into the Western glare and fussy officials count the waves and measure the winds and the day wanes and the trains that you had planned to take home depart. And have you ever been caught in a boatrace town when it poured buckets and the whole show had to go over to the next day? . . . All the best park benches are in the hands of speculators, etc.,

wrote George S. Chappell.

The advertisements and the cartoons set a scene of carefree affluence which was to take a plunge two years later, but there is not a care in the world in 1927. Assured young men smoke pipes and young women wear scarves fluttering in the breeze, rimless evening specs are offered, and movie cameras by Bell and Howell, Brooks Brothers homespun, flannels, straw and panama hats. The literary set's favourite hotel sends itself up from a *New Yorker* cartoon: 'Algonquin, Critics' honkin'.' Cecil B. de Mille's *King of Kings* has its New England premiere and the Jitney Plays announce the programme for their comedy, tragedy and fantasy on their automobile stage in New England, Long Island and northern New Jersey, including Jerome K.

Jerome's *Sunset*. The cover summarizes the age and the event, at least from the spectator's view: sailing galleys billowing along under a flurry of clouds and a rainbow, a bright sun in God's heaven and a gorgeous moon, swordfish dancing over the fern-bottomed deep. By Charles Child, 50 cents or half a crown in London and 15 francs in Paris. Putney-to-Mortlake was never quite like that.

Thus far the Boat Race has produced offspring and look-alikes as well as its own history and folk tales. But it has also inspired fiction to flesh out the adventures of the nervous or the prankster blues, the arrogant or humble blues, the mutinous or victimized blues. Factual accounts of the race may, as in other of life's courses, be stranger than fiction, but the event seldom embraces all the emotions and archetypes of the theatre on the same occasion. Fiction, though, has filled in most of the gaps unplugged in the race's real pageant. We have already seen that Oxbridge rowing found its way into the work of Thomas Hughes, Ian Hay, Shane Leslie, Max Beerbohm and Cuthbert Bede (the Rev. Edward Bradley). The Harvard–Yale match has inspired counterparts in boys' and undergraduate fiction also, such as the short stories of Waldron Kintzing Post about Harvard and adventures of Yale by Ralph D. Paine, whose hero in *Stroke Oar* is shanghaied to Hamburg and works his passage as a stoker to New York to arrive just in time to take his seat and crush the dastardly Crimsons.

The *Oxford Magazine* of 21 May 1936 carried a long poem written by 'Blair to his friend Michael', better stuff than much on rowing for all its heaviness and haughtiness. It comes close to translating the undergraduate emotions associated with the comradeship of the oar – the feel of the boat and the forming of the perfect machine unsullied by body contact or backers – into a parable for life. It captures much of the feeling of a group who have learned to do something well and cherish the thought afterwards, be they college, blues, or neither. In real life they seldom get on well without some friction, but in mythology they are supposed to meet by chance as they walk their separate paths of life down Piccadilly. Such encounters are not unusual; the proverb is a grand voyage from Isis to Tideway, with the bump, the headship, and Eights Week ever present in life hereafter:

> . . . Funny to meet old John in Piccadilly
> On my last leave! – He just said, 'Hullo, Bow!'
> We lunched together. What's become of Billy?

> He loved to pull the leg of poor old Six
> Who long ago was ferried over Styx. . . .

Wilfred Blair tackled the race itself, giving its different phases different poetic approaches in his 'Bards on the Boat Race' in the *Arena* magazine in 1912. He summoned the poets to produce a ballad drawing on their various approaches, appointing Milton as stakeboat man:

> Thus he. Whereat the coin, descending swift,
> What seemed the likeness of a head displayed. . . .

Browning as oarsman:

> Not a jest, not a jorum; we bent to our yoke,
> Neck by neck, swing by swing, never changing our stroke;

Meredith as spectator:

> Quicker fall the blades as the grim Stroke stretches
>   In his scant zephyr, calling on his crew,
> Arms out, he lengthens. O the bluish oar-blades!
>   O the stark aloofness of the star-skied Blue!

Browning is still pulling:

> 'Twas ding-dong at Crabtree; but as we draw near
> Harrod's Stores, rowing strong, we began to pull clear. . . .

Tennyson is coxing:

> Neat and low, neat and low,
>   Stroke of the 'Varsitee,
> Low, low, swing and row,
>   Stroke of the 'Varsitee!
>
> Swing and kick, swing and kick,
>   Hammersmith Bridge is past;
> Kick, kick, and feather quick,
>   Hammersmith Bridge is past.

Browning is having a rotten time:

> By the meadows Six fainted, and Cox cried, 'Jump clear!
> You are dead to the world, and you look pretty queer,
> We'll remember at Mortlake' – One felt the quick spring
> Of the boat, saw the splashed spray and widening ring,
> And spurted, with horrible heaves of the oar,
> As Six, Five, Four, Three, Two, and Bow swam ashore.

Anon. is a frantic coach on the launch:

> 'Why does your blade drap in sae deep,
>   Eightsmon, eightsmon?
> Why does your blade drap in sae deep,
>   And why sae bad row ye, O?'
> 'O I hae strained my rigger sair,
>   Coachie, coachie;
> O I hae strained my rigger sair,
>   And I canna feather free, O.'

Dobson is in trouble:

> I intended a spurt,
>   And it turned to a bucket.
> Oh, I'll lay my last shirt
> I intended a spurt. . . .

Meanwhile, Browning won the race on his own:

> Then I flung off my zephyr, as Seven fell slack,
> Seized hold of his oar at the small of my back,
> Stood up on my slide as I swung to and fro,
> Called to Cox to give ten, doing forty or so,
> Banged the rowlocks, sang songs (with the foe looking done),
> Till at length into Mortlake I spurted and won.

Byron wrote the epitaph:

> Last eve beheld them simply full of beans,
> Last night brought early bed, the dawning grey
> The needle – and who knows not what that means!

The morn the race itself – the close of day
Dinner's beneficently-big display!
The Empire last receives them, where when shent
They shake the earth anew with sterner fray –
Whence they are outed, bruised, and well content,
Isis and Cam – friend, foe – to one grim Vine St sent!

Rowing has been a popular subject of poets and rhymesters, but their collected works would be a voyage of crabbing, sour bell notes and a less than adequate reverence for timing and rhythm than the ingenious work of Wilfred Blair. Robert Henry Forster was another of the better bards to pen amusements about his sport. He was a force in Lady Margaret rowing in his day, and became captain of Thames RC, chairman of Putney Amateur Regatta, and a novelist. He wrote a superb series of rowing pieces for the *Eagle*, the magazine of St John's College, around the turn of the century, including 'The Debutante' concerning the conversation among boats in a Cam boathouse one night when visited by a galaxy of ghosts:

'Who is it?' whispered the new ship timidly.
'I'm ashamed of your ignorance,' cried the '88 ghost; 'but of course you're too young to know. This is the ghost of the '79 Swaddle, a much more distinguished lady than ever I was or you can hope to be.'
'Oh bother the distinction!' said the elder ghost; 'and yet I daresay I can claim some; I've been where only one other ship has been of all that ever raced.'
'Where was that?' cried a number of voices.
'In the 'Varsity dead heat,' was the answer. . . .

Forster's tale is ingenious and tells much of the craft of boatbuilding and the traditions of the sport in Cambridge which underlie the sustenance of the blues.

Ghosts there may have been, visions certainly, but so far there have been no deaths directly connected with the Boat Race. Except, that is, in David Winser's story *The Boat Race Murder* published in 1942. It is in the classic mould of the whodunnit, and concerns a crew who get a 'fizz' night at Ranelagh Club to boost their spirits, capturing an atmosphere of strain real enough in the last two weeks of practice. During a practice row, one man dies of heart failure, and the finger swings round to various members of the crew because substitution was in the air, providing everyone in the know with a motive. The story is peppered with B film dialogue of the time:

> 'Would you mind if we arrested Matthews and your cox?' the detective asked Solly, the coach.
> 'Yes, old chap,' said Solly. 'We can get another cox, but we haven't any more strokes. Leave them both if you can.'
> The detective looked serious. 'Evidence is bad,' he said.
> Solly leaned back in his chair. 'Trot it out,' he said. 'The cox and I will spoil it. The cox does the crossword in half an hour every morning. . . .'

The satisfactory ending of the story has never occurred in the real life of the race. But crews from the blues have had some spectacular real-life rewards in other parts of the world. Cambridge won a race in Brazil against four opponents in 1956, sponsored by the *Journal des Sports*. Ronnie Howard's 1959 Oxford crew, with two changes, went to Japan sponsored by the newspaper *Asahi Shimbun* and the Japan Amateur Rowing Association. The tour was in August and September and they were not fit enough to row several races, losing the final at Sapporo to Hitotsubashi and Tokyo universities, a length behind the first and half a length behind the second. A few days later Jumbo went missing after the British embassy dance, which Howard found very dull and continuing for too long. He was discovered asleep at the embassy. They had two more races at Kansai regatta and beat each of the Japanese university finalists in turn, first Kansai and then Kyoto. They were entertained royally and raced against Royal Hong Kong Yacht Club in small boats on the way home.

Both Oxford and Cambridge crews, again with several changes, returned to Japan in 1981 and re-enacted the Boat Race on the Sumida river in Tokyo. They were the guests of Channel 12 Television and were there to help celebrate the fiftieth boat race between Waseda and Keio universities, and on the choppy, concrete-lined river Oxford beat Cambridge for the second time before an immense colourful crowd kindled by sunshine, bands and cheerleaders. Nine helicopters whirled overhead in a dance of near death, setting up a fantastic din, almost matched by the flotilla of pursuing craft which came close to swamping the crews at the beginning of the race, and then couldn't keep up.

In 1975 both crews went to Paris and Cambridge beat Oxford on the Seine between the Pont de Sully and the Pont de la Concorde, spectactors lining the banks and the bridges and seeing the Seine Head of River race as well. Oxford crews have appeared at Orio in Spain and Miami in Florida, and several times during the seventies crews from both universities were the guests of honour at the Nile Rowing Festival, a fantastic pilgrimage to one of the places with a good claim to a very early place in rowing history. Two races were arranged involving Egyptian crews, one under the Christmas-time sun of Luxor and one in Cairo. For the inhabitants of Luxor, which claims to be the cradle of civilization and is just across the Nile from the Pharaohs' burial ground in the Valley of the Kings, the rowing is the high point of the year. They line the corniche in their thousands, enthralled by the ceremony of the oars in the Luxor temple, the lighting of an Olympic-type flame, and the parade of the giant foreign oarsmen who, with their sticks held aloft, march through the dignified columns of the temple and along the river bank headed by bands, fêted by buglers, and applauded by white-clad schoolgirls with garlands of flowers. An amazing museum of ancient ferries follows the race, the boats for which are also museum pieces. In ancient times the gods of Thebes processed along this stretch of water to the temple of Amun at Karnak, Isis no doubt included. Luxor in the 1980s is much as it was when Howard Carter found Tutankhamun's tomb in 1922, a watering place for tourists and archaeologists, backed by a dusty Arab and Bedouin town. Several blues found their way there to swim in the Winter Palace pool and pull on the Nile before the Egyptian ambitions broadened to invite internationally representative crews to their two-centre rowing festival.

14

First with the news
Newspapers, wireless and television

This was not simply an extraordinary event calling for full and fresh details, such as the death of the Emperor Napoleon tomorrow would be, or the outbreak of a Fenian insurrection in Ireland. On the contrary, it was a topic to which the attention of two continents had been directed for over a month, the interest constantly rising and everybody concerned having had ample time for all preparations for securing the earliest news. The leading newspapers of the United States and Great Britain were known to be looking forward to and making every possible arrangement for it.

The recipient of this lambast was Cyrus W. Field of the Trans-Atlantic Cable Company. His crime was that his company failed to get George W. Smalley's modest 2200-word report on the Oxford–Harvard race of Friday, 27 August 1869, to the *New York Tribune* in time for the Saturday editions. What made matters worse was that the paper did not publish a Sunday edition, so it missed out badly on the story that America awaited. The *New York Times* came out on the day after the race with five of its six front-page columns devoted to it, and at least thirteen other American papers had their own correspondents filing from the Thames. Unsurprisingly Smalley was beside himself when he learned that his dispatch had not been printed until the Monday edition of the *Tribune*, venting spleen in all directions and still writing to his editor, Whitelaw Reid, a month later: 'You may laugh at me if you like, but the disaster was a blow to me which I have not got over. It left me unfit to do anything but sit on the beach at Dieppe and curse the idiot who caused it.' It was Reid who fired off the complaint to the cable company.

Transmission of news by cable across the Atlantic was still in its infancy. The first cable was layed by the Great Eastern from Volunteer Bay, Ireland, and completed at Heart's Content, Newfoundland, on 28 July 1866. Smalley, who had rowed in the first Harvard–Yale match in 1852 for one of the two Yale crews in the race, then attended Harvard Law School, where he became a vehement campaigner against the repatriation of slaves from Massachusetts to their owners in the South, then became a lawyer in Boston before turning to journalism, could well have sent the first news through the new cable. After reporting the American Civil War for the *Tribune*, he was sent to Europe to cover the Austro-Prussian War, but the conflict lasted only for a few weeks and by the time he arrived the armistice had been signed. From London he cabled a message relaying this to the *Tribune*, forty-nine words for £49. This was sent on 1 August but still took two days to get from Heart's Content to New York.

The opening of the cable made a profound if gradual change in the way in which transatlantic journalism operated. It made foreign correspondents possible, enabling them to attend events abroad and sift newspapers at the point of sale, a great improvement both in the immediacy with which news travelled and in the methods of acquiring it. Previously American papers relied on analysing European papers after they had been brought by sea, and vice versa; by 1869 a combination of the old and the new methods was operated whereby important items were sent expensively by cable and more reflective articles by mail. Thus Smalley, whose knowledge of rowing told him that Oxford were going to win, answered the *New York Times*'s accusation that his Yale prejudices were getting the better of him by signing up three other commentators to help out with the *Tribune*'s coverage. As well he might, after filing pieces about the preparation for the race for weeks and weeks beforehand. Twenty dollars persuaded the Harvard secretary William Blaikie to put a Harvard view of the race into the *Tribune*. Thomas Hughes, already a contributor to the paper, agreed to send letters, a useful little coup because the Liberal MP was referee of the race. And another occasional *Tribune* contributor, the novelist and dramatist Charles Reade, was to write a description of the race which would be rushed aboard the steamship *Russia* on the day of the race. Smalley's first dispatch would be cabled, and his more considered view together with the contributions of Blaikie and Hughes would be sent by sea later.

The disaster of the cable delay was compounded by Charles Reade, who refused to write his report after Harvard lost the race. Smalley was professional enough to quote the man whose role as a foreign correspondent was brief: 'It could hardly be believed in the United States to what extent I, an Oxford man, sympathize with your gallant fellows.' It could well be believed what Smalley, managing editor Whitelaw Reid and the men at the *Tribune* thought of Reade.

Anyway, that was how the *Tribune* was beaten by its rivals on a day when the *Echo* in London got 25,000 copies of its extra onto the streets within threequarters of an hour of the end of the race. The *Illustrated London News* said that in the remote districts of Yorkshire, the savage valleys in the north, the out-of-the-way nooks in Wales, wherever tourists came across one another, the first eager question was about the race. The *Tribune* reported the mood of New York City, crowds gathering outside the newspaper offices' bulletin boards, Mayor Hall running up the flags on City Hall, curbstone operators noting bets in their stockbooks, and Wall Street patriotically giving up the legitimate business of the day. Newspapers on both sides of the ocean had reported the run-up to the race for four months and were to spend another month examining the entrails; this was the treatment that future international sports events and future wars and political crises were to receive, beginning with the Franco-Prussian War soon afterwards.

While the press was quick to reflect the snobbery of boat racing, the London *Times* (for which Smalley later became the New York correspondent) pointing out that the Harvard men 'are of the best families of New England, although one of them nominally "hails" from the Sandwich islands . . . ,' the newspapers also made perhaps legitimate, perhaps inflated claims which the event afforded for advances in understanding between nations so far apart. 'For the first time in the history of either people, the nation of England has been brought in close rapport with the nation of America,' said *London Society*. The *New York Times* dismissed the sceptics as to the race's importance: 'There are, perhaps, a few aberrant philosophers still in existence who will look down from their serene eminence on this memorable contest, and smile at what they regard as the folly and vanity of mankind. But philosophers never rule the world, and seldom comprehend the motive-power by which it is governed.'

Until the coming of wireless broadcasts of the Boat Race, the newspapers were the only conveyers of the result. Competing with one another, they went to considerable lengths to be first and to be best informed about all the minutiae of activity surrounding the day. In 1898 the *Westminster Gazette* published a piece among its extensive coverage of the race telling the public how it was that the papers moved their information from Putney and Mortlake to the world outside. Horse-drawn post offices were positioned near the Duke's Head in Putney and at the winning post, square-shaped tents being erected outside the vans as operating rooms. Two Wheatstone instruments, manned by operators, were set up in the tents and a third remained in the van, which also carried its own length of cable to plug into the main wires. Pencils and a heap of telegram forms were set out ready for the onslaught of the 'specials', whose messages would be sent in Morse on little rolls of green paper. 'Jove never sent his thunders smarter, nor did the youthful Mercury of the Greeks deliver his message with more alacrity, than do the Post Office officials despatch today the commonplace words "Oxford won . . . lengths" or "Cambridge won . . . lengths" along their line,' said the *Gazette*. Before that, though, the scene had to be set. The special correspondents were out testing the weather, estimating the crowd, finding the latest odds, monitoring the crews' last minutes of practice, reviewing the prospects and profiling the men. The Post Office's records from around this time show more than 120 messages sent from the temporary office at Putney and more than 250 from the permanent office there.

Once the race was under way a variety of methods was used to get the news out first. Reporters would employ boys to lie in wait for the press launch in rowing boats. The correspondent would write copy up to the last moment, usually in duplicate or triplicate by means of transfer paper, seal it in an airtight tin box and throw it to his boy, with a second version for good measure should the first bob away on the turbulence of the Tideway. The runner then rows off for the shore in a scrabble for the post office, where the copy is dispatched at 300–400 words a minute. Carrier pigeons are also used, some to nearby locations like Richmond or Barnes where company representatives take the messages to the post offices with less business than those close to the course. Others of the feathered runners are express long-distance fliers, winging away to a loft in London or more distant shires. Meanwhile siege has been lain to any telephone within hailing distance of the finishing post, and the Exchange Telegraph Company has left no stone unturned. They have set up their own field wire along the course,

have cyclists stationed at key points along it, and have placed signal-
men on loan from the Guards at strategic bankside points so that,
according to the editor John Boon, they can compile a runner with a
message each half a second. The result is known by their 'thousand and
one' newspaper clients a few seconds after reaching their Haymarket
headquarters, and in New York within half a minute. As the *Gazette*
says, 'You have barely time to cry out "Heigh presto" at Mortlake
before the London public knows which of the two crews are heroes of
the hour.'

Speed was everything to the newspapers. The *Cambridge Daily
News*, after telling its readers in 1906 that 'according to custom the
Varsity watermen, Walter Taylor (Oxford) and Cooie Phillips (Cambridge), together with the London and Leander watermen, Ted and
John Phelps, spent the night in watching the boats,' concluded its
report of the race with a blast on its own trumpet: 'Start was at three
minutes past 12. Time of winner 19 mins 24 secs. Race thus concluded
at 22 mins 24 secs past 12, and at 26 mins past 12 the *Cambridge Daily
News* was on sale with the result in the streets. A few minutes later a
second special edition was issued containing a full report of the race.'

Pigeons were employed by bookmakers and punters as well as
newspapers. Martin Cobbett recalls in his memoirs that many interesting coups had been brought off in the Boat Race by betting men, and
how for example the 'wise or cute men of Hampton Court and East
Molesey were broke to a pebble, thanks to the pigeon express and
finding mugs.' What happened, according to Cobbett, was that Cambridge came under Barnes Bridge with an impossible lead. 'Great as
was the enterprise on behalf of the stroke (C. B. Lawes) who dug his
oar in and hoicked it out at the rate of *x* to the minute, it seemed almost
as though, should he join the army of martyrs done to a turn in the
good cause, the tide would float what I believe I have heard described
as an octette up to the winning post before the followers could catch
them up. . . .' A pigeon reached Hampton Court, a light blue ribbon
tied round its foot, and pockets were emptied on the strength of the tip.
Meanwhile, however, Oxford came through to win by four lengths.
Cobbett's memory played him a trick in his recall, for assuming that he
named the Cambridge stroke correctly, the year was 1865, and the
light blues were in the lead at Hammersmith Bridge, not Barnes. But
this makes the tale more plausible. On many occasions the bookies'
runners would give false information or use private codes to relay the

progress of the race, and so there were several points where the punter could come unstuck.

Another ploy used in getting the result out first was the use of rockets. J. B. Booth describes the unfortunate results in *A Pink 'Un Remembers*:

A rival paper tried the effect of sound as a method of sending signals, and scored a success by means of rockets, which at a great height exploded a charge of gun-cotton. At the last moment the gentleman with the rockets heard that an opponent had also planned to send up rockets for himself, and promptly decided to help him. An assistant was instructed to buy some ordinary rockets, and hide in some quiet place adjacent to the rival's lair. If he saw one rocket go up, he was to fire two; if two went up he was to fire an assortment, to make things a trifle indefinite. The assistant was a firework enthusiast. Laying in a stock of three or four dozen, he eagerly awaited the first rocket from the enemy's camp. It came, and seizing the opportunity for enjoying himself, he indulged in a miniature Brock's Benefit and fired off his entire collection. The face of the rival, who had to receive the signals at Mortlake, when he saw the display, was tragic.

Betting on the Boat Race was, of course, one of the main reasons why the populace took the fixture to heart. It was as simple and as unpredictable – in the ordinary course of events – as backing two flies walking up the wall.

The 1980s are a very different picture regarding both the betting and the news gathering. The race is now sponsored by Ladbrokes the bookmakers and the punters are catered for almost exclusively by their shops. The newspapers still play an important role, but a changed one in the light of live radio and television broadcasts. The world no longer relies on the buzzing of the wires and the rushed Saturday sport editions to learn the result, but the newspapers on Sunday and Monday are the places where the analyses and the colouring of the incidents can be found, and often where a telling photograph will illuminate a point of weakness or strength. It is also the job of the reporters on those papers which cover rowing regularly to tell aficionados what is happening during the long weeks of preparation and to make their predictions of the result, to examine the conditions of the course and the men. Thus although the two weeks of Putney-based practice go largely unattended by the rowing fraternity and by the fans, who have better things to do than hang about on the embankment seeing very little for hours on end, the press launch run by the Newspaper Press Boat Fund is in daily attendance, usually with three or four motley lunatics huddled together in the driving rain or freezing sleet, or if they are lucky in a crisp and brilliant spring morning. They have pencils and 'Wet Notes' and rating watches and stopwatches and try to make some sense out of a series of three-minute pieces or a piece of pacing against another crew or a series of starts from a stakeboat. There you will find the huge frames of Desmond Hill of the *Daily Telegraph* (Oxford, 1940) and Richard Burnell of the *Sunday Times* (Oxford, 1939), the former in his point-to-point cloth cap and Leander scarf, the latter wearing a motorcycle helmet visor over his cossack hat and spectacles. Here you will find Geoffrey Page of the *Sunday Telegraph* displaying his unique knowledge of the Tideway learned as a schoolboy and then as captain of the arch rival Purples, London University; and the Press Association's veteran Bill Martin wearing a bright blue boiler suit and flexing his prodigious memory of heavies. Here you will find Jim Railton of *The Times* huddled in a scarlet-lined pea coat and wool skull cap and shades and mimicking anything that moves that day, and Christopher Dodd of the *Guardian* in walking boots and a disreputable old track suit pulled over every other garment, hands deep in pockets because he has usually lost his gloves and screwing his spectacled visage against the elements which they all curse. Sometimes there are others, sometimes hardly any, driven back and forth on the tide by the ever-cheerful Chas Newens. Sometimes, with good reason, a hip flask does the rounds, for most of these men have flu long before Boat Race day. Embarkation and disembarkation on the beach at Putney is one of the most undignified sights in the world today.

On the day itself there are two launches, *Enchantress* and *Aquarius*, with the numbers swollen by the *Financial Times*, the *Daily Mail*, the *Washington Post*, and so on, with photographers and film cameramen; and if the starting time is late in the day, there is a mad scramble for quotes at the finish and telephones which have usually been booked at houses nearby. At times like this the proceedings resemble the hectic pre-broadcasting days. But the style of the newspaper coverage began to change when the British Broadcasting Corporation started live commentary in 1927. It is personified by John Snagge, who followed forty-five Boat Races for the BBC and was there almost from the beginning, but Gully Nickalls and Sir John Squire were on the launch on that first memorable occasion.

Nickalls and Squire were on board the *Magician* with four engineers, an assistant, a pilot and a ship's engineer and about 1000 pounds weight of generator and batteries amounting to a transmitter. They had no idea whether what they were saying was being received on shore. The specially built transmitter sent its message via a horizontal aerial slung between masts to four reception points along the river, nobody really knowing if the range was right. Nickalls, who was auditioned for the part by being asked to read some random prose, presumed that all this proved was that he could read and speak. Eventually, according to his account, he and Squire were competing to pour words into the microphone, Squire by stamping on Nickalls's foot when he thought it was his turn. The broadcast was successful. Every word had gone out clearly, said Lance Sieveking, who was in charge of the technicalities, and the Director-General John Reith had sent his congratulations.

This was the second live outside commentary, the first being the England versus Scotland rugby match at Twickenham on 15 January that year. The significant thing about the Boat Race, however, was that the commentators had to move with the race. Snagge, a young broadcaster employed by the BBC, got his first chance in 1931 when the corporation decided to cultivate its own talent. A rowing man, like his father before him, from Winchester and New College, Oxford, he was not a blue, something which Fred Pitman admonished the BBC for without avail. He quickly became the famous voice of the Boat Race, instantly recognized by millions of listeners the world over, and although he devoted not much more than a day a year to it among his commentating and other duties, it is, perhaps unfairly, for the race that he is known. He certainly made it his own, a superb piece of wireless drama each year, ad-libbing the script through narrative description to moments of humour, farce, tragedy, a subtle interpreter of a plot which unfolded before him but which he did not write, which was supposed to be roughly the same on each occasion but which could surprise and baffle and bore. Snagge had rich vocal chords on his side, a deep Winchester and Oxford voice perfectly in keeping with a state or stately occasion but which never betrayed a hint of class, snobbery, patronization or crass ignorance. His knowledge of rowing he learned at New College, but his sense of occasion and human contact, his ability to keep a good story going and freeze an immense audience to the edge of their chairs when in reality the cause was clearly won or lost, he learned at Stoke-on-Trent.

There he began his broadcasting career as the announcer at the BBC's relay station, and for the local programmes he and the producer did their own thing. He read news bulletins supplied by the *Staffordshire Sentinel*, sang duets with the producer on their children's programme which ran a birthday club at 6d a mention, with proceeds to the local orthopaedic hospital, and ran a weekly show using local talent, including an orchestra and chorus formed for the programme. In his four years there Snagge learned more than in the rest of his time as a broadcaster. He learned how to cope with the people of a mining and pottery community whose language he did not understand, how to be with them, how to behave, how to enjoy their company, and how to find out who they were, what they did, what made them tick. When he went back to re-open the station nearly half a century later, several of them recognized him as he wandered about the town and the pubs incognito, remembered what he drank and where the conversation left off.

Snagge is very much a child of the live broadcast, mistrusting the recording where if something goes wrong everything can be done again. 'You cannot broadcast live, however experienced you are, without a butterfly in your stomach,' he says. It is a great challenge, requiring concentration and thinking ahead. 'You think, "So far I've got away with it . . . is this going to be my Waterloo? Am I going to drop the mother and father of a brick?" I'm always nervous.' His famous gaffe to the effect that he couldn't see who was in the lead but it was either Oxford or Cambridge he had no recollection of until he heard a recording afterwards, but he has never dried up, not even when somebody he has taken aboard has done so, like the Everest climber Tom Brocklebank (Cambridge, 1929–31), who at Hammersmith said only, 'As far as I'm concerned, it's all over,' and handed the microphone back. They've got the needle as badly as the crew, Snagge says. Or the Director of Outside Broadcasts, S. J. de Lotbiniere, who was the commentator in an aeroplane when the BBC first used one in 1939 to judge the distance between the crews, and when asked to take over by Snagge at Barnes by a question as to how far Cambridge were in front, said, 'Three and a half lengths; back to the launch.' Lotbiniere was feeling the dire effects of the tight-circling plane. But not drying up is experience, not brilliance, says Snagge. You could always have a blackout, or your memory could go.

During his long reign, now taken over by Brian Johnstone, the technicalities of the outside broadcast have changed beyond recognition. In the early days the commentator had no link with the land at all, but now he is not quite alone because he has two-way communication. No longer does he have to watch for an engineer's white handkerchief on the roof of Harrods depository to know if he's being received. There is now only one reception point and a small transmitter can range four to five miles from the launch, a miniaturization and improvement in broadcasting which owes a great deal to the Boat Race and the demands of its broadcasters. It is light years away from the shipload of batteries and the telephone line known as the Post Office Appointment to connect with the studio of pioneer days.

There have been some spectacular disasters in the broadcasting. One year the launch broke down at Duke's Meadows and was almost swamped by the pursuant steamers and Snagge couldn't see the end of the race. This was unfortunate for him because it was the 1952 win-by-a-canvas by Oxford, the closest finish of his lifetime. Until, that is, the last one on which he commentated when Francis collapsed in the Oxford boat and the dark blues won by a canvas. That is his most memorable race for that reason. He once did the commentary from the *Sir John Peel*, a police launch, perched beside the helmsman with the engineers still installing equipment in odd corners of the boat, because the BBC launch had slipped her moorings during the night before the race. She was found beached at Wandsworth but there was not time to test everything and make sure that the boat was undamaged. One year when Sir William Hailey, Director-General of the BBC, was on board, the press launch got caught in the wash of the BBC launch and during the confusion of the bump, the *Sunday Times* correspondent Edgar Tomlin jumped aboard. 'I am delighted to see there is still great enterprise in Fleet Street,' said Sir William when he learned the identity of the uninvited guest.

Snagge has got his feet wet, too, though mercifully not during a race but after the debacle of the sinking in 1951 when the tide was very high and the soaked crews came ashore at Putney. The water was over the embankment and he was piggybacked from one boathouse to another trying to inquire what was to be done about a result or a rerow. Eventually he rolled his trousers up and, still clutching his microphone, plied as a paddling messenger between camps until he was able to inform the world, and the Port of London Authority who had not been asked, that there would be another race on the following Monday.

He has had some strange experiences, such as watching the collapse of the 6-foot 6-inches Barnard in the Oxford boat of 1957. 'He just broke down, couldn't take it. It was a very strange thing, he just sat there doing nothing, and the stroke said afterwards that it was exactly like pressing the accelerator of a car and nothing happened at all.' He has lived by his own judgement without realizing it, when in the early days he used to gauge the distance between the boats at Duke's Meadows by a couple of flags run up on a pole at the bank. After several years he met the flagman in a bar, thanked him for his work, but joked that he didn't watch him any more because he, Snagge, was always right. 'I should bloody well hope my flags are accurate,' said the flagman, 'for I do it from what you say on the wireless.' He once extracted the secret of the blues which explains why an umpire is necessary and why he has to take a grip, on 'Children's Hour'. He was interviewing the only blue in the forthcoming race and asked him if he thought he had any advantage over the fifteen new oarsmen. Yes, said the artful blue: 'Any damn fool can start on the word "go" but it takes experience to start on the word "Are . . . ?" '

Snagge once got the BBC's engineers to consider if the losing crew have the disadvantage of having to row uphill. This arose from a letter to *The Times* in which such a theory was put, and the answer came back that it could be so, depending on the speed and the depth of the water. From the bows of a sailing boat in shallow water, they explained, you can see the water coming down towards you. The cavalcade of launches and steamers could have the effect of pulling the water down and thus causing the nearest racing boat, which does not pull water towards it, to row uphill.

It was great good fortune that Snagge turned down the proffered job as Controller for Northern Ireland in 1952, for he was to continue to be heard on the air during Boat Races, coronations and such events. Several years ago he presented a gold sovereign dating from 1829, the year of the first race, to the presidents to use for the toss. Finding one of the right year took him eighteen months, but he eventually located a mint one at £75 and a used one at £25 in a shop round the corner from Broadcasting House. When the dealer found out who Snagge was and why he wanted a coin, he said he would be prepared to sell the mint one for the worth of its weight in gold at the current price, if Snagge would take the gamble that it could come out at more than £75. The commentator took the plunge, the dealer weighed the coin, and Snagge paid just over £5 for it. He then unwittingly caused a problem by writing to the presidents asking them to accept the coin for the toss, which they did, and deciding with them that the winning club would be responsible for the coin until the next year. The Amateur Rowing Association heard of the scheme and pointed out that there was a danger of the Boat Race victors losing their amateur status if they kept the coin, because they would have competed for a money prize. It did not seem to matter that the coin was only vested in the club for a year. The problem was solved, says Snagge, by Gully Nickalls, who suggested that the *losing* crew should keep the coin because it was up to them to issue the challenge each year and because nobody could be deemed to lose amateur status by gaining a sovereign for losing a race.

What John Snagge has enjoyed about his years with the battling blues has been their enthusiasm for the race, their good manners, their goodness towards him. He was a man for his age, a period when a newfangled means of communication changed the role of the newspapers to that of views- and/or reviewspapers. Print was for opinion and, as important, analysis; wireless was for news and mystery, with Snagge as the assured narrator of who-will-do-it and whodunnit. Television has brought its own insight to the Boat Race audience. First you read, then you listened, now you see, warts and all. It has not invalidated either the newspapers or the radio, but it has removed much of an important ingredient in the event: mystique.

The Boat Race was first televised from the bank in 1938, eighteen months after the first transmission and a year after the first outside broadcast, the coronation of George VI. The occasion was almost wrecked by a workman at Muswell Hill whose pick severed a cable which cut off Alexandra Palace, the BBC's television headquarters, from telephonic communication. The cameraman near the finish transmitted messages to the Palace and the pictures were clear, but commentary there could be none. Eventually the wireless commentary was broadcast to television viewers while an animated diagram of progress was shown. The commentator Howard Marshall arrived hot foot at Ally Pally and spoke to the pictures received from the river bank in time for the finish, and sound was restored by Post Office engineers to get interviews with spectators at the end.

The real milestone in television, however, was passed in 1949, when the race was followed from beginning to end for the first time. This was made possible by the development of a ship-to-shore radio link. A hundred technicians and commentators and nine cameras were used altogether, and the deployment of every piece of outside broadcasting equipment was a great success, its results being picked up freakishly in Cape Town for about twenty minutes. The launch kept up for most of the distance, and there was another BBC triumph that day. For the first time they succeeded in producing a Telecine – a television recording – by photographing the screen during the race and the whole thing was repeated in the evening. This was the forerunner of video recording. The writing was thus put on the embankment wall for the newsreel companies like Movietone, for whom Gully Nickalls was doing the commentaries.

The Boat Race remains one of the BBC's largest outside broadcasts, in terms of the number of camera crews deployed and the number of viewers. Six million two hundred thousand people watched it in 1982, a low figure because of the sunny afternoon, but viewers in Australia, Italy, Japan, Korea, Portugal, Spain and the United States could also see it in its entirety, and those who get a glimpse of it in news bulletins, especially in a year with an incident like a sinking, can be counted in tens of millions. A helicopter now hovers overhead so that the full aerial reality of a four-length advantage at Barnes Bridge leaves no one in doubt as to the improbability of the losers making up the water, save by accident or act of God. But television is not yet the perfect medium for the race, and the race still gives it a challenge which has spurred its technical development. The BBC has tried taking commentators and monitor screens on the water without great success, and has not got over the problem that the viewer mostly gets a picture showing only one crew or a panorama in which they are both specks. That spells trouble for the commentators, too. They are in a hut beside Vesta Rowing Club, watching a bank of monitors with an assistant taking ratings, but they do not see what the radio and newspaper reporters see from the launches. The eyes of the cameras are not their eyes. They have a selection of images but no freedom to choose their own. The human eye is quick and receptive to incident, but the TV eye can only go where someone points it, and that may be too late. Thus they are often not much better placed than Marshall was in Alexandra Palace in 1938, though unquestionably the pictures, sound, assistance and information are all vastly improved on what he had. Wherever you put him, it is sometimes harder for the television commentator, despite his bank of monitors, to pick up the nuances which others who are out on the water can see. Although the camera does not lie, except by parallax, the orchestration of the cameras can leave a serious gap. Also, the temptation for commentators to talk all the time leaves them more opportunities for drying up or repeating themselves or stating the obvious simply because their vision is mostly accessible to their listeners. The radio man is still his own man, with his reminiscence, his imagination, his ingenuity and his notes to draw on. The newspaper man, even if he is in a hurry, can rework his material and check it before he makes it public. The television commentator is much more a prisoner of his medium when it comes to imagination; but on the other hand he has plenty of scope for reminiscence.

The challenge which reporting the race gives to television has spurred technical development in the youngest branch of the media just as it did for newspapers and wireless. Gyro heads have been developed for mounting cameras on vibrating boats. Filming from helicopters has been adapted to other outside broadcasts, both in sports events and in other spheres such as reviewing the Fleet or great processional occasions, and during the Boat Race itself the commentator has near-perfect aerial coverage for the entire time, a feat in itself. The BBC has experimented with several methods of electronic transmission. Originally, there were cameras only at the start and the finish and one on a launch. Then came a period which John Vernon, who directed the show from 1957 to 1977, reckons to have been the most effective, when the hiring of the *Everest*, which had an exceptionally strong cabin roof and was designed partially with the race in mind, enabled two cameras to be mounted on board. One of the most successful cameramen was Bill Wright, who became the begetter and first producer of the eggheads' quiz programme, 'Mastermind'. The commentators at that time, Desmond Hill and Peter West, and the director sailed as well in the company of the monitors. Cramped conditions eventually led to commentators, their keeper of the watches, and the director coming ashore, albeit backed by fifteen cameras, the most important of which are naturally those on the water and in the air. Harry Carpenter, a former rowing correspondent of the

Daily Mail replaced Peter West, and later Jim Railton replaced Desmond Hill. Now the senior national rowing coach, Penny Chuter, has replaced Railton, and Vernon has been succeeded by David Kenning. It remains essentially a live show, although parts of the build-up such as the toss and the crews coming out are sometimes videotaped so that they can be dovetailed with other items of the day's sporting events. There is still, though, at least one kick-back to the days of Honest John Phelps and the traditional lines of communication at the finish. The official time for the race is taken on the press launch, passed verbally to the judge, who writes it on a blackboard for the television director, who reads it off to the commentator.

Ever since the Boat Race began it has played a significant role in communication, from its own problems of timekeeping and judging the distance at the finish to informing its public who won and why, by print, sound, or vision. Its contribution has been enormous simply because of the challenge that it, a simple but long-distance event, throws up. No other sports event requires the reporter in whatever guise to observe the minute close-up detail of, say, quirky bladework which may give the clue to trouble and the immense panoply of the moving pageant, causing him to travel with it over four and a quarter miles. Ideally he needs the bird's eye view, the bowman's view, the coxswain's view, the umpire's view, the lady-on-Hammersmith-Bridge's view and the finishing judge's view all at once. Of course he cannot get them all. He can sometimes get close to several of them, but even television's vast technical resources have not got him all the way. The Boat Race is still a big challenge for the moving picture, even with the split screen, the action replay, and the use of more than one commentator. And it is still a challenge for any interpreter because each is in a slightly different place, each judges speed and light differently, and because boats, wind and tide change course and interact. So the fixture often retains some mystique even in an age when we think we can see it all.

PART FOUR
Needle

15

The antagonists
Separate development, common denominator

In 1982 the university boat clubs of Oxford and Cambridge prepared to race each other for the 128th time. The annual free show staged in London by two universities from the provinces was under way long before Cambridge's president, Roger Stephens, formally issued the challenge to Nick Conington, his opposite number at Oxford. Stephens had little short of revolution on his mind for his attempt to revive the fortunes of the Cam by reversing a run of six defeats, while Conington was looking to the many well-proven assets of an Oxford system which had given Cambridge six of the worst. From their elections by their college captains in May 1981 they would be single-minded about the main purpose of life until the afternoon of 27 March 1982. They, and a small band of others, would plan, organize, train and orchestrate the performing side in a fantastic display of eccentricity. As of so many sporting things, others could imitate but only an Englishman could have started it. Considering its world-wide millions of partisans, considering the institution which the simple race has become, considering the tradition which has grown up while it has slipped along with the times, the fact that both the clubs which stage it hardly exist comes as a surprise. Neither club has permanent members. In theory, each is composed only of members of the current eight.

Oxford University Boat Club owns no premises. It possesses some boats and a van and a few crews are formed each year, of whom the most important is the blue boat. All the aims that it may harbour developed as a step towards winning from Putney to Mortlake, or are very much secondary to doing so. Cambridge is very similar, the difference being that the Goldie boathouse is exclusively available to the club, a handsome bequest. Each crew is different each year, not just in personnel, but in character. Crews are unique and exclusive, whether they be good, bad or indifferent, notwithstanding that a few individuals span several years in blue boats.

The only constants are the professional boatmen of the two clubs, coaches who are theoretically invited to coach by the respective presidents each year, and a small number of old heavies, some of whom busybody but some of whom perform usefully by running sideshows such as dinners and weekends off, the things that make the boys feel they have support.

And so it came about in May 1981 that the two men pivotal to the 1982 Boat Race were Graeme Hall and Daniel Topolski, the chief coaches. It was to the thirty-five-year-old litigation lawyer Hall that Stephens sent his invitation to counsel his revolution, and it was to the capable hands of the thirty-nine-year-old freelance journalist Topolski that Conington offered the fortune of the dark blues. Both men are winning blues, both have won medals in British crews, indeed in the same one, and both have considerable experience of coaching international crews. Both men have needle burning deeply in them, and needle is the constant that has kept the Battle of the Blues alive annually, except for a few war years, since 1856.

Topolski first went rowing in Regent's Park, on the lake practically visible from the house where he was brought up and still lives. At Westminster School he wanted to play soccer, but his father, the energetic emigré Polish artist Feliks Topolski, persuaded him to go down to the Thames. Rowing more than soccer suited Feliks's idea of traditional amateur English sport. An Isis oarsman, Ian Ross, was running the school's rowing but the real inspiration for the young and light Topolski was the professional boatman Ted Phelps. 'I sculled a lot under his guidance and began to get quite fast. I was far too light, but he taught me technique and nous.'

Lightweight rowing was to play a considerable part in the lives of both Hall and Topolski, but in the days of their youth there was no recognized lightweight category in Britain or at official international level for adult oarsmen. Technique and nous were thus very essential ingredients for men under 12 stone if they were to excel, and Topolski found them early in his schoolboy career on the Tideway. He soon came to know the championship course well, its tides, its feel, its moods, because Westminster boated from Putney.

Phelps was advisor to Jumbo Edwards when he brought his Oxford crews to the Tideway. Jumbo was an old Westminster who sometimes did a bit of coaching for his old school, and, as we have seen, he kept the dark blue needle burnished sharp through long years of frustration in defeat. To a schoolboy he imparted enthusiasm and got through as a thinker.

Topolski earned his seat in Westminster's first eight, and as captain of boats the following year his crew was coached by Jumbo. They had some pacing outings with both Oxford and Cambridge blue boats, and went to Henley. In October 1964 he went up to New College, Oxford, to read geography and within four months was captain of boats there. Glandular fever interrupted his attempt to get a blue in 1965 but he joined an Isis four in the summer who reached the semifinal round of the Wyfolds at Henley. In 1966 he helped Isis to their seven-length win over Goldie. In 1967 he got into the blue boat. OUBC bought four new sculling boats and a second-hand one from the proceeds of providing two crews for the filming of *Half a Sixpence* and coaching Tommy Steele and other actors. President Jock Mullard sent his men sculling and Jumbo coached them in the eight at Wallingford for six weeks. Mullard had difficulty with his squad because Chris Albert and Fred Carr were removed from rowing by their tutors, and he was apprehensive about the Group Captain's relationship with the crew. After the first outing, however, they all ate out of the hand of the fêted flier. And they beat Cambridge by three and a quarter lengths in a boat built by Sims of Eel Pie Island, with Topolski in the number seven seat. At 11 stone 13 pounds he was a stone and a half lighter than the next lightest oarsmen in the race. As it turned out, they were the last winning Oxford crew to be coached by Jumbo. His record by Topolski's count was thirteen losers and five winners.

For the 1968 race John R. Bockstoce of Yale and St Edmund Hall was president and Topolski was in the bow seat, officially the lightest man in either boat at 11 stone 6 pounds. They may have had an American president but the thoughts of some of the Oxford men, Topolski included, were on the Olympic Games to be held in the airy heights of Mexico City. Jumbo was in charge, and Dan remembers complacency in the crew. They had five blues and they thought they were better than they were, and they went to Reading University's Head of River race and lost their place to the University of London. Only by a second, but they didn't realize that UL were a fast crew who, unbeknown to anybody at the time, were on their way to Mexico.

Furthermore, Goldie were only two seconds behind Oxford.

The Christ Church boatman George Harris and the OUBC boat-man Albert Andrews were both critical of the crew, but Bockstoce by his own later admission didn't heed their warnings. Meanwhile, Jumbo panicked after Reading. He experimented with extraordinary Italian rig, for which two, three, six and seven rowed on bow side, the rest on the other. The club had not bought a new boat to save money, and this could have been a mistake. Topolski reckons that gunwales were weak, causing him in the bow seat great trouble keeping his blade covered at the finish of the stroke. But some photographs show a chronic lack of togetherness which would have caused similar effect. They lost the race by three and a half lengths. The lightest man in the Cambridge boat that day was the one with the best view of Topolski's straining back, the second-year law student in the stroke seat. He weighed 11 stone 10 pounds but was officially 12 stone because he was told not to weigh in at under 12 stone. He was an old boy of Tiffin School in Kingston and an undergraduate at Downing, and his name was Graeme Hall.

It was a great moment for Hall, a man who had found enthusiasm and nous in quite different ways from Topolski. He also had the fanaticism of the convert, though his vision took place early in his life. 'When I was six or seven years old,' he says, 'I became aware that I wanted to row in the Boat Race.' He was living on the north side of Plymouth and there were no rowing connections in his family. He recalls supporting Oxford at the time. The Plymouth schoolboy became so wrapped up in the race that he couldn't bear to watch it on television. He was tall for his age, rode horses and played rugby at Devonport High School, and then the family moved to London and Graeme was sent to Tiffin. He contracted rheumatic fever during his fourth term there but went on to row three times in the Princess Elizabeth Cup at Henley. On the last two occasions he stroked the boat. He was coached by Keith Southern, the rowing master, who had been at Downing College, Cambridge, and in the school's first eight by Tim Shaw, a cox at Thames Rowing Club and now coach at Fitz-william College, Cambridge.

The rheumatic fever put Hall on penicillin for seven years and caused a technical hitch in his academic career. He secured a place to read engineering at Downing but couldn't take it up until he had passed a second language apart from French, having dropped Latin during his illness. He flunked German in his last year in the sixth, enrolled for every German course available at Kingston Technical College where, he says, they were very good, and emerged, speaking German, to a pre-university engineering job with Vickers in Swindon.

He joined Wallingford Rowing Club where he encountered the rough and tumble of club life for the first time, impressing them enough to become stroke of their eight. Here he met Jumbo. 'He was quite something because he was a big name, but he was very distant.' Hall sensed, he says, immediate prejudice against him because of his lack of experience and size, but he was impressed by how the club oarsmen got on with the job. They were self-disciplined, they worked hard, no allowances or excuses were made. Eventually there were four lighter men sitting behind Hall in the Wallingford eight who went to Henley's Thames Cup in 1966. They beat Crowland and then Burway and then lost the quarter final by two lengths to Harvard. The Americans went on to beat Isis, with Topolski in the bow seat, in the final. Hall went on with Wallingford to a round of pot-hunting in small boats at West Country regattas, an enjoyable and eye-opening preliminary to the world of big men he was to enter at Cambridge.

Hall realized from the start that if he was going to get anywhere he would have to keep out of things as much as possible at the beginning. It was the age of the big Ratzeburg eights, German crews compiled of huge men who were world beaters, and so the fashion was to find big men, race them against each other, get them super-fit and shoot them up and down the slides as if there was no tomorrow. The compilation of half-truths about the Germans filtered through to backwaters where people had big ideas. Hall entered for the CUBC trials, always conscious of the prejudice against oarsmen of his weight of around 12 stone, and lied about it. However, he found himself in the CUBC final sixteen where, he says, he was the lightest man by 20 pounds, and he was in the stroke seat of Goldie for the 1967 race, with Mike Tebay, a dropped blue, at seven. 'We were faster than the blue boat. The philosophy was to do ridiculously high rates in the boat which we called the Banham dung barge. We were coached by an American, Peter Conze, who used to yell, "Roll right up and go right in." ' They won the Bedford Head in record time with a record following stream, and they beat Isis by going as far as Hammersmith Bridge rating 36 strokes to the minute, 'where everyone stopped for a smoke'.

After that Hall, who began academic life at Cambridge by switching from engineering to law and made his mark at sculling by reaching the semifinals of the Colquhoun Sculls, stroked the Downing eight in the Ladies' Plate at Henley and then went back to rough and tumble for the summer, this time in the Thames skiffing regattas. The next year Downing had a good crew for the Cambridge Light Fours, and at CUBC the boatman, Alf Twinn, took a shine to Hall. 'He bawled and screamed at me for a month and got my rowing sorted out,' says Hall. Twinn had had a bad time with the previous president, Lindsay Henderson, who offended the waterman in him by applying a graphite finish to the blue boat's hull at Putney. This was the first of Banham's short boats with a rudder behind, and Henderson thought to borrow the latest idea from the treatment of racing yacht hulls. His crew lost the Boat Race, and Twinn never spoke to him again. When he got the boat back to the quiet of the Goldie boathouse, the boatman rubbed it down to the bare wood and revarnished it.

So Alf backed a good Goldie man and Hall beat his rival Jocelyn Cadbury, who had won the Ladies' Plate with First and Third Trinity, each time they met. He 'grabbed a bit off the start' on each occasion, and, at a Henley training camp under Derek Drury, Hall replaced Cadbury in the stroke seat of the A crew on the second day and never left it. He became a member of a crew who began as underdogs but developed tremendous spirit, a strong will to win, and were backed by considerable experience. Oxford were strong favourites at the start of the campaign and remained so until after their debacle at Reading, but by Boat Race day the punters were backing the light blues.

Their experience was decisive. Hall's apprenticeship with Wallingford was more than matched by Robin Winckless, who had rowed a lot with Kingston's Thames Cup eights, Nick Hornsby of London RC, and Chris Powell of the Leander cadets. Wally Church was the bow man who won the Ladies' in the same crew as Jocelyn Cadbury, and Geoffrey Leggett and the president, Pat Delafield, had rowed with Winckless and Hornsby for Leander in the Grand. Delafield provided the inspiration. He was a big, powerful Jesus man, a fast sculler who led by example. He emphasized sculling, which was the central plank of Tideway Scullers' School with whom Cambridge were forging links, and the squad did a lot of it, Hall being the only one who beat Delafield, and that only once. He cut into the tradition of Cambridge a little, dropping the high protein lunches of mince, poached eggs and spinach which made everyone feel rotten afterwards when they went to row. But they took breakfast and dinner together, went to Oxford to see the Varsity boxing match and dined in Vincents, a bold stroke of oneupmanship even though they as Hawks men enjoyed reciprocal membership. They partook of three traditional weekend treats, the lunch given by Harold Rickett at the Bell at Aston Clinton with a trip to Whipsnade Zoo; a weekend with another famous coach, Derek Mays-Smith, at Shiplake; and a weekend with the old blue Richie McEwen whose Texan wife served huge turkeys and sides of beef at their Hampshire farmhouse and wouldn't let the boys leave any.

During Putney training under Mike Muir-Smith they lived at the English Speaking Union. They were issued with blanket trousers and blazers for cold weather, which were traditional heavy-duty garments in Cambridge blue but made out of crumpled blanket. They dressed formally for dinner, eating like pigs with the CUBC silverware including the Paul Revere bowl on the table, and they were driven twice daily to the river. It was the era of miniskirts and, says Hall, the drives along the Kings Road were highlights of the day. But the Friday night before the race was an experience he could have done without. There were people to dinner as usual, but Hall didn't need them at such a time for his needle. They seemed to be there at breakfast and at lunch on the next day, questioning whether he should be eating all that he was eating. The stroke going for his first blue had to put up with his dislike of a lot of people around him as he worked through his own private ritual of doing every little thing in the right order. And he preferred to row on a full stomach as long as it wasn't filled immediately before the race.

His girlfriend kept a comprehensive cuttings book about the crew's activities, and by race day every paper except the *Evening Standard* and the *Sunday Times* were backing them. 'The papers don't matter in the early stages, but the press coming out on your side later is a help. It calms the nerves. If they're against you it's slightly nerve-racking.' At almost the last minute Hall was handed some typewritten 'Notes to Stroke', helpful hints for the race, 'as if I'm going to have time to take any notice during the race'. He was determined to lead off the start, the press having tipped Oxford to do so, and he remembers his number seven man, Geoffrey Leggett, screaming at him, 'For Christ's sake settle down!' when they were two thirds of a length up. Oxford pressed them before Harrods, and in the steering battle the dark blue cox Painter gave way just as the water got smooth. Cambridge went from half a length down to half a length up in twenty strokes, a burst exaggerated by their advantage of the Surrey bend. A minute later they had a length of clear water, just as they had planned.

The following year lacked such excitement. Hall was one of four blues in the crew, in the stroke seat again, doing the same programme, and the crew were strong favourites from the beginning of training. They had a higher cruising speed and less sprint, but nearly came croppers at Putney where Lou Barry of Tideway Scullers', then in the fore of British rowing, was the finishing coach for the first time. He took what was sent him from the Cam and worked them almost to their knees. 'You lot couldn't pull the skin off a rice pudding,' he told them after the last outing before the race, and Alf Twinn was furious. But they won their Boat Race.

By this time Topolski had left Oxford and was working for BBC Television, and he won the Henley Wyfolds with London RC and competed for Britain in the European championships. Hall set out to go there as well but his coxed four did not achieve selection, and he went skiffing instead. Both men continued their rowing, Hall desperately trying to become the Tideway Scullers' regular first-crew stroke. With the arrival of representative lightweight rowing on the international scene in 1974, men like Hall and Topolski were relieved of fighting their way into top-level crews against the very big men. With the Oxford blue Nick Tee and the London RC oarsman Chris Drury, they formed a four who finished seventh at the world lightweight championships in 1974, and second in 1975. Hall was to win a second silver medal in the British lightweight eight of 1976 before he retired because of pressure of work with Allen and Overy, with whom he is now a partner, whereas Topolski won a gold in the lightweight eight of 1977 and represented Britain again in double sculls in 1978. But it was in the coxless four, stroked by Hall, where the two men first competed together and where each got the measure of his future coaching opponent. Crucially, Hall learned that, to Topolski, training was racing. 'He didn't train. He only raced.' But they went for every opponent Topolski could find.

That was an attitude which probably hardened in Topolski in 1968 after he was dropped from the Oxford squad's attempt to get a four into the British team. He responded by forming a four himself. They did not get to the Games in Mexico, but in the course of trying they met the Oxford crews in trials, and that, Topolski says, is the only time he can remember being really antagonistic towards Oxford. 'They drop-ped me. I would do anything I could with London RC to beat them.'

George Harris, the boatman at Christ Church for just under fifty years, came across Topolski the undergraduate on the river. 'When he was here he certainly didn't know anything about coaching, but he had marvellous enthusiasm, unbearable at times,' Harris says. When the spicy Topolski and the sage Harris both joined OUBC's coaching team in 1973, George held Dan's hand. 'I knew then that unless he was an absolute idiot he was going to be brilliant. He knew what good rowing was, he was a good waterman, but the biggest thing about him was that he could tear a strip off any man in the crew and I could guarantee that five minutes after insulting that man right down to the ground there would be no ill feeling. That's the main reason why he's a good coach. It takes others much longer to get over that sort of thing.'

Topolski had coached a trial eight in 1971 and he and Hugh Matheson (Oxford, 1969) were spotted as young talents by their even younger charges. When Topolski was in India in 1972, Andy Hall wrote to him inviting him to coach in 1973. He accepted, and between then and 1982 became the most experienced Boat Race coach on the Tideway, as well as taking on the British women's team for the programme leading to the Moscow Olympic Games in 1980. He started out with Oxford in a difficult year and by methods which bore out Harris's shrewd assessment. His first aim was to make everyone far more competitive, and during the winter he dropped two men from the blue boat who had not shone in the tests which Topolski employed as indications of progress. One of them went off and sulked; the other was the president, Andy Hall. 'He galvanized himself and won every running race after that,' Topolski says. 'Each time he crossed the line he spat "You bastard" at me. He was back in the crew in two days.'

Andy Hall rowed for Oxford four times from 1970 to 1973 and lost them all. He was president for the last two of those years and he saw and took part in the desperate changes of policy to try and reverse the run of defeats. In the autumn of 1969 they were coached by Jumbo and Jumbo men and spent hours in the octologue 'learning about getting bell notes at the catch' (from the Fairbairn bible) and Moriarty (from the Jumbo book on how to recover at the end of the stroke: all the momentum of the body must be transferred to the oar handle by drawing it to a standstill while recovering the balance of the head and body by a powerful sweep-back of the outside shoulder while the back is straightening – as applied by Sherlock Holmes to pitch Professor Moriarty off the ledge above Reichenbach Falls while recovering his own balance).

Next year under Jerry Dale they did everything differently. The 'Radley coaches' took over: Ronnie Howard, Jock Mullard, Martin Kennard, with the American Bill Fink as finishing coach. They did a lot of work in sculling boats, were beaten by Goldie in the Reading Head, and met a superb Cambridge blue boat. When Andy Hall became president he switched back to the Jumbo school with Dick Fishlock as chief and finishing coach but with Jumbo as well. It was not a happy year or a happy result. He fought apathy of college captains and went for a compromise between all training and no coaching and all coaching and no training, and the crew never met any top-class competition. But the trials coaches Topolski and Harris were the men who stood out with Andy Hall, and he enlisted them as part of his team for his second year as president. He didn't appoint a chief coach because he feared a generation argument and because he had clearly finished the previous year out of sorts with his chief coach. But Dan Topolski was finishing coach and he more and more assumed the role of chief coach. Michael Barry, Derek Thurgood and Chris Blackwall completed the team. Thurgood and Andy Hall went to see the German guru of Ratzeburg, Karl Adam, who gave them an enormous work-load which he considered appropriate to a Boat Race crew, and a first-class oarsman, Dave Sawyier, arrived from Harvard.

Sawyier treated the whole matter like a fetish. 'He was a maniac who would pull his nuts off for ever. . . . His gungho attitude caused some problems. His demonic drive and determination were an invalu-able asset far outweighing the inconvenience of minor ructions. . . . He would train until he was coughing blood.' Those were the things people said of Sawyier. He would also go into a trance before a race, meditating in the dressing room, and woe betide a Topolski who broke it. He would read a magazine while the coaches were talking to the crew.

That crew took on everybody. They beat the University of London; they beat Tideway Scullers'; they were second to Leander at Reading; they beat the national squad; they were second in the Head to Leander; and they lost to Cambridge. There was controversy about the type of riggers they should use. They had a Stampfli boat with five-stay riggers and the coaches wanted them changed to Jumbo-style aerofoil ones.

The crew objected, the coaches gave in, the weather was foul, the warm-up was long, and in the race the boat filled up in two minutes while Sawyier set a rating of about 46, water everywhere. It took twenty men to lift it out at Mortlake, so they said.

Sawyier was president for the next race. He began his campaign by coming through the door at Leander where the coaches were assembled and saying, 'Before you say anything I must apologize for my behaviour last year.' He cut the ground from under the feet of those who were standing on their dignity. Topolski coached again. 'Sawyier didn't know any other coaches really, so there was luck in it for me,' he says. Both chief coach and president were more relaxed, but arguments occurred, including one about whether Sawyier should bring in the blues Nick Tee and Paddy Payne only six weeks before the race. The coaches opposed the move but Sawyier did it as a result of seat racing trials that he had introduced into Oxford's programme, an exercise by which two crews row over a set distance and then one person from each switches and they race again. The results show up the relative strengths of the men, although Tee and Payne had not been subjected to this test. Sawyier's crew lost the toss, were given the Surrey station, were driven at 35 for the first half of the race, beat Cambridge and broke the Boat Race and course record. In their wooden Salters boat they travelled at an average of more than fifteen miles per hour over the four and a quarter miles. They also broke Cambridge's run of six wins.

In the following year Tee was president and he invited Topolski again, though not as chief coach. He didn't want to offend the older coaches. Among the younger ones Hugh Matheson and Chris Blackwall were outstanding in different ways. Tee's aim was to run the coaches as a team. Dr Michael Barry, George Harris, Chris Blackwall, Hugh Matheson and Andy Hall were all involved, and they ran a diet of sculling, ergometer tests, running and seat racing. Oxford lost the race to a heavier crew, not helped by Andy Baird's gate springing open during the race, so that suddenly the bow man was sitting with his oar in his lap. He recovered remarkably quickly and began to send puddles down again. But the excellent Cambridge crew had taken enough of a lead to steal Oxford's water at Hammersmith, and that was that.

In spite of that defeat, Oxford's new coaching team were finding their spurs while activity on the Cam was lulled into complacency.

Although they were doing a lot of work the Cantabs were not searching for ideas or examining their approach to the race. They were turning out good crews who usually won. With the approval of the Oxford coaches, the new president Graham Innes invited Topolski to be chief coach for the 1976 race. Innes was convinced that the dark blues were gaining on Cambridge because they were getting more racing and training on the Tideway. He could see the results of Topolski's thinking, of the experience that Dan had gained in the lightweight four under Ron Needs and as an eager pupil of Bob Janousek, principal national coach and specifically in charge of the Amateur Rowing Association's Olympic programme. Topolski was at work adapting the national team training methods to the peculiar needs of the Boat Race, and with Innes he found an exceptionally strong crew, moulded in the early stages by George Harris in particular. They got a baptism from the University of London, who duffed them up in an angry and clash-ridden practice session. They underestimated the pride of London, their strong desire always to beat Oxford crews, and they paid for it. But another developing Oxford quality emerged. In a later encounter they did well against the national squad. They were displaying the trait of not giving up, which in crew psychology is sometimes as hard to achieve as it is vital. Confidence can be lost at several stages of the Boat Race programme and is very difficult to regain. Somebody – the president, the cox, the stroke, the coach – needs to sense the wind and do the right thing, and Topolski was showing that quality, not exclusively, but constantly.

He was doing it, too, without taking chances. Some calculated gambles, maybe, but no chances. Oxford for him were not the research laboratory sometimes entered by Jumbo. Experiments were to be made, yes, but their results must be proven before they were afforded a place in the scheme. Innes's crew, in beating Cambridge by six lengths, took the time for Putney to Mortlake to under seventeen minutes for the first time. Blackwall's Isis crew beat Goldie. We are beginning to win again, said the dark blues.

Topolski wouldn't believe, in that year of 1976, that he himself was too small to get into the Olympic quadruple sculling crew, but everybody else believed it, and they were right. He failed to make the lightweight eight too. He finished up representing England in the Home Countries International regatta at Cork. If rowing hadn't existed, it would have to have been invented for a regatta like that –

chaotic, joyous, quaint and uproarious. Everyone enjoyed themselves, Topolski included. His book on travelling round Africa was published that year. Bob Mason assembled a powerful squad for 1977, including the Harvard and US international Al Shealy, and the Australian lightweight international oarsman Andy Michelmore. Cambridge had only one blue oarsman, were lighter, lost the toss and the Surrey station, and were walloped off the start. Oxford's seven-length margin was their greatest for seventy-nine years. Colin Moynihan, the boxing blue, steered, and after Barnes Bridge he stole a look at the opposition and judged them ten lengths behind. 'Because I had a stake at the bookie on seven lengths I zigzagged up the final stretch to get it right,' he once claimed. He can lie as skilfully as he can needle and nurse a crew from the back seat, but he can't keep a straight face doing the former. He laughed all the way back to the betting shop.

That race was the first to be sponsored; the bookmaking and leisure activities group Ladbrokes began a five-year programme of financial aid to OUBC and CUBC worth £10,000–£12,000 to each of the clubs per annum. The sponsorship was increased when it was renewed for another five years in 1981, and it saved the Boat Race from running into crippling monetary difficulties and enabled the clubs to think ahead when buying boats and organizing their training. Topolski realized this more than anyone. Oxford acquired a fleet of Carbocraft carbon-fibre moulded boats under his direction, with riggers which owed something to the Jumbo aerofoil design, and the man who had started rowing on Regent's Park lake guided them to a series of wins which continued at least until 1982.

Each year had its drama and excitement: Cambridge sank in atrocious conditions when trailing at Barnes Bridge in 1978. In 1979 Cambridge suffered from illness in the last three weeks and the final straw was when the stroke John Woodhouse was ill on the morning of the race. The news was leaked little more than an hour before the race and reporters streamed from the Duke's Head to Joe Coral's betting shop in Putney High Street to empty their pockets on Oxford. The ailing of Woodhouse was a tragedy because Cambridge were under the direction of Bob Janousek, who was by now building Carbocraft racing shells after resigning as Britain's principal rowing coach after the Montreal Olympic Games. He had a world-wide reputation and the rowing world eagerly awaited the Janousek–Topolski battle on the Tideway – the coach with the most experience of Eastern European and Western European rowing against the most experienced Boat Race guru.

In 1980 Cambridge, with Woodhouse as president but without Janousek except as a bankside backroom figure, reduced the margin to a canvas. The crews clashed soon after the start, and again at Harrods, where they were level, Oxford's president Boris Rankov having won the toss and chosen Surrey. Oxford's number seven Thomas Barry, son of the coach Michael, lost part of his blade somewhere near here. They then took a good enough lead under 'normal circumstances' but found the circumstances not as they should be. Cambridge took their rating up at Corney Reach and came at them, and Oxford couldn't seem to answer. By Barnes Bridge the bow man Steve Francis had more or less stopped rowing. The Cambridge advance continued, Oxford had to give them water, and scrambled home with barely a canvas. Francis was lifted aboard *Bosporos* and given oxygen. Cambridge had a new finishing coach that year: Graeme Hall.

In 1981 the Boat Race was a foregone conclusion almost since October of the previous year. Quite simply, Oxford had an outstanding crew and Cambridge were mantled in unhappiness. The dark blues also introduced Sue Brown, the first woman to take part in the men's Boat Race. Her crew won by a twentieth-century record for Oxford of eight lengths, under Steve Royle as chief coach. Topolski was away for most of the winter months, but returned as finishing coach at Putney. He then re-organized the crew for Henley's Grand Challenge Cup and brought three experienced Thames Tradesmen and the ex-Oxford coxswain Berners-Lee on board. They won the Grand and failed to win the national title two weeks later, in both cases against the national squad. But they saw three blues – John Bland, Mark Andrews, and Chris Mahoney who was already a veteran of the silver medal Olympic crew of 1980 coached by Graeme Hall – gain admission to the British crew who were the synthesis of the Henley and national duel. They went to the world championships and finished second to the Soviet Union.

Topolski's record during this run of victories was complementing his Boat Race work. His own rowing reached its peak in the 1977 gold-medal-winning lightweight eight. 'That was the most self-sacrificing and satisfactory crew to row in,' he says. 'We all wanted a gold medal and nothing else.' For the final in Amsterdam the cox, Ray Penney, was substituted because he was a little over the minimum weight, and Pat Sweeney steered instead. They won their medals by seven-hundredths of a second over the Spanish, a result which showed the wisdom of the substitution and the narrow margins between victory and defeat in international rowing.

It was in the autumn of 1978 that Topolski became chief coach of the British women's squad until the Moscow Olympic Games, while he continued to compete at Henley each year. His progress with Oxford has really been based on his good judgement. He has added to the sense of watermanship which George Harris spotted in him several years before an ability to spot weaknesses and get the right person to sort them out if he is not able to do so himself. Many prominent coaches have been associated with OUBC during his time as chief coach.

As an example of the system which has evolved, listen to a recent president reporting back, as it were, to his successor:

After seat racing it was decided to spend three weeks on technique and blending the crew together – Michael Barry for one week, Nick Tee for two. The next two weeks were gut-busters under Hugh Matheson, who excels in these conditions. He flogs them through an enormous amount of work but still picks them up on technique. The final two weeks before handing over to Dan, George Harris does an excellent job of re-establishing rhythm and harmony through the boat, ready for Dan's fine-tuning on the Tideway.

Others associated with the team have been Steve Royle, Mike Spracklen, who is a prominent sculling coach and an expert on technique, particularly when it comes to blending lightweights and heavyweights, Father Mark Jabale of Belmont Abbey, who produced a gold-medal lightweight four for Britain in 1979, John Pilgrim-Morris, another sculling expert, and Ronnie Howard from Radley.

Through it all is Topolski, darting up and down between Oxford and London for meetings and discussions, attending as many sessions as possible, keeping an eye on Cambridge, and giving his attention to detail. He is a master of publicity, more by bringing the instincts of Topolski the media man into play at the right moments than by going out and seeking it, as he is often accused of doing by Cantabs. His view is that publicity is good for the Boat Race and good for rowing as long as it doesn't interfere with the crew. Besides, he says, 'the boys read the papers, and they begin to get annoyed if Cambridge are getting too much attention.' He knows when to talk to the press and when not to, when to encourage a little diversion and when not to, how and when to take the media men into his confidence. He knows how to tune in to the crew of the particular year, sensing when he must play the dominant-personality role or be the wisecracker, when to play the aloof coach, or sit at the table as one of the lads. In his period he has brought a lot of light into the corners of the dark blues.

Graeme Hall, for all the similarities of rowing career between himself and Topolski, is a totally different kind of person. As the helper-out with the national coaching team in 1980 he produced, at very short notice, an eight who won the silver medal in the Moscow Olympic Games in the year when he had first coached Cambridge's blue boat and smelt a strong whiff of victory. Things did not go so well in the next year. He had domestic problems and he was abroad on business for much of the crucial winter training. But in the 1981–82 Boat Race he was to be cast in a light blue revolution. The crews call him Grumpy, and have done for years, but he doesn't know why. He is introspective, occasionally seldom speaking to an oarsman for weeks on end, but only when he has nothing to tell him. He is quiet, distant at times, and elusive. This is coupled with a low tolerance for stupidity, or for people who don't make an effort, and, one senses, his dislike for putting himself in the public eye or indeed in the eye of the old heavies. His personality thus requires others to provide humour and relaxation in the Cambridge camp. He is shy where his opponent is a chameleon, but he is certainly a good coach who earns great respect from those who come under his influence. He does not lack humour or lay-back, either. It is just that he doesn't put them on display much near the water. At night he pounds the streets near his Barbican flat, training for the 1982 London Marathon. Nobody seeing the lone runner on Blackfriars Bridge would imagine that he was in charge of a unit in the most intricate of team sports. But that is the solitary profile of Graeme Hall, or rather, that is the effect of the needle on him. The surest and least wavering factor in the respective souls of OUBC and CUBC is that Topolski has dark blue needle, and Hall has light blue needle. Rowing reserves a special meaning for the needle match.

16

Opposite sides of Clarendon Drive
The Putney fortnight

Two weeks before the 1982 Boat Race the centre of operations moved to Clarendon Drive in Putney. Oxford occupied a house which they had rented there and, by chance, Cambridge found one barely a boat's length away on the opposite side of the road. It is this final period of preparation which finds the crews most in the public eye yet much of the time cocooned from the attention and pressures which are upon them. Boris Rankov, Oxford's 'grand old man' in the number five seat, whose fifth appearance this will be, says that these two weeks are the best part. 'Eat, sleep and row' is how he sums it up. That's all they do, all they are expected to do, and it is a pleasure and a privilege. Sue Brown, now steering the dark blues for the second time, curls up on the sofa in the warm sitting room which looks out onto a secluded Putney garden and says that the number of people involved in putting on the race is almost unbelievable, but you can go through the last fortnight almost unaware that there is so much activity round you. Reporters and photographers now turn up on the embankment each day, and BBC people survey the scene in preparation for their biggest regular outside broadcast.

Alf Twinn moves into digs to look after the Cambridge boat, and his counterpart from Oxford, Albert Andrews, travels down to tend his shell. Launches are at the ready for the coaches and the press. There are meals to be cooked, shopping to be done, old blues to be entertained, coaches, mechanics, doctors on call, reserve crews training in the background. The public does not take notice of the Boat Race practice like it used to do. It is years since a crew needed a police cordon to take their boat to the water on a practice day. But the river is busy. The Head of the River race is to take place on the Saturday before the Boat Race. It has become the largest single rowing race in the world with 420 eights expected to start, Britain's largest sports event except for the marathons which have recently become popular, and many of its competitors are out on the course when they get the chance. So the blue boats are watched, and they watch each other, and they retreat to the obscurity of Clarendon Drive between their outings.

Cambridge are fed and watered by John Pritchard, a member of the national rowing squad who did some coaching with the trial eights early in the season. At twenty-four years old, he has silver medals for rowing in the British eight in the 1980 Olympic Games and the 1981 world championships and so knows his sport as well as the cooking which he had to give up professionally at the same time as he gave up karate to become an oarsman. Now he is on holiday from his job at a solicitor's, and travels across the river from Fulham each day to feed his charges, having worked out a diet to suit their training and his own. They get steak on Monday and pasta on Friday, plenty of protein at the beginning of the period, with the emphasis changing to more easily burned off carbohydrates as the race approaches. For this fortnight he is allowed up to £10 per man per day for food, which is generous even for the voracious appetites of super-fit oarsmen. Improvisation is the key word in the kitchen which is designed for a much smaller family than the light blues. A trolley from a supermarket stands in a corner loaded with jam steamers and the like in which Pritchard makes giant lasagne and cooks mountains of chilli con carne.

The men who sit at his table, or rather squeeze round it, have worked extremely hard to get there. Eight of Cambridge's colleges are represented in the crew, the cox and four of the oarsmen are freshmen, and only one, the president Roger Stephens, has a blue. The other three were all members of the 1981 Goldie crew, although Simon Harris, the stroke of that boat and of this one, had to drop out with glandular fever before Goldie's race with Isis. They are light for a Boat Race crew, averaging 13 stone 3 pounds, although among them is the heaviest man of the two crews, Bruce Philp. Stephens announced the crew early in February and has not thus far made any changes, and the judgement day for the plan which he formulated several months before is approaching fast.

After six defeats in a row it was obvious that all was not well with Cambridge rowing. Stephens, a student reading land economy at

Emmanuel and the number three man in the unhappy 1981 crew, set out to start a revolution. He told the college captains who elected him in May 1981, seated round the octagonal table in the blues room above the Goldie boathouse, that the demands of CUBC would take precedence over the colleges' even during the summer if need be, and that all measures considered necessary for winning the Boat Race would be taken.

He spent several weeks in Cambridge during the long vacation, spending up to four hours a day on the paperwork required to extract money from the re-organized finance committee to buy two new eights from Empacher of West Germany, hire two fours, purchase a second minibus and new, more economical launches, and organize a coaching team after inviting Graeme Hall to be, once again, the chief and finishing coach. With office comes the furniture: the president's filing cabinet, the president's telephone, and the president's bookcase containing Harold Rickett's bound coaching logs, the CUBC's immaculate photo albums, and other miscellaneous items. Oarsman's customary ephemera hang on the walls – photos of college crews, blades announcing that Stephens won the Bushe Fox Challenge Cup for freshmen's sculls in 1979, and with S. Collinson of Trinity Hall the Lowe Double Sculls in 1980. There are a settee, two chairs, a bed, and a desk for the red telephone, a few tomes on economics and real property, a shelf of Complan, Build-up and Staminer, and a view of Emmanuel's charming duck pond.

From here, under posters of So Bracing Skegness, Andrews Liver Salts, and the Sport of Kings, Stephens wrestled with his finance committee to organize his budget of about £30,000 for the 1981–82 Boat Race. He contacted all the likely freshmen from rowing schools before the Michaelmas term began and arranged a training camp near his home at Molesey, Surrey. Then he went to the world championships in Munich as a spectator. His peep into the outside world of rowing in Munich, where German organization threatened to dampen high spirits but where the boats, the crews, and the arguments were new, sharp and fine-honed, where positive drug tests on Bulgarians were revealed, where strategy, enthusiasm, and occasionally cynicism coloured the later-night conversations, was to help Stephens put cloistered Cambridge rowing into perspective for the months ahead.

Stephens and Hall reviewed the whole strategy of Cambridge and set a programme which differed in several ways from what had been custom and practice more or less since Hall got his first blue in 1968. The number in the coaching team was reduced and confined to those who were prepared to commit themselves to long weekends before Christmas and three-week stints after Christmas. Thus the main team consisted of Hall with Bob Winckless, Donald Legget, and Mark Bathurst, with assistance during the run-up to the trial eights from Pritchard and the national women's coach Alan Inns. Hall and Winckless were together in the winning Cambridge crews of 1968 and 1969, Winckless being the only member of the coaching team to row three times in the race, losing his first one in 1967. Legget lost in 1963 and won in 1964, and Bathurst was in the losing crews of 1977 and 1978. Pritchard's pedigree was Leander Club's cadet training scheme after conversion from karate to rowing through the influence of a schoolmaster, Graeme Mulcahy, who taught him at St Clement Danes and introduced him to rowing at Quintin. The Olympic eight in Moscow in 1980 included Pritchard and were coached by Hall. They won silver medals. Inns, also from the 'non-rowing' St Clement Danes school, was for many years the chief coxswain of Lou Barry's club, the Tideway Scullers' School. Hall stroked eights for Barry after leaving Cambridge and came to know Inns, the most experienced cox on the Tideway.

Stephens asked a lot of his coaches. He asked them to commit themselves for a minimum of three weeks of full-time coaching between October and March. 'It's a big decision for busy men to take and you have to kick them a bit to get them to do it,' he says. But Hall the lawyer, Bathurst the Penguin editor, Winckless the IBM salesman, and Legget the leisure-wear supplier agreed, and Stephens produced a training schedule designed to make life easier for them and the Cambridge squad. The crews were on the water on Saturdays and Sundays when the coaches could see them, taking a rest on Mondays. Weight training was done at Fenners gymnasium before breakfast on Mondays, Wednesdays and Fridays, supervised by Sergeant Major Barry Woodruff, and followed by a training breakfast at Emmanuel sponsored by the Milk Marketing Board with some help from the Danepak bacon company and Heinz, who donated two thousand cans of beans. 'I was very keen to reintroduce the training table because in the previous year people were losing weight because they were not eating properly,' says the president. 'If you slap three pints of milk down in front of them and say "drink it" they'll do it.' The oarsmen paid £1.50 a week for four breakfasts, and the CUBC put in a contribution also.

'If I'm being honest,' Stephens says, 'I'm doing this for myself. I'm very competitive in whatever I do. I had to choose at Cambridge between rowing and chess. I've met some masters and I play a very attacking game. After myself, I'm doing it for Cambridge and the crew. Sometimes people are content with getting their blue, especially when the selection is so hard. There is a difference between this and being content only to win.'

As the term continued, the others had the opportunity of working out their motives and their limitations. The twelve who attended the October training camp were given the choice by the president of returning to their colleges for the fours and then coming to the CUBC squad, or training with the squad from the start, their college captains concurring for the sake of Cambridge rowing. They all chose to train with the squad from the start, and the process of finding another dozen started well before the Michaelmas term fours were done with. Woodruff laid down the weights programme, Hall laid down the water programme, and Stephens tried to organize it so that the boat club intruded as little as possible into their lives. You can't afford to row and do nothing else at Cambridge any more, so his idea was that you should be able to get the rowing over and done with so that you can make use of some of the other opportunities of the place. To cope with all this, though, requires discipline. 'You can't afford late nights, you can't afford to drink alcohol, you've got to force yourself to eat sometimes when you don't want to,' Stephens says.

A typical midweek training day started at 6.45 with a run to Grantchester and back from Fenners gym, followed by heavy weights and a game of basketball or fast circuits or some other exercise for coordination, all under the watchful eye of Sergeant Major Woodruff. The crews were driven to Ely in the afternoon where they rowed twelve to fifteen miles on the uncrowded desolate stretch of the Great Ouse. At the weekends two rowing outings per day replaced the gym and weight work. A two-week training camp on the Tideway took place during the Christmas vacation for the eighteen men left on the squad, which Stephens had reduced gradually from the sixty or so men who made themselves available at the beginning of the year. Holding the trials on the water where the Boat Race was to take place was another change in Cambridge's recent history, and holding them after the training camp instead of before was also a Stephens change. His aim throughout was to get a happy crew. 'I wouldn't knock last year's crew,' he said at the time, 'but it is enough to say that it wasn't a happy one. I want a happy crew. What we are really doing is turning schoolboys into high-endurance performers in a short period of time, and it's important to get on well together to do that.' He recognized that this was not enough, however, that happiness can let in failure. It is not enough to want a blue. You have to feel the needle as well, to want very much to win.

The trials were on an ugly day. It was a warning of what the elements can be like when the Putney and Hammersmith reaches are feeling unfriendly. There was snow, there was a biting wind, and there was exceptionally rough water at Putney and Hammersmith, and the coaches made the best of things by decreeing a course from the University of London's Chiswick boathouse to Hammersmith Pier. Stephens's boat *Blunder* was beaten by 11½ seconds by *Thud* in a race which lasted for almost fifteen minutes, both crews beating the press launch by a considerable margin. Little could be learned from the exercise, but Hall and Stephens certainly had a good idea of who were heading for blues without the benefits of this blustery inclement day.

By this time Stephens had had considerable experience of dropping people. That was the hardest job for him. 'It's very hard because having made it to the squad they've all come through about fifty people, and then when you tell them that they're not good enough they look so shattered. It's hard to shatter someone's individual dreams.' But they all knew from the start that such standards and methods would be applied. The squad spent much time in fours at Ely, the composition of the crews changing quite often. As they went faster individuals stood out as being not able to cope with the extra speed of the boat. That's when to drop them, Stephens says. All the training was underlined with endurance. Strength for endurance, fitness for endurance, rowing for endurance, and mind for endurance; and high morale developed in the squad. 'We tried very hard to establish confidence early on. When you get low morale people start blaming others for the boat not going well, and it becomes a vicious circle.' Stephens remembered getting his blue the previous year, when during the last few weeks the despondency in the crew meant that they were never going to improve.

Not long after the trials the president separated the blue from the Goldie and announced his crew. In the bows was Paul St John Brine from Thame in Oxfordshire, St Edward's School and LMBC. In front of him was Alan Knight from Hampton and Clare, whose home was in Teddington, Middlesex. Then came Stephens himself, representing King's College School, Wimbledon and Emmanuel. Nick Bliss from Burnley, Barnard Castle School and Corpus Christi sat in the number four seat. At five was Bruce Philp of Brentford, Bryanston and Downing. At six was Charlie Heard from King Swinford in the West Midlands, Shrewsbury and the second man from the LMBC. Ewan Pearson from the King's School, Canterbury, and Jesus was at seven, and stroke was Simon Harris from Desborough School, Maidenhead (a school named after the lord who had rowed in the dead heat), and Queens'. The coveted coxswain's seat was secured by Ian Bernstein, soon to become known as Gonzo after a character in the television 'Muppet Show'. He was from City of London School and Emmanuel, and, although a freshman medical student, had done several seasons steering on the Tideway with his school and the club to which they are attached, London RC.

The four freshmen were Knight, Philp, Heard and Pearson. Bliss learned all his rowing at Cambridge. They were all fair or blond except for the stroke, Harris. They were young, relatively inexperienced, but fit and compatible, and they tackled a series of encounters on the Tideway to bring them up to match peak.

This was another feature about Stephens's Cambridge which was different from recent policy on the Cam. During the last few years Oxford were frequently seen on the Tideway, Cambridge more rarely prior to the final two weeks of practice. But Stephens's crew came out fighting. He sought the best opposition he could get and his men remained undaunted by it. They experienced plenty of side-by-side racing. On 13 February they took on the re-formed national light-weight squad who were weaker than observers had come to expect. Cambridge took a length a minute off them in the first two minutes of each row. On the next day they met the University of London in an encounter which turned a little acrimonious. London had on board Richard Budgett, who had won a bronze medal in coxed pairs at the world championships in 1981 but when up at Cambridge had failed to be noticed during trials, while a fully-fledged Cambridge blue, Graham Phillips, was fighting for a place in London's second crew.

That was the measure of London's challenge, and many of their men had rowed in their world-beating under-23 crew in the previous summer.

So there was needle. Cambridge got the better of London in the first two of four three-minute pieces, finishing about a third of a length up. In the third Bernstein had the advantage again, but adopted kamikaze tactics and forced London to stop rather than concertina their boat on Barnes Bridge, and this experience wound up London's cox Greg 'Patsy' Fagan and his crew. They powered ahead when the fourth piece started and as the boats moved downstream towards Hammersmith Fagan took much of Bernstein's water, pointless aggression but giving the Cambridge boys experience of riding in someone else's wash, and London held a length lead on the outside of the bend. Cambridge, though, showed that they might be new but they weren't brittle. They were not behaving like Tideway rookies.

Two weeks later they were back at Putney again, this time against the very best opposition available, the heavyweight eight from the national training squad, coached by Penny Chuter. This crew were beginning their build-up to the Head of the River race three weeks later. They included Cambridge's chef, Pritchard, and between them they had won seventeen medals in various world and Olympic events. On the Saturday they took more than five lengths off Cambridge in a total of fourteen and a half minutes' rowing, and on the Sunday sharpened up to take a total of more than eight lengths in two four-minute pieces. But Cambridge and Bernstein acquitted themselves well against such a fit and experienced boatload of old hands, showing the following press men that they rowed well together when on level terms with another crew, went a bit ragged when dropped, but were capable of pressing the accelerator.

They returned to the Thames at Kingston two weeks later and as expected won the Kingston Head of River by a wide margin ahead of Isis. The course from Hampton to Kingston was shortened to four miles because of the strong stream, which eventually flooded the road, and the race was a good feather to stick in a blue cap. The Oxford crew were watching on the bank, and by this time their president, Nick Conington, who had been causing problems because he had been out of the boat for some time with illness, knew that he still had the glandular fever from which he had suffered more than twelve months before. The diagnosis of the recurring illness was known in at least two corners of the Kingston Rowing Club bar, but the Oxford crew didn't know, or if they did, Conington didn't know that they knew and didn't want them to know. His coach Dan Topolski had decided already that Conington would have to stay in the bow seat where he had sat since his latest comeback. He had set out as the stroke man, but a vulnerable stroke was much too risky. A bow man who goes out to lunch is less trouble for the rest than a collapsed occupant of any other stateroom. Topolski had reckoned Conington to be sufficiently recovered three weeks earlier, reassured that he had been cleared by tests for glandular fever.

That was 13 March, two weeks before Boat Race day, and now Stephens's men are in Clarendon Drive with Pritchard doing his damnedest to feed them well. Graeme Hall is in residence too, nicknamed KP because he is the kitchen porter, rushing about tending the greens and carving the carcasses. The phone is constantly in use, mostly to girlfriends, but Malcolm Harrison, the secretary, tries to field as many of the incoming calls as possible, dealing with press inquiries, keeping people away from the house, fixing up the old blues dinner at Hurlingham, to which the regular rowing correspondents have been invited. This is another welcome change from recent Cambridge practice. Harrison is more of a manager than a secretary and is quietly and supremely efficient, an excellent public-relations man for the crew. Driver, messenger, porter, switchboard operator, and untier of knotty problems, his contribution to the programme and the household, for that is what it has become, is immense, and a release for the president and the coach. Hall has taken the phone off the hook. There is confidence, there is laughter, there is needle, and there is a conviction about winning.

Bernstein, the cox, is surprised about this, for one. He probably owes his place in the crew to his experience of the Tideway. Although one of the crew's five freshmen, he was at the City of London School in Blackfriars, there coaxed down to the river by one of his teachers, John Milbourne. He began rowing but turned to coxing, and because City of London boat from London Rowing Club, and because clubs never have enough coxes, he soon found himself sitting in the stern of club boats. He had a baptism of fire when he was thirteen. The first club crew he steered was after eight weeks of coxing. They were in fact a national lightweight eight with Graeme Hall at stroke. 'I was just going zigzag all over the river, and I remember coming under Barnes

Bridge Graeme nearly got out of his seat and belted me one for making a complete cock-up of things generally.' That was in the 1976–77 lightweight crew who went on to great things without Bernstein. After that he would steer the school crew and then hang about to take a club crew out in the evening, doing his homework on the two-hour train journey home to Kenton, Middlesex.

In 1979 Bernstein coxed in the lightweight squad for three months, and learned more than he'd ever learned before by watching Ron Needs, the coach, at work. 'I learned about rowing technique because he knew what he was talking about and he showed a lot of films.' Then, his services not required by Needs, he joined Tideway Scullers' and coxed them in the Head, and came under the influence of Lou Barry. That was where Bernstein really learned about the course, because Lou took him over it and over it, drawing little sketch maps of the bank, and pointed out where there were bays or where the bank comes out, causing a cox to go off the stream. Barry had walked across the river at low tide with a sounding stick and told him where the deepest points were. He taught Bernstein to imagine where the line is and stick to it without cutting across or going wide. The knack according to Bernstein is to be able to plot your line in your mind. 'Lou was so absolute. He knew where it was because he'd walked across and found out. There was no according-to-so-and-so. He had found out himself with a sounding stick.' Barry spent a lot of time on how the course changes with the height of the tide. The position of the stream doesn't move much according to speed, but it does according to the wind.

At the crucial bend at Hammersmith Bridge the deepest point is well over to the Surrey bank. That's about the only bend you don't take on the outside, according to the Bernstein tune. It is like that because it's been dredged for barges. As the tide rises the line moves to the outside of the bends, the exception being near the bandstand and Emanuel School boathouse where there are shoals on the Surrey shore. The line is near Middlesex there and moves towards the centre, but not by very much.

Armed with all that, Bernstein became a medical student at Emmanuel College, Cambridge. He thought there weren't enough good people there to produce a good crew, especially coming up with his most recent experience fresh in his mind, steering a London RC elite eight which ran smoothly in some Continental regattas. He was depressed and originally took the attitude that he was doing it on the Cam to get a blue.

'As they got better,' Bernstein says, 'and as I saw what the coaches could do, and they are some of the best coaches I have met, my attitude changed from the slight possibility of a win to: "If things don't go wrong we *will* win." ' He saw eight men, mediocre to start with, lacking in Boat Race experience, but all, even the freshmen, with considerable rowing experience behind them, turned into a good crew, and selected the way they had been told they would be selected. The eight most compatible people would be there, and here they are in Clarendon Drive.

'From the stories that go round the table,' Bernstein says, 'this crew is incredibly concordant. People are aware of how easy it is to get on each other's nerves, and they've got a lot of self-control. We are all aware how easily we could wreck it by arguing.' They had followed the training programme laid down by Hall. They were seen by Pritchard and Inns before Christmas. Donald Legget made some changes and produced the blue boat which Stephens approved and announced. Mark 'Cutie' Bathurst took over for his stint, his job being to get the boat moving. And he got it moving in raceable form. Bob Winckless was next. He had problems because Pearson was ill for a day or two, but he made them move faster still. Now it was up to Hall to do the fine tuning. And he was excited by what he saw. 'I think the coaches built in as much aggression as there's ever been in any Cambridge crew,' Bernstein says.

The little medical student's attitude to his opponent was interesting. He didn't think Miss Brown possessed outstanding qualities as a cox. He wasn't admitting to any worries about racing against her. But he felt that he owed it to his crew to see that they had everything in their favour, so he was dieting like crazy to try and get under seven stone. His normal weight was 8 stone 2 pounds. Before Christmas he had been down to 7 stone 8 pounds by simply exercising and eating carefully. He estimated his normal racing weight to be 7 stone 6 pounds. But now he was sleeping fourteen hours a day and living, under doctor's and medical don's advice but with no pressure from CUBC, on the Cambridge Diet of flavoured powder mixed in a half-pint of water, hot for chicken or beef soup, cold for banana, strawberry, vanilla, or chocolate. He was taking in only 300 calories a day, and hating it. 'I don't feel like doing anything. The flavours are fairly disgusting. After the weigh-in I'll have to eat more and put a couple of pounds back on so that I can think clearly. I've got to be on the ball. But if I can weigh in under seven stone – Sue Brown will be 6 stone x pounds – the crew will be impressed. It wasn't required of me. It's self-imposed.'

The coxswain, then, will not be happy until at least after the official weigh-in eight days before the race. His assessment of the piecing together of the crew and the roles of the coaches is largely confirmed by the oarsmen. Nick Bliss, known to the others as Body Bliss, said that Pritchard and Inns found a definite stern four at the Molesey pre-Christmas training camp. 'Pritchard you listen to because he's got such a rowing pedigree. He helped me a lot. Inns was excellent on rhythm and movement in the boat.' Bliss would perhaps find a chord with Pritchard because they both came to rowing from something else, Pritchard from karate and Bliss from swimming, rugby and cross-country. He was at a non-rowing school at Barnard Castle in County Durham, and although the Tees was on his doorstep he learned all his rowing at Corpus Christi, Cambridge. Now reading law in his fourth year at Cambridge, he packed in a half-blue in swimming for the university, rugby and cricket appearances for his college, two appearances in the Ladies' Plate at Henley, and rowed for Goldie in 1981. He is the only pure-bred Cam oarsman in the crew. 'Everyone regards me as a total barbarian at Cambridge because I have a northern accent,' he says. 'It's quite useful, is that: they don't expect great things of me. Rowing fits in with my streak of fanaticism. I definitely have a streak of that. And I'm a perfectionist. I want to do something properly.' He says his president has made a really good job of it. 'He's given Cambridge rowing a real kick in the pants, which is what it needed. Last year was pathetic. You were almost ashamed of working hard.' Last year, he says, he would have liked to have rowed in the Oxford boat. The double humiliation for Cambridge had been an outstanding bunch of opponents added to a below-par crew.

Ewan Pearson, Cambridge's number seven man, is surprised to be there. He is one of the freshmen, reading natural sciences but with a long-term aim of doing medicine. He rowed at King's, Canterbury, because he couldn't stand rugby or cross-country, and he chose to aim for Cambridge because he knew that he didn't have a chance of getting into a representative London University crew, and he liked the idea of joining the underdogs. From Jesus College, he was the last man in,

Cambridge take their shell to the water during practice, Putney

Graeme Hall strokes Cambridge in 1968

Daniel Topolski training in the Oxford crew, 1967

Hall coaching on the Tideway

Topolski coaching on the Tideway

Oxford, right, approach Hammersmith Bridge one second ahead of Cambridge in 1982

The Boat Race Course, finish on the left and start on the right

The Cambridge Cox has yet to effect his turn

Roger Stephens, Cambridge president in 1982, in the Eights Room of the Goldie boathouse

Top left: Boris Rankov of Oxford became the first oarsman to win five consecutive Boat Races. *Right:* John Pritchard cooking for Cambridge. *Below left:* Suzi Grimsdale cooking for Oxford. *Right:* Nick Conington, Oxford president, watches his opponents

Alf Twinn, boatman to Cambridge

Albert Andrews, boatman to Oxford, with Alan Kirkpatrick

Miss Brown meets Ian 'Gonzo' Bernstein at the Boat Race Ball, 1982

having a fight to show up well on weights and ergometer. But he's got rhythm, one of the others said. He has swung his way into the number seven seat behind lightweight Harris from Desborough School in Maidenhead. An engineer, Harris did a lot of rowing before arriving at Cambridge, much of it with Maidenhead RC. 'Sometimes you stand next to him,' said Bruce Philp, the 15 stone 6 foot 2 inch number five man, 'and think, how can a chap like this stroke the blue boat? But he is a maniac. He'll row on to Twickenham unless someone tells him to stop.' Harris weighs 11½ stone and is 5 feet 9 inches and, like several good lightweights before him, has developed a really long stroke to reserve such a key seat for himself.

Charles Heard is in the number six seat, a first-generation oarsman but always a Cambridge man because his parents met at the university. He took up rowing at Shrewsbury because he didn't like soccer, and found four good coaches for each of his four school years, working under the rowing master Nick Bevan. The possibility of continuing rowing was a major consideration in his applying to St John's.

Philp completes the stern four. Another freshman, he is from Bryanston where the twisting one-lane rowing stretch attracted him because he enjoyed sculling in such an idyllic place tucked away in Dorset, because he didn't want to play cricket, because he was big, because not knowing anything about rowing, it intrigued him, because the top school oarsmen were a social elite. With the boy he shared a study with at school, Julian Rodd, Philp rowed in a pair and they almost reached the national junior teams, but they never won anything, dogged by illness or meeting someone just a fraction faster each time they got their act together. So while Rodd is rowing for Queen Mary College, London, having failed a London University trial, Philp finds himself in Cambridge's blue boat for another crack at a medal. Like Pearson, he is reading natural sciences and wants to change to medicine. In 1981 he rowed for his old boys, the Bryanston Buffaloes, in the Head of the River race, and went off trekking in Nepal and India. He returned after three months, having lost more than 2 stone, to find Stephens's letter inviting him to the pre-term training camp at Molesey. During a summer maths course at Cambridge – 'Rowing had taken a toll on A levels and I failed maths' – he asked the college boatman at Downing about getting a blue. 'You have to be Superman to get into CUBC,' the man told him. He went off travelling again, to Italy and France, and then started training at Molesey. 'It was a strong squad. There were maniacs like Harris and Bliss. There were a lot of Goldie caps. But Roger said to me, "You might be able to get your blue" and that was like a blinding light to me, so I stuck it. We got our trial caps before we even got to college. It's like stepping into a man-trap. You can't get out for a variety of reasons.'

Philp enjoyed Cambridge, felt obliged to do all the work, to go to the lectures and practicals. 'Creativity gets axed in the neck if you're a scientist and a rower,' he said. He is a prodigious reader of fiction. 'Physically,' he says, 'it is great to see how far you can push yourself, to have a body that's in good shape. The Boat Race is mind over matter at this stage, being able to walk to the edge of the abyss and look down and carry on rowing.' He would like to win the race for Hall, apart from anything else. He feels immense responsibility for winning. 'I know we can crush them,' he says, and in the next sentence, 'I'm pretty terrified by the whole thing. Every time we walk down and see those BBC platforms we think, "Oh Christ, is that for us?" I'm looking forward to the adrenaline rush I'll get. . . . Reputedly there are millions watching. I have one niggling doubt. What happens if I die at Barn Elms?' He is going into the race thinking about Rob Clay, Oxford's stroke. 'I'm unlucky in that people say, "I think of your opposite man, you're better than him." Well, I've got Rankov, so I think about Clay. I think we can crush Clay.'

Bliss sits behind Philp, and Stephens behind Bliss, and Alan Knight behind Stephens. Knight took up rowing at Hampton after a couple of mediocre rugby years. He wanted something to be good at and something to make him big and strong because his older sister was always beating him up, he says. His father rowed a bit, but Knight only found out two years after he himself had taken it up. To the Hampton coaches Richard Hooper and Steve Gunn he attributes attitude and technique respectively. He went to Clare with no particular rowing ambitions, but he found that this interest, which conflicted with all his other fondnesses, came out on top.

In the bows is Paul St John Brine, another Lady Margaret oarsman, another with no family connection with the sport, another refugee from physical contact games — scared of rugby, bored by cricket, terrified of fast hockey balls. But he had notions of messing about in boats which his coaches at St Edward's, John Lever and Mike Rose-wall, converted to fitness and strength, etc., and Brine rowed for the British junior team in the coxed four of 1977, and Goldie in 1980.

By seat and by weight at nearly 15 stone Rankov is Oxford's answer to Philp. At twenty-seven years of age he is the senior of both crews by a considerable margin. He doesn't know whether he is a stabilizing influence on the dark blues or not. He is in his fifth Boat Race, a junior research fellow in Roman archaeology at St Hugh's, and sharing the children's room at Oxford's Clarendon Drive headquarters with Steve Foster, reading classics at Pembroke, who is one of his students. Rankov was persuaded to return to training after Christmas by president Nick Conington, and his late bid for fitness is no longer regarded as a joke by the light blues. 'Rankov is not going to crack first' is a belief voiced in the Cambridge camp. 'It's been very nice only having half of it this time,' Rankov says. 'I haven't had time to get depressed about it, which I usually have in other years. This stage is wonderful, always. A terrific fortnight. Wonderful way to spend two weeks, eat and row.'

If he wins he will be the first oarsman to win five times, equalling C. R. W. Tottenham's five steering wins for Oxford from 1864 to 1868 and beating Muttlebury of Cambridge who rowed from 1886 to 1890 but lost one of his five. Geographically he is Oxford's answer to Cambridge's northcountryman Bliss, although his Yorkshire accent is softer than Bliss's Durham. He is, though, a first-generation Yorkshireman. His father is Yugoslav, his mother is half Czech and half Sudetan; both were sent to Bradford during the Second World War as refugees to work in textiles. His father is now a pharmaceutical salesman living in Henley-on-Thames, his medical studies in Budapest having been rudely and permanently interrupted many years before; but the family was in Bradford during Boris's upbringing, and he got the top classical scholarship to Corpus Christi, Oxford.

'At Bradford Grammar School the good athletes tended not to come down to the river,' Boris said. 'You rowed if you couldn't do anything else. The joke is Ken Wootton who was there. He's now a national rowing coach.' Boris went down to the Aire, and learned his rowing on the 650-metre stretch of water with a weir at either end, not wide enough for two eights abreast, and situated roughly between what is now the Damart Thermal Underwear chimney and the symbolic llama of Sir Titus Salt's alpaca spinning mill. Training for head races was really fun, recalls Rankov. You had to spin the boat round fourteen times. After winning his scholarship he took a year off, bought a sculling boat in Lucerne, Switzerland's rowing mecca, and obtained some coaching from a German friend of his uncle.

At Oxford he rowed for Isis in 1974 and 1975, but did not reach the blue boat until 1978. From the relative tranquillity of the domestic headquarters he still finds the coming race exciting, feeling the press attention on the crew and appreciating that the coaching is being done from the *Bosporos* and not from a rubber duck or a bicycle. But the race to him now is just another race. The first one was different. 'There are millions of witnesses to see you make a mistake. The first one for a lot of people is a question of one stroke after another until you get to the end without cocking it up.'

In 1978 there was little hint that this man, who collected a first in Greats in the same year as he first became a blue, would become the rock of a dark blue crew. Andy Michelmore, who was president at the time, recalls the patience which one of the coaches, George Harris, showed towards Rankov and others whom Michelmore regarded as 'problem' members of his crew. Harris had an endearing touch which was not to be found in Topolski or Christopher Blackwall, the other coaches.

By rowing as a junior fellow at St Hugh's in 1981 Rankov became the first representative of a women's college in the men's Boat Race in the same year that Sue Brown became the first woman to compete in the men's race. Cambridge made a half-hearted attempt to keep him out under the eligibility rules in 1982, but Oxford resisted the press-ure. The rules are slightly hazy anyway, because the university regu-lations differ in the two places. They say that you have to have matriculated, be in residence, and be reading for a degree. Rankov fitted all three. The rule was fixed like that in 1975 when Cambridge wanted David Sturge in as a postgraduate, and Oxford wanted Nick Tee. Eventually Sturge got glandular fever and didn't row. 'It was changed as much for their benefit as it was for ours. That's the way it stands,' Rankov says.

He is studying a particular grade of Roman army officer for his PhD, interested in the process of Romanization of the provinces of the Roman empire, and the Roman army was important in that. But not in his eating and rowing fortnight. He already knows, from the press reports and the observations of the Oxford coaches, that there is a possibility of being led by Cambridge early on in the race. 'My worst moment was in 1980,' he says. Not at the end of the race when Cambridge came up to within a canvas of Oxford after Steve Francis, the Oxford bow, stopped being effective somewhere around Barnes Bridge, but near the mile post when Cambridge were a seat or two ahead. 'For the first time Cambridge had been up on *me*. It was a mixture of horror and disbelief . . . this can't be happening. I was thinking of the burn that was coming at Harrods that was the answer to it all.' And he remembers the race of 1979 as being murder. He came in late that year because of a back injury. Cambridge's stroke John Woodhouse fell sick on the morning of the race, so Oxford did not need a miracle to win. It looked easy, everyone said it was easy, but for Rankov it was murder. 'The tide was low so there was little help from it. We pulled our balls off to keep going. It was like rowing through glue.'

Rankov got his first blue late in his undergraduate career, and in four trips from Putney to Mortlake the highly strung inexperienced problem boy had become dependable old Boris, unstoppable, unflappable, friendly, tolerant of the reporters' repeated questions, the anchor man of the dark blues. He was president in 1980. The Cambridge men appeared slightly in awe of him, refusing to believe that a late entry who had, by his own admission, done no training at all for five months could take a stone off in a very short time and show match fitness. Yet by 7 February, when Oxford had a particularly violent outing with the University of London, Rankov had recovered the old power, stamina and aggression behind his oar.

Like Cambridge, but also like they themselves had done during the years in which Topolski was in charge, Oxford were to be seen every second weekend after Christmas on the Tideway. In fact in 1982 the rowing correspondents were kept busier than they could remember, scarcely a Saturday or Sunday passing without an encounter of one or other worth watching. Oxford's president Conington took two months from his trial eights on 9 December to name his crew, largely because he was convinced that he must persuade some of the blues still in residence to return to the boat. At the beginning of the year Conington and the coxswain, Sue Brown, were the only ones who made themselves available. Then before Christmas Richard Yonge, who had stood against Conington for the presidency, reappeared. John Bland and Mark Andrews, veterans now of Great Britain's silver-medal-winning eight, both made it clear that academy would prevail. So did Richard Emerton. But Rankov's door was opened when Conington knocked on it, and he didn't take a great deal of persuading.

He was still rankled about not getting a trial in that British eight. 'But that's life,' he said, pointing out that the national coach Penny Chuter had a week to make a crew from a galaxy of talent. 'Six Oxford men were invited down, and Richard Yonge and I weren't.'

Conington's crew was settled a couple of weeks before he announced it. Robert Clay of Eton and New College was in the bow, sitting behind his twin brother Hugh from the same school and Magdalene; Steve Foster, the classicist from Brentwood and Pembroke, was at number three; Alan Kirkpatrick from Durham University and Oriel sat in front of him; Yonge, who learned his rowing at King's School, Canterbury, and University College and Hospital, London, and was now at New College, was in the engine room at number five; Rankov at six; Nick Holland from Radley and Oriel at seven; and Conington himself, from Hampton and Oriel, in the stroke seat. Sue Brown of Taunton and Wadham was steering.

The crew were in the wars before the line-up was officially announced. Of the weekend of 7 and 8 February *The Times* correspondent Jim Railton began his piece: 'Each time the universities of Oxford and London meet on the Tideway an interesting conflict is guaranteed. They set out to destroy themselves, but yesterday Oxford, after a searching test of character, came out on top.' And Conington came out of the boat, injuring his back and turning as grey as the day's mood. London's crew were steered by Adrian Ellison, who adopted single-minded collision tactics when seated in the rear of his battleship. Neither Steve Higgins for Oxford on the Saturday nor Sue Brown on Sunday showed much inclination for the art of steering either, preferring to go for ramming. Between them the crews put modern oars through a severe test of strength from which the oars emerged intact but several tempers did not.

Oxford showed that they were not prepared to lie down and that they had reserves of power on which to draw when under severe pressure. This was particularly evident on the second day when, with Conington taken out of the boat into the coach's rubber duck, Holland moved to stroke, necessitating changing sides, and London University's junior international Reimbold found himself plucked off the bank to take the Oxford bow seat. It was an unhappy experience for him because he had been a hospital case of acute angina only three weeks before. He was replaced by the coach Topolski who applied himself as he would expect his crew to do, and while learning that he was older than he thought, he helped them to a desperate half-length lead in the third and final effort of the day. Boris Rankov was punching the air at the end, air which remained thick with the whiff of cordite for a long time afterwards. It even seeped under the door of UL's friendly and hospitable tearoom.

During the next fortnight Oxford were trained at Marlow under Mike Spracklen, a coach who is expert at putting polish on rowing technique. He did not get much of a chance, though, because Conington was injured and the secretary Steve Foster was out of the boat for two days with a virus infection. They got back together in time to meet the lightweights on the Tideway on 20 February and dealt with them even more summarily than Cambridge had done on the previous weekend, but on the Sunday Conington was too weak to go on. He was sent for blood tests and ordered to rest by the chief coach, Topolski.

Conington returned to the boat by the time the Reading University Head of River race came up on 6 March, though the crew was in a much different order. The president was in the bow, Rob Clay had moved to the stroke seat but remained on the bow side of the boat, Holland had moved back to number two, Kirkpatrick moved from four to seven, Foster from three to six, so the line-up now read from the bow: Conington, Holland, Hugh Clay, Yonge, Rankov, Foster, Kirkpatrick, Rob Clay, with Brown steering. They restored their confidence by winning at Reading, where Oxford had come unstuck the year before because the fin fell off their boat, leaving them entangled with the bank. But the opposition this time was, unusually, not very strong.

Desmond Hill in the *Daily Telegraph* reflected the collywobbles of the dark blue seers when he discussed the question of who should stroke:

> The agonising and immediate problem is surely not just which one but whether either of the two current candidates should stroke the boat. Both Conington's and Clay's techniques are so faulty, above all in uncovered finishes, one wonders if an alternative leader might not be beneficial. Clay, a youth international, handled last year's Isis–Goldie race with coolness and maturity. Conington stroked the national youth eight for two years but, hard trier that he is, there is a suspicion his rhythm is more effective over 1500 metres than 4¼ miles. However

great the gamble, there must be a case for giving Holland a further trial. When he changed sides in mid-outing a month ago to relieve the injured Conington as stroke, he successfully fought off all London University's assaults. The most obvious solution is bent over his books.

The return of John Bland, twice winner of the Boat Race, plus the Henley Grand and a silver medal in Britain's eight, 'could put Oxford's seventh successive victory beyond doubt,' concluded Hill.

At Reading, though, Topolski was convinced that the new order should remain although Conington seemed to have recovered. Persistent illness, particularly in the president, could be a worrying factor, therefore best to leave him in the bows where, should disaster strike, substitution would be less of a problem. And if Conington survived until the race and then ran into trouble, he would cause less of it in the bow than if he were disrupting men both in front and behind him. There was still time, of course, for the president to put himself out of the boat, but he seemed all right. But it was after his Reading race that Conington realized that his glandular fever might be persistent, and when he was watching Isis and Cambridge at Kingston a few days later he knew that his fitness for the 27 March, Boat Race day, was a gamble. Topolski was unaware of the exact nature of his trouble.

The order remained and the crew met no more opposition until they arrived at Clarendon Drive for the last two weeks. In Oxford they had dined at Merton, a modern tradition which speaks well of the cuisine. Here at Putney Susie Grimsdale, late of La Petite Cuisine School of Richmond, comes in every day to do the cooking, a welcome relief for her from the stuffier directors' lunches which she normally produces as a freelance cook. Like Pritchard across the road, she has to improvise in the small domestic kitchen; sometimes she is cooking for sixteen people. What makes up for working while stepping round crates of milk and Robinson's and straddling boxes of vitamins, is that they eat everything she can produce.

Oxford invite the rowing correspondents to dinner, and their coaches and wives, and the old blues. These are light-hearted gatherings on the whole, and the vibrations round the dinner table are of application and firm conviction of victory by a crew somewhat rough-hewn and not in the class of the 1981 eight, but strong and single-minded. Throughout their troubled training in the last two months they never gave up on an opponent, and it was this quality which would earn them the press's nomination as favourites on the morning of the race.

The Oxford crew's backgrounds and rowing experiences are diverse. Conington, a final-year physics student at Oriel, is from Hampton school where he was a good athlete as well as an oarsman, and could well have run for Oxford instead of pulled. His idol at school was Chris Mahoney, whom he followed to Oriel, to the blue boat, and to the presidency. He does not carry authority obviously or particularly openly, probably not the man to orchestrate a revolution and carry people with him, but an adequate leader in the more passive situation in which he finds himself. He has, after all, well-proven coaches and methods, Boris the anchor, a winning run, and an experienced crew. He is also quietly efficient, the sort of man who sends his thank-you letters promptly and who willingly visits his old school to encourage the next generation, and the infant school in Feltham where his mother is headmistress. The latter school took to the Boat Race, decking out its hall in dark and light blue and following the fortunes of the crews. Conington conducted operations from his shared flat in Boars Hill outside Oxford, running up the hill before breakfast, dealing with the administration in the morning and picking the crew up in the OUBC minibus outside the gates of Trinity at one o'clock to drive them to their training water, be it Henley, Radley, Pangbourne, or Marlow. Just as Cambridge almost never train in Cambridge, Oxford are almost never seen in Oxford. Too crowded, they say.

Alan Kirkpatrick is from the Royal Methodist College, Belfast, where he learned to row and won the Irish Schools Championships in 1977. He then went to Durham University and is now reading for an MSc in agricultural economics at Oriel. He is a first-generation oarsman, although there is a long history of rowing in Belfast. Richard Yonge took up rowing at King's School, Canterbury, because he was not good at ball games, then did three years of medicine at University College, London, where he came under the influence of the coach Jeff Easton. He was in the University College and Hospital four who lowered the record to Fawley in the Henley Wyfolds before they lost the race to Potomac in 1976. Then he moved to Oxford Polytechnic to take his degree, and is now at New College studying respiratory physiology.

Nick Holland, Radley College oarsman, chose to read engineering at Oriel because of the college's rowing reputation. Like the Clays, he is from a rowing background, first being taught by his godfather Ronald Bradbeer and subsequently by Jock Mullard at Radley. He runs amiably about the house in Clarendon Drive giving people cups of tea and loading the dishwasher, the only duty expected of the crew in the life of their kitchen.

The Clay twins are far from identical and are closest to the traditional idea of rowing blues, coming from Eton and with an elder brother, Henry, who rowed for Cambridge from 1974 to 1976, winning in his presidential year of 1975, and wound up in the British Olympic eight of 1980. Their father, John, lost with Oxford in 1949 and 1950. Hugh stands 6 feet 4½ inches and Robert is 6 feet 1 inch. They both rowed in British youth eights in 1978 and 1979; both go sailing. Hugh is reading jurisprudence at Magdalen and Rob ancient and modern history at New.

Steve Foster is the only man who learned his rowing at Oxford. From Brentwood School with a classics scholarship to Pembroke, he went down to the Isis in his first term and has rowed every term since, fired by making three bumps in his college's second boat in his first summer. He got a trial cap in the 1980–81 year, reaching the Isis boat, and now, in his penultimate term, is in the blue boat, a refugee from soccer at which he was hopeless and from swimming at which, like Nick Bliss, the Cambridge novice-to-blue, he was good. And there is Sue Brown, now with most of the spotlights turned away after the press's relentless pursuit of her the previous year, coming up for her biochemistry finals in Wadham with an almost completed dissertation entitled 'A Purification of Multiplication Stimulating Activity from Buffaloe Rat Liver Conditioned Medium'; and an ambition to return to Japan to teach for a year or two.

In the last fortnight the crews have the opportunity to watch each other more, if they wish to. Topolski spent considerable time watching Cambridge's outings on the Tideway during the weekends of build-up. Somehow, whenever the light blues were having a race, the wiry and wily Oxford coach happened to be out in his sculling boat. Or he was leaning over Hammersmith Bridge. Or he was lurking about at London Rowing Club to chat with reporters and ask questions when they came off the water after following a Cambridge outing. He did not, of course, have the monopoly of the watching; Hall, for one, picked his moments for a run along the towpath or a discreet solo voyage in Cambridge's motorized bath. But Topolski was paying unusually close attention to what he saw as well as to the results which he logged in his mind.

On 17 March, Cambridge had a return encounter with London University, who had revamped their crew and were much sharper. Amidst a Wagnerian storm the crews clashed before they started. Fagan for London got the better of the steering and his crew got the better of the light blues, but the latter did show a facility in rough water to burn after two minutes, which could be a crucial moment in the Boat Race.

On the next day Oxford, without Yonge, who absented himself for an interview, met the national squad's second crew, most of whom were limbering up for the Head of River race in which they were rowing for Kingston, and were beaten. On 20 March the Head was run from Mortlake to Putney, a grand procession of 420 eights won by the national squad, who lowered the record by seven seconds to 17 minutes 10 seconds, disappointed that they did not get it down a lot farther. Oxford had a light morning outing and went to Peacock Vane in Ventnor, Isle of Wight, a comfortable hotel run by the former Isis oarsman John Wolfenden, where they relaxed over an excellent meal and a change of surroundings, but where Topolski had to rescue Holland from over-zealous teasing over his nickname of Ron the Projectionist. It is at this point that some of the men reveal their little anxieties by digging at the others, and the coach, who remembers being a victim during his own blue days, keeps a watchful eye in case things get out of hand.

Cambridge's break was taken at a large house near Henley-on-Thames, where their titled landlady and her daughters treated them to a royal repast and the Sunday afternoon was spent watching the Cambridge lightweights, the Cambridge women, and the Cambridge women's reserves beat Oxford from the regatta finish to the island. A huge crowd rushed up and down the towpath to cheer their crews and there was buoyant mood abroad amongst light blues in the CUWBC's tea party in Leander Club's river-view restaurant afterwards. Three–nil, three–nil, said the voices of Girton, the ex-lacrosse players and swimmers who had put one over on Oxford with oars. It was a good omen, and the women gave the men a carnation. Too bad that the men's minibus was in collision with a Mini near Birfield Heath on their way back to their Henley house. They were unscathed but the other driver was injured. Their boat trailer had been hit in Hammersmith the week before. Having had a smooth programme all through their training they were now encountering small disasters.

Cambridge dined their blues and the press together at Hurlingham Club and were then ordered off to early beds while the heavies and the speculators heavied and speculated. It was an enjoyable evening, even Hall managing to hide his tension with smiles. They went to see *Anyone for Denis?* They watched video movies, as did Oxford, and then on an evening ebb tide two days before D-day they hit a submerged chest just off Chiswick Eyot, tearing off the fin and slitting the kevlar skin of their German boat. They waded ashore and were taken to Putney on the Cambridge launch while Hall towed the shell back. Immediately he and Alf Twinn, their boatman, got to work on the damage, and soon after dinner the crew took the boat out for a paddle in the dark, to test the repair and restore their assurance before a good night's sleep.

That was after they had met a much improved national lightweight eight again, the last of their practice encounters, on 23 March. Oxford met the same crew, who came like lambs to slaughter, the next day. Cambridge had taken about eleven seconds off the lightweights, so Oxford took about eighteen seconds off over the same course, from Hammersmith to the University Stone. They also set an official record of 6 minutes 46 seconds for the distance, about six seconds faster than Cambridge claimed for the distance rowed the previous evening, but six seconds slower than Cambridge claimed in an unofficial piece after the Head. All this, however, was the war of nerves, with both camps rubbishing the other's statistics or pointing out the differences of tide, wind, time of day, state of tiredness of the lightweights, etc.

Basically, the cameras were ready, the stage was set, the selection was settled, the training was done, and the world was getting impatient for their annual few minutes of partisan vicarious rowing. There was very little that could be done to alter the crews in lung, heart, or head now. All things being equal, Oxford would win through their one advantage: weight. All other things being equal. If they lost their heads, they would probably lose. Cambridge's good-luck gift from their girls, the red carnation, was still blooming in the refreshing water of their bidet in Clarendon Drive.

17
Rankov's fifth symphony
1982: The 128th Boat Race

Looking downstream from Chiswick Bridge at 10 a.m. on Boat Race day 1982 is a mysterious, misty experience. It is still very early in the day, for the race is not scheduled until 2.30 p.m. from Putney. The water, the meadows to the left and the brewery to the right are enshrouded in white vapour, but it is warm. The sun is up behind the television mast on the Surrey and western side of the bridge, promising a gorgeous day. Four single scullers in diamond formation emerge briefly from the bridge and glide into the opaque middle distance, almost suspended between ether and water, and they are followed by a four who have scullers as vanguard, rearguard and flankers. Workmen are busy hanging a Ladbrokes Hotels banner from the bridge and smoke rises from Watney's. The towpath is almost deserted, and the tide is low, low, so that even from the path which is damp from the latest high tide there is a bird's eye view of the passing boats.

There is a trailer camp of BBC vehicles under the Surrey side of the bridge, and Capital Radio's bus is drawn up outside the Ship. It is too early for signs of life from the pub but a swarthy Italian has been hiking along the path pinning cards advertising his restaurant on the trees. There is a stream of quiet scullers on the river, warming up for their Head of River race which will attract nearly five hundred of them on the next Saturday, and at each boathouse, crews are going afloat or coming ashore. The mist is lifting from Duke's Meadows and the bandstand in the civil servants' playing fields which has served as a landmark for Boat Race crews for many years.

A small fair and flea market is being set up between Mortlake and Barnes; there is utter inactivity at the police launch moorings near Barnes's latticed railway bridge, and every now and then a dog-walker or pram-pusher passes a television camera going through its paces at some strategic spot on the bank, while antennae reach for the sky and discs on poles are prepared to trap and plot the expected trial by oar. There are men working in the yard of Lep's waterside warehouse in Chiswick, but lower down the jarring note of their chainsaw gives way to the peels of St Nicholas's parish church, cheery and ushering in the fresh morning. The foliage is fresh too, the birds are singing, the motorway which hems Chiswick Mall to the Thames is out of sight, earshot and mind, and even the airliners dropping towards Heathrow float overhead with the sound turned down. Under the pale blue flawless sky weeping willows cascade to the high-tide mark, shading the crocuses and daffodils in the neat gardens which hug the Middlesex bank between beach and Mall. Filtered by the trees are the elegant frontages of fine old houses, bow-window and brass-knocker country, a houseboat in front of them here, a palm tree in the garden there. Chiswick Eyot stands exposed almost to its roots, with a green fringe on top. A gull stands statuesque on a post. A rusty moped lies near the water's edge on the Surrey shingle.

Where Chiswick turns to Hammersmith the houses back onto the river with gardens leading to an abrupt drop at this stage of the tide. Some have derricks and steps. The Black Lion is tucked behind them, and the park between it and the Old Ship is speckled with people enjoying the bright Saturday morning. From a town house by the pub comes the first real hint of impending events: a large sheet proclaiming 'Oxford' hangs from its balcony. There is a driftwood fire on the beach by Furnivall Gardens. West of Hammersmith Bridge a policeman on a motorcycle rides slowly up the towpath. Harrods furniture depository still looks gloomy on such a day as this. A television cameraman is already in position at Fairbairn's mile post, and at the Sea Scout hut at Barn Elms boxes of pop and crisps are arriving in the arms of willing helpers. By now it is almost eleven o'clock and the embankment at Putney is busy and expectant.

The rowing-club bars are opening for business, the tables are out on the lawn of the Constitutional Club, the panoramic windows of the Duke's Head are open and the first imbibers at the Star and Garter are bagging the window seats for a gallery view of the start. Men wearing earphones are looking for people with stopwatches and stroke timers. The police have not yet cordoned off the boathouses used by the crews, but they stand guard in front of them. At Oxford's the policeman is black and half as high again as Albert Andrews, the OUBC boatman, who is showing his ruddy countenance to the sun and not quite disguising his tension. He is wearing his cloth cap, black trousers and a smart double-breasted black jacket, and his black shoes are every bit as shined as the policeman's boots.

Reporters and supporters and heavies gather in small groups, those who have launch tickets checking from time to time that they haven't left them in their other jacket. Alan Mays-Smith (Cambridge, 1955–56), the London representative of the race who is responsible for liaison with Ladbrokes, the BBC and the Port of London Authority, is settling last-minute queries. There is little sign of activity at Barclay's Bank boathouse where Cambridge are billeted, and the doors at NatWest, the dark blue headquarters, are firmly shut. Sue Brown, however, is on the embankment passing the time of day with Mike Muir-Smith, the umpire, and Dan Topolski, the Oxford coach, is also in evidence. Soon the Oxford launch *Bosporos* crunches her nose onto the beach and Miss Brown and Mr Topolski climb aboard so that Bert Green, who is driving, can take the coxswain over the course for the last time when it doesn't matter. The ex-Oxford coach, Dick Fishlock, and his two small boys are invited aboard for the ride, and they sit in the bows while Brown and Topolski sit on the gunwale alongside Green who is amidships. Putney is serene, clean and colourful as *Bosporos* slips away, now moving upstream with the incoming tide, or what there is of it. They sail and hunt the stream as far as Chiswick, talking very little. It's 12.50 and Bert says there is going to be a lot of water because it's already reached the foot of the Fulham wall. Brown is wearing a green sun visor, and for much of the return trip she sits demurely cross-legged on the deck, facing the stern, watching the limp flag while the course rolls out from under her. 'We didn't learn anything from that,' Topolski says. 'On this occasion we just went out because it's traditional.' Camera work.

On the embankment a youth sells favours from a cardboard egg box which he has hung round his neck. Bills on the trees advertise Boat Race reports and rowing news from the rivals of Fleet Street, and a lad on roller skates swirls and pirouettes through the crowds selling a competitor to the official programme. It is *Rowling*, Vol. 1, No. 1, and besides containing the names of the crews it has the results of the eights Head of the River race which was held a week earlier. It will take the magazine *Rowing*, which *Rowling* mercilessly satirizes, several weeks to come up with that information. *Rowling* also has a hilarious analysis of an East German oarsman. In cutaway section it shows his carbon-fibre reinforced limbs and solid hardwood skull, cold-cured backbone, kevlar-impregnated stomach and the silicon chip which he has for a brain. At this moment there are eight men in the NatWest Bank's changing rooms and eight more just arriving at Barclay's in their minibus who are trying to kid themselves that they are just like that. But their chosen sport is much more human.

While the Isis and Goldie crews are warming up on the water the two presidents meet for the toss, performed with the aid of the 1829 gold sovereign presented to the Boat Race by John Snagge. Oxford win and Conington chooses Surrey. Umpire Muir-Smith is asked by David Coleman of the BBC what his hopes are for the race. 'I expect them to stay on their stations and keep out of trouble,' he says, echoing what he had told the coxswains the day before when pointing out to them the undesirability of clashing. Stephens of Cambridge tells Coleman and the millions of viewers on the Grandstand programme: 'We're out to give them a licking today. If we keep nibbling at them all the way we should be onto a win. We're much fitter than they are. We know that.' Asked about the toss, he says, 'I don't think it's too important today. I think it's going to be a close race all the way. I don't think either crew is sufficiently powerful to put in tactical bursts and take advantage of bends.' Conington agrees about the toss, saying that it isn't too important but that 'it's going to affect the way both crews are going to race this race. I think the outcome will be the same whatever station we chose. I think we're a very fast crew and a difficult crew to beat.'

The interviews continue, the presidents being probed about weight, aggression, motivation. Conington: 'I really can't see how they can be fitter than us. There's a lot more to it than that.' Stephens: 'We're not worried about being lighter. The crew's getting better and better. We're looking for the race of our lives.' Conington: 'We're not the prettiest crew to watch, but we've got a lot of power, a lot of strength.' Stephens: 'It's not personal hatred towards the Oxford camp . . . so much work has been put in.'

Partly they tell the viewers what they have to believe, partly they echo the predictions in the press. The newspapers which cover rowing regularly all predict an Oxford win this day, although all have more than a good word to say for Cambridge. Penny Chuter, the senior national rowing coach, who is to share the television commentary with Harry Carpenter, echoes their opinions as she explains the map of the course to viewers. 'Oxford are stronger,' she says. 'In theory they should win.'

Soon after the crews have carried their boats to the water and embarked for the quiet warm-up reach downstream from Putney Bridge, cheered by their supporters as they paddle pristine in the sunshine, there is a little drama as Goldie on the Middlesex station take a flier at the start of their match with Isis. The umpire, Nick Tee, calls them back again and the second start gets off cleanly to a roar from the banks. Goldie go into an immediate lead but Isis overhaul them before the crews are clear of the Putney boathouses and disappear from view and thoughts.

The blue boats slip quietly through Putney Bridge to take up their stations. Oxford have six red Cambridge lions along their gunwale, like a Spitfire with its tally of swastikas. The calm water makes no difficulties for getting attached to the stakeboats, and precisely on time Mike Muir-Smith, standing in the umpire's launch *Scorpio*, asks the crews if they are ready. Sue Brown's hand is raised for a short while as Oxford straighten up on the Surrey station, and then the boats are away cleanly on the 'Go!'

The flotilla of launches sets off in line abreast behind them, Chas Newens keeping *Scorpio* close and between the crews, the rest abreast and churning up a sizable wake as all eyes are on the crucial first ten strokes. By now Putney is floating on an ocean of spectators, lining the bridge and the embankment from the railings to the Lower Richmond Road, enveloping the Star and Garter and the Duke's Head, packed on the rowing club balconies. Bishop's Park on the Fulham bank is also lined, and the biggest crowd for a decade is rewarded by Cambridge's Harris setting a rate of 35 strokes to the minute and edging relentlessly ahead of the heavier dark blues. After the first minute Harris may see Oxford's Rankov and Yonge, in the five and four seats respectively, if he cares to look, and his crew are still moving up at the mile post. Harris is driving them to their main chance on the Middlesex station of the smooth highway: to get far enough in front of their sluggish opponents to take their water by Hammersmith and so to give themselves the advantage of the long bend which favours Oxford's station. Cambridge's coxswain Ian Bernstein is doing his bit as well, pressing Sue Brown farther and farther towards the Surrey shore in the hope that she will move too far over and allow Bernstein to straddle the stream, such as it is.

Brown maybe does go a little too far. Cambridge settle to 34, one stroke a minute slower than Oxford, and move out to threequarters of a length in front, but it is not yet enough. Dan Topolski in the bows of *Bosporos* is getting agitated, while Hall and the Cambridge blues in the *Amaryllis* see none of this because their propeller has caught two plastic Tesco bags right at the start, and they are now vainly attempting to catch up behind the lumbering large boats, the *Queen Elizabeth* and the *Hurlingham*. The rest of the flotilla is still in line approaching Hammersmith, however: the *Clivanda* with Brian Johnston and the BBC radio team, the *Enchantress* with the timekeepers and the press, the *Magician* and the *Majestic* with the old blues, and the *Aquarius* with more newspaper men and photographers. Hammersmith Bridge is closed to spectators but the Mall is packed to the gunwales with them, as is the towpath.

Cambridge are a second ahead at the mile and extending their lead, but approaching Harrods Oxford begin to pull back the deficit, imperceptibly at first. Rob Clay stroking them on bow side maintains an expression every bit as determined as Harris's, and the rate which he sets remains constant at 35. But the work in the water is hardening, and Sue Brown begins to edge out towards Cambridge. Bernstein appears to give water readily, and as the two crews approach the bridge they look as if they are level. The difference between the ratings remains at one pip, although both strokes have raised their striking slightly. The other difference is that Miss Brown has steered into a perfect position for shooting the bridge, the wake of the Carbocraft describing an even arc towards the shadow ready to take the sharp turn without requiring overtime from the rudder. Perhaps she is not in the advantageous position for the stream, but Bernstein is veering towards the centre of the span with much turning left to do. When the flag dips as the boats reach the bridge Oxford are one second ahead, or not much more than a canvas. By the time both shells are clear of the bridge, Oxford are a length ahead and streaking away, dropping their rating. Suddenly they have changed the whole pattern of the race and left the Cambridge coxswain near the centre of the river with a choice of tucking in behind the dark blues or continuing on course in the diminishing hope of getting effective help from the stream.

The thousands at Hammersmith, the millions allowed a helicopter's eye view, and not least the Oxford coaching team, have seen a burn as brilliant as it was devastating. Seconds before, Topolski was wondering whether his men had heard him right at the prerace talk. 'Go somewhere between Harrods and Hammersmith Bridge,' he had told them, wherever they felt necessary. Or, more precisely, where Clay felt it was necessary. They were expecting to be led in the early stages, for they knew Cambridge were more nimble than themselves. They didn't, however, expect to be led by quite so much. From the *Bosporos* and the other launches they appeared not to be going at all. What were they waiting for? Cambridge hadn't got their water but were set to remain on terms. Clay turned on the power, not the rate of stroke, and it did the trick subtly and efficiently and, at the last moment, dramatically. First you see a neck-and-neck struggle, for struggle it was; now you see a procession.

But the race is by no means over at this point. The Oxford burn has taken so much out of them that they doubt whether they can raise another, so the danger is still that Harris will wear them down by a succession of changes of gear, and they will be unable to respond. An unlikely scenario for sure, but a possible one, for this is where Cambridge's fitness can reap dividends. Oxford gradually move down from 36 to 33 but they continue to draw away. Bernstein keeps Cambridge outside their opponents and takes a little scenic deviation towards Chiswick Eyot, and at Chiswick Steps the gap between the boats is nine seconds or about three lengths. Oxford's burn and bend has handed them at least ten seconds and Cambridge need the hand of fate to help them now. They have lost any control over where Miss Brown might steer their opponents and for a while they are in the worst position, washed down by an opponent in the stream. Their rowing does not suffer but they are outmanoeuvred, and fate does not extend a hand. Oxford make what use they like of the Middlesex bend after Barnes Bridge, where, with a slack stream, corner-cutting is probably no bad thing, and in spite of Cambridge's gallant finishing burst they are able to extend their lead by a further two seconds. The verdict of three and a quarter lengths brings them their seventh consecutive win, makes Boris Rankov the first oarsman to win five races, and leaves the score at Oxford 59, Cambridge 68, with one dead heat. Cambridge reached the mile first in 3 minutes 47 seconds (Oxford 3.48), while Oxford's times were 6 minutes 53 seconds to Hammersmith (6.54), 11 minutes 2 seconds to Chiswick Steps

(11.11), 15 minutes 10 seconds at Barnes Bridge (15.20), and 18 minutes 21 seconds to the finish (18.32).

All the way the banks are thick with people, and by the Ibis and Quintin boathouses at the finish is a great crush as the crews come ashore, Cambridge dejected and neglected outside Ibis and Oxford jubilant and elated outside Quintin. An Isis man, flushed with his own five-second win over Goldie, lifts Sue Brown out of the boat and holds her up for the photographers and microphones. It is a struggle to put the boat away, a struggle to think or hear or be heard. Reporters dash about trying to get quotations, or simply to get somebody to say something coherent. Men from the sponsoring Ladbrokes group dash about trying to get the crew to the lawn to receive their medals and the trophy, which depicts an oarsman labouring over an oar in a manner foreign to any known coaching manual. Parents and girlfriends look for sons and boyfriends and corks pop in the Quintin changing room.

At Ibis a huge television set begins the first of several replays in the bar, but behind the scenes is the heavy, empty pall of defeat. Some of these light blue men have never won anything. They have applied themselves to physical endurance and sometimes pain for six months. Nineteen minutes ago they were utterly convinced that together they were going to achieve their individual ambitions of winning this race, an ambition for self and a crock of secondary desires, such as reward for CUBC, their college, university, school or coach. They gave their all and they are slumped in a silent, sweaty slough, heads in hands, and the hardest weeping. Harris, the lightweight who strokes, has wet eyes, and so does Bliss, the law student who is leaving Cambridge, and so does president Stephens, who scored a new symphony for the orchestra in the summer before and who is also leaving Cambridge. Graeme Hall, the coach, has never felt so bad in his brooding way about a loss. Even the sandwiches curl in distress. Later, as they pack their yellow shell onto its trailer, a reporter murmurs consolation to Harris. 'There's always next year,' says Harris, forcing a twitchy smile.

18

Another end, another beginning
The pageant presses on

The road to next year began pretty soon after the ball at the Savoy on the night of 27 March, which some of the blues dread and few are in a fit state to enjoy. Nick Conington, for example, was found asleep on a couch elsewhere in the hotel, victim of exhaustion and fever rather than bacchanalian excesses and euphoria. The Cambridge crew all went to Sunday lunch at their president's parental home after the ball, and it was not many weeks before Simon Harris was elected president at Cambridge for the 1983 Boat Race, and word filtered to the press that the light blues would not be returning to their college boats for the Mays. At Cambridge this is like the principals of the orchestra not showing up for the last night of the Proms. Blues have traditionally returned to help the college out, but Harris and Graeme Hall had other tunes, other occasions on their minds. The best way to recover from the devastating emptiness of the Ibis locker room was to keep as much of the CUBC flagship together as possible for a year when five of them would no longer be freshmen, to distance themselves from the main event of the Cam year which their club would organize, and to race through a hard summer. With John Kinsella at two and Chris Roberts at four from the Goldie crew in place of Bliss and Brine, they won their first medals at Mannheim regatta in Germany, won the Metropolitan regatta at Thorpe in Surrey, and were allowed to compete in the Thames Cup at Henley, a second-class competition, on the grounds that in spite of being a representative university boat they had seven freshmen on board. At Henley the crew beat Hollingworth Lake in the first round, Star Club of Bedford in the second, Tideway Scullers' School in the third, Leander in the semifinal, and lost to the Charles River Rowing Association of the United States in the final. Bliss and

Brine turned up as well, the former rowing for the Pembroke and Corpus, Cambridge, composite Ladies' Plate crew who beat Leeds and Newcastle universities before losing to Harvard, and the latter in a St Thomas's Hospital coxless four in the Wyfold Cup, beaten by Thames Tradesmen in the first round.

Most of the Oxford blues took part in Eights Week with their colleges, Oriel retaining the Head with Conington, Kirkpatrick and Holland on board. Most of them turned up at Henley, too, although Dan Topolski's already deeply contemplated plans for the 1983 Boat Race did not include any attempt to keep the eight or parts of it together for the summer. The new president, Richard Yonge, appeared with Holland, Topolski himself and Jerry Dale, a former Oxford president, in the Wyfold fours, losing to London RC in the first round. Boris Rankov and Rob Clay survived one round of the Goblets before being beaten by Paul Wensley and Paul Reynolds of the University of London and Kingston. Kirkpatrick turned up as a substitute in the Isis crew in the Ladies' Plate. They beat Queen's University, Belfast, and then three American universities in succession, Santa Clara, Georgetown and Harvard, before losing the final to the University of London's second crew. Hugh Clay and Foster did not compete, and Conington and Susan Brown were part of a British composite crew of more than twenty whom the Amateur Rowing Association sent to the dragon boat races in Hong Kong.

Also seen at Henley was a manifestation of the lessons of Pindar which Charles Wordsworth, co-founder of the Boat Race, recommended to his students at St Andrews so many years before. Pindar's code included not being envious of your opponents' success, to be generous towards them. It is hard to reconcile these with the needle sometimes, but there in the Goblets were two men who had opposed each other to the brink of bitterness during the previous year's Boat Race. The respective presidents of Oxford and Cambridge for 1981, Chris Mahoney and James Palmer, were rowing as a pair representing Molesey and Eton Vikings.

Cambridge were not through yet. Their aim was the under-23 championship of the world, for which they had secured the British nomination. The seating order was changed by the time they arrived in Vienna for the regatta two weeks after Henley, Kinsella moving into the stroke seat. They were leading just before halfway along the course on a lake parallel to the Danube, when he had a mishap with his oar, which separated him from the handle. They had to stop before they could recover. The Danes, who were their most dangerous opponents, went into the lead and the Germans, French and Spanish got ahead as well, and although Cambridge moved up rapidly approaching the line they had to settle for fourth. Hall couldn't bear to watch the race, so he settled them at the start and cycled off for the finish, being told threequarters of the way along that his men were leading. He couldn't believe what he saw when he turned round at the end. But it was true. The light blues thus lost the Match des Seniors, but at least they had won a crop of races and some medals after the Boat Race.

They had, too, given Oxford a run for their money. In the cold print of the statistics it is easy to assume that because Oxford have won seven races in a row, Cambridge are a pushover. Nothing could be farther from the truth. Topolski's crews have had to fight to gain their run of victories, and 1982 was a nerve-racking year. What with Holland unhappy about his place, with Yonge missing outings for interviews or exams, with Rankov being unfit at Christmas, and with president Conington invalided out of the boat during training and always vulnerable to sickness, he could have done without the constant pressure of Stephens's revolutionary cadre for the six months leading to the race. But life isn't like that, nor is the needle. Thirteen men have been added to the blues' register, having taken part in the Boat Race or passed Mortlake Brewery in it, whichever definition one prefers. And in the light of the facts that Cambridge have more wins than Oxford and that, roughly calculated, they were 133 lengths ahead of Oxford by 1983 in the great partisan needle match since 1829, then the blues and we watchers can only agree with *Punch* in toasting the future: Oxford won, Cambridge too.

Results

Year	Winner	Time min. sec.		Distance
1829	Oxford	14	30	Easily
1836	Cambridge	36	0	1 min.
1839	Cambridge	31	0	1 min. 45 sec.
1840	Cambridge	29	30	¾ length
1841	Cambridge	32	30	1 min. 5 sec.
1842	Oxford	30	10	13 sec.
1845	Cambridge	23	30	30 sec.
1846	Cambridge	21	5	3 lengths
1849	Cambridge	22	0	Easily
1849	Oxford	—		Foul
1852	Oxford	21	36	27 sec.
1854	Oxford	25	29	11 strokes
1856	Cambridge	25	45	½ length
1857	Oxford	22	50	32 sec.
1858	Cambridge	21	23	22 sec.
1859	Oxford	24	40	Camb. sank
1860	Cambridge	26	5	1 length
1861	Oxford	23	30	47 sec.
1862	Oxford	24	40	30 sec.
1863	Oxford	23	6	45 sec.
1864	Oxford	21	40	27 sec.
1865	Oxford	21	24	4 lengths
1866	Oxford	25	35	3 lengths
1867	Oxford	22	39	½ length
1868	Oxford	20	56	6 lengths
1869	Oxford	20	4†	3 lengths
1870	Cambridge	22	4	1½ lengths

Year	Winner	Time min. sec.		Distance
1871	Cambridge	23	10	1 length
1872	Cambridge	21	15	2 lengths
1873	Cambridge	19	35†	3 lengths
1874	Cambridge	22	35	3½ lengths
1875	Oxford	22	2	10 lengths
1876	Cambridge	20	20	Easily
1877	Dead heat	24	8	—
1878	Oxford	22	15	10 lengths
1879	Cambridge	21	18	3 lengths
1880	Oxford	21	23	3¾ lengths
1881	Oxford	21	51	3 lengths
1882	Oxford	20	12	7 lengths
1883	Oxford	21	18	3½ lengths
1884	Cambridge	21	39	2½ lengths
1885	Oxford	21	36	2½ lengths
1886	Cambridge	22	30	⅔ length
1887	Cambridge	20	52	2½ lengths
1888	Cambridge	20	48	7 lengths
1889	Cambridge	20	14	3 lengths
1890	Oxford	22	3	1 length
1891	Oxford	21	48	½ length
1892	Oxford	19	10†	2¼ lengths
1893	Oxford	18	45†	1 length 4 ft
1894	Oxford	21	39	3½ lengths
1895	Oxford	20	50	2¼ lengths
1896	Oxford	20	1	⅖ length
1897	Oxford	19	12	2½ lengths
1898	Oxford	22	15	Easily
1899	Cambridge	21	4	3¼ lengths
1900	Cambridge	18	45	20 lengths
1901	Oxford	22	31	⅖ length
1902	Cambridge	19	9	5 lengths
1903	Cambridge	19	33	6 lengths
1904	Cambridge	21	37	4½ lengths
1905	Oxford	20	35	3 lengths
1906	Cambridge	19	25	3½ lengths
1907	Cambridge	20	26	4½ lengths
1908	Cambridge	19	20	2½ lengths
1909	Oxford	19	50	3½ lengths
1910	Oxford	20	14	3½ lengths

Year	Winner	Time min.	sec.	Distance
1911	Oxford	18	29†	2¾ lengths
1912	Oxford[1]	22	5	6 lengths
1913	Oxford	20	53	¾ length
1914	Cambridge	20	23	4½ lengths
1920	Cambridge	21	11	4 lengths
1921	Cambridge	19	45	1 length
1922	Cambridge	19	27	4½ lengths
1923	Oxford	20	54	¾ length
1924	Cambridge	18	41	4½ lengths
1925	Cambridge	21	50	Oxford sank
1926	Cambridge	19	29	5 lengths
1927	Cambridge	20	14	3 lengths
1928	Cambridge	20	25	10 lengths
1929	Cambridge	19	24	7 lengths
1930	Cambridge	19	9	2 lengths
1931	Cambridge	19	26	2½ lengths
1932	Cambridge	19	11	5 lengths
1933	Cambridge	20	57	2¼ lengths
1934	Cambridge	18	3†	4¼ lengths
1935	Cambridge	19	48	4½ lengths
1936	Cambridge	21	6	5 lengths
1937	Oxford	22	39	3 lengths
1938	Oxford	20	30	2 lengths
1939	Cambridge	19	3	4 lengths
1946	Oxford	19	54	3 lengths
1947	Cambridge	23	1	10 lengths
1948	Cambridge	17	50†	5 lengths
1949	Cambridge	18	57	¼ length
1950	Cambridge	20	15	3½ lengths
1951	Cambridge[2]	20	50	12 lengths
1952	Oxford	20	23	Canvas
1953	Cambridge	19	54	8 lengths
1954	Oxford	20	23	4½ lengths
1955	Cambridge	19	10	16 lengths
1956	Cambridge	18	36	1¼ lengths
1957	Cambridge	19	1	2 lengths
1958	Cambridge	18	15	3½ lengths
1959	Oxford	18	52	6 lengths
1960	Oxford	18	59	1¼ lengths
1961	Cambridge	19	22	4¼ lengths

Year	Winner	Time min. sec.		Distance
1962	Cambridge	19	46	5 lengths
1963	Oxford	20	47	5 lengths
1964	Cambridge	19	18	6½ lengths
1965	Oxford	18	7	4 lengths
1966	Oxford	19	12	3¾ lengths
1967	Oxford	18	52	3¼ lengths
1968	Cambridge	18	22	3½ lengths
1969	Cambridge	18	4	4 lengths
1970	Cambridge	20	22	3½ lengths
1971	Cambridge	17	58	10 lengths
1972	Cambridge	18	36	9½ lengths
1973	Cambridge	19	21	13 lengths
1974	Oxford	17	35†	5½ lengths
1975	Cambridge	19	27	3¾ lengths
1976	Oxford	16	58†	6½ lengths
1977	Oxford	19	28	7 lengths
1978	Oxford	18	58	Camb. sank
1979	Oxford	20	33	3½ lengths
1980	Oxford	19	20	Canvas
1981	Oxford	18	11	8 lengths
1982	Oxford	18	21	3¼ lengths

Cambridge 68, Oxford 59, one dead heat
[1] Rerow. In first race both crews sank
[2] Rerow. In first race Oxford sank
† Race records

ISIS *v.* GOLDIE RESULTS

Year	Winner	Time min. sec.		Distance
1965	Isis	18	45	7 lengths
1966	Isis	19	22	7 lengths
1967	Goldie	19	11	2 lengths
1968	Goldie	18	44	5½ lengths
1969	Goldie	18	50	2 lengths
1970	Goldie	19	58	14 lengths
1971	Goldie	18	37	15 lengths

Results

Year	Winner	Time min.	sec.	Distance
1972	Goldie	19	19	2½ lengths
1973	Goldie	18	13	5 lengths
1974	Goldie	17	51	4 lengths
1975	Isis	21	16	9½ lengths
1976	Isis	17	34	2½ lengths
1977	Goldie	19	35	7 lengths
1978	Goldie	19	37	1¼ lengths
1979	Goldie	22	50	12 lengths
1980	Isis	19	3	5 lengths
1981	Isis	19	1	4½ lengths
1982	Isis	18	43	1⅔ lengths

Goldie 11, Isis 7

Crew Lists

The first race was from Hambleden Lock to the bridge at Henley-on-Thames. The next five, those in 1836, 1839 and 1840–42, were from Westminster to Putney. The rest were rowed from Putney to Mortlake except in 1846, 1856 and 1863 when the ebb tide from Mortlake to Putney was used. Weights are unreliable, an accurate weigh-in taking place only since 1976. The crew in the left-hand column had the Surrey station. † denotes the winner of the toss. * denotes an old blue.

ABBREVIATIONS

Oxford

Ball. – Balliol College
BNC – Brasenose College
CCC – Corpus Christi College
Ch.Ch. – Christ Church
Ex. – Exeter College
Linc. – Lincoln College
Magd. – Magdalen College
Mert. – Merton College
New C. – New College
Pemb. – Pembroke College
Qu. – Queen's College
St Cath. – St Catherine's College
St Ed. H. – St Edmund Hall
St Joh. – St John's College
Trin. – Trinity College
Univ. – University College
Wadh. – Wadham College
Worc. – Worcester College

Cambridge

CCC – Corpus Christi College
Chr. – Christ's College
Dow. – Downing College
Emm. – Emmanuel College
Fitz. – Fitzwilliam College
LMBC – Lady Margaret Boat Club
   (St John's College)
Magd. – Magdalene College
Pemb. – Pembroke College
Pet. – Peterhouse
Qu. – Queens' College
St Cath. – St Catharine's College
St Joh. – St John's College (see LMBC)
Selw. – Selwyn College
Sid. S. – Sidney Sussex College
1 Trin. – First Trinity BC
2 Trin. – Second Trinity BC
3 Trin. – Third Trinity BC
1 & 3 Trin. – First and Third Trinity BC
Trin. H. – Trinity Hall

1 Wednesday, 10 June 1829, at 7.56 p.m.

Berks		Bucks	
CAMBRIDGE †		OXFORD	
A. B. E. Holdsworth, Charterhouse and 1 Trin., bow	10. 7	J. Carter, Shrewsbury and St Joh., bow	
A. F. Bayford, Kensington GS and Trin H.	10. 8	J. E. Arbuthnot, Shrewsbury and Ball.	
C. Warren, Hammersmith and 2 Trin.	10.10	J. E. Bates, Westminster and Ch.Ch.	
C. Merivale, Harrow and LMBC	11. 0	C. Wordsworth, Harrow and Ch.Ch.	11.10
T. Entwisle, Rugby and Trin. H.	11. 4	J. J. Toogood, Harrow and Ball.	14.10
W. T. Thompson, Ruthin and Jesus	11.10	T. F. Garnier, Winchester and Worc.	
G. A. Selwyn, Eton and LMBC	11.13	G. B. Moore, Westminster and Ch.Ch.	12. 4
W. Snow, Eton and LMBC, str.	11. 4	T. Staniforth, Eton and Ch.Ch., str.	12. 0
B. R. Heath, Eton and 1 Trin., cox	9. 4¾	W. R. Fremantle, Westminster and Ch.Ch., cox	8. 2
Average	11. 1½		

Oxford won easily in 14 min. 30 sec.

2 Friday, 17 June 1836 at 4.20 p.m. (stations not recorded)

CAMBRIDGE		OXFORD	
W. H. Solly, Harrow and 1 Trin., bow	11. 0	G. Carter, Shrewsbury and St Joh., bow	10. 0
F. S. Green, Shrewsbury and Caius	11. 2	E. Stephens, Blundell's and Ex.	10. 7
E. S. Stanley, Eton and Jesus	11. 4	Sir W. Baillie, Bt, Eton and Ch.Ch.	11. 7
P. Hartley, Charterhouse and Trin. H.	12. 0	T. Harris, Rugby and Magd.	12. 4
W. M. Jones, Westminster and Caius	12. 0	Sir J. V. Isham, Bt, Eton and Ch.Ch.	12. 0
J.H. Keane, Rugby and 1 Trin.	12. 0	J. Pennefather, Harrow and Ball.	12.10
A. W. Upcher, Private and 2 Trin.	12. 0	W. S. Thomson, Ruthin and Jesus	13. 0
A. K. B. Granville, St Paul's and CCC, str.	11. 7	F. L. Moysey, Westminster and Ch.Ch., str.	10. 6
T. S. Egan, Rottingdean and Caius, cox	9. 0	E. W. L. Davies, Cowbridge and Jesus, cox	10. 3
Average	11. 8⅝	Average	11. 7¾

Cambridge won by nearly a minute in 36 min. 0 sec.

3 Wednesday, 3 April 1839, at 4.47 p.m.

Surrey		Middlesex	
CAMBRIDGE		**OXFORD †**	
A. H. Shadwell, Eton and LMBC, bow	10. 7	S. Lee, Reading and Qu., bow	10. 4
W. W. Smyth, Westminster and 2 Trin.	11. 0	J. Compton, Private and Mert.	11. 5
J. Abercombie, Tonbridge and Caius	10. 7	S. E. Maberly, Eton and Ch.Ch.	11. 4
A. Paris, Cheam and CCC	11. 4	W. J. Garnett, Eton and Ch.Ch.	12.10
C. T. Penrose, Rugby and 1 Trin.	12. 0	R. G. Walls, Rugby and BNC	13. 0
W. H. Yatman, Winchester and Caius	10.10	R. Hobhouse, Eton and Ball.	12. 0
W. B. Brett, Westminster and Caius	12. 0	P. L. Powys, Eton and Ball.	12. 0
*E. S. Stanley, Eton and Jesus, str.	10. 6	C. Bewicke, Westminster and Univ., str.	12. 0
*T. S. Egan, Rottingdean and Caius, cox	9. 0	W. W. Ffooks, Sherborne and Ex., cox	10. 2
Average	11. 0¾	Average	11.10½

Cambridge won by 1 min. 45 sec. in 31 min. 0 sec.

4 Wednesday, 15 April 1840, at 1.30 p.m.

CAMBRIDGE		OXFORD †	
*A. H. Shadwell, Eton and LMBC, bow	10. 7	J. G. Mountain, Eton and Mert., bow	11. 0
W. Massey, Harrow and 1 Trin.	11. 0	I. J. I. Pocock, Eton and Mert.	11. 2
S. B. Taylor, Dr Pinckney's and 1 Trin.	11. 7	*S. E. Maberly, Eton and Ch.Ch.	11. 4
J. M. Ridley, Eton and Jesus	12. 8	W. Rogers, Eton and Ball.	12.10
G. C. Uppleby, Shrewsbury and Magd.	11.12	*R. G. Walls, Rugby and BNC	12. 7
F. C. Penrose, Winchester and Magd.	12. 1	E. Royds, Rugby and BNC	12. 4
H. C. Jones, Shrewsbury	11. 9	G. Meynell, Shrewsbury and BNC	11.10
C. M. Vialls, Westminster and 3 Trin., str.	11. 6	J. J. T. Somers-Cocks, Westminster and BNC, str.	11. 3
*T. S. Egan, Rottingdean and Caius, cox	9. 0	W. B. Garnett, Shrewsbury and BNC, cox	9. 7
Average	11. 8	Average	11.10½

Cambridge won by ¾ length in 29 min. 30 sec.

5 Wednesday, 14 April 1841, at 6.10 p.m.

OXFORD		CAMBRIDGE †	
R. Bethell, Eton and Ex., bow	10. 6	W. R. Croker, Private and Caius, bow	9.12
E. V. Richards, Westminster and Ch.Ch.	11. 2	Hon. L. W. Denman, Shrewsbury and Magd.	10.12
*J. G. Mountain, Eton and Mert.	10. 9	A. M. Ritchie, Private and 1 Trin.	11.10
*E. Royds, Rugby and BNC	11.13	*J. M. Ridley, Eton and Jesus	12. 7
H. W. Hodgson, Westminster and Ball.	11.10	R. H. Cobbold, Shrewsbury and Pet.	12. 4
W. Lea, Rugby and BNC	11. 7	*F. C. Penrose, Winchester and Magd.	12. 0
G. Meynell, Shrewsbury and BNC	11.11	Hon. G. Denman, Repton and 1 Trin.	10. 7
*J. J. T. Somers-Cocks, Westminster and BNC, str.	11. 4	*C. M. Vialls, Westminster and 3 Trin., str.	11. 7
*C. B. Wollaston, Ottery St Mary and Ex., cox	9. 2	J. M. Croker, Private and Caius, cox	10. 8
Average	11. 4⅛	Average	11. 5⅝

Cambridge won by 1 min. 5 sec. in 32 min. 30 sec.

6 Saturday, 11 June 1842, at 3.43 p.m.

CAMBRIDGE		OXFORD †	
F. E. Tower, Harrow and LMBC, bow	10. 2	F. T. M. M'Dougall, King's Coll., Lon., and Magd. H.,[1] bow	9. 8
* Hon. L. W. Denman, Shrewsbury and Magd.	10.11	Sir R. Menzies, Bt, Edin. Univ. and Univ.	11. 3
W. Watson, Private and Jesus	10.13	E. A. Breedon, Private and Trin.	12. 4
* F. C. Penrose, Winchester and Magd.	11.10	W. B. Brewster, Eton and St Joh.	12.10
* R. H. Cobbold, Shrewsbury and Pet.	12. 6	.G. D. Bourne, Eton and Oriel	13.12
J. Royds, Rugby and Chr.	11. 7	J. C. Cox, Winchester and Trin.	11. 8
*Hon. G. Denman, Repton and 1 Trin.	10. 9	G. E. Hughes, Rugby and Oriel	11. 6
*J. M. Ridley, Eton and Jesus, str.	12. 0	F. N. Menzies, Edin. Univ. and Univ., str.	10.12
A. B. Pollock, Westminster and 3 Trin., cox	9. 7	A. T. W. Shadwell, Eton and Ball., cox	10. 4
Average	11. 3¾	Average	11. 9⅝

Oxford won by 13 sec. in 30 min. 10 sec.
[1]Magdalen Hall, now Hertford.

7 Saturday, 15 March 1845, at 6.01 p.m.

OXFORD		CAMBRIDGE †	
M. Haggard, Westminster and Ch.Ch., bow	10. 3	G. Mann, Private and Caius, bow	10. 7
W. Chetwynd-Stapleton, Eton and Mert.	10.12	W. Harkness, Eton and LMBC	10. 0
W. H. Milman, Westminster and Ch.Ch.	11. 0	W. S. Lockhart, King's Coll., Lon., and Chr.	11. 3
H. Lewis, Private and Pemb.	11. 7	W. P. Cloves, Private and 1 Trin.	12. 0
W. Buckle, Winchester and Oriel	13.12	F. M. Arnold, Rugby and Caius	12. 0
F. C. Royds, Rugby and BNC	11. 5	R. Harkness, Eton and LMBC	11. 0
F. M. Wilson, Eton and Ch.Ch.	12. 3	J. Richardson, Shrewsbury and 1 Trin.	12. 0
F. E. Tuke, Eton and BNC, str.	12. 2	C. G. Hill, Sherborne and 2 Trin., str.	10.11
F. J. Richards, Eton and Mert., cox	10.10	H. Munster, King's Coll., Lon., and 1 Trin., cox	9. 2
Average	11. 9	Average	11. 2⅝

Cambridge won by 30 sec. in 23 min. 30 sec.

8 Friday, 3 April 1846, at 11.10 a.m.

OXFORD †		CAMBRIDGE	
H. S. Polehampton, Eton and Pemb., bow	10. 9	G. F. Murdoch, Eton and LMBC, bow	10. 2
E. C. Burton, Westminster and Ch.Ch.	11. 0	G. F. Holroyd, Winchester and 1 Trin.	11. 1
W. U. Heygate, Eton and Mert.	11. 8	S. T. Clissold, Eton and 3 Trin.	12. 0
E. H. Penfold, Maidstone and St Joh.	11. 8	*W. P. Cloves, Private and 1 Trin.	12.12
J. W. Conant, Eton and St Joh.	12. 4	E. Wilder, Eton and Magd.	13. 2
* F. C. Royds, Rugby and BNC	11. 9	*R. Harkness, Eton and LMBC	11. 6
* W. Chetwynd-Stapleton, Eton and Mert.	10.12	E. P. Wolstenholme, Halifax and 1 Trin.	11. 1
* W. H. Milman, Westminster and Ch.Ch., str.	11. 0	*C. G. Hill, Sherborne and 2 Trin., str.	11. 1
C. J. Soanes, King's Coll., Lon., and St Joh., cox	9.13	T. B. Lloyd, Shrewsbury and LMBC, cox	9. 8
Average	11. 4½	Average	11. 8⅜

Cambridge won by 3 lengths in 21 min. 5 sec. First race in outriggers.

9 Thursday, 29 March 1849 (i), at 5.40 p.m.

OXFORD		CAMBRIDGE †	
D. Wauchope, Edin. Acad. and Wadh., bow	10. 4	H. Proby, Cheam and 2 Trin., bow	9.13
J. W. Chitty, Eton and Ball.	11. 2	W. J. H. Jones, Bedford and 2 Trin.	10.13
H. H. Tremayne, Eton and Ch.Ch.	11. 5	A. de Rutzen, Eton and 3 Trin.	11. 8
*E. C. Burton, Westminster and Ch.Ch.	11. 0	C. J. Holden, Eton and 3 Trin.	11. 8
C. H. Steward, Rugby and Oriel	12. 0	W. L. G. Bagshawe, Eton and 3 Trin.	11.10
A. Mansfield, Private and Ch.Ch.	11. 8	W. H. Waddington, Rugby and 2 Trin.	11.10
E. J. Sykes, Eton and Worc.	11. 0	W. C. Hodgson, Rugby and 1 Trin.	11. 2
W. G. Rich, Westminster and Ch.Ch., str.	10. 0	J. C. Wray, King's Coll., Lon., and 2 Trin., str.	10.12
*C. J. Soanes, King's Coll., Lon., and St Joh., cox	10. 8	G. Booth, Rugby and 1 Trin., cox	10. 7
Average	11. 0⅝	Average	11. 2

Cambridge won easily in 22 min. First race over present distance.

10 Saturday, 15 December 1849 (ii), at 2.44 p.m.

CAMBRIDGE		OXFORD †	
A. Baldry, Putney Coll. and 1 Trin., bow	10.10	J. J. Hornby, Eton and BNC, bow	11. 8
H. E. Pellew, Eton and 3 Trin.	11.11	W. Houghton, Private and BNC	11. 2
*A. de Rutzen, Eton and 3 Trin.	11. 8	J. Wodehouse, Private and Ex.	11. 7
*C. J. Holden, Eton and 3 Trin.	11.11	*J. W. Chitty, Eton and Ball.	11. 9
*W. L. G. Bagshawe, Eton and 3 Trin.	12. 0	J. Aitken, Eton and Ex.	12. 1
H. J. Miller, Eton and 3 Trin.	12. 0	*C. H. Steward, Rugby and Oriel	12. 2
*W. C. Hodgson, Rugby and 1 Trin.	11. 3	*E. J. Sykes, Eton and Worc.	11. 2
*J. C. Wray, King's Coll., Lon., and Clare, str.	11. 0	*W. G. Rich, Westminster and Ch.Ch., str.	10. 2
*G. Booth, Rugby and 1 Trin., cox	10. 8	R. W. Cotton, Westminster and Ch.Ch., cox	9. 0
Average	11. 5¾	Average	11. 5⅞

Oxford won on a foul.

11 Saturday, 3 April 1852, at 1.45 p.m.

CAMBRIDGE †		OXFORD	
E. Macnaghten, Trin. Coll. Dublin and 1 Trin., bow	11. 0	K. Prescot, Macclesfield and BNC, bow	10. 0
H. Brandt, Rugby and 1 Trin.	11. 5	R. Greenall, Liverpool Coll. and BNC	10.12
H. E. Tuckey, RFGS, Marlborough and LMBC	11. 3	P. H. Nind, Eton and Ch.Ch.	11. 2
H. B. Foord, Rugby and 1 Trin.	12. 6	R. J. Buller, Eton and Ball.	12. 4
E. Hawley, Oakham and Sid. S.	12. 5	H. Denne, Eton and Univ.	12. 8
W. S. Longmore, Blundell's and Sid. S.	11. 4	*W. Houghton, Private and BNC	11. 8
W. A. Norris, Eton and 3 Trin.	11. 9	W. O. Meade-King, Eton and Pemb.	11.11
F. W. Johnson, Eton and 3 Trin, str.	11. 8	*J. W. Chitty, Eton and Ball., str.	11. 7
C. H. Crosse, Rugby and Caius, cox	9. 7	*R. W. Cotton, Westminster and Ch.Ch., cox	9. 2
Average	11. 8½	Average	11. 6½

Oxford won by 6 lengths in 21 min. 36 sec.

12 Saturday, 8 April 1854, at 10.40 a.m.

CAMBRIDGE		OXFORD †	
R. C. Galton, Rugby and 1 Trin., bow	9.10	W. F. Short, Winchester and New C., bow	10. 5
S. Nairne, Clapton GS and Emm.	10. 2	A. Hooke, Worc. Col. Sch. and Worc.	10. 0
J. C. Davis, Eton and 3 Trin.	11. 1	W. Pinckney, Eton and Ex.	11. 2
S. Agnew, Edin. Univ. and 1 Trin.	10.12	H. B. H. Blundell, Eton and Ch.Ch.	11. 8
E. Courage, Harrow and 1 Trin.	11.13	T. A. Hooper, Marlborough and Pemb.	11. 5
H. F. Johnson, Eton and 3 Trin.	10.13	*P. H. Nind, Eton and Ch.Ch.	10.12
H. Blake, Norwich and CCC	11. 1	G. L. Mellish, Eliz. Coll., Guernsey, and Pemb.	11. 2
J. Wright, Westminster and LMBC, str.	10. 2	*W. O. Meade-King, Eton and Pemb., str.	11. 8
C. T. Smith, Private and Caius, cox	9.12	T. H. Marshall, Eton and Ex., cox	10. 3
Average	10.10¼	Average	11. 0

Oxford won by 11 strokes in 25 min. 29 sec.

13 *Saturday, 15 March 1856, at 11 a.m.*

OXFORD		CAMBRIDGE †	
P. Gurdon, Radley and Univ., bow	10. 8	J. P. King-Salter, Private and Trin. H., bow	9.13
W. F. Stocken, St Paul's and Ex.	10. 1	F. C. Alderson, Eton and 3 Trin.	11. 3
R. I. Salmon, Durham and Ex.	10.10	R. Lewis-Lloyd, Eton and 3 Trin.	11.12
A. B. Rocke, Shrewsbury and CCC	12. 8	E. H. Farrie, Clapton GS and Trin. H.	12.10
R. N. Townsend, Crewkerne GS and Pemb.	12. 8	H. Williams, Marlborough and LMBC	12. 8
A. P. Lonsdale, Eton and Ball.	11. 4	J. M'Cormick, Liverpool and LMBC	13. 0
G. Bennett, Winchester and New C.	10.10	H. Snow, Eton and LMBC	11. 8
J. T. Thorley, St Paul's and Wadh., str.	9.12	H. R. M. Jones, Eton and 3 Trin., str.	10. 7
F. W. Elers, Tonbridge and Trin., cox	9. 2	W. Wingfield, Rossall and 1 Trin., cox	9. 0
Average	11. 0⅝	Average	11. 9⅜

Cambridge won by ½ length in 25 min. 45 sec.

Start at Barker's Rails (about 3 min. longer than present course).

14 *Saturday, 4 April 1857, at 11.10 a.m.*

CAMBRIDGE		OXFORD †	
A. P. Holme, Grange Sch., Sunderland, and 2 Trin., bow	11. 8	R. W. Risley, Radley and Ex., bow	11. 3
A. Benn, Cheltenham and Emm.	11. 5	*P. Gurdon, Radley and Univ.	10.13
W. H. Holley, Private and Trin. H.	11. 8	J. Arkell, Durham and Pemb.	11. 1
A. L. Smith, Private and 1 Trin.	11. 2	R. Martin, Marlborough and Ch.Ch.	11.13
J. J. Serjeantson, Rugby and 1 Trin.	12. 4	W. H. Wood, Louth GS and Univ.	11.10
*R. Lewis-Lloyd, Eton and Magd.	11.11	E. Warre, Eton and Ball.	12. 4
P. P. Pearson, Charterhouse and LMBC	11. 4	*A. P. Lonsdale, Eton and Ball.	11. 9
*H. Snow, Eton and LMBC, str.	11. 8	*J. T. Thorley, St Paul's and Wadh., str.[1]	10. 1
R. Wharton, Eton and Magd., cox	9. 2	*F. W. Elers, Tonbridge and Trin., cox	9. 0
Average	11. 8	Average	11. 5

Oxford won by 32 sec. in 22 min. 50 sec.

Oxford were stroked on bow side, the boat being the first of carvel construction, without keel, to be used in the Boat Race.

15 Saturday, 27 March 1858, at 1 p.m.

OXFORD		CAMBRIDGE †	
*R. W. Risley, Radley and Ex., bow	11. 8	H. H. Lubbock, Private and Caius, bow	11. 4
*J. Arkell, Durham and Pemb.	11. 3	*A. L. Smith, Private and 1 Trin.	11. 4
C. G. Lane, Westminster and Ch.Ch.	11.10	W. J. Havart, Rugby and LMBC	11. 4
W. G. G. Austin, Radley and Magd.	12. 9	D. Darroch, Harrow and 1 Trin.	12. 1
E. Lane, Private and Ball.	11.12	*H. Williams, Marlborough and LMBC	12. 4
*W. H. Wood, Louth GS and Univ.	12. 6	*R. Lewis-Lloyd, Eton and Magd.	11.13
*E. Warre, Eton and Ball.	13. 2	A. H. Fairbairn, Rugby and 2 Trin.	11.12
*J. T. Thorley, St Paul's and Wadh., str.	10. 3	J. Hall, Eton and Magd., str.	10. 7
H. S. Walpole, Eton and Ball., cox	9. 8	*R. Wharton, Eton and Magd., cox	9. 0
Average	11.11⅞	Average	11. 7⅞

Cambridge won by 22 sec. in 21 min. 23 sec.

16 Friday, 15 April 1859, at 11 a.m.

CAMBRIDGE		OXFORD †	
N. Royds, Rugby and 1 Trin, bow	10. 6	H. F. Baxter, Hereford Cath. Sch. and BNC, bow	10.12
H. J. Chaytor, Durham and Jesus	10.13	R. F. Clarke, Merchant Taylors' and St Joh.	11.13
*A. L. Smith, Private and 1 Trin.	11.11	*C. G. Lane, Westminster and Ch.Ch.	11. 9
*D. Darroch, Harrow and 1 Trin.	12. 4	Hon. V. Lawless, Eton and Ball.	12. 3
*H. Williams, Marlborough and LMBC	12. 6	G. Morrison, Eton and Ball.	13. 1
*R. Lewis-Lloyd, Eton and Magd.	11. 9	*R. W. Risley, Radley and Ex.	11. 2
G. A. Paley, Clapham GS and LMBC	11. 7	G. G. T. Thomas, Eton and Ball.	11. 4
*J. Hall, Eton and Magd., str.	10. 2	*J. Arkell, Durham and Pemb., str.	10.12
J. T. Morland, Harrow and 1 Trin., cox	9. 0	A. J. Robarts, Eton and Ch.Ch., cox	9. 1
Average	11. 5½	Average	11. 8¾

Cambridge sank, Oxford finished in 24 min. 40 sec.

17 *Saturday, 31 March 1860, at 8.28 a.m.*

CAMBRIDGE		OXFORD †	
S. Heathcote, Bath Coll. and 1 Trin., bow	10. 3	J. N. McQueen, Glenalmond and Univ., bow	11. 7
*H. J. Chaytor, Durham and Jesus	11. 4	G. Norsworthy, Winchester and Magd.	11. 0
D. Inglis, Edin. Acad. and 1 Trin.	10.13	T. F. Halsey, Eton and Ch.Ch.	11.11
J. S. Blake, Marlborough and CCC	12. 9	J. F. Young, Harrow and CCC	12. 8
M. Coventry, King's Coll., Lon., and Trin. H.	12. 8	*G. Morrison, Eton and Ball.	12.13
B. N. Cherry, Durham and Clare	12. 1	*H. F. Baxter, Hereford Cath. Sch. and BNC	11. 7
*A. H. Fairbairn, Rugby and 2 Trin.	11.10	C. I. Strong, Harrow and Univ.	11. 2
*J. Hall, Eton and Magd., str.	10. 4	*R. W. Risley, Radley and Ch.Ch., str.	11. 8
*J. T. Morland, Harrow and 1 Trin., cox	9. 0	*A. J. Robarts, Eton and Ch.Ch., cox	9. 9
Average	11. 6½	Average	11.10½

Cambridge won by 1 length in 26 min. 5 sec.

18 *Saturday, 23 March 1861, at 11 a.m.*

OXFORD		CAMBRIDGE †	
W. Champneys, Charterhouse and BNC, bow	10.11	G. H. Richards, Rugby and 1 Trin., bow	10. 4
E. B. Merriman, Winchester and Ex.	10. 1	*H. J. Chaytor, Durham and Jesus	11. 3
H. E. Medlicott, Harrow and Wadh.	12. 4	W. H. Tarleton, Dedham and LMBC	11. 0
W. Robertson, Geelong GS and Wadh.	11. 3	*J. S. Blake, Marlborough and CCC	12.10
*G. Morrison, Eton and Ball.	12. 8	*M. Coventry, King's Coll., Lon., and Trin. H.	13. 3
A. R. Poole, Rugby and Trin.	12. 3	H. H. Collings, Eton and 3 Trin.	10.11
H. G. Hopkins, Rugby and CCC	10. 8	R. U. P. Fitzgerald, Westminster and Trin. H.	11. 2
W. M. Hoare, Eton and Ex., str.	10.10	*J. Hall, Eton and Magd., str.	10. 6
S. O. B. Ridsdale, Tonbridge and Wadh., cox	9. 0	T. K. Gaskell, Westminster and 3 Trin., cox	8. 3
Average	11. 4¼	Average	11. 4⅞

Oxford won by 47 sec. in 23 min. 30 sec.

19 Saturday, 12 April 1862, at 12.08 p.m.

CAMBRIDGE		OXFORD †	
P. F. Gorst, Brighton and LMBC, bow	10. 4	W. B. Woodgate, Radley and BNC, bow	11. 6
J. G. Chambers, Eton and 3 Trin.	11. 8	O. S. Wynne, Eton and Ch.Ch.	11. 3
E. Sanderson, Lancaster GS and CCC	10.10	W. B. R. Jacobson, Winchester and Ch.Ch.	12. 4
W. C. Smyly, Harrow and 1 Trin.	11. 5	R. E. L. Burton, Eton and Ch.Ch.	12. 5
*R. U. P. Fitzgerald, Westminster and Trin. H.	11. 3	*A. Morrison, Eton and Ball.	12. 8½
*H. H. Collings, Eton and 3 Trin.	11. 2	A. R. Poole, Rugby and Trin.	12. 5
J. G. Buchanan, Private and 1 Trin.	10.12	C. R. Carr, Durham and Wadh.	11. 2½
*G. H. Richards, Rugby and 1 Trin., str.	10. 5	*W. M. Hoare, Eton and Ex., str.	11. 1
F. H. Archer, King's Sch. Canterbury and CCC, cox	5. 2	F. E. Hopwood, Eton and Ch.Ch., cox	7. 3
Average	10.13⅛	Average	11.11⅜

Oxford won by ½ min in 24 min. 40 sec.

20 Saturday, 28 March 1863, at 10.25 a.m.

CAMBRIDGE †		OXFORD	
J. C. Hawkshaw, Westminster and 3 Trin., bow	11. 0	R. Shepherd, Tonbridge and BNC, bow	10. 0½
*W. C. Smyly, Harrow and 1 Trin.	11. 4	F. H. Kelly, Rugby and Univ.	11. 5½
R. H. Morgan, Llandovery and Emm.	11. 3	*W. B. R. Jacobson, Winchester and Ch.Ch.	12. 4
J. B. Wilson, Giggleswick and Pemb.	11.10	*W. B. Woodgate, Radley and BNC	11.11
C. H. La Mothe, King Wm Coll. and LMBC	12. 3	*A. Morrison, Eton and Ball.	12. 4
R. A. Kinglake, Eton and 3 Trin.	12. 0	W. Awdry, Winchester and Ball.	11. 4
*J. G. Chambers, Eton and 3 Trin.	11. 6	*C. R. Carr, Durham and Wadh.	11. 3½
J. Stanning, Rugby and 1 Trin., str.	10. 6	*W. M. Hoare, Eton and Ex., str.	11. 7½
F. H. Archer, King's Sch. Canterbury and CCC, cox	5. 9½	*F. E. Hopwood, Eton and Ch.Ch., cox	8. 4½
Average	11. 5¾	Average	11. 8½

Oxford won by ¾ min. in 23 min. 6 sec. Start at Barker's Rails (as in 1856).

21 Saturday, 19 March 1864, at 11.30 a.m.

CAMBRIDGE		OXFORD †	
*J. C. Hawkshaw, Westminster and 3 Trin., bow	11. 3	C. R. Roberts, Marlborough and Trin., bow	10. 9
E. V. Pigott, Marlborough and CCC	11. 9	*W. Awdry, Winchester and Ball.	11. 4½
H. S. Watson, Manchester GS and Pemb.	12. 4	*F. H. Kelly, Rugby and Univ.	11. 9
W. W. Hawkins, St Pet., York, and LMBC	12. 0	J. C. Parson, Marlborough and Trin.	12. 9
*R. A. Kinglake, Eton and 3 Trin.	12. 4	*W. B. R. Jacobson, Winchester and Ch.Ch.	12. 3½
G. Borthwick, Uppingham and 1 Trin.	12. 1	A. E. Seymour, Charterhouse and Univ.	11. 3
D. F. Steavenson, King Wm Coll. and Trin. H.	12. 1	M. M. Brown, Radley and Trin.	11. 3
J. R. Selwyn, Eton and 3 Trin., str.	11. 0	D. Pocklington, Eton and BNC, str.	11. 5
*F. H. Archer, King's Sch., Canterbury, and CCC, cox	6. 6	C. R. W. Tottenham, Eton and Ch.Ch., cox	7. 3
Average	11.11½	Average	11. 7½

Oxford won by 27 sec. in 21 min. 40 sec.

Start moved to University Stone, 400 ft upstream of Putney Bridge. Finish moved same distance upstream.

22 Saturday, 8 April 1865, at 1.03 p.m.

CAMBRIDGE		OXFORD †	
H. Watney, Rugby and LMBC, bow	11. 1	R. T. Raikes, Radley and Mert., bow	11. 0
M. H. L. Beebee, Rossall and LMBC	10.12	H. P. Senhouse, Eton and Ch.Ch.	11. 1
*E. V. Pigott, Marlborough and CCC	11.12	E. F. Henley, Sherborne and Oriel	12.13
*R. A. Kinglake, Eton and 3 Trin.	12. 8	G. G. Coventry, Private and Pemb.	11.12
*D. F. Steavenson, King Wm Coll. and Trin. H.	12. 4	*A. Morrison, Eton and Ball.	12. 6
*G. Borthwick, Uppingham and 1 Trin.	11.13	T. Wood, Louth GS and Pemb.	12. 2
W. R. Griffiths, Eton and 3 Trin.	11. 8	H. Schneider, Magd. Coll. Sch. and Trin.	11.10
C. B. Lawes, Eton and 3 Trin., str.	11. 7	*M. M. Brown, Radley and Trin., str.	11. 4
*F. H. Archer, King's Sch., Canterbury, and CCC, cox	7. 3	*C. R. W. Tottenham, Eton and Ch.Ch., cox	7.13
Average	11. 9⅞	Average	11.11¼

Oxford won by 4 lengths in 21 min. 24 sec.

23 Saturday, 24 March 1866, at 7.48 a.m.

CAMBRIDGE		OXFORD †	
J. Still, Winchester and		*R. T. Raikes, Radley and	
Caius, bow	11. 7	Mert., bow	11. 0
*J. R. Selwyn, Eton and 3 Trin.	11. 6	F. Crowder, Rugby and BNC	11.11
J. U. Bourke, St Columba's,		W. L. Freeman, Cheltenham	
Dublin, and 1 Trin.	12. 3	and Mert.	12. 7
H. J. Fortescue, Eton and		F. Willan, Eton and Ex.	12. 2
Magd.	12. 5		
*D. F. Steavenson, King Wm		*E. F. Henley, Sherborne and	
Coll. and Trin. H.	12. 7	Oriel	13. 0
*R. A. Kinglake, Eton and		W. W. Wood, Eton and Univ.	12. 4
3 Trin.	12.11		
*H. Watney, Rugby and LMBC	10.10	*H. P. Senhouse, Eton and	
		Ch.Ch.	11. 3
*W. R. Griffiths, Eton and		*M. M. Brown, Radley and	
3 Trin., str.	11.12	Trin., str.	11. 5
A. Forbes, Sedbergh and		*C. R. W. Tottenham, Eton and	
LMBC, cox	8. 0	Ch.Ch., cox	7.13
Average	11.12⅞	Average	11.12¾

Oxford won by 3 lengths in 25 min. 35 sec.

24 Saturday, 13 April 1867, at 8.58 a.m.

CAMBRIDGE		OXFORD †	
W. H. Anderson, Repton and		W. P. Bowman, Eton and	
1 Trin., bow	11. 0	Univ., bow	10.12
J. M. Collard, Private and		J. H. Fish, Durham and Worc.	12. 1½
LMBC	11. 4		
*J. U. Bourke, St Columba's,		E. S. Carter, Durham and	
Dublin, and 1 Trin.	12. 9	Worc.	11. 8
Hon. J. H. Gordon, St Andrews		*W. W. Wood, Eton and Univ.	12. 8
Univ. and 1 Trin.	12. 3		
F. E. Cunningham, Eton and		J. C. Tinné, Eton and Univ.	13. 5½
King's	12.12		
*J. Still, Winchester and Caius	11.12	*F. Crowder, Rugby and BNC	11.12
*H. Watney, Rugby and LMBC	11. 0	*F. Willan, Eton and Ex.	12. 1½
*W. R. Griffiths, Eton and		R. G. Marsden, Eton and	
3 Trin., str.	12. 0	Mert., str.	11.11
*A. Forbes, Sedbergh and		*C. R. W. Tottenham, Eton and	
LMBC, cox	8. 2	Ch.Ch., cox	8. 7
Average	11.12	Average	12. 0½

Oxford won by ½ length in 22 min. 39 sec.

25 Saturday, 4 April 1868, at 12 noon

OXFORD		CAMBRIDGE †	
W. D. Benson, Eton and		W. H. Anderson, Repton and	
Ball., bow	10.13	1 Trin., bow	11. 2
A. C. Yarborough, Eton and		J. P. Nichols, Westminster and	
Linc.	11. 8	3 Trin.	11. 3
R. Ross of Blandensburg,		J. G. Wood, Private and	
Radley and Ex.	11. 8	Emm.	12. 6
*R. G. Marsden, Eton and Mert.	11.13	W. H. Lowe, Durham and Chr.	12. 4
*J. C. Tinné, Eton and Univ.	13. 7	H. T. Nadin, Leicester and	
		Pemb.	12.11
*F. Willan, Eton and Ex.	12. 5	W. F. MacMichael, Ripon and	
		Dow.	12. 2
*E. S. Carter, Durham and Worc.	11. 8	*J. Still, Winchester and Caius	12. 1
S. D. Darbishire, Univ. Coll.		W. J. Pinckney, Rugby and	
Sch. and Ball., str.	11. 3	1 Trin., str.	10.10
*C. R. W. Tottenham, Eton and		T. D. Warner, CEGS	
Ch.Ch., cox	8. 7	Melbourne and Trin. H., cox	8. 4
Average	11.11⅝	Average	11.11⅞

Oxford won by 6 lengths in 20 min. 56 sec.

26 Wednesday, 17 March 1869, at 3.58 p.m.

CAMBRIDGE		OXFORD †	
J. A. Rushton, Edin. Acad. and		S. H. Woodhouse, Eton and	
Emm., bow	11. 5	Univ., bow	10.13
J. H. Ridley, Eton and Jesus	11.10	R. Tahourdin, Shrewsbury and	
		St Joh.	11.11
J. W. Dale, Tonbridge and		T. S. Baker, Lancing and Qu.	12. 8
LMBC	11.12		
F. J. Young, Leeds GS and Chr.	12. 4	*F. Willan, Eton and Ex.	12. 2½
*W. F. MacMichael, Ripon and		*J. C. Tinné, Eton and Univ.	13.10½
Dow.	12. 4		
*W. H. Anderson, Repton and		*A. C. Yarborough, Eton and	
1 Trin.	11. 4	Linc.	11.11
*J. Still, Winchester and Caius	12. 1	*W. D. Benson, Eton and Ball.	11. 7
J. H. D. Goldie, Eton and		*S. D. Darbishire, Univ. Coll.	
LMBC, str.	12. 1	Sch. and Ball., str.	11. 9
H. E. Gordon, Twickenham		D. A. Neilson, Harrow and	
and 1 Trin., cox	7. 7	St Joh., cox	7.10
Average	11.12⅛	Average	12. 0¼

Oxford won by 3 lengths in 20 min. 4 sec.

27 Wednesday, 6 April 1870, at 5.14 p.m.

OXFORD †		CAMBRIDGE	
R. W. B. Mirehouse, Eton and Univ., bow	11. 0	E. S. L. Randolf, Westminster and 3 Trin., bow	10.11½
A. G. P. Lewis, Eton and Univ.	11. 2½	*J. H. Ridley, Eton and Jesus	11. 9½
*T. S. Baker, Lancing and Qu.	12. 9	*J. W. Dale, Tonbridge and LMBC	12. 2½
J. E. Edwards-Moss, Eton and Ball.	13. 0	E. A. A. Spencer, Rossall and 2 Trin.	12. 4½
F. E. H. Payne, Cheltenham and St Joh.	12.10	*W. H. Lowe, Durham and Chr.	12. 7½
*S. H. Woodhouse, Eton and Univ.	11. 4	E. L. Phelps, Wimbledon and Sid. S.	12. 1½
*W. D. Benson, Eton and Ball.	11.13	J. F. Strachan, Norwich and Trin. H.	11.13
*S. D. Darbishire, Univ. Coll. Sch. and Ball., str.	11.11	*J. H. D. Goldie, Eton and LMBC, str.	12. 0
F. H. Hall, Canterbury and CCC, cox	7. 7	H. E. Gordon, Twickenham and 1 Trin., cox	7.12
Average	11.13¼	Average	11.13¼

Cambridge won by 1½ lengths in 22 min. 4 sec.

28 Saturday, 1 April 1871, at 10.08 a.m.

CAMBRIDGE		OXFORD †	
J. S. Follett, Eton and 3 Trin., bow	11. 6½	* S. H. Woodhouse, Eton and Univ., bow	11. 6½
John B. Close, Private and 1 Trin.	11. 8	E. Giles, Westminster and Ch.Ch.	11.13½
H. J. Lomax, Marlborough and 1 Trin.	12. 2	*T. S. Baker, Lancing and Qu.	13. 3½
*E. A. A. Spencer, Rossall and 2 Trin.	12. 9	E. C. Malan, Sherborne and Worc.	13. 1
*W. H. Lowe, Durham and Chr.	12.10	*J. E. Edwards-Moss, Eton and Ball.	12. 8½
*E. L. Phelps, Wimbledon and Sid. S.	12. 1	*F. E. H. Payne, Cheltenham and St Joh.	12. 9½
*E. S. L. Randolf, Westminster and 3 Trin.	11.10	J. M. Clintock-Bunbury, Eton and BNC	11. 8
*J. H. D. Goldie, Eton and LMBC, str.	12. 6½	R. Lesley, Radley and Pemb., str.	11.10½
*H. E. Gordon, Twickenham and 1 Trin., cox	7.13	*F. H. Hall, King's Sch., Canterbury, and CCC, cox	7.10½
Average	12. 1⅜	Average	12. 4⅛

Cambridge won by 1 length in 23 min. 10 sec.

29 Saturday, 23 March 1872, at 1.35 p.m.

OXFORD		CAMBRIDGE †	
J. A. Ornsby, Doncaster and Linc., bow	10.13	James B. Close, Wellington and 1 Trin., bow	11. 3
C. C. Knollys, Private and Magd.	10.13	C. W. Benson, Eton and 3 Trin.	11. 4
*F. E. H. Payne, Cheltenham and St Joh.	12.11	G. M. Robinson, Repton and Chr.	11.12
A. W. Nicholson, Winchester and Magd.	12. 1	*E. A. A. Spencer, Rossall and 2 Trin.	12. 8½
*E. C. Malan, Sherborne and Worc.	13. 0	C. S. Read, Radley and 1 Trin.	12. 8
R. S. Mitchison, Eton and Pemb.	12. 1½	*John B. Close, Private and 1 Trin.	11.10
*R. Lesley, Radley and Pemb.	11.12	*E. S. L. Randolf, Westminster and 3 Trin.	11.11
T. H. A. Houblon, Radley and Ch.Ch., str.	10. 5	*J. H. D. Goldie, Eton and LMBC, str.	12. 4½
*F. H. Hall, King's Sch., Canterbury, and CCC, cox	7.12	C. H. Roberts, St Paul's and Jesus, cox	6. 6
Average	11.10½	Average	11.12⅞

Cambridge won by 2 lengths in 21 min. 15 sec.

30 Saturday, 29 March 1873, at 2.32 p.m.

OXFORD †		CAMBRIDGE	
*C. C. Knollys, Private and Magd., bow	10.12½	*James B. Close, Wellington and 1 Trin., bow	11. 3
J. B. Little, King Ed. VI Sch., Norwich, and Ch.Ch.	10.13	E. Hoskyns, Haileybury and Jesus	11. 2
M. G. Farrer, Eton and BNC	12. 4	J. E. Peabody, Private and 1 Trin.	11. 7
*A. W. Nicholson, Winchester and Magd.	12. 9	W. C. Lecky-Browne, Radley and Jesus	12. 1½
*R. S. Mitchison, Eton and Pemb.	12. 7½	T. S. Turnbull, Private and Trin. H.	12.12½
W. E. Sherwood, Magd. Coll. Sch. and Ch.Ch.	11. 1	*C. S. Read, Radley and 1 Trin.	12.13
*J. A. Ornsby, Doncaster and Linc.	11. 1½	*C. W. Benson, Eton and 3 Trin.	11. 5
F. T. Dowding, Eton and St Joh., str.	11. 0	H. E. Rhodes, Eton and Jesus, str.	11. 1½
G. E. Frewer, Eton and St Joh., cox	7. 6	C. H. Candy, Cheltenham and Caius, cox	7. 5
Average	11. 7⅞	Average	11.11

Cambridge won by 3 lengths in 19 min. 35 sec. First year on sliding seats.

31 Saturday, 28 March 1874, at 11.14 a.m.

OXFORD		CAMBRIDGE †	
H. W. Benson, Eton and BNC, bow	11. 0	P. J. Hibbert, Shrewsbury and LMBC, bow	11. 0
J. S. Sinclair, Repton and Oriel	11. 5½	G. F. Armytage, Geelong GS and Jesus	11. 6
*W. E. Sherwood, Magd. Coll. Sch. and Ch.Ch.	11. 8	*James B. Close, Wellington and 1 Trin.	10.13
A. R. Harding, Radley and Mert.	11. 1½	A. S. Estcourt, Marlborough and Trin. H.	11. 8
J. Williams, Liverpool and Linc.	13. 0½	*W. C. Lecky-Browne, Radley and Jesus	12. 3
*A. W. Nicholson, Winchester and Magd.	12.10	J. A. Aylmer, Liverpool Coll. and 1 Trin.	12.10
H. J. Stayner, Somerset Coll., Bath, and St Joh.	11.10½	*C. S. Read, Radley and 1 Trin.	12.12
J. P. Way, Somerset Coll., Bath, and BNC, str.	10. 9	*H. E. Rhodes, Eton and Jesus, str.	11. 5
W. F. A. Lambert, Merchant Taylors' and Wadh., cox	7. 4	*C. H. Candy, Cheltenham and Caius, cox	7. 7
Average	11. 9⅛	Average	11.10⅝

Cambridge won by 3½ lengths in 22 min. 35 sec.

32 Saturday, 20 March 1875, at 1.13 p.m.

OXFORD		CAMBRIDGE †	
H. M'D. Courtney, Highgate and Pemb., bow	10.13	*P. J. Hibbert, Shrewsbury and LMBC, bow	11. 2
H. P. Marriott, Winchester and BNC	11.13	W. B. Close, Wellington and 1 Trin.	11.10
J. E. Bankes, Eton and Univ.	11.11	G. C. Dicker, Winchester and 1 Trin.	11. 7½
A. M. Mitchison, Eton and Pemb.	12.10	W. G. Michell, Wellington and 1 Trin.	11.12
*H. J. Stayner, Somerset Coll., Bath, and St Joh.	12. 2	E. A. Phillips, Shrewsbury and Jesus	12. 5
*J. M. Boustead, Harrow and Univ.	12. 3	*J. A. Aylmer, Liverpool Coll. and 1 Trin.	12.10
T. C. Edwards-Moss, Eton and BNC	12. 5	*C. W. Benson, Eton and 3 Trin.	11. 6
*J. P. Way, Somerset Coll., Bath, and BNC, str.	10.12	*H. E. Rhodes, Eton and Jesus, str.	11. 8
E. O. Hopwood, Qu. Eliz. Sch., Kirkby Lonsdale, and Ch.Ch., cox	8. 3	G. L. Davis, St Pet., York, and Clare, cox	6.10
Average	11.12⅛	Average	11.11

Oxford won by 10 lengths in 22 min. 2 sec. Cambridge damaged a side.

33 *Saturday, 8 April 1876, at 2.02 p.m.*

CAMBRIDGE		OXFORD †	
P. W. Brancker, Radley and Jesus, bow	11. 3½	*H. M'D. Courtney, Highgate and Pemb., bow	11. 2
T. W. Lewis, King's Coll., Lon., and Caius	11. 8	F. R. Mercer, Tonbridge and CCC	11. 6½
*W. B. Close, Wellington and 1 Trin.	11. 8	W. H. Hobart, Uppingham and Ex.	11.11
C. Gurdon, Haileybury and Jesus	12. 9¾	*A. M. Mitchison, Eton and Pemb.	13. 0
L. G. Pike, Highgate and Caius	12. 9	*J. M. Boustead, Harrow and Univ.	12. 6
T. E. Hockin, Radley and Jesus	12. 8	*H. J. Stayner, Som. Coll., Bath, and St Joh.	12. 2½
*H. E. Rhodes, Eton and Jesus	11.13	*H. P. Marriott, Winchester and BNC	11. 9½
C. D. Shafto, Durham and Jesus, str.	11. 9½	*T. C. Edwards-Moss, Eton and BNC, str.	12. 3¼
*G. L. Davis, St Pet., York, and Clare, cox	6.13	W. D. Craven, King's Coll., Lon., and Worc., cox	7. 6½
Average	11.13⅞	Average	11.13⅞

Cambridge won easily in 20 min. 20 sec. Course probably 60 yd too long.

34 *Saturday, 24 March 1877, at 8.27 a.m.*

CAMBRIDGE		OXFORD †	
B. G. Hoskyns, Haileybury and Jesus, bow	10.11	D. J. Cowles, Merchant Taylors' and St Joh., bow	11. 2½
*T. W. Lewis, King's Coll., Lon., and Caius	11. 9	*J. M. Boustead, Harrow and Univ.	12. 8
J. C. Fenn, Cheltenham and 1 Trin.	11. 7	H. Pelham, Haileybury and Magd.	12. 7
*W. B. Close, Wellington and 1 Trin.	11. 9½	W. H. Grenfell, Harrow and Ball.	12.10
*L. G. Pike, Highgate and Caius	12. 8	*H. J. Stayner, Somerset Coll., Bath, and St Joh.	12. 3¾
*C. Gurdon, Haileybury and Jesus	12.13	Hon. A. J. Mullholland, Eton and Ball.	12. 5¾
*T. E. Hockin, Radley and Jesus	12.11	*T. C. Edwards-Moss, Eton and BNC	12. 1
*C. D. Shafto, Durham and Jesus, str.	12. 0	*H. P. Marriott, Winchester and BNC, str.	11.13
*G. L. Davis, St Pet., York, and Clare, cox	7. 2	F. M. Beaumont, Eton and New C., cox	6. 6½
Average	11.13¾	Average	12. 2⅞

Dead heat. Time 24 min. 8 sec. Oxford cracked an oar.

35 Saturday, 13 April 1878, at 10.15 a.m.

OXFORD †		CAMBRIDGE	
W. A. Ellison, Eton and Univ., bow	10.13	Ll. R. Jones, Durham and Jesus, bow	10. 9
*D. J. Cowles, Merchant Taylors' and St Joh.	11. 5	J. A. Watson-Taylor, Eton and Magd.	11. 9¾
H. B. Southwell, Charterhouse and Pemb.	12. 8½	T. W. Barker, Harrow and 1 Trin.	12. 6
*W. H. Grenfell, Harrow and Ball.	12.10½	R. J. Spurrell, Ipswich and Trin. H.	11.13½
*H. Pelham, Haileybury and Magd.	12.11	*L. G. Pike, Highgate and Caius	12. 8½
G. F. Burgess, Blackheath and Keble	13. 3½	*C. Gurdon, Haileybury and Jesus	12.10½
*T. C. Edwards-Moss, Eton and BNC	12. 3	*T. E. Hockin, Radley and Jesus	12. 4½
*H. P. Marriott, Winchester and BNC, str.	12. 2½	*E. H. Prest, Durham and Jesus, str.	10.12¾
*F. M. Beaumont, Eton and New C., cox	7. 0½	*G. L. Davis, St Pet., York, and Clare, cox	7. 5
Average	12. 3⅝	Average	11.12¾

Oxford won by 40 sec. in 22 min. 15 sec.

36 Saturday, 5 April 1879, at 12.45 p.m.

OXFORD †		CAMBRIDGE	
J. H. T. Wharton, Magd. Coll. Sch. and Magd., bow	11. 4	*E. H. Prest, Durham and Jesus, bow	11. 0
H. M. Robinson, Harrow and New C.	11. 1	H. Sandford, Shrewsbury and LMBC	11. 7
H. W. Disney, Finchley and Hert.	12. 5½	A. H. S. Bird, Haileybury and 1 Trin.	11. 8
*H. B. Southwell, Charterhouse and Pemb.	12. 9	*C. Gurdon, Haileybury and Jesus	13. 2
T. C. Burrowes, Winchester and Trin.	12. 9	*T. E. Hockin, Radley and Jesus	12. 1
G. D. Rowe, Marlborough and Univ.	11.12	C. Fairbairn, Geelong GS and Jesus	12. 4
*W. H. Hobart, Uppingham and Ex.	11.11	T. Routledge, Allhallows and Emm.	12. 6
*H. P. Marriott, Winchester and BNC, str.	12. 3	R. D. Davis, Private and 1 Trin., str.	12. 4
*F. M. Beaumont, Eton and New C., cox	7. 4	*G. L. Davis, St Pet., York, and Clare, cox	7. 7
Average	11.13¾	Average	12. 0½

Cambridge won by 3 lengths in 21 min. 18 sec.

37 *Monday, 22 March 1880, at 10.40 a.m.* (postponed from Saturday, 20 March)

CAMBRIDGE		OXFORD †	
*E. H. Prest, Durham and Jesus, bow	10.12	R. H. J. Poole, Durham and BNC, bow	10. 6
*H. Sandford, Shrewsbury and LMBC	11. 5½	D. E. Brown, Harrow and Hert.	12. 6
W. Barton, Wellington, NZ, and LMBC	11. 3½	F. M. Hargreaves, St Pet., York, and Keble	12. 2
W. M. Warlow, Monmouth GS and Qu.	12. 0	*H. B. Southwell, Charterhouse and Pemb.	13. 0
C. N. L. Armytage, Geelong GS and Jesus	12. 2½	R.S. Kindersley, Clifton and Ex.	12. 8
*R. D. Davis, Private and 1 Trin.	12. 8½	*G. D. Rowe, Marlborough and Univ.	12. 3
R. D. Prior, Bedford and Qu.	11.13	*J. H. T. Wharton, Magd. Coll. Sch. and Magd.	11.10
W. W. Baillie, Private and Jesus, str.	11. 2½	L. R. West, Eton and Ch.Ch., str.	11. 1
B. S. Clarke, Giggleswick and LMBC, cox	7. 0	C. W. Hunt, Merchant Taylors' and CCC, cox	7. 5
Average	11. 9½	Average	11.13

Oxford won by 3¾ lengths in 21 min. 23 sec.

38 *Friday, 8 April 1881, at 8.24 a.m.*

CAMBRIDGE		OXFORD †	
R. C. M. G. Gridley, Eton and 3 Trin., bow	10. 7	*R. H. J. Poole, Durham and BNC, bow	10.11
*H. Sandford, Shrewsbury and LMBC	11.10½	R. A. Pinckney, Eton and Ex.	11. 3
*J. A. Watson-Taylor, Eton and Magd.	12. 3½	A. R. Paterson, Loretto and Trin.	12. 7
P. W. Atkin, Mill Hill and Jesus	11.13	E. Buck, Malvern and Hert.	11.11
E. Lambert, Cheltenham and Pemb.	12. 0	*R. S. Kindersley, Clifton and Ex.	13. 3
A. M. Hutchinson, Durham and Jesus	11.13	*D. E. Brown, Harrow and Hert.	12. 7
C. W. Moore, Durham and Chr.	11. 9	*J. H. T. Wharton, Magd. Coll. Sch. and Magd.	11.10
E. C. Brooksbank, Eton and Trin. H., str.	11. 8	*L. R. West, Eton and Ch.Ch., str.	11. 0½
H. Woodhouse, Manchester GS and Trin. H., cox	7. 2	E. H. Lyon, Charterhouse and Hert., cox	7. 0
Average	11. 9¾	Average	11.11¾

Oxford won by 3 lengths in 21 min. 51 sec.

39 *Saturday, 1 April 1882, at 1.02 p.m.*

OXFORD		CAMBRIDGE †	
G. C. Bourne, Eton and New C., bow	10.13	*Ll. R. Jones, Durham and Jesus, bow	10.13½
R. S. de Haviland, Eton and CCC	11. 1½	*A. M. Hutchinson, Durham and Jesus	11.12½
G. S. Fort, Uppingham and Hert.	12. 3½	J. C. Fellowes, Mannamead and 1 Trin.	12. 6¾
*A. R. Paterson, Loretto and Trin.	12.12	*P. W. Atkin, Mill Hill and Jesus	11. 3
*R. S. Kindersley, Clifton and Ex.	13. 4½	*E. Lambert, Cheltenham and Pemb.	11.10½
*E. Buck, Malvern and Hert.	12. 0	S. Fairbairn, Geelong GS and Jesus	12. 3
*D. E. Brown, Harrow and Hert.	12. 6	*C. W. Moore, Durham and Chr.	11. 6½
A. H. Higgins, Magd. Coll. Sch. and Magd., str.	9. 6½	S. P. Smith, Repton and 1 Trin., str.	11. 0½
*E. H. Lyon, Charterhouse and Hert., cox	7.12	P. L. Hunt, Highgate and Cavendish, cox	7. 5
Average	11.11⅛	Average	11.11

Oxford won by 7 lengths in 20 min. 12 sec.

40 *Saturday, 15 March 1883, at 5.39 p.m.*

OXFORD †		CAMBRIDGE	
*G. C. Bourne, Eton and New C., bow	10.11½	* R. C. M. G. Gridley, Eton and 3 Trin., bow	10. 7
*R. S. de Haviland, Eton and CCC	11. 4	F. W. Fox, Grove House Sch. and 1 Trin.	12. 2
*G. S. Fort, Uppingham and Hert.	12..0	* C. W. Moore, Durham and Chr.	11.13
E. L. Puxley, Eton and BNC	12. 6½	*P. W. Atkin, Mill Hill and Jesus	12. 1
D. H. McLean, Eton and New C.	13. 2½	F. E. Churchill, Eton and 3 Trin.	13. 4
*A. R. Paterson, Loretto and Trin.	13. 1	S. Swann, Marlborough and Trin. H.	12.12
G. Q. Roberts, HS Hobart and Hert.	11. 1	*S. Fairbairn, Geelong GS and Jesus	13. 4
*L. R. West, Eton and Ch.Ch., str.	11. 0	F. C. Meyrick, Eton and Trin. H., str.	11. 7
*E. H. Lyon, Charterhouse and Hert., cox	8. 1	*P. L. Hunt, Highgate and Cavendish, cox	8. 1
Average	11.12	Average	12. 2¾

Oxford won by 3½ lengths in 21 min. 18 sec.

41 Monday, 7 April 1884, at 12.45 p.m.

OXFORD †		CAMBRIDGE	
A. G. Shortt, Private and Ch.Ch., bow	11. 2	*R. C. M. G. Gridley, Eton and 3 Trin., bow	10. 6
L. Stock, Felsted and Ex.	11. 0	G. H. Eyre, St Pet., York, and CCC	11. 3½
C. R. Carter, Cheltenham and CCC	12.10	F. Straker, Harrow and Jesus	12. 2
P. W. Taylor, Derby and Linc.	13. 1	*S. Swann, Marlborough and Trin. H.	13. 3
*D. H. McLean, Eton and New C.	12.11½	*F. E. Churchill, Eton and 3 Trin.	13. 2½
*A. R. Paterson, Loretto and Trin.	13. 4	E. W. Haig, Eton and 3 Trin.	11. 6¾
W. C. Blandy, Marlborough and Ex.	10.13	*C. W. Moore, Durham and Chr.	11.12¾
W. D. B. Curry, Trin. Coll., Stratford, and Ex., str.	10. 4	F. I. Pitman, Eton and 3 Trin., str.	11.11½
F. J. Humphreys, Radley and BNC, cox	7. 9	C. E. Tyndale Biscoe, Bradford and Jesus, cox	8. 2
Average	11.12¾	Average	11.13

Cambridge won by 2½ lengths in 21 min. 39 sec.

42 Saturday, 28 March 1885, at 12.26 p.m.

OXFORD		CAMBRIDGE †	
W. S. Unwin, Magd. C. Sch. and Magd., bow	10.10½	N. P. Symonds, Hereford and LMBC, bow	10. 8
J. S. Clemons, Launceston CES, Tasmania, and CCC	11. 9	W. K. Hardacre, Eton and Trin. H.	10. 8
*P. W. Taylor, Derby and Linc.	13. 6½	W. H. W. Perrott, Private and 1 Trin.	12. 2½
*C. R. Carter, Cheltenham and CCC	13. 2	*S. Swann, Marlborough and Trin. H.	13. 3½
H. McLean, Eton and New C.	12.12	*F. E. Churchill, Eton and 3 Trin.	13. 2½
F. O. Wethered, Eton and Ch.Ch.	12. 6	*E. W. Haig, Eton and 3 Trin.	11. 8
*D. H. McLean, Eton and New C.	13. 1½	R. H. Coke, Westminster and Trin. H.	12. 4
H. Girdlestone, Bath Coll. and Magd., str.	12. 7	*F. I. Pitman, Eton and 3 Trin., str.	11.11½
*F. J. Humphreys, Radley and BNC, cox	8. 2	G. Wilson, Charterhouse and 1 Trin., cox	7.11
Average	12. 6¾	Average	11.13

Oxford won by 2½ lengths in 21 min. 36 sec.

43 Saturday, 3 April 1886, at 1.38 p.m.

OXFORD †		CAMBRIDGE	
*W. S. Unwin, Magd. C. Sch. and Magd., bow	10.11	C. J. Bristowe, Repton and Trin. H., bow	10. 8½
L. S. R. Byrne, Eton and Trin.	11.11½	*N. P. Symonds, Hereford and LMBC	10.10
W. St L. Robertson, Geelong GS and Wadh.	11. 7½	J. Walmsley, Uppingham and Trin. H.	12. 1
*C. R. Carter, Cheltenham and CCC	13. 0½	A. D. Flower, Bedford Mod. and Clare	12. 8½
*H. McLean, Eton and New C.	12.12	*S. Fairbairn, Geelong GS and Jesus	13. 9
*F. O. Wethered, Eton and Ch.Ch.	12. 6	S. D. Muttlebury, Eton and 3 Trin.	13. 3
*D. H. McLean, Eton and New C.	13. 0	C. Barclay, Eton and 3 Trin.	11. 3
*H. Girdlestone, Bath Coll. and Magd., str.	12. 9¼	*F. I. Pitman, Eton and 3 Trin., str.	11.10½
W. E. Maynard, Haileybury and Ex., cox	7.12	G. H. Baker, Vict. Coll., Douglas, and Qu., cox	6. 9
Average	12. 3¾	Average	11.13¾

Cambridge won by ⅔ length in 22 min. 30 sec.

44 Saturday, 26 March 1887, at 3.05 p.m.

CAMBRIDGE †		OXFORD	
R. McKenna, King's Coll., Lon., and Trin. H., bow	10. 7	W. F. C. Holland, Eton and BNC, bow	10. 9
C. T. Barclay, Eton and 3 Trin.	11. 1	G. Nickalls, Eton and Magd.	12. 1
P. Landale, Hawthorne GS and Trin. H.	12. 0½	S. G. Williams, Marlborough and CCC	12. 5
J. R. Orford, Shrewsbury and King's	13. 0	H. R. Parker, Eton and BNC	13. 3
*S. Fairbairn, Geelong GS and Jesus	13. 5½	*H. McLean, Eton and New C.	12. 8½
*S. D. Muttlebury, Eton and 3 Trin.	13. 6½	F. O. Wethered, Eton and Ch.Ch.	12. 5
*C. Barclay, Eton and 3 Trin.	11. 8	*D. H. McLean, Eton and New C.	12. 9
*C. J. Bristowe, Repton and Trin. H., str.	10. 7½	A. F. Titherington, Charterhouse and Qu., str.	12. 2
G. H. Baker, Vict. Coll., Douglas, and Qu., cox	7. 1	L. J. Clarke, Marlborough and Ex., cox	7. 9
Average	11.13¼	Average	12. 3½

Cambridge won by 2½ lengths in 20 min. 52 sec. Oxford broke an oar.

45 *Saturday, 24 March 1888, at 10.56 a.m.*

CAMBRIDGE		OXFORD †	
R. H. Symonds-Taylor, Hereford and Trin. H., bow	10. 7	*W. F. C. Holland, Eton and BNC, bow	11. 0
L. Hannen, Radley and Trin. H.	11. 3	A. P. Parker, Private and Magd.	11.11
R. H. P. Orde, Richmond, Yorks, and 1 Trin.	11. 7	M. E. Bradford, Eton and Ch.Ch.	11. 9
C. B. P. Bell, Shrewsbury and Trin. H.	12.13½	S. R. Fothergill, Eton and New C.	12.10
*S. D. Muttlebury, Eton and 3 Trin.	13. 7	H. Cross, Bedford and Hert.	13. 0½
*P. Landale, Hawthorne GS and Trin. H.	12. 4	*H. R. Parker, Eton and BNC	13. 5
F. H. Maugham, Dover and Trin. H.	11. 5	*G. Nickalls, Eton and Magd.	12. 4
J. C. Gardner, Rugby and Emm., str.	11. 7	L. Freere, Eton and BNC, str.	10. 0½
J. R. Roxburgh, Edin. Coll. and Trin. H., cox	8. 2	A. H. Stewart, Eton and New C., cox	7.13½
Average	11.12	Average	11.13¾

Cambridge won by 7 lengths in 20 min. 48 sec.

46 *Saturday, 30 March 1889, at 1.15 p.m.*

CAMBRIDGE †		OXFORD	
*R. H. Symonds-Taylor, Hereford and Trin. H., bow	10.10½	H. E. L. Puxley, Eton and CCC, bow	11. 8½
*L. Hannen, Radley and Trin. H.	11. 4	R. P. P. Rowe, Clifton and Magd.	11. 9
		T. A. Cook, Radley and Wadh.	12. 2
*R. H. P. Orde, Richmond, Yorks, and 1 Trin.	11.10		
*C. B. P. Bell, Shrewsbury and Trin. H.	13. 1	F. C. Drake, Winchester and New C.	12.12
*S. D. Muttlebury, Eton and 3 Trin.	13. 9	Lord Ampthill, Eton and New C.	12.11
*P. Landale, Hawthorne GS and Trin. H.	12. 8	*H. R. Parker, Eton and BNC	13.11
*F. H. Maugham, Dover and Trin. H.	11. 5½	*G. Nickalls, Eton and Magd.	12. 5
*J. C. Gardner, Rugby and Emm., str.	11.10	*W. F. C. Holland, Eton and BNC, str.	10.12
T. W. Northmore, Rossall and Qu., cox	7.13	J. P. Heywood-Lonsdale, Eton and New C., cox	8. 2½
Average	12. 0¼	Average	12. 3½

Cambridge won by 3 lengths in 20 min. 14 sec.

47 Wednesday, 26 March 1890, at 4.44 p.m.

CAMBRIDGE †		OXFORD	
G. Elin, Eton and 3 Trin., bow	10. 9	*W. F. C. Holland, Eton and BNC, bow	11. 1
J. M. Sladen, Harrow and Trin. H.	11.12	P. D. Tuckett, Marlborough and Trin.	11. 2
E. T. Fison, Repton and CCC	12. 6½	*H. E. L. Puxley, Eton and CCC	11. 7
J. F. Rowlatt, Fettes and Trin. H.	11.12	C. H. St J. Hornby, Harrow and New C.	12. 5
A. S. Duffield, Rugby and Trin. H.	12. 9	*Lord Ampthill, Eton and New C.	13. 5
*S. D. Muttlebury, Eton and 3 Trin.	13. 9	*G. Nickalls, Eton and Magd.	12.10
G. Francklyn, Eton and 3 Trin.	11.12½	*R. P. P. Rowe, Clifton and Magd.	11.10
*J. C. Gardner, Rugby and Emm., str.	11.12½	W. A. L. Fletcher, Eton and Ch.Ch., str.	13. 0
*T. W. Northmore, Rossall and Qu., cox	7.10½	*J. P. Heywood-Lonsdale, Eton and New C., cox	8. 0
Average	12. 1½	Average	12. 1½

Oxford won by 1 length in 22 min. 3 sec.

48 Saturday, 21 March 1891, at 11.09 a.m.

CAMBRIDGE		OXFORD †	
J. W. Noble, Haileybury and Caius, bow	11. 5¾	W. M. Poole, Bedford Mod. and Magd., bow	10. 7½
E. W. Lord, Brisbane GS and Trin. H.	10.10¼	*R. P. P. Rowe, Clifton and Magd.	11.11
* G. Francklyn, Eton and 3 Trin.	12. 3	V. Nickalls, Eton and Magd.	12. 9
* E. T. Fison, Repton and CCC	12. 7½	*G. Nickalls, Eton and Magd.	12. 5
W. Landale, Harrow and Trin. H.	12.11	F. Wilkinson, Trin. Coll., Melbourne, and BNC	13. 8
* J. F. Rowlatt, Fettes and Trin. H.	11.12	*Lord Ampthill, Eton and New C.	13. 5
* C. T. Fogg-Elliot, Durham and Trin. H.	11. 4	*W. A. L. Fletcher, Eton and Ch.Ch.	13. 2
* G. Elin, Eton and 3 Trin., str.	10.13	C. W. Kent, Private and BNC, str.	10.11
* J. V. Braddon, Shrewsbury and Trin. H., cox	7.12	*J. P. Heywood-Lonsdale, Eton and New C., cox	8. 6
Average	11.10	Average	12. 3¾

Oxford won by ½ length in 21 min. 48 sec.

49 Saturday, 9 April 1892, at 12.19 p.m.

CAMBRIDGE		OXFORD †	
*E. W. Lord, Brisbane GS and Trin. H., bow	10.12	H. B. Cotton, Eton and Magd., bow	9.13
R. G. Neill, Greenock Coll. and Jesus	11.11	J. A. Ford, Winchester and BNC	11. 9
*G. Francklyn, Eton and 3 Trin.	12. 3	W. A. S. Hewett, Haileybury and Univ.	12. 2
*E. T. Fison, Repton and CCC	12. 6½	F. E. Robeson, Eton and Mert.	13. 7½
*W. Landale, Harrow and Trin. H.	13. 1	*V. Nickalls, Eton and Magd.	13. 1
G. C. Kerr, Durham and 1 Trin.	12. 1	*W. A. L. Fletcher, Eton and Magd.	13. 8
*C. T. Fogg-Elliot, Durham and Trin. H.	11. 8½	*R. P. P. Rowe, Clifton and Magd.	12. 0
*G. Elin, Eton and 3 Trin., str.	10.10	C. M. Pitman, Eton and New C., str.	11.12
*J. V. Braddon, Shrewsbury and Trin. H., cox	7.13	*J. P. Heywood-Lonsdale, Eton and New C., cox	8. 9
Average	11.11⅞	Average	12. 3

Oxford won by 2¼ lengths in 19 min. 10 sec.

50 Wednesday, 22 March 1893, at 4.35 p.m.

CAMBRIDGE †		OXFORD	
G. A. H. Branson, Bedford and 1 Trin., bow	10. 9½	*H. B. Cotton, Eton and Magd., bow	9.12
R. F. Bayford, Eton and Trin. H.	11. 9	*J. A. Ford, Winchester and BNC	11.13
*C. T. Fogg-Elliot, Durham and Trin. H.	11.10½	J. A. Morrison, Eton and New C.	12. 4½
E. H. M. Waller, Highgate and CCC	12. 5½	H. Legge, Haileybury and Trin.	12.13½
L. A. E. Ollivant, Charterhouse and 1 Trin.	13. 3½	*V. Nickalls, Eton and Magd.	13. 4
*G. C. Kerr, Durham and 1 Trin.	12. 6	*W. A. L. Fletcher, Eton and Ch.Ch.	13. 8½
*R. O. Kerrison, Eton and 3 Trin.	12. 0	*C. M. Pitman, Eton and New C.	12. 0½
T. G. E. Lewis, Eton and 3 Trin., str.	11.12	M. C. Pilkington, Eton and Magd., str.	11.11
C. T. Agar, Westminster and 3 Trin., cox	7. 5	L. Portman, Wellington and Univ., cox	7. 7
Average	12. 0	Average	12. 3⅛

Oxford won by 1 length 4 feet in 18 min. 45 sec.

51 Saturday, 17 March 1894, at 9.12 a.m.

OXFORD †		CAMBRIDGE	
*H. B. Cotton, Eton and Magd., bow	9.13	A. H. Finch, Eton and 3 Trin., bow	11. 0
*M. C. Pilkington, Eton and Magd.	12. 4	N. W. Paine, Eton and 3 Trin.	11. 1
W. Burton Stewart, Loretto and BNC	13. 5	Sir Charles Ross, Bt, Eton and 3 Trin.	11. 8
*J. A. Morrison, Eton and New C.	12. 5	H. M. Bland, Eton and 3 Trin.	11. 5
E. G. Tew, Shrewsbury and Magd.	13. 7	*L. A. E. Ollivant, Charterhouse and 1 Trin.	13. 5¾
T. H. E. Stretch, Radley and New C.	12. 4	*C. T. Fogg-Elliot, Durham and Trin. H.	11. 8
W. E. Crum, Eton and New C.	12. 0	*R. O. Kerrison, Eton and 3 Trin.	11.12
*C. M. Pitman, Eton and New C., str.	12. 0	*T. G. E. Lewis, Eton and 3 Trin., str.	11.12
*L. Portman, Wellington and Univ., cox	8. 5	F. C. Begg, Clifton and Trin. H., cox	8. 0
Average	12. 3	Average	11.10

Oxford won by 3½ lengths in 21 min. 39 sec.

52 Saturday, 30 March 1895, at 4.08 p.m.

OXFORD †		CAMBRIDGE	
*H. B. Cotton, Eton and Magd., bow	9.13	T. B. Hope, Eton and Trin. H., bow	10.11
*M. C. Pilkington, Eton and Magd.	12. 4	F. C. Stewart, Harrow and Trin. H.	12. 1½
C. K. Phillips, Eton and New C.	11.12	H. A. Game, Harrow and 1 Trin.	12. 2
*T. H. E. Stretch, Radley and New C.	12. 4	W. S. Adie, Lon. Int. Coll. and 1 Trin.	13. 2½
*W. Burton Stewart, Loretto and BNC	13. 7½	T. J. G. Duncanson, Harrow and Emm.	13. 3
C. D. Burnell, Eton and Magd.	13. 0½	R. Y. Bonsey, Forest Sch. and LMBC	12. 4
*W. E. Crum, Eton and New C.	12. 2	A. S. Bell, Eton and Trin. H.	11. 2
*C. M. Pitman, Eton and New C., str.	12. 0	D. A. Wauchope, Repton and Trin. H., str.	11. 9
C. P. Serocold, Eton and New C., cox	8. 1	*F. C. Begg, Clifton and Trin. H., cox	8. 9
Average	12. 1⅞	Average	12. 0¾

Oxford won by 2¼ lengths in 20 min. 50 sec.

53 *Saturday, 28 March 1896, at 1.03 p.m.*

CAMBRIDGE †		OXFORD	
*T. B. Hope, Eton and Trin H., bow	11. 1	J. J. J. de Knoop, Eton and New C., bow	11. 1½
*H. A. Game, Harrow and 1 Trin.	12. 4	*C. K. Phillips, Eton and New C.	12. 5½
D. Pennington, Bath Coll. and Caius	12. 7	E. C. Sherwood, Magd. Coll. Sch. and Magd.	12.12
*R. Y. Bonsey, Forest Sch. and LMBC	12.10	*C. D. Burnell, Eton and Magd.	13.10
W. A. Bieber, Clifton and Trin. H.	12.12	E. R. Balfour, Edin. Acad. and Univ.	13. 6
*T. J. G. Duncanson, Harrow and Emm.	13.12	R. Carr, Eton and Magd.	12. 8½
*A. S. Bell, Eton and Trin. H.	11.13	W. E. Crum, Eton and New C.	12. 3
W. J. Fernie, Malvern and Trin. H., str.	11.13	H. G. Gold, Eton and Magd., str.	11. 5½
T. R. Paget-Tomlinson, Aldenham and Trin. H., cox	8. 4½	H. R. K. Pechell, Eton and BNC, cox	7.13½
Average	12. 5½	Average	12. 6½

Oxford won by ⅖ length in 20 min. 1 sec.

54 *Saturday, 3 April 1897, at 2.24 p.m.*

OXFORD		CAMBRIDGE †	
*J. J. J. de Knoop, Eton and New C., bow	11. 6	D. E. Campbell-Muir, Blair Lodge and Trin. H., bow	11. 5
G. O. C. Edwards, Eton and New C.	12. 1	* A. S. Bell, Eton and Trin. H.	12. 1
*C. K. Phillips, Eton and New C.	12. 0½	E. J. D. Taylor, Bath Coll. and Caius	12.13
*C. D. Burnell, Eton and Magd.	13. 9	B. H. Howell, Mil. Coll., USA, and Trin. H.	12. 9
*E. R. Balfour, Edin. Acad. and Univ.	13. 8½	* W. A. Bieber, Clifton and Trin. H.	13. 1
*R. Carr, Eton and Magd.	12.11½	* D. Pennington, Bath Coll. and Caius	12. 9
*W. E. Crum, Eton and New C.	12. 3	W. Dudley Ward, Eton and 3 Trin.	12. 6
*H. G. Gold, Eton and Magd., str.	11.11	* W. J. Fernie, Malvern and Trin. H., str.	11.13
*H. R. K. Pechell, Eton and BNC, cox	8. 0½	E. C. Hawkins, Charterhouse and Caius, cox	8. 1
Average	12. 6¼	Average	12. 5⅜

Oxford won by 2½ lengths in 19 min. 12 sec.

55 Saturday, 24 March 1898, at 3.47 p.m.

CAMBRIDGE		OXFORD †	
W. B. Rennie, Giggleswick and Emm., bow	11. 7	R. O. Pitman, Eton and New C., bow	11. 0
J. F. Beale, Harrow and 1 Trin.	12. 2¾	*G. O. C. Edwards, Eton and New C.	12. 7½
H. G. Brown, Harrow and 1 Trin.	13.11¾	*C. K. Phillips, Eton and New C.	12. 0½
S. V. Pearson, Manchester GS and Emm.	12. 9½	F. W. Warre, Eton and Ball.	12.12
A. W. Swanston, Loretto and Jesus	12.10	*C. D. Burnell, Eton and Magd.	14. 0
R. B. Etherington-Smith, Repton and 1 Trin.	12.11¼	*R. Carr, Eton and Magd.	13. 1
C. J. D. Goldie, Eton and 3 Trin.	12. 0	A. T. Herbert, Bedford GS and Ball.	12.10½
*A. S. Bell, Eton and Trin. H., str.	12. 2¼	*H. G. Gold, Eton and Magd., str.	11.10½
*E. C. Hawkins, Charterhouse and Caius, cox	8. 4	*H. R. K. Pechell, Eton and BNC, cox	8. 1
Average	12. 6½	Average	12. 7

Oxford won easily in 22 min. 15 sec.
Cambridge waterlogged

56 Saturday, 25 March 1899, at 12.58 p.m.

CAMBRIDGE †		OXFORD	
W. H. Chapman, Eton and 3 Trin., bow	11. 2	* R. O. Pitman, Eton and New C., bow	10.10
N. L. Calvert, Geelong GS and Trin. H.	11.13	C. W. Tomkinson, Eton and Ball.	12. 0
*C. J. D. Goldie, Eton and 3 Trin.	12. 1½	A. H. D. Steel, Eton and Ball.	12.11½
J. E. Payne, New Coll., Eastbourne, and Pet.	12.10½	H. J. Hale, Eton and Ball.	12. 9
*R. B. Etherington-Smith, Repton and 1 Trin.	12.10	C. E. Johnston, Eton and New C.	13. 0
R. H. Sanderson, Harrow and 1 Trin.	12.10	*F. W. Warre, Eton and Ball.	12.13
*W. Dudley Ward, Eton and 3 Trin.	12. 9½	*A. T. Herbert, Bedford GS and Ball.	12.13
J. H. Gibbon, Eton and 3 Trin., str.	11. 3½	*H. G. Gold, Eton and Magd., str.	11.11½
G. A. Lloyd, Eton and 3 Trin., cox	8. 5	G. S. Maclagan, Eton and Magd., cox	8. 1
Average	12. 2¼	Average	12. 5

Cambridge won by 3¼ lengths in 21 min. 4 sec.

57 *Saturday, 31 March 1900, at 2 p.m.*

OXFORD †		CAMBRIDGE	
H. H. Dutton, St Pet., Adelaide, and Magd., bow	10. 9½	S. P. Cockerell, Eton and 3 Trin., bow	11.10
R. H. Culme-Seymour, Eton and New C.	11. 7½	C. J. M. Adie, Fettes and 1 Trin.	12. 3
*C. E. Johnston, Eton and New C.	12.12	B. W. D. Brooke, Winchester and 1 Trin.	11.10¼
*C. W. Tomkinson, Eton and Ball.	11.13	* J. E. Payne, New Coll., Eastbourne, and Pet.	13. 0
Lord Grimston, Eton and Ch.Ch.	13.10¾	* R. B. Etherington-Smith, Repton and 1 Trin.	12.11¼
H. B. Kittermaster, Shrewsbury and Ch.Ch.	14. 6	* R. H. Sanderson, Harrow and 1 Trin.	12.13¼
T. B. Etherington-Smith, Repton and Oriel	11. 5¾	* W. Dudley Ward, Eton and 3 Trin.	12. 9
C. P. Rowley, Winchester and Magd., str.	11.12½	* J. H. Gibbon, Eton and 3 Trin., str.	11. 8
*G. S. Maclagan, Eton and Magd., cox	8. 5	* G. A. Lloyd, Eton and 3 Trin., cox	9. 0
Average	12. 4⅜	Average	12. 4⅝

Cambridge won by 20 lengths in 18 min. 45 sec.

58 *Saturday, 30 March 1901, at 10.31 a.m.*

CAMBRIDGE †		OXFORD	
R. H. Nelson, Eton and 3 Trin., bow	11. 3	F. O. J. Huntley, Radley and Univ., bow	11. 7
*B. C. Cox, Harrow and Trin. H.	12. 0	H. C. de J. Du Vallon, Malvern and BNC	12. 4½
B. W. D. Brooke, Winchester and 1 Trin.	11. 9½	J. Younger, Winchester and New C.	12.11½
C. W. H. Taylor, Eton and 3 Trin.	12. 7½	A. de L. Long, Winchester and New C.	12. 9½
G. Parker, Radley and 1 Trin.	12. 5½	*H. J. Hale, Eton and Ball.	12.10
H. B. Grylls, Rugby and 1 Trin.	12. 7	*F. W. Warre, Eton and Ball.	12. 7½
E. F. Duncanson, Harrow and Emm.	12. 5	*T. B. Etherington-Smith, Repton and Oriel	11. 4½
G. M. Maitland, Marlborough and 1 Trin., str.	12. 1	*R. H. Culme-Seymour, Eton and New C., str.	11. 8½
E. A. O. A. Jamieson, Glenalmond and 1 Trin., cox	8. 6	*G. S. Maclagan, Eton and Magd., cox	8. 3
Average	12. 1¼	Average	12. 2⅝

Oxford won by ⅖ length in 22 min. 31 sec.

59 Saturday, 22 March 1902, at 12.45 p.m.

CAMBRIDGE †		OXFORD	
*W. H. Chapman, Eton and 3 Trin., bow	11. 2	G. C. Drinkwater, Rugby and Wadh., bow	11. 7
T. Drysdale, St Paul's and Jesus	12. 2	D. Milburn, Hill Sch., USA, and Linc.	12. 4½
P. H. Thomas, Eton and 3 Trin.	12. 5	* J. Younger, Winchester and New C.	12.12½
*C. W. H. Taylor, Eton and 3 Trin.	12. 8	* H. J. Hale, Eton and Ball.	13. 1
F. J. Escombe, Clifton and Trin. H.	12. 8	J. G. Milburn, Hill Sch., USA, and Linc.	13. 3½
*H. B. Grylls, Rugby and 1 Trin.	12.10	* A. de L. Long, Winchester and New C.	13. 0¼
J. Edwards-Moss, Eton and 3 Trin.	12. 4	H. W. Adams, St Paul's and Univ.	12. 1½
*R. H. Nelson, Eton and 3 Trin., str.	11. 5	*F. O. J. Huntley, Radley and Univ., str.	11. 7½
C. H. S. Wasbrough, Radley and Trin. H., cox	8. 1	*G. S. Maclagan, Eton and Magd., cox	8. 5
Average	12. 2	Average	12. 6½

Cambridge won by 5 lengths in 19 min. 9 sec.

60 Wednesday, 1 April 1903, at 3.35 p.m.

OXFORD †		CAMBRIDGE	
C. A. Willis, Eton and Magd., bow	11. 4	*W. H. Chapman, Eton and 3 Trin., bow	11. 3
A. K. Graham, Eton and Ball.	10.12	*P. H. Thomas, Eton and 3 Trin.	12. 8½
*A. de L. Long, Winchester and New C.	12.11	S. R. Beale, Marlborough and 1 Trin.	11. 2
F. S. Kelly, Eton and Ball.	11.12	*C. W. H. Taylor, Eton and 3 Trin.	12.11
*H. W. Adams, St Paul's and Univ.	12. 1	J. S. Carter, Eton and King's	13. 4
*D. Milburn, Hill Sch., USA, and Linc.	12.10	*H. B. Grylls, Rugby and 1 Trin.	12.13
*G. C. Drinkwater, Rugby and Wadh.	11.11	*J. Edwards-Moss, Eton and 3 Trin.	12. 9
E. G. Monier-Williams, Winchester and Univ., str.	12. 5	*R. H. Nelson, Eton and 3 Trin., str.	11. 5
F. T. H. Eyre, Bedford and Keble, cox	6. 6	B. G. A. Scott, St Paul's and Trin. H., cox	8. 6
Average	11.13½	Average	12. 3½

Cambridge won by 6 lengths in 19 min. 33 sec.

61 *Saturday, 26 March 1904, at 7.45 a.m.*

CAMBRIDGE †		OXFORD	
H. Sanger, Dunstable and LMBC, bow	10. 7	T. G. Brocklebank, Eton and Trin., bow	10. 9¼
S. M. Bruce, CEGS, Melbourne, and Trin. H.	12. 0	R. W. Somers-Smith, Eton and Mert.	10. 8
B. C. Johnstone, Eton and 3 Trin.	12. 1	A. J. S. H. Hales, Rugby and CCC	12. 3¾
A. L. Lawrence, Rugby and 1 Trin.	12.13¾	H. W. Jelf, Eton and Ch.Ch.	12. 6
R. V. Powell, Eton and 3 Trin.	12. 2¾	P. C. Underhill, St Edward's and BNC	12. 9
*P. H. Thomas, Eton and 3 Trin.	12. 7	A. R. Balfour, Edin. Acad. and Univ.	12. 0
H. D. Gillies, Wanganui, NZ, and Caius	10. 5	E. P. Evans, Radley and Univ.	13. 0½
M. V. Smith, Eton and Trin. H., str.	10. 5½	*A. K. Graham, Eton and Ball., str.	11. 0
*B. G. A. Scott, St Paul's and Trin. H., cox	8. 4	E. C. T. Warner, Eton and Ch.Ch., cox	7.10
Average	11. 8¾	Average	11. 9¾

Cambridge won by 4½ lengths in 21 min. 37 sec.

62 *Saturday, 1 April 1905, at 11.30 a.m.*

OXFORD		CAMBRIDGE †	
*R. W. Somers-Smith, Eton and Mert., bow	10. 9	*H. Sanger, Dunstable and LMBC, bow	10. 9
H. M. Farrer, Eton and Ball.	11. 5	W. B. Savory, Private and 1 Trin.	12. 9
*A. J. S. H. Hales, Rugby and CCC	12. 0	*B. C. Johnstone, Eton and 3 Trin.	12. 4
*A. R. Balfour, Edin. Acad. and Univ.	12. 0	*P. H. Thomas, Eton and 3 Trin.	12. 4½
L. E. Jones, Eton and Ball.	13. 9½	E. P. W. Wedd, Cheltenham and Caius	13. 1
*E. P. Evans, Radley and Univ.	13. 2½	B. R. Winthrop-Smith, Eton and 3 Trin.	12. 7
*A. K. Graham, Eton and Ball.	11. 3½	*R. V. Powell, Eton and 3 Trin.	12. 3
H. C. Bucknall, Eton and Mert., str.	11. 1½	C. H. S. Taylor, Rugby and Caius, str.	10. 4
L. P. Stedall, Harrow and Mert., cox	8. 0	R. Allcard, Eton and 3 Trin., cox	8. 6
Average	11.12⅝	Average	12. 0

Oxford won by 3 lengths in 20 min. 35 sec.

63 *Saturday, 7 April 1906, at 12 noon*

OXFORD †		CAMBRIDGE	
G. M. A. Graham, Eton and New C., bow	10.13½	G. D. Cochrane, Eton and 3 Trin., bow	10. 8½
C. H. Illingworth, Radley and Pemb.	12. 0	J. H. F. Benham, Fauconberge and Jesus	11. 6
J. Dewar, Rugby and New C.	12. 4½	H. M. Goldsmith, Sherborne and Jesus	12. 6½
*L. E. Jones, Eton and Ball.	13.13	M. Donaldson, Charterhouse and 1 Trin.	13. 9½
*A. G. Kirby, Eton and Magd.	13. 7½	*B. C. Johnstone, Eton and 3 Trin.	12. 6½
*E. P. Evans, Radley and Univ.	13. 6	*R. V. Powell, Eton and 3 Trin.	12. 6½
A. C. Gladstone, Eton and Ch.Ch.	10. 7½	E. W. Powell, Eton and 3 Trin.	11. 6
*H. C. Bucknall, Eton and Mert., str.	11. 4½	D. C. R. Stuart, Cheltenham and Trin. H., str.	11. 1½
*L. P. Stedall, Harrow and Mert., cox	8. 5	A. G. L. Hunt, Ipswich and LMBC, cox	8. 0
Average	12. 3½	Average	11.13⅜

Cambridge won by 3½ lengths in 19 min. 25 sec. Stroked on bow side.

64 *Saturday, 16 March 1907, at 3 p.m.*

OXFORD †		CAMBRIDGE	
W. T. Heard, Fettes and Ball., bow	11. 0	A. B. Close-Brooks, Winchester and 1 Trin., bow	11. 0
*H. C. Bucknall, Eton and Mert.	11. 8	* J. H. F. Benham, Fauconberge and Jesus	12. 5½
G. E. Hope, Eton and Ch.Ch.	12.13	* H. M. Goldsmith, Sherborne and Jesus	12. 6
R. M. Peat, Sedbergh and Trin.	11.11	J. S. Burn, Harrow and 1 Trin.	12. 9½
J. A. Gillan, Edin. Acad. and Magd.	12. 7	H. G. Baynes, Leighton Park and 1 Trin.	14. 0
*A. G. Kirby, Eton and Magd.	13.10	* B. C. Johnstone, Eton and 3 Trin.	12. 9
E. H. L. Southwell, Eton and Magd.	12. 1	* E. W. Powell, Eton and 3 Trin.	11. 6
*A. C. Gladstone, Eton and Ch.Ch., str.	11. 0	* D. C. R. Stuart, Cheltenham and Trin. H., str.	11. 1
A. W. F. Donkin, Eton and Magd., cox	8. 5	R. F. R. P. Boyle, Bradfield and Trin. H., cox	8.10
Average	12. 1	Average	12. 2⅞

Cambridge won by 4½ lengths in 20 min. 26 sec. Stroked on bow side.

65 Saturday, 4 April 1908, at 3.30 p.m.

OXFORD †		CAMBRIDGE	
Hon. R. P. Stanhope, Eton and		F. H. Jerwood, Oakham and	
Magd., bow	9.10	Jesus, bow	11.10
C. R. Cudmore, St Pet.,		G. E. Fairbairn, Eton and	
Adelaide and Magd.	12. 0	Jesus	11.13
*E. H. L. Southwell, Eton and		O. A. Carver, Charterhouse and	
Magd.	12. 3	1 Trin.	12.10
A. E. Kitchin, Tonbridge and		H. E. Kitching, Uppingham and	
St Joh.	12. 7	Trin. H.	13. 2
*A. G. Kirby, Eton and Magd.	13. 7	* J. S. Burn, Harrow and 1 Trin.	12.10½
A. McCulloch, Winchester and		E. G. Williams, Eton and	
Univ.	12. 9½	3 Trin.	13. 0½
H. R. Barker, Eton and Ch.Ch.	12. 0½	*E. W. Powell, Eton and 3 Trin.	11. 6
*A. C. Gladstone, Eton and		* D. C. R. Stuart, Cheltenham	
Ch.Ch., str.	11. 3½	and Trin. H., str.	11. 2
*A. W. F. Donkin, Eton and		* R. F. R. P. Boyle, Bradfield and	
Magd., cox	8. 7	Trin. H., cox	8.10
Average	11.13¾	Average	12. 3¼

Cambridge won by 2½ lengths in 19 min. 20 sec. Stroked on bow side.

66 Saturday, 3 April 1909, at 12.38 p.m.

CAMBRIDGE †		OXFORD	
R. W. M. Arbuthnot, Eton and		* A. C. Gladstone, Eton and	
3 Trin., bow	10. 2	Ch.Ch., bow	11. 6½
H. E. Swanston, Loretto and		* H. R. Barker, Eton and Ch.Ch.	12. 5
Jesus	12. 4		
G. L. Thomson, Univ. Coll.		* C. R. Cudmore, St Pet.,	
Sch. and Trin. H.	12. 6	Adelaide, and Magd.	12. 4
* H. E. Kitching, Uppingham		A. S. Garton, Eton and Magd.	13. 8½
and Trin. H.	12.12		
*E. G. Williams, Eton and 3 Trin.	13. 0	D. Mackinnon, Rugby and	
		Magd.	13. 3½
J. B. Rosher, Charterhouse and		* J. A. Gillan, Edin. Acad. and	
1 Trin.	14. 0	Magd.	13. 1
E. S. Hornidge, Sherborne and		* A. G. Kirby, Eton and Magd.	13.10½
Trin. H.	13. 0		
*D. C. R. Stuart, Cheltenham		R. C. Bourne, Eton and New C.,	
and Trin. H., str.	11. 2	str.	10.13
G. D. Compston, Dulwich and		* A. W. F. Donkin, Eton and	
Trin. H., cox	8.10	Magd., cox	8. 8
Average	12. 5	Average	12. 8¼

Oxford won by 3½ lengths in 19 min. 50 sec.

67 Wednesday, 23 March 1910, at 12.30 p.m.

OXFORD		CAMBRIDGE †	
M. B. Higgins, Melbourne Univ. and Ball., bow	11. 8	*R. W. M. Arbuthnot, Eton and 3 Trin., bow	10. 5
R. H. Owen, Dulwich and Wadh.	12. 6½	R. Davies, Hymer's Coll., Bath, and St Cath.	11.11½
N. Field, Wellington and BNC	13. 8½	F. E. Hellyer, Winchester and 1 Trin.	12. 3½
E. Majolier, Eton and Ch.Ch.	13. 0½	C. P. Cooke, Geelong GS and Trin. H.	12. 9½
*D. Mackinnon, Rugby and Magd.	13. 2½	*E. G. Williams, Eton and 3 Trin.	13. 2½
*A. S. Garton, Eton and Magd.	13.11	*J. B. Rosher, Charterhouse and 1 Trin.	14. 4
P. Fleming, Eton and Magd.	12. 6	C. R. le Blanc Smith, Eton and 3 Trin.	12. 6½
*R. C. Bourne, Eton and New C., str.	11. 0	H. J. S. Shields, Loretto and Jesus, str.	11. 5½
*A. W. F. Donkin, Eton and Magd., cox	8. 8	C. A. Skinner, Durban HS and Jesus, cox	8. 5
Average	12. 8⅞	Average	12. 4½

Oxford won by 3½ lengths in 20 min. 14 sec.

68 Saturday, 1 April 1911, at 2.36 p.m.

OXFORD†		CAMBRIDGE	
C. E. Tinné, Eton and Univ., bow	12. 2½	S. E. Swann, Rugby and Trin. H., bow	11. 8
L. G. Wormald, Eton and Magd.	12. 7	P. V. G. Van der Byl, Diocesan Coll., Rondebosch, and Pemb.	12. 2½
R. E. Burgess, Eton and Magd.	12. 2½	*F. E. Hellyer, Winchester and 1 Trin.	12. 0
E. J. H. V. Millington-Drake, Eton and Magd.	12. 8	C. F. Burnand, Downside and 1 Trin.	12. 4
C. W. B. Littlejohn, Melbourne Univ. and New C.	12.13½	*C. R. le Blanc Smith, Eton and 3 Trin.	13. 3
*A. S. Garton, Eton and Magd.	13. 8	*J. B. Rosher, Charterhouse and 1 Trin.	14. 6½
*D. Mackinnon, Rugby and Magd.	13. 5½	*G. E. Fairbairn, Eton and Jesus	11.13
*R. C. Bourne, Eton and New C., str.	10.13	*R. W. M. Arbuthnot, Eton and 3 Trin., str.	10. 8
H. B. Wells, Winchester and Magd., cox	8. 5	*C. A. Skinner, Durban HS and Jesus, cox	8.12
Average	12. 7½	Average	12. 3⅞

Oxford won by 2¾ lengths in 18 min. 29 sec.

69 Saturday, 30 March 1912 at 11.40 a.m., and Monday, 1 April, at 12.40 p.m.

CAMBRIDGE		OXFORD †	
*R. W. M. Arbuthnot, Eton and		F. A. H. Pitman, Eton and	
3 Trin., bow	10. 9	New C., bow	11.11½
*D. C. Collins, Wellington, NZ,		*C. E. Tinné, Eton and Univ.	12. 4
and 1 Trin.	11. 7¾		
H. M. Heyland, Wellington and		*L. G. Wormald, Eton and	
Pemb.	12. 4¼	Magd.	12. 9
R. S. Shove, Uppingham and		E. D. Horsfall, Eton and Magd.	12. 6
1 Trin.	12. 6½		
J. H. Goldsmith, Rossall and		A. H. M. Wedderburn, Eton	
Jesus	12.13½	and Ball.	13.11
*C. R. le Blanc Smith, Eton and		A. F. R. Wiggins, Eton and	
3 Trin.	13. 3	New C.	12.11
L. S. Lloyd, Eton and 3 Trin.	10. 5½	*C. W. B. Littlejohn, Melbourne	
		Univ. and New C.	12. 8
*S. E. Swann, Rugby and Trin.		*R. C. Bourne, Eton and New C.,	
H., str.	11. 6	str.	11. 0½
*C. A. Skinner, Durban HS and		*H. B. Wells, Winchester and	
Jesus, cox	8. 3	Magd., cox	8. 7
Average	11.12¼	Average	12. 5⅞

In first race Cambridge sank and Oxford were waterlogged. In rerow Oxford won by
6 lengths in 22 min. 5 sec.

70 Thursday, 13 March 1913, at 4.38 p.m.

CAMBRIDGE †		OXFORD	
G. A. Fisher, Winchester and		E. R. Burgess, Eton and Magd.,	
Jesus, bow	11. 2	bow	11. 6
*S. E. Swann, Rugby and Trin.		C. L. Baillieu, Melbourne GS	
H.	11. 9½	and Magd.	12. 4
H. Roper, Blundell's and Sid. S.	12.10½	R. P. Hankinson, Winchester	
		and New C.	11.13
W. M. Askwith, Bedford and		H. K. Ward, Sydney Univ. and	
CCC	13.10	New C.	12. 6
C. S. Clark, Bedford and Pemb.	12.13	*A. H. M. Wedderburn, Eton	
		and Ball.	13.10
*R. S. Shove, Uppingham and		*A. F. R. Wiggins, Eton and	
1 Trin.	12. 8	New C.	12.12
C. E. V. Buxton, Eton and		*L. G. Wormald, Eton and	
3 Trin.	12. 0	Magd.	12. 8
G. E. Tower, Eton and 3 Trin.,		*E. D. Horsfall, Eton and	
str.	11.11¼	Magd., str.	12. 6
L. E. Ridley, Eastbourne and		*H. B. Wells, Winchester and	
Jesus, cox	8. 6	Magd., cox	8. 8
Average	12. 4½	Average	12. 6⅜

Oxford won by ¾ length in 20 min. 53 sec.

71 *Saturday, 28 March 1914, at 2.20 p.m.*

CAMBRIDGE		OXFORD †	
D. I. Day, Repton and LMBC, bow	11. 6	R. W. Fletcher, Eton and Ball., bow	11.10½
*S. E. Swann, Rugby and Trin. H.	11.13	B. Burdekin, Cheltenham and New C.	12. 4
P. C. Livingstone, Vancouver and Jesus	13. 7	*H. K. Ward, Syd. Univ. and New C.	12. 9
J. A. Ritson, Rugby and 1 Trin.	13. 7	*E. D. Horsfall, Eton and Magd.	12. 7½
K. G. Garnett, St Paul's and 1 Trin.	13.12	J. B. Kindersley, Clifton and Ex.	12. 9½
*C. S. Clark, Bedford and Pemb.	13. 1	*A. F. R. Wiggins, Eton and New C.	12.13
*C. E. V. Buxton, Eton and 3 Trin.	12. 2½	G. W. Titherington, Radley and Qu.	12.10
*G. E. Tower, Eton and 3 Trin., str.	11.12	*F. A. H. Pitman, Eton and New C., str.	11.12½
*L. E. Ridley, Eastbourne and Jesus, cox	8. 7	*H. B. Wells, Winchester and Magd., cox	8. 8
Average	12. 9¼	Average	12. 6

Cambridge won by 4½ lengths in 20 min. 23 sec.

72 *Saturday, 27 March 1920, at 5.40 p.m.*

CAMBRIDGE		OXFORD †	
H. O. C. Boret, Eton and 3 Trin., bow	12. 1	S. Earl, Eton and Magd., bow	12. 6½
J. H. Simpson, Bedford and Pemb.	13. 0	N. H. McNeil, Scotch Coll., Melbourne, and Ball.	12. 0
A. F. W. Dixon, Monkton Combe and Chr.	12.11	A. T. M. Durand, Eton and Magd.	13. 0
R. I. L. McEwen, Eton and 3 Trin.	13. 8	A. C. Hill, Shrewsbury and St Joh.	13. 8½
H. B. Playford, St Paul's and Jesus	13. 8	D. T. Raikes, Radley and Mert.	13. 7
J. A. Campbell, Melbourne CEGS and Jesus	13. 5	W. E. C. James, Eton and Magd.	13. 8½
A. Swann, Rugby and Trin. H.	12. 0½	H. W. B. Cairns, Adelaide HS and Ball.	12. 0
P. H. G. H.-S. Hartley, Eton and LMBC, str.	10.10¼	M. H. Ellis, Shrewsbury and Keble, str.	10. 4½
R. T. Johnstone, Eton and Chr., cox	8.11	W. H. Porritt, Wyggeston and Magd., cox	8. 9½
Average	12. 9	Average	12. 7¾

Cambridge won by 4 lengths in 21 min. 11 sec.

73 Wednesday, 30 March 1921, at 5 p.m.

OXFORD †		CAMBRIDGE	
M. H. Ellis, Shrewsbury and Keble, bow	10. 6	*H. O. C. Boret, Eton and 3 Trin., bow	12. 7
P. C. Mallam, Lancing and Qu.	11. 6¾	A. G. W. Penney, Repton and Pemb.	13. 4
*S. Earl, Eton and Magd.	12. 5	A. B. Ritchie, RN Coll., Dartmouth, and Trin H.	13. 7
F. B. Lothrop, Harvard Univ. and Trin.	13. 5	A. D. B. Pearson, Winchester and 1 Trin.	13. 7
*W. E. C. James, Eton and Magd.	13. 6	*H. B. Playford, St Paul's and Jesus	13.10
R. S. C. Lucas, Eton and Magd.	13. 7½	*J. A. Campbell, Melbourne CEGS and Jesus	13. 2
G. O. Nickalls, Eton and Magd.	12. 6	Hon. J. W. H. Fremantle, Eton and 3 Trin.	12. 0
*D. T. Raikes, Radley and Mert., str.	13. 4	*P. H. G. H.-S. Hartley, Eton and LMBC, str.	11. 1
*W. H. Porritt, Wyggeston and Magd., cox	8.10	L. E. Stephens, Felsted and Trin H., cox	8.11
Average	12. 7½	Average	12.11¾

Cambridge won by 1 length in 19 min. 45 sec.

74 Saturday, 1 April 1922, at 4.40 p.m.

OXFORD		CAMBRIDGE †	
*P. C. Mallam, Lancing and Qu., bow	11. 6	T. D. A. Collet, Oundle and Pemb., bow	12. 3
A. C. Irvine, Shrewsbury and Mert.	12. 8	A. J. Hodgkin, Leighton Pk and 1 Trin.	12. 6½
*S. Earl, Eton and Magd.	12. 6½	K. N. Craig, Cheltenham and Pemb.	12. 8½
J. E. Pedder, Shrewsbury and Worc.	12. 9	* A. D. P. Pearson, Winchester and 1 Trin.	13.10½
*G. O. Nickalls, Eton and Magd.	12. 8	* H. B. Playford, St Paul's and Jesus	13.10½
*D. T. Raikes, Radley and Mert.	13. 6½	B. G. Ivory, Bedale's and Pemb.	13. 8
G. Milling, Radley and Mert.	11.10	* Hon. J. W. H. Fremantle, Eton and 3 Trin.	12. 6½
A. V. Campbell, Eton and Ch.Ch., str.	11. 5½	* P. H. G. H.-S. Hartley, Eton and LMBC, str.	11. 6
*W. H. Porritt, Wyggeston and Magd., cox	8.10	* L. E. Stephens, Felsted and Trin. H., cox	9. 4
Average	12. 4	Average	12.11

Cambridge won by 4½ lengths in 19 min. 27 sec.

75 Saturday, 24 March 1923, at 5.10 p.m.

OXFORD †		CAMBRIDGE	
*P. C. Mallam, Lancing and Qu., bow	11.12	W. F. Smith, Shrewsbury and 1 Trin., bow	11. 7½
P. R. Wace, King's Sch., Cant, and BNC	12. 6½	F. W. Law, St Paul's and LMBC	12.12
*A. C. Irvine, Shrewsbury and Mert.	12.10½	* K. N. Craig, Cheltenham and Pemb.	13. 0
R. K. Kane, Harvard Univ. and Ball.	13. 9½	S. H. Heap, Eton and Jesus	13. 7½
G. J. Mower-White, Rugby and BNC	13.11½	* B. G. Ivory, Bedale's and Pemb.	13.10
* J. E. Pedder, Shrewsbury and Worc.	13. 3½	* T. D. A. Collet, Oundle and Pemb.	12. 7
*G. O. Nickalls, Eton and Magd.	12.12	R. E. Morrison, Eton and 3 Trin.	12. 1
W. P. Mellen, Middx., Concord, USA and BNC, str.	10.12	T. R. B. Sanders, Eton and 3 Trin., str.	11.12
G. D. Clapperton, Magd. Coll. Sch. and Magd., cox	7.11	R. A. L. Balfour, Eton and 3 Trin., cox	8. 8
Average	12. 8½	Average	12. 8⅞

Oxford won by ¾ length in 20 min. 54 sec.

76 Saturday, 5 April 1924, at 2.23 p.m.

CAMBRIDGE †		OXFORD	
G. E. G. Goddard, Imp. Ser. Coll. and Jesus, bow	11. 9½	*P. C. Mallam, Lancing and Qu., bow	11.11½
J. S. Herbert, Eton and King's	11. 9	* P. R. Wace, King's Sch., Cant., and BNC	12. 1½
J. A. Macnabb, Eton and 3 Trin.	11.11¾	W. F. Godden, Shrewsbury and Trin.	12.12
G. L. Elliot-Smith, St Pet., York, and LMBC	13. 2	R. E. Eason, Abingdon and All Souls	13. 1½
G. H. Ambler, Shrewsbury and Clare	12. 2	* G. J. Mower-White, Rugby and BNC	13. 9½
*T. D. A. Collet, Oundle and Pemb.	12. 4	* J. E. Pedder, Shrewsbury and Worc.	13. 2
C. R. M. Eley, Eton and 3 Trin.	11. 4	G. E. G. Gadsden, Eton and Ch.Ch.	11.10
A. B. Stobart, RN Coll., Dartmouth, and Pemb., str.	11.10½	* W. P. Mellen, Middx, Concord, USA, and BNC, str.	10.10
J. A. Brown, Clifton and Caius, cox	7. 7	* G. D. Clapperton, Magd. Coll. Sch. and Magd., cox	7. 9½
Average	11.13⅝	Average	12. 5½

Cambridge won by 4½ lengths in 18 min. 41 sec.

77 Saturday, 28 March 1925, at 3.41 p.m.

OXFORD		CAMBRIDGE †	
A. H. Franklin, Merchant		*G. E. G. Goddard, Imp. Ser. Coll.	
Taylors' and Linc., bow	11. 9½	and Jesus, bow	11. 2
C. E. Pitman, Eton and Ch.Ch.	11. 7	*W. F. Smith, Shrewsbury and	
		1 Trin.	11. 7
E. C. T. Edwards, Westminster		H. R. Carver, Eton and 3 Trin.	12.13
and Ch.Ch.	12. 3½		
M. R. Grant, Winchester and		*J. S. Herbert, Eton and King's	11. 9
Ch.Ch.	11. 8		
*G. J. Mower-White, Rugby and		*G. H. Ambler, Shrewsbury and	
BNC	13. 4	Clare	12. 7
J. D. W. Thomson, Eton and		*G. L. Elliot-Smith, St Pet., York,	
Univ.	12.10	and LMBC	13. 4
*G. E. G. Gadsden, Eton and		S. K. Tubbs, Shrewsbury and	
Ch.Ch.	11.12	Caius	11.12
*A. V. Campbell, Eton and		A. G. Wansbrough, Eton and	
Ch.Ch., str.	11. 9	King's, str.	11. 7
R. Knox, Highgate and Ball.,		*J. A. Brown, Clifton and	
cox	8. 2	Caius, cox	7.13
Average	12. 0⅞	Average	12. 0½

Oxford waterlogged. Cambridge finished in 21 min. 50 sec.

78 Saturday, 27 March 1926, at 12.27 p.m.

OXFORD †		CAMBRIDGE	
P. W. Murray-Threipland, Eton and		M. F. A. Keen, Haileybury and	
Ch.Ch., bow	12. 5	LMBC, bow	11. 9
T. W. Shaw, Shrewsbury and		*W. F. Smith, Shrewsbury and	
Ch.Ch.	12. 7½	1 Trin.	11. 8
G. H. Crawford, Harrow and		*G. H. Ambler, Shrewsbury and	
BNC	13. 0	Clare	12. 5
W. Rathbone, Radley and		R. B. T. Craggs, Shrewsbury	
Ch.Ch.	13. 9	and LMBC	11.13
H. R. A. Edwards, Westminster		L. V. Bevan, Bedford and	
and Ch.Ch.	13. 5	LMBC	13. 9
*J. D. W. Thomson, Eton and		J. B. Bell, Geelong GS and Jesus	13. 2
Univ.	13. 5½		
*E. C. T. Edwards, Westminster and		*S. K. Tubbs, Shrewsbury and	
Ch.Ch.	12. 9	Caius	12. 4
*C. E. Pitman, Eton and Ch.Ch.,		E. C. Hamilton-Russell, Eton	
str.	11. 1	and 3 Trin., str.	11. 8
Sir J. H. Croft, Bt, Eton and		*J. A. Brown, Clifton and Caius,	
BNC, str.	8. 5½	cox	8. 6½
Average	12.10½	Average	12. 3¾

Cambridge won by 5 lengths in 19 min. 29 sec.

79 Saturday, 2 April 1927, at 1.30 p.m.

OXFORD †		CAMBRIDGE	
N. E. Whiting, Radley and		Hon. J. S. Maclay, Winchester	
Worc., bow	11. 9	and 1 Trin., bow	11. 9
P. Johnson, Tonbridge and		T. E. Letchworth, Downside	
Magd.	11.11	and Chr.	12. 7
*E. C. T. Edwards, Westminster		J. C. Holcroft, Radley and	
and Ch.Ch.	12.10	Pemb.	12. 5
*J. D. W. Thomson, Eton and		R. Beesly, Oundle and 1 Trin.	12.11½
Univ.	13. 6		
*W. Rathbone, Radley and		*L. V. Bevan, Bedford and	
Ch.Ch.	13.13	LMBC	13. 3½
H. T. Kingsbury, Yale Univ.		*J. B. Bell, Geelong GS and	
and Qu.	14. 2	Jesus	13. 3
*T. W. Shaw, Shrewsbury and		*S. K. Tubbs, Shrewsbury and	
Ch.Ch.	12. 7	Caius	12. 3
A. M. Hankin, Bromsgrove		R. J. Elles, Marlborough and	
and Worc., str.	10.11	Trin. H., str.	11. 9
*Sir J. H. Croft, Bt, Eton and		*J. A. Brown, Clifton and Caius,	
BNC, cox	8.12	cox	8.10½
Average	12. 8⅝	Average	12. 6⅜

Cambridge won by 3 lengths in 20 min. 14 sec.

80 Saturday, 31 March 1928, at 9.45 a.m.

CAMBRIDGE		OXFORD †	
R. G. Michell, Shrewsbury and		M. C. Graham, Shrewsbury	
Caius, bow	11. 4	and Magd., bow	11. 3
N. M. Aldous, St Joh., Leather-		*T. W. Shaw, Shrewsbury and	
head, and Selw.	11.13	Ch.Ch.	12.10
M. H. Warriner, Harrow and		* N. E. Whiting, Radley and	
1 Trin.	13. 0	Worc.	11.11
*R. Beesly, Oundle and 1 Trin.	13. 4	H. C. Morphett, Geelong GS	
		and BNC	12. 3
*J. C. Holcroft, Radley and		G. M. Brander, Edin. Acad. and	
Pemb.	12.13	Ex.	13. 9
J. B. Collins, Eton and 3 Trin.	14. 3	G. E. Godber, Bedford and	
		New C.	12.12
R. A. Symonds, Bedford and		* P. W. Murray-Threipland, Eton	
LMBC	11.12	and Ch.Ch.	12.12
*T. E. Letchworth, Downside		W. S. Llewellyn, Eton and	
and Chr., str.	12. 9	Ball., str.	12. 3
A. L. Sulley, Denstone and		* Sir J. H. Croft, Bt, Eton and	
Selw., cox	8. 6	BNC, cox	9. 4
Average	12. 9	Average	12. 9⅝

Cambridge won by 10 lengths in 20 min. 25 sec.

81 Saturday, 23 March 1929, at 12.12 p.m.

CAMBRIDGE †		OXFORD	
E. N. Norman-Butler, Eton and		P. D. Barr, Radley and Trin.,	
3 Trin., bow	12. 0	bow	11. 5
*R. J. Elles, Marlborough and		*G. E. Godber, Bedford and	
Trin. H.	12. 4½	New C.	12. 4½
R. A. Davies-Cooke, Eton and		C. F. Juel-Brockdorff, Svend-	
3 Trin.	12. 1½	borg, Denmark, and Pemb.	12.12
*R. Beesly, Oundle and 1 Trin.	13. 6	J. M. Macdonald, Winchester	
		and Magd.	12.12½
*M. H. Warriner, Harrow and		*H. C. Morphett, Geelong GS	
1 Trin.	13. 6	and BNC	12. 4
*J. B. Collins, Eton and 3 Trin.	14. 6	J. A. Ingles, Tasmania Univ.	
		and Magd.	13.10
C. E. Wool-Lewis, Westminster		D. E. Tinné, Eton and Univ.	12. 0
and 3 Trin.	12. 2½		
T. A. Brocklebank, Eton and		A. Graham, Eton and BNC, str.	11. 2½
3 Trin., str.	11.12		
*A. L. Sulley, Denstone and		G. V. Stopford, Radley and New	
Selw., cox	8.10	C., cox	8.10
Average	12.10	Average	12. 4½

Cambridge won by 7 lengths in 19 min. 24 sec.

82 Saturday, 12 April 1930, at 12.30 p.m.

OXFORD †		CAMBRIDGE	
M. J. Waterhouse, Eton and		D. Haig-Thomas, Eton and	
Ball., bow	12. 8	LMBC, bow	11. 4
R. V. Low, Winchester and		H. R. N. Rickett, Eton and	
Univ.	12. 2½	3 Trin.	12. 6
N. K. Hutton, Fettes and Univ.	12.11	W. A. Prideaux, Eton and	
		3 Trin.	12. 6
C. M. Johnston, Shrewsbury		P. N. Carpmael, Oundle and	
and BNC	12.11	Jesus	12. 7
*H. R. A. Edwards, Westminster		*M. H. Warriner, Harrow and	
and Ch.Ch.	13. 6	1 Trin.	13.10
L. Clive, Eton and Ch.Ch.	13. 0½	*J. B. Collins, Eton and 3 Trin.	14. 5
*D. E. Tinné, Eton and Univ.	12. 1	A. S. Reeve, Brighton and Selw.	12. 1
C. F. Martineau, Harrow and		*T. A. Brocklebank, Eton and	
Univ., str.	10.13	3 Trin., str.	11.11½
H. A. G. Durbridge, Malvern		R. E. Swartwout, Middx,	
and Univ., cox	8. 7	Concord, USA, and 1 Trin.,	
		cox	7. 8
Average	12. 6½	Average	12. 8

Cambridge won by 2 lengths in 19 min. 9 sec.

83 Saturday, 21 March 1931, at 2.29 p.m.

CAMBRIDGE		OXFORD †	
*D. Haig-Thomas, Eton and LMBC, bow	11. 4½	W. L. Garstang, Oundle and Trin., bow	11. 2
*W. A. Prideaux, Eton and 3 Trin.	12. 6	G. M. L. Smith, Winchester and BNC	11.11
R. H. H. Symonds, Bedford and LMBC	11.12½	*D. E. Tinné, Eton and Univ.	12. 4
G. Gray, Bolton and Qu.	13. 5	*C. M. Johnston, Shrewsbury and BNC	12. 9
*P. N. Carpmael, Oundle and Jesus	13. 0	R. A. J. Poole, Eton and BNC	13. 2
*H. R. N. Rickett, Eton and 3 Trin.	12.10	*L. Clive, Eton and Ch.Ch.	13. 2½
C. J. S. Sergel, Monkton Combe and Clare	12. 7	*W. D. C. Erskine-Crum, Eton and Ch.Ch.	12. 1½
*T. A. Brocklebank, Eton and 3 Trin., str.	11. 6	R. W. G. Holdsworth, Shrewsbury and BNC, str.	11.10½
J. M. Ranking, Cheltenham and Pemb., cox	6.13	E. R. Edmett, Herne Bay and Worc., cox	8. 0
Average	12. 4⅝	Average	12. 3½

Cambridge won by 2½ lengths in 19 min. 26 sec.

84 Saturday, 19 March 1932, at 10.28 a.m.

CAMBRIDGE †		OXFORD	
*D. Haig-Thomas, Eton and LMBC, bow	11. 6	G. A. Ellison, Westminster and New C., bow	11. 8½
K. M. Payne, Eton and 3 Trin.	12. 5	* G. M. L. Smith, Winchester and BNC	11. 9
T. G. Askwith, Haileybury and Pet.	11. 8½	J. de R. Kent, Sherborne and BNC	11. 8½
W. A. T. Sambell, Melbourne GS and Pemb.	12. 6½	* C. M. Johnston, Shrewsbury and BNC	12. 4½
*C. J. S. Sergel, Monkton Combe and Clare	12. 9	* W. D. C. Erskine-Crum, Eton and Ch.Ch.	12. 6
*H. R. N. Rickett, Eton and 3 Trin.	12.11½	* R. A. J. Poole, Eton and BNC	13. 2½
D. H. E. McCowen, Cheltenham and Pemb.	12. 1½	W. H. Migotti, Radley and Worc.	11. 5½
L. Luxton, Melbourne GS and Pemb., str.	12. 2¼	C. A. Chadwyck-Healey, Eton and Trin., str.	11. 6¼
* J. M. Ranking, Cheltenham and Pemb., cox	6.13	T. E. Pritchard, Clifton and Ex., cox	8. 2
Average	12. 2¾	Average	11.13¼

Cambridge won by 5 lengths in 19 min. 11 sec. (course short by at least a minute).

85 Saturday, 1 April 1933, at 4.02 p.m.

CAMBRIDGE †		OXFORD	
W. L. R. Carbonell, Shrewsbury and St Cath., bow	12. 4½	* W. H. Migotti, Radley and Worc., bow	11.11½
J. E. Gilmour, Eton and Trin. H.	12. 0½	M. H. Mosley, Shrewsbury and Trin.	12. 0¼
*T. G. Askwith, Haileybury and Pet.	12. 0½	* W. D. C. Erskine-Crum, Eton and Ch.Ch.	12. 9½
R. B. F. Wylie, Shrewsbury and Clare	12.10	J. M. Couchman, Sherborne and Ch.Ch.	12. 9
*C. J. S. Sergel, Monkton Combe and Clare	12.10	P. Hogg, Sherborne and New. C.	12. 9
*W. A. T. Sambell, Melbourne and Pemb.	12. 5	P. R. S. Bankes, Oundle and Ch.Ch.	13.12
C. M. Fletcher, Eton and 3 Trin.	12. 9½	* G. A. Ellison, Westminster and New C.	11.12½
T. Frame-Thomson, Eton and 3 Trin., str.	12. 0	* R. W. G. Holdsworth, Shrewsbury and BNC, str.	11.13¼
R. N. Wheeler, Clifton and Sid. S., cox	7.12	C. Komarakul-Na-Nagara, St Paul's and Magd., cox	8. 4½
Average	12. 5	Average	12. 6⅛

Cambridge won by 2¼ lengths in 20 min. 57 sec.

86 Saturday, 17 March 1934, at 2.16 p.m.

CAMBRIDGE †		OXFORD	
A. D. Kingsford, Uppingham and Pemb., bow	11. 8	* W. H. Migotti, Radley and Worc., bow	12. 3½
C. K. Buckle, Eastbourne and Magd.	12. 4½	* R. W. G. Holdsworth. Shrewsbury and BNC	11.13¾
W. G. R. M. Laurie, Monkton Combe and Selw.	13. 6	* P. Hogg, Sherborne and New C.	12.13¾
*K. M. Payne, Eton and 3 Trin.	12. 6	* J. M. Couchman, Sherborne and Ch.Ch.	13. 3¼
D. J. Wilson, Melbourne GS and Clare	13. 0½	* P. R. S. Bankes, Oundle and Ch.Ch.	14. 9
*W. A. T. Sambell, Melbourne GS and Pemb.	12. 5½	J. H. Lascelles, Chr. Coll., NZ, and Ball.	11.12½
J. H. T. Wilson, Shrewsbury and Pemb., str.	12.13	G. I. F. Thomson, Shrewsbury and Ball.	12. 0½
N. J. Bradley, Monkton Combe and Pemb., str.	14. 1¼	A. V. Sutcliffe, Shrewsbury and Trin., str.	14. 2
J. N. Duckworth, Lincoln and Jesus, cox	7.13	C. G. F. Bryan, Eton and Worc., cox	7.13
Average	12.10¾	Average	12.12½

Cambridge won by 4¼ lengths in 18 min. 3 sec.

87 Saturday, 6 April 1935, at 2.47 p.m.

CAMBRIDGE †		OXFORD	
T. R. M. Bristow, Dulwich and Pemb., bow	12. 4	R. Hope, Eton and New C., bow	12. 2
E. A. Szilagyi, St Paul's and Jesus	12. 3	D. M. de R. Winser, Winchester and CCC	11. 9½
*A. D. Kingsford, Uppingham and Pemb.	12. 4	E. E. D. Tomlin, Whitgift and Univ.	12. 5
J. H. C. Powell, Eton and 3 Trin.	12. 0	*P. R. S. Bankes, Oundle and Ch.Ch.	14. 3
D. G. Kingsford, Uppingham and Pemb.	13. 1½	D. R. B. Mynors, Eton and New C.	13. 0
M. P. Lonnon, Westminster and 3 Trin.	12. 8	*J. M. Couchman, Sherborne and Ch.Ch.	12.13½
*J. H. T. Wilson, Shrewsbury and Pemb.	12.13	B. J. Sciortino, Shrewsbury and Univ.	12.10
*W. G. R. M. Laurie, Monkton Combe and Selw., str.	13. 7	*A. V. Sutcliffe, Shrewsbury and Trin., str.	14. 5
*J. N. Duckworth, Lincoln and Jesus, cox	7.13	*C. G. F. Bryan, Eton and Worc., cox	7.11
Average	12. 8⅝	Average	12.13

Cambridge won by 4½ lengths in 19 min. 48 sec.

88 Saturday, 4 April 1936, at 11.40 a.m.

OXFORD †		CAMBRIDGE	
M. G. C. Ashby, Oundle and New C., bow	12. 0	T. S. Cree, Geelong GS and Jesus, bow	12. 2
J. S. Lewes, King's Sch., Paramatta, and Ch.Ch.	12. 7½	H. W. Mason, Clifton and Trin. H.	12. 8
K. V. Garside, Bradfield and St Joh.	12.12	G. M. Lewis, Malvern and Pemb.	13. 0
S. R. C. Wood, Geelong GS and BNC	12. 7	D. W. Burnford, St Paul's and Jesus	13. 4
*B. J. Sciortino, Shrewsbury and Univ.	12.11	* M. P. Lonnon, Westminster and 3 Trin.	13. 6
J. D. Sturrock, Winchester and Magd.	14. 1½	* D. G. Kingsford, Uppingham and Pemb.	13. 7
J. C. Cherry, Westminster and BNC	13. 7	* J. H. T. Wilson, Shrewsbury and Pemb.	13. 0
*D. M. de R. Winser, Winchester and CCC, str.	11.12	* W. G. R. M. Laurie, Monkton Combe and Selw., str.	13. 6
M. A. Kirke, Sherborne and Keble, cox	8. 7	* J. N. Duckworth, Lincoln and Jesus, cox	8. 7
Average	12.10¾	Average	13. 0½

Cambridge won by 5 lengths in 21 min. 6 sec.

9 Wednesday, 24 March 1937, at 11.35 a.m.

CAMBRIDGE		OXFORD	
*T. S. Cree, Geelong GS and Jesus, bow	11. 8	* M. G. C. Ashby, Oundle and New C., bow	12. 4
*H. W. Mason, Clifton and Trin. H.	11.10	* D. M. de R. Winser, Winchester and CCC	12. 0
M. Bradley, Monkton Combe and Pemb.	13. 1	R. R. Stewart, Eton and Magd.	13. 0
D. M. W. Napier, Eton and Magd.	12. 9	R. G. Rowe, Eton and Univ.	12.11
*M. P. Lonnon, Westminster and 3 Trin.	12.12	J. P. Burrough, St Edward's and St Ed. H.	13. 7
T. B. Langton, Radley and Jesus	13. 4	*J. D. Sturrock, Winchester and Magd.	14. 4
A. Burrough, St Paul's and Jesus	12. 1	* J. C. Cherry, Westminster and BNC	13.11
R. J. L. Perfitt, KCS Wimbledon and Trin. H., str.	12. 0½	A. B. Hodgson, Eton and Oriel, str.	12. 2
T. H. Hunter, Harvard Univ. and Trin. H., cox	8. 0	G. J. P. Merifield, King Ed. VI Soton, and St Ed. H., cox	7.11
Average	12. 5¾	Average	12.13½

Oxford won by 3 lengths in 22 min. 39 sec.

90 Saturday, 2 April 1938, at 1.45 p.m.

CAMBRIDGE †		OXFORD	
B. T. Coulton, Dulwich and Jesus, bow	10.13	J. L. Garton, Eton and Magd., bow	11.12
A. M. Turner, Cranleigh and CCC	11.12	H. M. Young, Westminster and Trin.	12.12
* A. Burrough, St Paul's and Jesus	12. 7	*R. R. Stewart, Eton and Magd.	12.13
*T. B. Langton, Radley and Jesus	13. 9	H. A. W. Forbes, St Paul's and Magd.	13. 2
J. L. L. Savill, Radley and Jesus	12.13	*J. P. Burrough, St Edward's and St Ed. H.	13. 7
G. Keppel, Princeton Univ. and Trin. H.	13. 6	F. A. L. Waldron, Shrewsbury and Trin.	13.10
A. Campbell, Barrow GS and Selw.	12. 4	*J. C. Cherry, Westminster and BNC	13.12
D. S. M. Eadie, Oundle and 1 Trin., str.	12. 1	* A. B. Hodgson, Eton and Oriel, str.	12. 0
*T. H. Hunter, Harvard Univ. and Trin. H., cox	8. 7	*G. J. P. Merifield, King Ed. VI, Soton, and St Ed. H., cox	8. 1
Average	12. 6½	Average	12.13¾

Oxford won by 2 lengths in 20 min. 30 sec.

91 *Saturday, 1 April 1939, at 11.01 a.m.*

CAMBRIDGE		OXFORD †	
C. N. C. Addison, Roxburgh and Pemb., bow	12. 0½	G. Huse, Latymer Upper Sch. and Oriel, bow	12. 7
*A. M. Turner, Cranleigh and CCC	12. 3	*J. L. Garton, Eton and Magd.	11. 7
*A. Burrough, St Paul's and Jesus	12. 7	A. G. Slemeck, St Edward's and St Ed. H.	13. 1
*J. L. L. Savill, Radley and Jesus	13. 2	*R. R. Stewart, Eton and Magd.	13. 4
H. Parker, Tabor Acad. and Trin. H.	12.13	R. D. Burnell, Eton and Magd.	14. 1½
J. Turnbull, Geelong GS and Clare	13.12	*F. A. L. Waldron, Shrewsbury and Trin.	14. 4
M. Buxton, Eton and 3 Trin.	12.13	*H. A. W. Forbes, St Paul's and Magd.	13. 5
C. B. Sanford, Eton and Trin. H., str.	12. 1	J. R. Bingham, Bedford and Pemb., str.	11. 2
H. T. Smith, Eton and Magd., cox	8.11	H. P. V. Massey, Upper Canada Coll. and Ball., cox	5. 2
Average	12.10	Average	12.12½

Cambridge won by 4 lengths in 19 min. 3 sec.

92 *Saturday, 30 March 1946, at 11 a.m.*

CAMBRIDGE †		OXFORD	
J. S. Paton-Philip, Perse and LMBC, bow	12. 0	R. M. T. Raikes, Radley and Trin., bow	11. 2
T. J. Sullivan, Oundle and Clare	12. 0	R. T. Turner Warwick, Bedale's and Oriel	11. 0
P. L. P. Macdonnell, Upper Canada Coll. and Trin. H.	13. 2½	J. M. Barrie, Dulwich and Qu.	12. 7
D. J. D. Perrins, Dauntsey's and Jesus	12. 2	R. M. A. Bourne, Eton and New C.	11.13
G. E. C. Thomas, Shrewsbury and Jesus	13. 9	J. R. L. Carstairs, St Edward's and Ch.Ch.	12. 9
J. G. Gosse, St Pet., Adelaide, and Trin. H.	12. 3	J. R. W. Gleave, Uppingham and Magd.	12. 4
M. S. Allman-Ward, Oundle and Chr.	13. 4	P. N. Brodie, Oundle and Oriel	11. 7
J. H. Neame, Lincoln HS, Oregon, and Trin. H., str.	11. 7	A. J. R. Purssell, Oundle and Oriel, str.	11.13
G. H. C. Fisher, Kingswood and 1 & 3 Trin., cox	9. 1½	R. Ebsworth Snow, Bradfield and Magd., cox	9. 1
Average	12. 7	Average	11.12¼

Oxford won by 3 lengths in 19 min. 54 sec.

93 Saturday, 29 March 1947, at 6.15 p.m.

OXFORD †		CAMBRIDGE	
D. G. Jamison, Radley and		A. P. Mellows, Monkton Combe	
Magd., bow	11. 9½	and Clare, bow	11.12
P. H. Mathews, St Edward's and		D. J. C. Meyrick, Eton and Trin.	
St Ed. H.	11.11	H.	11. 0
D. A. M. Mackay, Owen's and		N. S. Rogers, Brentwood and	
Linc.	13. 3	Jesus	12. 9
T. D. Raikes, Radley and Trin.	12. 3	P. J. Garner, Bedford and	
		King's	11.12
*J. R. W. Gleave, Uppingham and		W. A. D. Windham, Bedford	
Magd.	12. 5	and Chr.	13. 4
*R. M. A. Bourne, Eton and		I. M. Lang, Monkton Combe	
New C.	11. 4	and Caius	13. 8
*P. N. Brodie, Oundle and Oriel	11. 4	A. S. F. Butcher, City of Lon.	
		Sch. and Qu.	11.13
*A. J. R. Purssell, Oundle and		G. C. Richardson, Winchester	
Oriel, str.	11.12	and Magd., str.	12.10
Alastair Palgrave-Brown,		*G. H. C. Fisher, Kingswood and	
Shrewsbury and Qu., cox	8.10	1 & 3 Trin., cox	8.10
Average	11.13½	Average	12. 5

Cambridge won by 10 lengths in 23 min. 1 sec.

94 Saturday, 27 March 1948, at 3.30 p.m.

OXFORD		CAMBRIDGE †	
G. C. Fisk, Geelong GS and		*A. P. Mellows, Monkton Combe	
Oriel, bow	12. 1½	and Clare, bow	12. 1
*J. R. W. Gleave, Uppingham		*D. J. C. Meyrick, Eton and	
and Magd.	12. 7	Trin. H.	11. 4
A. D. Rowe, Eton and Trin.	12.12	P. A. de Giles, Wellington and	
		Qu.	12. 3
W. W. Woodward, Shore Sch.,		*G. C. Richardson, Winchester	
NSW, and BNC	13. 3½	and Magd.	12.11
R. A. Noel, Oundle and Ch.Ch.	12.13½	A. B. C. Harrison, Geelong GS	
		and 1 & 3 Trin.	13.12
R. L. Arundel, Marlborough		E. A. P. Bircher, Radley and	
and Mert.	14. 4	Chr.	13. 8
*P. N. Brodie, Oundle and Oriel	11. 8	M. C. Lapage, Monkton Combe	
		and Selw.	13. 0
*A. J. R. Purssell, Oundle and		C. B. R. Barton, St Columba's,	
Oriel, str.	11.11½	Dublin, and Jesus, str.	11.11
R. G. B. Faulkner, Radley and		K. T. Lindsay, Liverpool Coll.	
Trin., cox	9. 0	and Jesus, cox	8.13
Average	12. 9⅜	Average	12. 8

Cambridge won by 5 lengths in 17 min. 50 sec.

95 Saturday, 26 March 1949, at 11.30 a.m.

CAMBRIDGE		OXFORD †	
G. S. S. Ludford, Latymer Upper Sch. and Jesus, bow	11. 2	*G. C. Fisk, Geelong GS and Oriel, bow	11. 9½
A. L. Macleod, Shrewsbury and LMBC	12. 4	A. J. M. Cavenagh, Winchester and Magd.	11. 1
C. B. M. Lloyd, Shore Sch. and LMBC	13. 0	W. J. H. Leckie, Edin. Acad. and BNC	12.12
J. R. la T. Corrie, Winchester and 1 & 3 Trin.	13. 3	*R. L. Arundel, Marlborough and Mert.	14. 0
*E. A. P. Bircher, Radley and Clare	13. 7	*A. D. Rowe, Eton and Trin.	12.11½
P. M. O. Massey, Oundle and LMBC	13. 8	*T. D. Raikes, Radley and Trin.	12.10½
D. V. Lynch Odhams, Westminster and Jesus	13. 1	J. M. Clay, Eton and Magd.	12.12½
D. M. Jennens, Oundle and Clare, str.	12. 4½	C. G. V. Davidge, Eton and Trin., str.	12.13
T. R. Ashton, Monkton Combe and Chr., cox	9. 3	*Alastair Palgrave-Brown, Shrews. and Qu., cox	8. 9
Average	12.10¾	Average	12. 8¾

Cambridge won by ¼ length in 18 min. 57 sec.

96 Saturday, 1 April 1950, at 12.30 p.m.

OXFORD †		CAMBRIDGE	
J. G. C. Blacker, Eton and Ball., bow	12. 2	H. H. Almond, Shrewsbury and LMBC, bow	10. 6
P. Gladstone, Eton and Ch.Ch.	12.11	*D. M. Jennens, Oundle and Clare	12. 4
H. J. Renton, Eton and Magd.	12. 4	*A. L. Macleod, Shrewsbury and LMBC	12. 9
*J. M. Clay, Eton and Magd.	12. 7½	*P. M. O. Massey, Oundle and LMBC	13. 9
*G. C. Fisk, Geelong GS and Oriel	11.10½	W. T. Arthur, Wits. Univ., SA, and LMBC	13. 0
J. Hayes, Shrewsbury and New. C.	13. 0	*E. A. P. Bircher, Radley and Chr.	13. 6
D. N. Callender, Eton and Trin.	12. 4	*C. B. M. Lloyd, Shore Sch., NSW and LMBC	12. 9
*A. J. M. Cavenagh, Winchester and Magd., str.	11. 3	J. L. M. Crick, Marlborough and LMBC, str.	12. 8
J. E. C. Hinchliffe, King's Sch., Canterbury, and Trin., cox	8. 6	A. C. R. Armstrong-Jones, Eton and Jesus, cox	8. 8
Average	12. 3½	Average	12. 8¼

Cambridge won by 3½ lengths in 20 min. 15 sec.

97 Saturday, 24 March 1951 at 1.45 p.m., and Monday, 26 March at 2.30 p.m.

OXFORD †		CAMBRIDGE	
J. F. E. Smith, Eton and New C., bow	11.11	*H. H. Almond, Shrewsbury and LMBC, bow	10. 4
A. J. Smith, Melbourne GS and Mert.	12.11	D. D. Macklin, Felsted and LMBC	11.11
*H. J. Renton, Eton and Magd.	13. 1½	J. G. P. Crowden, Bedford and Pemb.	12. 7½
L. A. F. Stokes, Winchester and New C.	13. 3	R. F. A. Sharpley, Shrewsbury and LMBC	13. 5
M. J. Hawkes, Bedford and New C.	12.11½	E. J. Worlidge, Marlborough and LMBC	12.13½
C. G. Turner, Winchester and New C.	14. 6	*C. B. M. Lloyd, Shore Sch., NSW, and LMBC	12.12½
*D. N. Callender, Eton and Trin.	12. 6½	*W. A. D. Windham, Bedford and Chr.	12.12
*C. G. V. Davidge, Eton and Trin., str.	13. 7½	*D. M. Jennens, Oundle and Clare, str.	12. 7
G. Carver, Yale Univ. and Ball., cox	8. 7	J. F. K. Hinde, Malvern and Pemb., cox	9. 4
Average	13. 0½	Average	12. 5½

In first race Oxford sank, and umpire declared 'No race'. In rerow Cambridge won by 12 lengths in 20 min. 50 sec.

98 Saturday, 29 March 1952, at 3.15 p.m.

OXFORD		CAMBRIDGE †	
N. W. Sanders, Radley and Mert., bow	10. 7	E. J. N. T. Coghill, Gordonstoun and Pemb., bow	12. 4
*P. Gladstone, Eton and Ch.Ch.	12.12	G. A. H. Cadbury, Eton and King's	12. 2
C. D. Milling, Radley and Mert.	12. 1	*J. G. P. Crowden, Bedford and Pemb.	12. 8
*L. A. F. Stokes, Winchester and New C.	13. 0	G. T. Marshall, Bryanston and King's	13. 6½
M. L. Thomas, Clifton and Jesus	13. 6	J. R. Dingle, Chr. Hosp. and LMBC	14. 0
K. H. Keniston, Harvard Univ. and Ball.	13. 6	*R. F. A. Sharpley, Shrewsbury and LMBC	13. 8
H. M. C. Quick, Shrewsbury and Mert.	13. 4	N. B. M. Clack, Wycliffe and LMBC	12. 9
*C. G. V. Davidge, Eton and Trin., str.	12. 7	J. S. M. Jones, Shrewsbury and LMBC, str.	11.12½
D. R. Glynne-Jones, Magd. Coll. Sch. and Jesus, cox	8.12	*J. F. K. Hinde, Malvern and Pemb., cox	9. 3
Average	12. 9	Average	12.11½

Oxford won by a canvas in 20 min. 23 sec.

99 *Saturday, 28 March 1953, at 12 noon*

CAMBRIDGE †		OXFORD	
J. A. N. Wallis, Bryanston and LMBC, bow	11.12½	R. A. Byatt, Gordonstoun and New C., bow	12. 4
*J. S. M. Jones, Shrewsbury and LMBC	12. 3	*A. J. Smith, Melbourne GS and Mert.	12. 9
J. R. A. Macmillan, Eton and 1 & 3 Trin.	13. 0½	J. M. Wilson, St Edward's and Trin.	13. 3
*G. T. Marshall, Bryanston and King's	13. 5	E. C. B. Hammond, Clifton and BNC	13. 2
D. A. T. Leadley, Bedford Mod. and Emm.	13. 3½	*M. L. Thomas, Clifton and Jesus	13.10
L. B. McCagg, Harvard Univ. and Emm.	13. 0	D. T. H. Davenport, Radley and Univ.	13. 1
J. M. King, Derby and LMBC	12. 8½	*H. M. C. Quick, Shrewsbury and Mert.	13. 5
P. D. Hall, Berkhamsted and CCC, str.	12. 6	J. S. Howles, Newcastle RGS and Univ., str.	12. 0
B. M. Eddy, Carlisle GS and Pemb., cox	8.10	W. R. Marsh, St Edward's and Univ., cox	8.10
Average	12.10	Average	12.13

Cambridge won by 8 lengths in 19 min. 54 sec.

100 *Saturday, 3 April 1954, at 12.45 p.m.*

OXFORD †		CAMBRIDGE	
R. A. Wheadon, Cranleigh and Ball., bow	11.13	*J. A. N. Wallis, Bryanston and LMBC, bow	12. 0
E. V. Vine, Geelong GS and BNC	12. 0	J. C. G. Stancliffe, Harrow and Pemb.	12. 3
J. A. Gobbo, Melbourne Univ. and Magd.	12. 9	D. K. Hill, Shrewsbury and Jesus	12. 6
R. D. T. Raikes, Radley and Mert.	12. 6	K. A. Masser, Shrewsbury and Trin. H.	14. 0
*H. M. C. Quick, Shrewsbury and Mert.	13.12	M. G. Baynes, Bryanston and Trin. H.	13. 1
J. G. McLeod, Sydney Univ. and New C.	12. 1	C. M. Davies, Bryanston and Clare	13.13
E. O. G. Pain, Sydney Univ. and Linc.	12. 0	J. N. Bruce, St Paul's and Clare	12. 1
J. J. H. Harrison, Shrewsbury and Trin., str.	11. 9	M. J. Marshall, Eton and Jesus, str.	11.10
*W. R. Marsh, St Edward's and Univ., cox	8.12	J. W. Tanburn, Charterhouse and Jesus, cox	8. 9
Average	12. 4½	Average	12. 9½

Oxford won by 4½ lengths in 20 min. 23 sec.

101 Saturday, 26 March 1955, at 2.20 p.m.

OXFORD †		CAMBRIDGE	
* J. A. Gobbo, Melbourne Univ.		* D. K. Hill, Shrewsbury and	
and Magd., bow	12.10	Jesus, bow	12. 4
* E. V. Vine, Geelong GS and		P. du Bois, Harvard Univ. and	
BNC	11.13	1 & 3 Trin.	13. 3
* J. M. Wilson, St Edward's and		A. A. M. Mays-Smith, Eton and	
Trin.	13. 5	1 & 3 Trin.	14. 0
D. P. Wells, Stowe and Magd.	13. 2	* K. A. Masser, Shrewsbury and	
		Trin. H.	13.12
* R. D. T. Raikes, Radley and		S. G. D. Tozer, Winchester and	
Mert.	12. 3	1 & 3 Trin.	13.12
* J. McLeod, Sydney Univ. and		R. A. G. Monks, Harvard Univ.	
New C.	12.10	and 1 & 3 Trin.	13. 9½
* E. O. G. Pain, Sydney Univ. and		J. J. Vernon, Radley and	
Linc.	12. 0	Trin. H.	12. 4
G. Sorrell, St Paul's and Ch.Ch.,		A. R. Muirhead, Glenalmond	
str.	11.12	and LMBC, str.	12. 2
I. A. Watson, Shrewsbury and		G. T. Harris, High Wycombe	
Keble, cox	9. 3	RGS and Jesus, cox	9. 4
Average	12. 5½	Average	13. 2½

Cambridge won by 16 lengths in 19 min. 10 sec.

102 Saturday, 24 March 1956, at 11.30 a.m.

CAMBRIDGE †		OXFORD	
J. A. L. Russell, Marlborough		* E. V. Vine, Geelong GS and	
and Clare, bow	12. 4	BNC, bow	11.12
J. F. Hall-Craggs, Shrewsbury		* J. G. McLeod, Sydney Univ. and	
and LMBC	12. 7	New C.	12. 0
M. J. H. Nightingale,		N. Paine, King's Sch.,	
Tonbridge and Trin. H.	13. 6	Canterbury, and Trin.	12. 0
A. A. M. Mays-Smith, Eton		K. L. Mason, KCS, Wimbledon,	
and 1 & 3 Trin.	14. 5½	and Qu.	12. 4
I. W. Welsh, Shrewsbury and		R. Barrett, St Edward's and	
Qu.	13. 2	Pemb.	14. 5
* K. A. Masser, Shrewsbury and		D. A. Cross, Winchester and	
Trin. H.	13.12	Ball.	13. 4
* M. G. Baynes, Bryanston and		R. H. Carnegie, Melbourne	
Trin. H.	13. 3	Univ. and New C.	13. 6
M. G. Delahooke, Univ. Coll.		B. S. Mawer, Epsom and Mert.,	
Sch. and Jesus, str.	12.11	str.	12. 0
J. P. M. Denny, Downside and		B. E. B. K. Venner, St Edward's	
Jesus, cox	10. 0	and St Ed. H., cox	9. 2
Average	13. 2½	Average	12. 9

Cambridge won by 1¼ lengths in 18 min. 36 sec.

103 *Saturday, 30 March 1957, at 12.30 p.m.*

CAMBRIDGE		OXFORD †	
M. H. Bartlett, Radley and Pet., bow	11. 8	* G. Sorrell, St Paul's and Ch.Ch., bow	12. 1
C. J. Pumphrey, Winchester and Magd.	12. 1	S. F. A. Miskin, St Paul's and Univ.	12. 8
J. A. Pitchford, Tonbridge and Ch.	13. 8	R. L. Howard, Shrewsbury and Worc.	13. 5
T. P. A. Norman, Eton and 1 & 3 Trin.	13. 6	A. H. Stearns, Bedford and Mert.	13.12
J. R. Meadows, Yale Univ. and Jesus	14. 0	P. F. Barnard, Eton and Ch.Ch.	14. 3
* M. G. Delahooke, Univ. Coll. Sch. and Jesus	13. 0	* R. Barrett, St Edward's and Pemb.	14. 5
J. M. Thompson, Radley and Pemb.	12. 5	* R. H. Carnegie, Melbourne Univ. and New C.	13.10
F. C. S. Clayre, Dean Close and Qu., str.	12. 6	* K. L. Mason, KCS, Wimbledon, and Qu., str.	11. 9
R. C. Milton, Harvard Univ. and Emm., cox	9. 4	A. Said, Peshawar Univ. and Pemb., cox	7.11
Average	12.11¼	Average	13. 3

Cambridge won by 2 lengths in 19 min. 1 sec.

104 *Saturday, 5 April 1958, at 1.30 p.m.*

CAMBRIDGE †		OXFORD	
A. T. Denby, Radley and Magd., bow	12. 4	* G. Sorrell, St Paul's and Ch.Ch., bow	11.13
J. R. Giles, Winchester and Emm.	12. 7	M. J. W. Hall, Winchester and Linc.	12. 5
* J. A. Pitchford, Tonbridge and Chr.	13.10	J. H. Ducker, Monkton Combe and St Ed. H.	12.13
R. D. Carver, Eton and 1 & 3 Trin.	13. 3	* S. F. A. Miskin, St Paul's and Univ.	12.13
R. B. Ritchie, Geelong GS and CCC	14. 2	F. D. M. Badcock, Harrow and Ch.Ch.	13. 3
P. D. Rickett, Eton and 1 & 3 Trin.	13. 6	R. Rubin, Yale Univ. and Mert.	14. 8
D. C. Christie, Eton and Pemb.	13.12	J. L. Fage, Wrekin and St Ed. H.	12.13
M. B. Maltby, Bedford and Pemb., str.	12. 9	D. C. R. Edwards, Downside and Ch.Ch., str.	13. 2
J. S. Sulley, Radley and Selw., cox	8. 8	J. G. Rowbotham, Winchester and Hert., cox	9. 0
Average	13. 3	Average	13. 0

Cambridge won by 3½ lengths in 18 min. 15 sec.

105 Saturday, 28 March 1959, at 3.15 p.m.

CAMBRIDGE †		OXFORD	
J. R. Owen, Bedford and St Joh., bow	11. 8	S. C. H. Douglas-Mann, Westminster and St Ed. H., bow	12. 5
*J. R. Giles, Winchester and Emm.	12. 8	A. T. Lindsay, Eton and Magd.	12. 8
T. C. Heywood-Lonsdale, Eton and Trin.	13. 6	*R. L. Howard, Shrewsbury and Worc.	13.10
B. M. P. Thompson-McCausland, Eton and Trin.	12. 9	D. C. Rutherford, Rugby and Magd.	13. 0
G. H. Brown, Shrewsbury and Trin. H.	13. 9	*J. L. Fage, Wrekin, and St Ed. H.	13. 3
J. Beveridge, St Paul's and Jesus	13. 1	*D. C. R. Edwards, Downside and Ch.Ch.	13. 2
*D. C. Christie, Eton and Pemb.	14. 2	D. W. Shaw, Shrewsbury and Keble	13. 0
*M. B. Maltby, Bedford and Pemb., str.	12. 9	J. R. H. Lander, Shrewsbury and Ch.Ch., str.	12. 4
*J. S. Sulley, Radley and Selw., cox	8. 9	*J. G. Rowbotham, Winchester and Hert., cox	9. 1
Average	12.13¾	Average	12.12¾

Oxford won by 6 lengths in 18 min. 52 sec.

106 Saturday, 2 April 1960, at 4.15 p.m.

CAMBRIDGE		OXFORD †	
*J. R. Owen, Bedford and LMBC, bow	11. 8	R. C. I. Bate, Tonbridge and St Ed. H., bow	12. 5
S. R. M. Price, Westminster and 1 & 3 Trin.	12. 0	R. L. S. Fishlock, King's Sch., Canterbury, and St Ed. H.	12. 0
F. P. T. Wiggins, Univ. Coll. Sch. and LMBC	12.12½	T. S. Swayze, Harvard Univ. and Wadh.	13. 2
J. Parker, Shrewsbury and LMBC	12. 8	*A. T. Lindsay, Eton and Magd.	12.10
G. H. Brown, Shrewsbury and Trin. H.	13.11½	I. L. Elliott, Canford and Keble	13. 8
*J. Beveridge, St Paul's and Jesus	13. 2	*D. C. Rutherford, Rugby and Magd.	12.12
*E. T. C. Johnstone, Shrewsbury and LMBC	12.12	J. R. Chester, Monkton Combe and Keble	12. 5
P. W. Holmes, Portora Royal Sch. and LMBC, str.	12. 5	C. M. Davis, Eton and Linc., str.	12. 6
R. T. Weston, Dulwich and Selw., cox	9. 1	P. J. Reynolds, Uppingham and St Ed. H., cox	8. 4
Average	12. 9	Average	12. 9

Oxford won by 1¼ lengths in 18 min. 59 sec.

107 Saturday, 1 April 1961, at 2.10 p.m.

OXFORD †		CAMBRIDGE	
*R. C. I. Bate, Tonbridge and St Ed. H., bow	12. 5	R. G. Nicholson, Shrewsbury and St Cath., bow	12. 0
C. P. M. Gomm, Cheltenham and Ball.	12.12	J. E. Gobbett, St Paul's and St Cath.	12. 7
J. O. B. Sewall, Harvard Univ. and BNC	13. 4	R. J. Fraser, Radley and Jesus	13. 7
*I. L. Elliott, Canford and Keble	13. 5	A. J. Collier, Univ. Coll. Sch. and LMBC	13. 0
J. C. D. Sherratt, St Edward's and St Ed. H.	12.12	D. W. G. Calder, St Paul's and St Cath.	12.13
G. V. Cooper, Eton and Keble	13. 0	*J. Beveridge, St Paul's and Jesus	13. 5
*J. R. Chester, Monkton Combe and Keble	12. 8	M. W. Christian, Harvard Univ. and 1 & 3 Trin.	12. 8
*C. M. Davis, Eton and Linc., str.	12. 7	M. Hoffman, Harvard Univ. and 1 & 3 Trin., str.	12. 5
*P. J. Reynolds, Uppingham and St Ed. H., cox	8. 4	*R. T. Weston, Dulwich and Selw., cox	8.12
Average	12.12	Average	12.11

Cambridge won by 4¼ lengths in 19 min. 22 sec.

108 Saturday, 7 April 1962, at 3.45 p.m.

CAMBRIDGE †		OXFORD	
*R. G. Nicholson, Shrewsbury and St Cath., bow	12. 4	N. D. Tinné, Eton and Keble, bow	12. 7
C. J. T. Davey, Eton and Jesus	11. 6	D. D. S. Skailes, Eton and Keble	13. 4
R. A. Napier, Winchester and LMBC	13. 0	J. Y. Scarlett, Eton and Ch.Ch.	13.10
*A. J. Collier, Univ. Coll. Sch. and LMBC	13. 4	R. A. Morton Maskell, Bryanston and Keble	13. 8
J. M. S. Lecky, Brit. Col. Univ. and Jesus	14. 1	*J. C. D. Sherratt, St Edward's and St Ed. H.	13. 4
H. B. Budd, Yale Univ. and 1 & 3 Trin.	15. 1	T. W. Tennant, Eton and New C.	13.12
J. N. L. Tollemache, Eton and 1 & 3 Trin.	13. 9	P. C. D. Burnell, Eton and Magd.	12.13
Lord Chewton, Eton and 1 & 3 Trin., str.	11. 3	*C. M. Davis, Eton and Linc., str.	12. 6
R. Walmsley, Fettes and Qu., cox	9. 0	C. M. Strong, Shrewsbury and Keble, cox	8. 6
Average	13. 0	Average	13. 2¾

Cambridge won by 5 lengths in 19 min. 46 sec.

109 Saturday, 23 March 1963, at 11.30 a.m.

OXFORD †		CAMBRIDGE	
S. R. Morris, Radley and St		P. J. Webb, Monkton Combe	
Ed. H., bow	11.11	and Qu., bow	11. 0
N. V. Bevan, Shrewsbury and		M. V. Bevan, Bedford and	
Ball.	12.11	Dow.	12. 9½
*R. A. Morton Maskell,		A. V. Cooke, King's Sch.,	
Bryanston and Keble	13. 9	Chester, and Jesus	12.13½
M. Q. Morland, Radley and		B. J. R. Jackson, Wits. Univ.,	
Linc.	13. 7	SA, and Clare	12. 7½
R. C. T. Mead, Eton and		J. Maasland, St Kentigern,	
Keble	13. 7	NZ, and Qu.	14. 1½
*D. D. S. Skailes, Eton and Keble	13. 6	M. H. Beckett, Bedford and Qu.	13. 0½
P. A. V. Roff, Melbourne		D. F. Legget, Radley and	
Univ. and New C.	12. 9	Trin. H.	12. 6
C. D. Spencer, Yale Univ. and		*Lord Chewton, Eton and 1 & 3	
Ch.Ch., str.	12.11	Trin., str.	10.12
*C. M. Strong, Shrewsbury and		F. G. G. de Rancourt, Eton and	
Keble, cox	8.13	1 & 3 Trin., cox	9. 0
Average	13. 0⅛	Average	12. 6½

Oxford won by 5 lengths in 20 min. 47 sec.

110 Saturday, 28 March 1964, at 2.20 p.m.

CAMBRIDGE †		OXFORD	
*D. F. Legget, Radley and Trin.		J. Leigh-Wood, Eton and	
H., bow	12.10	Keble, bow	12. 3
*M. V. Bevan, Bedford and Dow.	13. 2	D. W. Steel, Eton and Keble	13. 7
M. Muir-Smith, Sir Wm		D. W. A. Cox, Bryanston and	
Borlase's and Chr.	14. 0	St Pet.	13. 7
J. W. Fraser, Radley and Jesus	14. 2	* M. Q. Morland, Radley and	
		Linc.	14. 6
*J. M. S. Lecky, Brit. Coll. Univ.		R. C. T. Mead, Eton and Keble	14. 0
and 1 & 3 Trin.	14. 3		
J. R. Kiely, Amherst, USA, and		D. D. S. Skailes, Eton and Keble	14. 3
1 & 3 Trin.	14. 0		
A. Simpson, Bedford and Qu.	12.13	D. G. Bray, St Edward's and	
		Keble	13. 1
*C. J. T. Davey, Eton and		* D. C. Spencer, Yale Univ. and	
Jesus, str.	11. 8	Ch.Ch., str.	13. 5
R. G. Stanbury, Shrewsbury		M. J. Leigh, Eton and Keble,	
and LMBC, cox	8.10	cox	8.12
Average	13. 4¾	Average	13. 7½

Cambridge won by 6½ lengths in 19 min. 18 sec.

111 Saturday, 3 April 1965, at 2.50 p.m.

OXFORD †		CAMBRIDGE	
*S. R. Morris, Radley and St. Ed. H., bow	12. 8	J. A. Fell, Winchester and Pemb., bow	13. 0
D. J. Mills, King's Sch., Cant., and St Ed. H.	13. 8	D. J. Roberts, King's Sch., Chester, and St Cath.	13. 6
R. D. Clegg, Tiffin and St Ed. H.	12.12	M. W. J. Carter, Rossall and Pemb.	13.11½
*M. Q. Morland, Radley and Linc.	13. 8	*J. W. Fraser, Radley and Jesus	14. 4
W. R. Fink, Yale Univ. and Keble	13. 2	R. G. Ward, Charterhouse and Qu.	14.10
H. W. Howell, Yale Univ. and St Ed. H.	14. 5	W. E. Church, Eton and 1 & 3 Trin.	13.10
*D. C. Spencer, Yale Univ. and Ch.Ch.	13. 0	D. P. Moore, Geelong GS and St Cath.	13. 3
E. S. Trippe, Yale Univ. and St Ed. H., str.	13. 5	M. A. Sweeney, Becket Sch. and LMBC, str.	12. 8
*M. J. Leigh, Eton and Keble, cox	9. 0	*R. G. Stanbury, Shrewsbury and LMBC, cox	9. 2
Average	13. 4¼	Average	13. 8⅝

Oxford won by 4 lengths in 18 min. 7 sec.

112 Saturday, 26 March 1966, at 4.15 p.m.

OXFORD †		CAMBRIDGE	
R. A. D. Freeman, King's Sch., Cant., and Magd., bow	13. 0	M. E. K. Graham, Wycliffe and LMBC, bow	13. 7
*R. D. Clegg, Tiffin and St Ed. H.	13. 3	M. D. Tebay, KCS, Wimbledon and 1 & 3 Trin.	13. 4
F. C. Carr, Eton and Keble	13. 4	J. H. Ashby, Harvard Univ. and 1 & 3 Trin.	13. 2
C. H. Freeman, King's Sch., Cant., and Keble	14. 3	P. G. R. Delafield, St Ed. and Jesus	14. 8
J. K. Mullard, Radley and Keble	13. 7	*R. G. Ward, Charterhouse and Qu.	14.12
P. G. Tuke, Radley and Keble	13.11	P. H. Conze, Yale Univ. and 1 & 3 Trin.	12.10
E. C. Meyer, Canford and Univ.	13. 4	L. M. Henderson, St Ed. and Selw.	13. 6
M. S. Kennard, Radley and St Ed. H., str.	12.11	*M. A. Sweeney, Becket Sch. and LMBC, str.	12.10
J. B. Rogers jr, Yale Univ. and Ball., cox	9. 1	I. A. B. Brooksby, Radley and LMBC, cox	9. 0
Average	13. 5⅜	Average	13. 7

Oxford won by 3¾ lengths in 19 min. 12 sec.

113 Saturday, 30 March 1967, at 1.15 p.m.

OXFORD †		CAMBRIDGE	
J. R. Bockstoce, Yale Univ. and St Ed. H., bow	14. 0	*L. M. Henderson, St Ed. and Selw., bow	13. 5
*M. S. Kennard, Radley and St Ed. H.	13. 0	C. D. C. Challis, St Paul's and Selw.	13. 6
*C. H. Freeman, King's Sch., Cant., and Keble	14. 0	R. D. Yarrow, Durham and LMBC	13. 9
J. E. Jensen, Yale and New C.	15. 4	G. C. M. Leggett, Portora and St Cath.	13. 3
*J. K. Mullard, Radley and Keble	13.10	*P. G. R. Delafield, St Ed. and Jesus	14. 9
C. I. Blackwall, Radley and Keble	13. 6	N. J. Hornsby, Tonbridge and Trin. H.	14. 9
D. Topolski, Westminster and New C.	11.13	D. F. Earl, Norwich and LMBC	13.11
P. G. Saltmarsh, Shrewsbury and Keble, str.	14. 0	R. N. Winckless, Tiffin and Fitz., str.	13. 9
P. D. Miller, King's Sch., Cant., and St Cath., cox	9. 6	W. R. Lawes, Tonbridge and Pemb., cox	8.13
Average	13. 9¼	Average	13.11

Oxford won by 3¼ lengths in 18 min. 52 sec.

114 Saturday, 30 March 1968, at 3.40 p.m.

CAMBRIDGE †		OXFORD	
R. C. W. Church, King's Sch., Cant., and 1 & 3 Trin., bow	12. 3	* D. Topolski, Westminster and New C., bow	11. 6
*R. N. Winckless, Tiffin and Fitz.	13. 9	* M. S. Kennard, Radley and St Ed. H.	13. 1½
J. H. Reddaway, Oundle and Fitz.	13. 8	J. P. W. Hawksley, Emanuel and Ball.	12. 6
C. S. Powell, St Paul's and Dow.	14.13	D. G. C. Thomson, Westminster and Keble	13.12
*P. G. R. Delafield, St Ed. and Jesus	14. 7	*P. G. Saltmarsh, Shrewsbury and Keble	13. 6
*N. J. Hornsby, Tonbridge and Trin. H.	14. 5	* J. R. Bockstoce, Yale Univ. and St Ed. H.	14. 3
*G. C. M. Leggett, Portora and St Cath.	12.12	* W. R. Fink, Yale Univ. and Keble	13. 5
G. F. Hall, Tiffin and Dow., str.	12. 0	P. C. Prichard, Winchester and New C., str.	12.13
C. J. Gill, Oundle and Fitz., cox	8. 9	A. W. Painter, Shrewsbury and Hert., cox	8. 2
Average	13. 7½	Average	13. 1¼

Cambridge won by 3½ lengths in 18 min. 22 sec.

115 Saturday, 30 March 1969, at 3.30 p.m.

CAMBRIDGE †		OXFORD	
C. M. Robson, Kingston GS and		F. J. L. Dale, Emanuel and	
Clare, bow	11. 9	Keble, bow	13. 4
*R. N. Winckless, Tiffin and Fitz.	13.13	K. B. Gee, Hampton GS and	
		Worc.	12. 4
C. W. Daws, Winchester and		D. M. Higgs, Oxted County	
1 & 3 Trin.	13. 4	and Ball.	13. 5
D. L. Cruttenden, The Leys and		H. P. Matheson, Eton and	
St Cath.	15.11	Keble	14. 8
*C. S. Powell, St Paul's and Dow.	14.12	J. M. Duncan, Shrewsbury and	
		Keble	13.10
*N. J. Hornsby, Tonbridge and		W. R. C. Lonsdale, Monkton	
Trin. H.	14. 9	Combe and Keble	13.10
T. M. Redfern, Shrewsbury and		N. D. C. Tee, Emanuel and Ball.	12. 0
Fitz.	13. 2		
*G. F. Hall, Tiffin and Dow., str.	11.12	*P. G. Saltmarsh, Shrewsbury	
		and Keble, str.	13.12
C. B. Murtough, St Geo. and		A. T. Calvert, Univ. Tasmania	
Fitz., cox	8. 6	and New C., cox	9. 0
Average	13. 9	Average	13. 6½

Cambridge won by 4 lengths in 18 min. 4 sec.

116 Saturday, 28 March 1970, at 4.35 p.m.

CAMBRIDGE †		OXFORD	
J. F. S. Hervey-Bathurst, Eton		R. J. D. Gee, Univ. Tasmania	
and 1 & 3 Trin., bow	13. 1½	and St Joh., bow	13. 8
C. L. Baillieu, Radley and Jesus	13. 5	J. K. G. Dart, Radley and	
		Ch.Ch.	12.10
A. C. Buckmaster, Charterhouse		*D. M. Higgs, Oxted County	
and Clare	13. 8	and Ball.	13. 9
C. J. Rodrigues, Univ. Coll. Sch.		S. E. Wilmer, Yale Univ. and	
and Jesus	13. 2	Ch.Ch.	13.11
C. J. Dalley, Winchester and		*F. J. L. Dale, Emanuel and	
Qu.	14. 5½	Keble	13.11
*D. L. Cruttenden, The Leys and		A. J. Hall, Hampton GS	
St Cath.	16. 0	and Keble	15. 7
C. M. Lowe, Shrewsbury and		*N. D. C. Tee, Emanuel and	12. 4
Fitz.	13. 7	Ball.	
S. N. S. Robertson, Radley and		*W. R. C. Lonsdale, Monkton	
Fitz., str.	12. 3½	Combe and Keble, str.	13.10
N. G. Hughes, Winchester and		*A. T. Calvert, Univ. Tasmania	
Qu., cox	8. 9	and New C., cox	8.12
Average	13. 9¼	Average	13. 8

Cambridge won by 3½ lengths in 20 min. 22 sec.

117 Saturday, 27 March 1971, at 2 p.m.

CAMBRIDGE †		OXFORD	
G. J. O. Phillpotts, St Paul's and Clare, bow	11.11	S. D. Hunt, Radley and Keble, bow	12.10
*C. L. Baillieu, Radley and Jesus	13. 5	K. Bolshaw, King's Sch., Chester, and Ch.Ch.	12.11
*J. F. S. Hervey-Bathurst, Eton and 1 & 3 Trin.	13. 4	S. D. Nevin, Westminster and Ch.Ch.	13. 8
N. W. James, Latymer Upper Sch. and Jesus	13.10	C. R. W. Parish, Eton and Ch.Ch.	13.10
B. A. Sullivan, King's Sch., Chester, and Selw.	14. 7	D. R. d'A. Willis, Radley and St Pet.	15. 0
D. L. Maxwell, Eton and Jesus	13. 1	*A. J. Hall, Hampton and Keble	14.13
S. R. Waters III, Univ. of Penn. and 1 & 3 Trin.	13. 8	*F. J. L. Dale, Emanuel and Keble	13. 3
*C. J. Rodrigues, Univ. Coll. Sch. and Jesus, str.	13. 6	*J. P. W. Hawksley, Emanuel and Ball., str.	12.10
*N. G. Hughes, Winchester and Qu., cox	8.11	M. T. Eastman, Radley and Ch.Ch., cox	8.11
Average	13. 6	Average	13. 8

Cambridge won by 10 lengths in 17 min. 58 sec.

118 Saturday, 1 April 1972, at 3.25 p.m.

OXFORD †		CAMBRIDGE	
M. A. Magarey, Adelaide Univ. and Magd., bow	13. 8	R. J. S. Clarke, Emanuel and St Cath., bow	13. 1
*K. Bolshaw, King's Sch., Chester, and Ch.Ch.	12.11	*C. L. Baillieu, Radley and Jesus	13.13
*D. R. d'A. Willis, Radley and St Pet.	14.12	S. G. I. Kerruish, Eton and Fitz.	12.10
*A. J. Hall, Hampton and Keble	15. 3	J. A. Hart, Hampton and Fitz.	13. 5
D. R. Payne, Hampton and Ball.	12.10	*N. W. James, Latymer Upper Sch. and Jesus	14. 0
*J. P. W. Hawksley, Emanuel and Ball.	12.12	G. A. Cadwalader, Univ. of Penn. and LMBC	14.10
Hon. P. D. E. M. Moncreiffe, Eton and Ch.Ch.	11. 6	M. J. Hart, Hampton and Pet.	14. 2
M. G. C. T. Baines, Eton and Keble, str.	12. 3	*D. L. Maxwell, Eton and Jesus, str.	14. 6
E. Yalouris, Harvard Univ. and Mert., cox	8.12	*N. G. Hughes, Winchester and Qu., cox	9. 1
Average	13. 2⅞	Average	13.11⅛

Cambridge won by 9½ lengths in 18 min. 36 sec.

119 Saturday, 7 April 1973, at 4.20 p.m.

OXFORD †		CAMBRIDGE	
R. G. A. Westlake, Stowe and Ch.Ch., bow	12.13	J. D. Lever, Westminster and 1 & 3 Trin., bow	12.10
J. S. Ollivant, Eton and Worc.	12. 3	H. R. Jacobs, Winchester and Pemb.	13. 6
*M. R. Magarey, Adelaide Univ. and Magd.	14. 1	R. P. B. Duncan, Shrewsbury and St Cath.	13.10
P. D. P. Angier, Westminster and CCC	11.13	*C. L. Baillieu, Radley and Jesus	13.10
S. G. Irving, Magd. Coll. Sch. and Keble	13. 8	D. P. Sturge, Radley and LMBC	13.10
*A. J. Hall, Hampton and Keble	14.13	M. O'K. Webber, King's Sch., Cant., and Jesus	13.10
*D. R. Payne, Hampton and Ball.	12.12	S. C. Tourek, Dartmouth Univ. and 1 & 3 Trin.	14. 4
D. R. Sawyier, Harvard Univ. and Ch.Ch., str.	13. 8	*M. J. Hart, Hampton and Pet., str.	13.12
*E. Yalouris, Harvard Univ. and Mert., cox	8.10	M. D. Williams, Oundle and Trin. H., cox	9. 3
Average	13. 3½	Average	13. 9

Cambridge won by 13 lengths in 19 min. 21 sec.

120 Saturday, 4 April 1974, at 1.30 p.m.

OXFORD		CAMBRIDGE †	
*N. D. C. Tee, Emanuel and Ball., bow	12. 1	*R. P. B. Duncan, Shrewsbury and St Cath., bow	13. 8
G. S. Innes, Pangbourne and Oriel	13. 2	*H. R. Jacobs, Winchester and Pemb.	13. 6
D. D. Rendel, Eton and St Cross	13.10	D. J. Walker, Bootham and Clare	13. 9
*S. D. Nevin, Westminster and Ch.Ch.	13.13	D. B. Sprague, Durham and Emm.	13. 2
G. P. G. Stoddart, Winchester and Univ.	13. 0	J. H. Smith, Winchester and Caius	14.12
P. J. Marsden, Monmouth and Linc.	13. 6	J. H. Clay, Eton and Pemb.	13. 4
*D. R. Payne, Hampton and Ball.	13. 5	T. F. Yuncken, Melbourne Univ. and Pemb.	12.12
*D. R. Sawyier, Harvard Univ. and Ch.Ch., str.	14. 2	N. C. A. Bradley, Shrewsbury and Pemb., str.	12. 3
G. E. Morris, Bedford and Oriel, cox	8.12	H. J. H. Wheare, Magd. Coll. Sch. and Jesus, cox	8.11
Average	13. 5	Average	13. 5¼

Oxford won by 5½ lengths in 17 min. 35 sec.

121 Saturday, 29 March 1975, at 3 p.m.

OXFORD †		CAMBRIDGE	
A. G. H. Baird, Radley and Ch.Ch., bow	13. 1	C. Langridge, Sir Wm Borlase's and 1 & 3 Trin., bow	13. 7
M. G. C. Harris, St Ed. and Oriel	11. 8	*N. C. A. Bradley, Shrewsbury and Pemb.	12.11
D. R. H. Beak, Radley and Oriel	13. 2	*J. H. Clay, Eton and Pemb.	13. 4
C. J. A. N. Money-Coutts, Eton and Keble	14. 7	A. F. U. Powell, Tiffin and St Cath.	13. 2
J. E. Hutchings, Univ. of Manitoba and Ch.Ch.	14. 2	*S. C. Tourek, Dartmouth Univ and 1 & 3 Trin.	14. 8
R. S. Mason, Eton and Keble	14. 1	J. Macleod, Bradford and LMBC	14. 5
*N. D. C. Tee, Emanuel and Ball.	11. 8	P. J. Robinson, Durham and LMBC	13. 6
*G. S. Innes, Pangbourne and Oriel, str.	13. 7	A. N. Christie, The Leys and LMBC, str.	14. 7
J. N. Calvert, Thirsk and St Ed. H., cox	8. 2	D. J. T. Kitchin, Oundle and Fitz., cox	8.12
Average	13. 2¾	Average	13. 9¾

Cambridge won by 3¾ lengths in 19 min. 27 sec.

122 Saturday, 20 March 1976, at 4 p.m.

OXFORD †		CAMBRIDGE	
*D. R. H. Beak, Radley and Oriel, bow	13. 6	D. J. Searle, Radley and St Cath., bow	12. 7
*G. S. Innes, Pangbourne and Oriel	13.10	R. R. A. Breare, Eton and Pemb.	14. 6
A. D. Edwards, King's Sch., Worc., and St Pet.	14. 0	M. R. Gritten, RMA Sandhurst and Qu.	14. 0
*R. S. Mason, Eton and Keble	14. 6	M. P. Wells, Aylesbury GS and Selw.	14.12
S. G. H. Plunkett, Meth. Coll., Belfast, and Qu.	16. 5	P. B. Davies, Tonbridge and 1 & 3 Trin.	14. 1
K. C. Brown, Cornell Univ. and Ch.Ch.	14. 5	R. M. Cashin, Harvard Univ. and 1 & 3 Trin.	14.12
A. J. Wiggins, Wallingford Sch. and Keble	13. 5	*J. H. Clay, Eton and Pemb.	12.11
*A. G. H. Baird, Radley and Ch.Ch., str.	12.10	R. Harpum, RMA Sandhurst and Jesus, str.	12. 4
*J. N. Calvert, Thirsk and St Ed. H., cox	9. 4	J. P. Manser, Westminster and Sid. S., cox	9. 5
Average	14. 0⅝	Average	13.10⅛

Oxford won by 6½ lengths in 16 min. 58 sec.

123 *Saturday, 19 March 1977, at 1 p.m.*

OXFORD †		CAMBRIDGE	
P. S. T. Wright, Hampton and Oriel, bow	12.11	N. G. Burnet, Bedford and Clare, bow	11.11
G. E. G. Vardey, St George's and Ball.	12.10	R. A. Waterer, Radley and Sid. S.	13. 1
M. M. Moran, Univ. Brit. Coll. and Keble	14. 4	*D. J. Searle, Radley and St Cath.	12. 6
*R. S. Mason, Eton and Keble	14. 8	A. E. Cooke-Yarborough, Eton and Caius	14. 4
*C. J. A. N. Money-Coutts, Eton and Keble	15. 2	R. C. Ross, King's Sch., Chester, and LMBC	14. 1
A. W. Shealy, Harvard Univ. and Univ.	14. 6	C. M. Horton, Eton and Dow.	14. 0
*A. J. Wiggins, Wallingford and Keble	13. 3	M. D. Bathurst, Merchant Taylors', Crosby and Pemb.	13. 6
A. G. Michelmore, Melbourne Univ. and New C., str.	12. 3	S. J. Clegg, Shrewsbury and St Cath., str.	12.10
C. B. Moynihan, Monmouth and Univ., cox	7. 9	*J. P. Manser, Westminster and Sid. S., cox	9.11
Average	13. 9½	Average	13. 3½

Oxford won by 7 lengths in 19 min. 28 sec.

124 *Saturday, 25 March 1978, at 2.45 p.m.*

OXFORD †		CAMBRIDGE	
T. J. Sutton, Oundle and St Cath., bow	14. 2	*M. D. Bathurst, Merchant Taylors', Crosby and Pemb., bow	13. 4
R. A. Crockford, Prince Henry's, Evesham, and CCC	13. 2	*S. J. Clegg, Shrewsbury and St Cath.	13. 6
J. R. Crawford, Winchester and Pemb.	14. 0	W. M. R. Dawkins, Westminster and 1 & 3 Trin.	14. 5
N. B. Rankov, Bradford and CCC	14. 3	*C. M. Horton, Eton and Dow.	14. 1
*M. M. Moran, Univ. Brit. Coll. and Keble	14. 2	*R. C. Ross, King's Sch., Chester, and LMBC	14. 7
*A. W. Shealy, Harvard Univ. and Univ.	14. 2	*A. E. Cooke-Yarborough, Eton and Caius	14. 8
J. W. Wood, Hampton and Pemb.	12.10	A. N. de M. Jelfs, John Mason, Abingdon and Fitz.	13. 3
*A. G. Michelmore, Melbourne Univ. and New C., str.	12. 3	R. N. E. Davies, Shrewsbury and St Cath., str.	12. 2
J. Fail, Bedford Mod. and Oriel, cox	7.13	G. Henderson, Radley and Dow., cox	8. 5
Average	13. 8¼	Average	13. 9¾

Cambridge sank. Oxford finished in 18 min. 58 sec.

125 *Saturday, 17 March 1979, at 2 p.m.*

OXFORD †		CAMBRIDGE	
P. J. Head, Hampton and Oriel, bow	12. 4	*S. J. Clegg, Shrewsbury and St Cath., bow	13. 0
*R. A. Crockford, Prince Henry's, Evesham, and CCC	13. 4	A. H. Gray, Shrewsbury and Pemb.	13. 1
R. J. Moore, Tiffin and St Ed. H.	13. 3	A. G. Phillips, City of London and Jesus	12.12
*N. B. Rankov, Bradford and CCC	14. 5	J. S. Palmer, Eton and Pemb.	14. 2
*J. R. Crawford, Winchester and Pemb.	14. 0	*A. N. de M. Jelfs, John Mason and Fitz.	13. 4
C. J. Mahoney, Hampton and Oriel	13. 4	P. W. Cross, Cheadle Hulme and Dow.	12.11
*A. J. Wiggins, Wallingford and Keble	13. 5	*R. C. Ross, King's, Chester, and LMBC	14. 4
M. J. Desirens, Wallingford and Keble, str.	12. 9	*R. N. E. Davies, Shrewsbury and St Cath., str.	12. 5
C. P. Berners-Lee, Emanuel and Wadh., cox	7. 9	*G. Henderson, Radley and Dow., cox	8. 8
Average	13. 4⅛	Average	13. 4

Oxford won by 3½ lengths in 20 min. 33 sec.

126 *Saturday, 5 April 1980, at 4.45 p.m.*

OXFORD †		CAMBRIDGE	
S. R. W. Francis, St Paul's and CCC, bow	13.12	L. W. J. Baart, Shrewsbury and Caius, bow	13. 4
N. A. Conington, Hampton and Oriel	13. 0	M. F. Panter, Kingston and LMBC	14. 1
M. D. Andrews, Abingdon and Magd.	14. 0½	T. W. Whitney, Dartmouth Coll., USA, and Jesus	13. 7
J. L. Bland, King Edward VI, Stafford, and Mert.	13.11	J. H. C. Laurie, Eton and Selw.	13.12
*N. B. Rankov, Bradford and CCC	14. 3	*A. G. Phillips, City of London and Jesus	13. 5½
*C. J. Mahoney, Hampton and Oriel	13. 6	J. W. Woodhouse, Shrewsbury and Selw.	13. 9
T. C. M. Barry, Radley and Oriel	13. 4½	*J. S. Palmer, Eton and Pemb.	14. 8
*M. J. Desirens, Wallingford and Keble, str.	12.13	A. D. Dalrymple, Eton and Dow., str.	12. 8
J. S. Mead, St Edward's and St Ed. H., cox	8. 3½	C. J. Wigglesworth, Bryanston and Jesus, cox	7.13½
Average	13. 8½	Average	13. 8½

Oxford won by a canvas in 19 min. 20 sec.

127 *Saturday, 4 April 1981, at 1 p.m.*

CAMBRIDGE †		OXFORD	
*L. W. J. Baart, Shrewsbury and Caius, bow	13. 2	*P. J. Head, Hampton and Oriel, bow	12. 6
*M. F. Panter, Kingston and LMBC	13.12	*N. A. Conington, Hampton and Oriel	12.10
R. J. Stephens, King's Coll. Sch., Wimbledon, and Emm.	13. 5	R. P. Yonge, UCH and New C.	14. 4
M. J. S. Clark, Shrewsbury and Dow.	13. 9	R. P. Emerton, Abingdon and Ch.Ch.	13. 1
M. P. Cowie, Cheltenham GS and Fitz.	13. 7	*N. B. Rankov, Bradford and St Hugh's	14. 5
*A. G. Phillips, City of London and Jesus	13. 0	*C. J. Mahoney, Hampton and Oriel	13. 8
*J. S. Palmer, Eton and Pemb.	14. 5	*M. D. Andrews, Abingdon and Magd.	14. 1
*A. D. Dalrymple, Eton and Dow., str.	12.12	*J. L. Bland, King Edward VI, Stafford, and Mert., str.	14. 1
*C. J. Wigglesworth, Bryanston and Jesus, cox	8. 0	Miss S. Brown, Taunton and Wadh., cox	6. 8
Average	13. 6½	Average	13. 8

Oxford won by 8 lengths in 18 min. 11 sec.

128 *Saturday, 27 March 1982, at 2.30 p.m.*

OXFORD †		CAMBRIDGE	
*N. A. Conington, Hampton and Oriel, bow	12.10	P. St J. Brine, St Edward's and LMBC, bow	12. 9
G. R. N. Holland, Radley and Oriel	13.12	A. R. Knight, Hampton and Clare	12. 8
H. E. Clay, Eton and Magd.	14. 2	*R. J. S. Stephens, KCS, Wimbledon, and Emm.	13.12
*R. P. Yonge, UCH and New C.	14. 8	N. J. Bliss, Barnard Castle and CCC	13.10
*N. B. Rankov, Bradford and St Hugh's	14.12	B. M. Philp, Bryanston and Dow.	15. 3
S. J. L. Foster, Brentwood and Pemb.	13.11	C. D. Heard, Shrewsbury and LMBC	14.10
A. K. Kirkpatrick, Durham Univ. and Oriel	14. 8	E. M. G. Pearson, King's, Canterbury, and Jesus	12. 1
R. C. Clay, Eton and New C., str.	13. 6	S. A. Harris, Desborough and Qu., str.	11. 5
*Miss S. Brown, Taunton and Wadh., cox	6.11	I. Bernstein, City of London and Emm., cox	7. 2
Average	13.13⅞	Average	13. 3¾

Oxford won by 3¼ lengths in 18 min. 21 sec.

Oarsmen

The following is a list from the Boat Race's official history and, updated to 1982, of those who have rowed in representative university crews, or were non-rowing presidents, or rowed in the Isis–Goldie races. The two races in 1849 are shown as '49i and '49ii

(L)   Matches against Leander Club
(H)   At Henley Regatta, up to 1859. After 1859 no Oxford or Cambridge crew competed at Henley until 1960
(T)   At the Thames Regatta
(W)   Wartime races, 1940–45
(P)   Peace Regatta, Henley, 1919
(AP) Allied Peace Regatta, Paris, 1919
(O)   Olympic Games
(I–G) Isis *v.* Goldie races
      Italic type denotes that the oarsman did not row in an official Boat Race, and did not gain a blue

OXFORD

Adams, H. W., St Paul's and Univ., 1902, '03

Aitken, J., Eton and Ex., 1849ii, '50 (H), '51 (H)

Albert, C. E., Yale Univ. and St Ed. H., 1966 (I–G)

Allen, M. J. S., Downside and Ex., 1972 (I–G)

Alloway, M. B., St Paul's and Trin., 1976 (I–G)

Ampthill, Lord, Eton and New C., 1889–91

Andrews, M. D., Abingdon and Magd., 1980, '81

Angier, P. D. P., Westminster and CCC, 1973

Arbuthnot, J. E., Shrewsbury and Ball., 1829

Archer-Houblon, T. H., Radley and Ch.Ch., 1872

Arkell, J., Durham and Pemb., 1857, '57 (H), '58, '59, '59 (H)

Arundel, R. L., Marlborough and Mert., 1948, '49

Ashby, M. G. C., Oundle and New C., 1936, '37

Atherton, G. A., Bedford Mod. and Oriel, 1977 (I–G), 78 (I–G)

Austin, W. G. G., Radley and Magd., 1858

Awdry, W., Winchester and Ball., 1863, '64

Badcock, F. D. M., Harrow and Ch.Ch., 1958

Baillie, Sir W., Bt, Eton and Ch.Ch., 1836

Baillieu, C. L., Melbourne GS and Magd., 1913

Baines, M. G. C. T., Eton and Keble, 1972

Baird, A. G. H., Radley and Ch.Ch., 1974 (I–G), '75, '76

Baker, T. S., Lancing and Qu., 1869–71

Baker, W. R., Cornell Univ. and St Ed. H., 1977 (I–G)

Balfour, A. R., Edinburgh Academy and Univ., 1904, '05

Balfour, E. R., (Repton), Edinburgh Academy and Univ., 1896, '97

Balguy, F. St J., Eton and BNC, 1852 (H)

Bankes, J. E., Eton and Univ., 1875

Bankes, P. R. S., Oundle and Ch.Ch., 1933–35

Baring, M. F. R., Eton and Ch.Ch., 1979 (I–G)

Barker, H. R., Eton and Ch.Ch., 1852 (H)

Barker, H. R., Eton and Ch.Ch., 1908, '09

Barnard, P. F., Eton and Ch.Ch., 1957

Barnes, D. M. P., King's Sch., Canterbury, and St Ed. H., 1965 (I–G)

Barr, P. D., Radley and Trin., 1929

Barrett, R., St Edward's and Pemb., 1956, '57

Barry, J. M., Dulwich and Qu., 1946

Barry, T. C. M., Radley and Oriel, 1978 (I–G), '79 (I–G), '80

Bate, R. C. I., Tonbridge and St Ed. H., 1960, '60 (O), '61

Bates, J. E., Westminster and Ch.Ch., 1829

Baxter, H. F., Hereford Cath. Sch. and BNC, 1859, '59 (H), '60

Beak, D. R. H., Radley and Oriel, 1975, '76

Beaumont, F. M., Eton and New C., 1877–79

Bennett, G., Winchester and New C., 1856

Benson, H. W., Eton and BNC, 1874

Benson, W. D., Eton and Ball., 1868–70, president '71 but did not row

Berners-Lee, C. P., Emanuel and Wadh., 1978 (I–G), '79

Berrisford, E. A., King Edward VII Sch., and Qu., 1919 (P), president '20 but did not row

Bethell, R., Eton and Ex., 1841

Bevan, N. V., Shrewsbury and Ball., 1963

Bewicke, C., Westminster and Univ., 1839

Bingham, J. R., Bedford and Pemb., 1939

Blacker, J. G. C., Eton and Ball., 1950

Blackwall, C. I., Radley and Keble, 1966 (I–G), '67

Blackwell, N. S., 1968 (I–G)

Bland, J. L., King Edward VI, Stafford, and Mert., 1978 (I–G), '80, '81

Blandy, W. C., Marlborough and Ex., 1884

Bloomfield, M. C. B., Merchant Taylors', Northwood and New C., 1982 (I–G)

Blundell, H. B. H., Eton and Ch.Ch., 1854

Bockstoce, J. R., Yale Univ. and St Ed. H., 1967, '68

Bolshaw, K., King's Sch., Chester, and Ch.Ch., 1971, '72

Bolton, E. de V., Radley and Trin., 1940 (W)

Bourne, G. C., Eton and New C., 1882, '83

Bourne, G. D., Eton and Oriel, 1842, '43 (H), '43 (T)

Bourne, R. C., Eton and New C., 1909–12

Bourne, R. M. A., Eton and New C., 1946, '47

Boustead, J. M., Harrow and Univ., 1875–77

Bowman, W. P., Eton and Univ., 1867

Bradford, M. E., Eton and Ch.Ch., 1888

Brander, G. M., Edinburgh Academy and Ex., 1928

Bray, D. G., St Edward's and Keble, 1964

Breedon, E. A., Private and Trin., 1842, '45 (H), '45 (T)

Brewster, W. B., Eton and St Joh., 1842, '43 (H), '43 (T) (not in Eton Register)

Brocklebank, T. G., Eton and Trin., 1904

Brodie, P. N., Oundle and Oriel, 1946–48

Brooks, J. M. H., Radley and New C., 1943 (W), '44 (W)

Brown, D. E., Harrow and Hert., 1880–82

Brown, K. C., Cornell Univ. and Ch.Ch., 1976

Brown, M. M., Radley and Trin., 1864–66

Brown, S. (Miss), Taunton and Wadh., 1981, '82

Bryan, C. G. F., Eton and Worc., 1934, '35

Buchanon, P. M. R., St Edward's and Ch.Ch., 1982 (I–G)

Buck, E., Malvern and Hert., 1881, '82

Buckle, W., Winchester and Oriel, 1844 (T), '45, '45 (H), '45 (T)

Bucknall, H. C., Eton and Mert., 1905–07

Buller, R. J., (Manningham), Eton and Ball., 1852, '53 (H)

Burdekin, B., Cheltenham and New C., 1914

Burgess, E. R., Eton and Magd., 1913

Burgess, G. F., Blackheath and Keble, 1878

Burgess, N. D. V., Radley and Oriel, 1976 (I–G), '77 (I–G)

Burgess, R. E., Eton and Magd., 1911

Burnell, C. D., Eton and Magd. 1895–98

Burnell, P. C. D., Eton and Magd., 1962

Burnell, R. D., Eton and Magd., 1939

Burns, A. G., St Paul's and Keble, 1969 (I–G), '71 (I–G)

Burns, T. H. S., St Paul's and Keble, 1943 (W)

Burrough, J. P., St Edward's Sch. and St Ed. H., 1937 '38

Burrows, J. C., Winchester and Trin., 1879

Burton, E. C., Westminster and Ch.Ch., 1846, '47 (H), '48 (H), '49i, '51 (H)

Burton, R. E. L., Eton and Ch.Ch., 1862

Burton, Stewart, W., *see* Stewart, W. Burton

Byatt, R. A., Gordonstoun and New C., 1953

Byrne, L. S. R., Eton and Trin., 1886

Cairns, H. W. B., Adelaide HS and Ball., 1920

Callender, D. N., Eton and Trin., 1950, '51

Callender, I. A., Eton and Keble, 1981 (I–G)

Calvert, A. J., Tasmania Univ. and New C., 1968 (I–G), '69, '70

Calvert, J. N., Thirsk and St Ed. H., 1974 (I–G), '75, '76

Campbell (-Douglas), A. V., Eton and Ch.Ch., 1922, '25

Carlise, I. O., Shrewsbury and New C., 1945 (W)

Carnegie, R. H., Melbourne Univ. and New C., 1956, '57

Carpenter, T. J., Cheltenham and Magd., 1979 (I–G)

Carr, C. R., Durham and Wadh., 1862, '63, president in '64 but did not row

Carr, F. C., Eton and Keble, 1965 (I–G), '66

Carr, R., Eton and Magd., 1896–98

Carstairs, J. R. L., St Edward's Sch. and Ch.Ch., 1944 (W), '45 (W), '46

Carter, C. R., (Eton), Cheltenham and CCC, 1884–86

Carter, E. S., Durham and Worc., 1867, '68

Carter, G., Shrewsbury and St Joh., 1836

Carter, J., Shrewsbury and St Joh., 1829

Carver, G., Yale Univ. and Ball., 1951

Cavenagh, A. J. M., Winchester and Magd., 1949, '50

Chadwyck-Healey, C. A., Eton and Trin., 1932

Chamberlayne, M. J. T., Harrow and Oriel, 1970 (I–G)

Champneys, W., Charterhouse and BNC, 1861

Chapman, M. C. G., Reigate GS and Pemb., 1981 (I–G)

Cheales, H. J., Eton and Ex., 1850 (H)

Cherry, J. C., Westminster and BNC, 1936–8

Chester, J. R., Monkton Combe and Keble, 1960, '60 (O), '61

Chetwynd-Stapleton, H. E., Eton and Univ., 1843 (T)

Chetwynd-Stapleton, W., Eton and Mert., 1844 (H), '44 (T), 45, '45 (H), '45 (T), '46, 46 (H)

Chitty, J. W., Eton and Ball., 1849i, '49ii, '50 (H), '51 (H), '52, '53 (H)

Clapperton, G. D., Magd. Coll. Sch. and Magd., 1923, '24

Clapperton, J. S., Magd. Coll. Sch. and Univ., 1919 (P)

Clark, R. W., King's Sch., Canterbury and St Ed. H., 1966 (I–G)

Clarke, L. J., Marlborough and Ex., 1887

Clarke, R. F., Merchant Taylors' and St Joh., 1859

Clay, H. E., Eton and Magd., 1981 (I–G), '82

Clay, J. M., Eton and Magd., 1949, '50

Clay, R. C., Eton and New C., 1981 (I–G), '82

Clegg, R. D., Tiffin and St Ed. H., 1965, '66

Clemons, J. S., Launceston CE Sch., Tasmania, and CCC, 1885

Clive, L., Eton and Ch.Ch., 1930, '31

Cobb, S. M., Shrewsbury and St Pet., 1970 (I–G)

Codrington, J. E., RFGS Marlborough and BNC, 1855 (H)

Collin, R. C. L. S., Trent Coll. and Worc., 1973 (I–G)

Collins, R. M., Radley and Trin., 1948 (O)

Colton, J. H. E., Clifton and St Ed. H., 1973 (I–G), '74 (I–G)

Compton, J., Private and Mert., 1839

Conant, J. W., Eton and St Joh., 1845 (H), '45 (T), '46, '46 (H)

Conington, N. A., Hampton and Oriel, 1980–82

Cook, T. A., Radley and Wadh., 1889

Cooper, G. V., Eton and Keble, 1960 (O), '61

Cotton, H. B., Eton and Magd., 1892–95

Cotton, R. W., Westminster and Ch.Ch., 1849ii, '50 (H), '52

Couchman, J. M., Sherborne and Ch.Ch., 1933–35

Courtney, H. M'D., Highgate and Pemb., 1875, '76

Coventry, G. G., Private and Pemb., 1865

Cowles, D. J., Merchant Taylors' and St Joh., 1877, '78

Cox, D. W. A., Bryanston and St Pet., 1964

Cox, J. C., Winchester and Trin., 1842, '43 (H), '43 (T)

Craig, D. H., Sydney Univ. and Magd., 1975 (I–G)

Craster, T. H., Durham and Univ., 1855 (H)

Craven, W. D., King's Coll., London, and Worc., 1876

Crawford, G. H., Harrow and BNC, 1926

Crawford, J. R., Winchester and Pemb., 1977 (I–G), '78, '79

Crawley, J. D., King's Sch., Peterborough, and Oriel, 1971 (I–G)

Crockford, R. A., Prince Henry's, Evesham, and CCC, 1977 (I–G), '78, '79

Croft, Sir J. H., Bt, Eton and BNC, 1926–28

Cross, D. A., Winchester and Ball., 1956

Cross, H., Bedford and Hert., 1888

Crowder, F., Rugby and BNC, 1866, '67

Crum, W. D. C., Erskine-, Eton and Ch.Ch., 1931–33

Crum, W. E., Eton and New C., 1894–97

Cudmore, C. R., St Peter's, Adelaide, and Magd., 1908, '09

Culme-Seymour, R. H., Eton and New C., 1900, '01

Curry, W. D. B., Trin. Coll., Stratford, and Ex., 1884

Dale, F. J. L., Emanuel and Keble, 1969–71

Darbishire, S. D., Univ. Coll. Sch. and Ball., 1868–70, '69 (*v.* Harvard)

Dart, J. K. G., Radley and Ch.Ch., 1969 (I–G), '70

Davenport, D. T. H., Radley and Univ., 1953

Davidge, C. G. V., Eton and Trin., 1949, president in '50 but did not row, '51, '52

Davies, E. W. L., Cowbridge and Jesus, 1836

Davis, C. M., Eton and Linc., 1960, '60 (O), '61, '62

Day, C. E., Yale Univ. and Keble, 1969 (I–G)

Deakin, J. C. B., Beaumont and Hert., 1940 (W)

de Hamel, F. A., *see* Hamel

de Haviland, R. S., Eton and CCC, 1882, '83, president in '84 but did not row

de Knoop, J. J. J., Eton and New C., 1896, '97

Denne, H., Eton and Univ., 1852, '53 (H)

Denne, R. H., Eton and Univ., 1855 (H)

Desirens, M. J., Wallingford and Keble, 1979, '80

Dewar, J., Rugby and New C., 1906

Disney, H. W., Finchley and Hert., 1879

Dodds-Parker, *see* Parker

Donkin, A. W. F., Eton and Magd., 1907–10

Douglas-Mann, S. C. H., Westminster and St Ed. H., 1959

Dowding, F. T., Eton and St Joh., 1873

Drake, F. C., Winchester and New C., 1889

Drinkwater, G. C., Rugby and Wadh., 1902, '03

Dry, W. J., Private and Wadh., 1844 (H), '44 (T)

Ducker, J. H., Monkton Combe and St Ed. H., 1958

Dudley, M., Truro Coll. and Ex., 1973 (I–G)

Duncan, J. M., Shrewsbury and Keble, 1967 (I–G), '68 (I–G), '69

Dunsten, F. D. J., South Shields and Ball., 1971 (I–G)

Durand, A. T. M., Eton and Magd., 1919 (P), '20

Durbridge, H. A. G., Malvern and Univ., 1930

Dutton, H. H., St Peter's, Adelaide, (Lancing) and Magd., 1900

du Vallon, H. C. de J., Malvern and BNC, 1901

Earl, S., Eton and Magd., 1919 (P), 1920–22

Eason, R. E., Abingdon and All Souls', 1924

Eastman, M. T., Radley and Ch.Ch., 1970 (I–G), '71

Ebsworth-Snow, R., Bradfield and Magd., 1944 (W), '45 (W), '46

Edmett, E. R., Herne Bay and Worc., 1931

Edwards, A. D., King's Sch., Worcester, and St Pet., 1975 (I–G), '76

Edwards, D. C. R., Downside and Ch.Ch., 1958, '59

Edwards, E. C. T., Westminster and Ch.Ch., 1925–27

Edwards, G. O. C., Eton and New C., 1897, '98

Edwards, H. R. A., Westminster and Ch.Ch., 1926, '30

Edwards-Moss, J. E., Eton and Ball., 1870, '71

Edwards-Moss, T. C., Eton and BNC, 1875–78

Elers, F. W., Tonbridge and Trin., 1856, '57, '57 (H)

Elliott, I. L., Canford and Keble, 1960, '60 (O), '61

Ellis, M. H., Shrewsbury and Keble, 1920, '21

Ellison, G. A., Westminster and New C., 1932, '33, president '34 but did not row

Ellison, W. A., Eton and Univ., 1878

Emerton, R. P., Abingdon and Ch.Ch., 1980 (I–G), '81

Erskine-Crum, *see* Crum

Etherington-Smith, T. B., Repton and Oriel, 1900, '01

Evans, E. P., Radley and Univ., 1904, '06

Everett, C. H., Bruton and Ball., 1855 (H)

Eyre, F. T. H., Bedford and Keble, 1903

Fage, J. L., Wrekin and St Ed. H., 1958, '59

Fail, J., Bedford Mod. and Oriel, 1976 (I–G), '78

Fanning, P. L., Radley and Qu., 1940 (W)

Farrer, H. M., Eton and Ball., 1905

Farrer, M. G., Eton and BNC, 1873

Faulkner, R. G. C., Radley and Trin., 1948

Fay, C. K., Sydney Univ. and St Ed. H., 1970 (I–G)

Ferguson, S. B., Dartmouth, USA, and Jesus, 1971 (I–G)

Ffooks, W. W., Sherborne and Ex., 1839

Field, N., Wellington and BNC, 1910

Fink, W. R., Yale Univ. and Keble, 1965, '68

Fish, J. H., Durham and Worc., 1867

Fisher, F. G., Harvard Univ. and Worc., 1972 (I–G)

Fishlock, R. L. S., King's Sch., Canterbury, and St Ed. H., 1960, '60 (O)

Fisk, G. C., Geelong GS and Oriel, 1948–50

Fitzherbert, D. H., Eton and Trin., 1977 (I–G)

Fleming, P., Eton and Magd., 1910

Fletcher, R. W., Eton and Ball., 1914

Fletcher, W. A. L., Eton and Ch.Ch., 1890–93

Forbes, H. A. W., St Paul's and Magd., 1938, '39

Ford, J. A., Winchester and BNC, 1892, '93

Fort, G. S., Uppingham and Hert., 1882, '83

Foster, S. J. L., Brentwood and Pemb., 1981 (I–G), '82

Fothergill, S. R., Eton and New C., 1888

Francis, S. R. W., St Paul's and CCC, 1980, '82 (I–G)

Franklin, A. H., Merchant Taylors' and Linc., 1925

Freeman, C. H., King's Sch., Canterbury, and Keble, 1966, '67

Freeman, R. A. D., King's Sch., Canterbury, and Magd., 1966

Freeman, W. L., Cheltenham and Mert., 1866

Fremantle, W. R., Westminster and Ch.Ch., 1829

Freere, L., Eton and BNC, 1888

Frewer, G. E., Eton and St Joh., 1873

Gadsden, G. E. G., Eton and Ch.Ch., 1924, '25

Garnett, W. B., Shrewsbury and BNC, 1840

Garnett, W. J., Rugby, Eton and Ch.Ch., 1839

Garnier, T. F., Winchester and Worc., 1829

Garside, K. V., Bedford and St Joh., 1936

Garstang, W. L., Oundle and Trin., 1931

Garton, A. S., Eton and Magd., 1909–11

Garton, J. L., Eton and Magd., 1938, '39

Gee, K. B., Hampton GS and Worc., 1969

Gee, R. J. D., Tasmania Univ. and St Joh., 1967 (I–G), '68 (I–G), '70

Giles, E., Westminster and Ch.Ch., 1871

Gillan, A. J. A., Shrewsbury and New C., 1943 (W)

Gillan, J. A., Edinburgh Academy and Magd., 1907, '09

Girdlestone, H., Bath College and Magd., 1885, '86

Gladstone, A. C., Eton and Ch.Ch., 1906–09

Gladstone, P., Eton and Ch.Ch., 1950, '52

Gleave, J. M., Uppingham and Linc., 1978 (I–G), '79 (I–G)

Gleave, J. R. W., Uppingham and Magd., 1946–48

Glynne-Jones, D. R., Magd. Coll. Sch. and Jesus, 1952

Gobbo, J. A., Melbourne Univ. and Magd., 1954, '55

Godber, G. E., Bedford and New C., 1928, '29

Godden, W. F., Shrewsbury and Trin., 1924

Gold, H. G., Eton and Magd., 1896–99

Gomm, C. P. M., Cheltenham and Ball., 1961

Graham, A., Eton and BNC, 1929

Graham, A. K., Eton and Ball., 1903–05

Graham, G. M. A., Eton and New C., 1906

Graham, J., Princeton Univ. and Worc., 1981 (I–G)

Graham, M. C., Shrewsbury and Magd., 1928

Grant, M. R., Winchester and Ch.Ch., 1925

Greenall, R., Liverpool Coll. and BNC, 1851 (H), '52, '52 (H)

Grenfell, W. H., (Lord Desborough), Harrow and Ball., 1877, '78, president in '79 but did not row

Griffiths, E. G. S., Cheltenham and Worc., 1847 (H)

Grimston, Visc., (Earl of Verulam), Eton and Ch.Ch., 1900

Gurdon, P., Radley and Univ., 1856, '57, '57 (H)

Haggard, M., Westminster and Ch.Ch., 1845, '46 (H), '47 (H), '48 (H)

Hale, H. J., Eton and Ball., 1899, '01, '02

Hales, A. J. S. H., Rugby and CCC, 1904, '05

Hall, A. J., Hampton GS and Keble, 1970–73

Hall, F. H., King's Sch., Canterbury, and CCC, 1869 (*v.* Harvard), '70–72

Hall, M. J. W., Winchester and Linc., 1958

Halsey, T. F., Eton and Ch.Ch., 1860

Hamel, F. A. de, Shrewsbury and New C., 1943 (W), '44 (W)

Hammond, E. C. B., Clifton and BNC, 1953

Hankin, A. M., Bromsgrove and Worc., 1927

Hankinson, R. P., Winchester and New C., 1913

Harding, A. R., Radley and Mert., 1874

Harding, N. F. C., Sir Wm Borlase's and Worc., 1980 (I–G)

Hargreaves, F. M., St Peter's, York, and Keble, 1880

Harris, M. G. C., St Edward's and Oriel, 1973 (I–G), '74 (I–G), '75

Harris, T., Rugby and Magd., 1836

Harris-Burland, W. M., Nottingham Univ. and Keble, 1972 (I–G)

Harrison, J. J. H., Shrewsbury and Trin., 1954

Hawkes, M. J., Bedford and New C., 1951

Hawkesley, J. P. W., Emanuel and Ball., 1968, '71, '72

Hayes, J., Shrewsbury and New C., 1950

Head, P. J., Hampton and Oriel, 1978 (I–G), '79, '80

Healey, J. A. D., Oundle and BNC, 1948 (O)

Healey, J. R., Shrewsbury and Wadh., 1982 (I–G)

Heard, W. T., Fettes and Ball., 1907

Henley, E. F., Sherborne and Oriel, 1865, '66

Herbert, A. T., (Lord Lucas), Bedford GS and Ball., 1898, '99

Hewett, W. A. S., Haileybury and Univ., 1892

Heygate, W. U., Eton and Mert., 1846

Heywood-Lonsdale, A. P., Eton and Ch.Ch., 1856, '57, '57 (H)

Heywood-Lonsdale, J. P., Eton and New C., 1889–92

Hicks, H. D., Mount Allison Univ., Canada, and Ex., 1940 (W)

Higgins, A. H., Magd. Coll. Sch. and Magd., 1882

Higgins, M. B., Melbourne Univ. and Ball., 1910

Higgins, S. E., Newcastle RGS and Ex., 1981 (I–G)

Higgs, D. M., Oxted County Sch. and Ball., 1969, '70

Hill, A. C., Shrewsbury and St Joh., 1920

Hill, R. D., Radley and New C., 1940 (W)

Hinchliffe, J. E. C., King's Sch., Canterbury, and Trin., 1950

Hoare, W. M., Eton and Ex., 1861–63

Hobart, W. H., Uppingham and Ex., 1876, '79

Hobbs, K. S., Wallasey GS and St Ed. H., 1967 (I–G)

Hobhouse, R., Eton and Ball., 1839

Hodgson, A. B., Eton and Oriel, 1937, '38

Hodgson, H. W., Westminster and Ball., 1841

Hogg, P., Sherborne and New C., 1933, '34

Holdsworth, R. W. G., Shrewsbury and BNC, 1931, '33, '34

Holland, G. R. N., Radley and Oriel, 1980 (I–G), '82

Holland, W. F. C., Eton and BNC, 1887–90

Hooke, A., Worcester Coll. Sch. and Worc., 1854, '55 (H)

Hooper, T. A., Marlborough and Pemb., 1854

Hope, G. E., Eton and Ch.Ch., 1907

Hope, R., Eton and New C., 1935

Hopkins, H. G., Rugby and CCC, 1861

Hopwood, E. O., Qu. Eliz. Sch., Kirkby
Lonsdale, and Ch.Ch., 1875

Hopwood, F. E., Eton and Ch.Ch.,
1862, '63

Hornby, C. H., St J., Harrow, and New
C., 1890

Hornby, J. J., Eton and BNC, 1849ii,
'50 (H), '51 (H)

Horsfall, E. D., Eton and Magd.,
1912–14, 1919 (P)

Houblon, T. H. Archer *see*
Archer-Houblon

Houghton, W., Private and BNC,
1849ii, '50 (H), '51 (H), '52

Howard, R. L., Shrewsbury and Worc.,
1957, '59

Howell, H. W., Yale Univ. and Keble,
1965

Howles, J. S., Newcastle RGS and
Univ., 1953

Hudson, A. W., Westminster and Ball.,
1977 (I–G)

Hughes, G. E., Rugby and Oriel, 1842,
'43 (H), '43 (T)

Humphreys, F. J., Radley and BNC,
1884, '85

Hunt, C. W., Merchant Taylors' and
CCC, 1880

Hunt, S. D., Radley and Keble, 1971,
'72 (I–G)

Huntley, F. O. J., Radley and Univ.,
1901, '02

Huse, G., Latymer Upper Sch. and Oriel,
1939, '40 (W)

Hutchings, J. E., Manitoba Univ. and
Ch.Ch., 1974 (I–G), '75

Hutton, N. K., Fettes and Univ., 1930

Illingworth, C. H., Radley and Pemb.,
1906

Imeson, D., Judd Sch. and St Ed. H.,
1976 (I–G)

Ingles, J. A., Tasmania Univ. and Magd.,
1929

Innes, G. S., Pangbourne and Oriel,
1974–76

Irvine, A. C., Shrewsbury and Mert.,
1922, '23

Irving, S. G., Magd. Coll. Sch. and
Keble, 1971 (I–G), 72 (I–G), '73

Isham, Sir J. V., Bt, Eton and Ch.Ch.,
1836

Jacobson, W. B. R., Winchester and
Ch.Ch., 1862–64

James, I. C., Doncaster GS and Qu.,
1973 (I–G)

James, Hon. W. E. C., (Lord
Northbourne), Eton and Magd., 1919
(P), 1920, '21

Jamison, D. G., Radley and Magd.,
1943 (W), '44 (W), '45 (W), '47

Jelf, H. W., Eton and Ch.Ch., 1904

Jenk, J. M. S., Westminster and Keble,
1981 (I–G)

Jensen, J. E., Yale Univ. and New C.,
1967

Johnson, P., Tonbridge and Magd.,
1927

Johnson, P. M., Dulwich and Jesus,
1971 (I–G)

Johnson, W. N. G., Radley and Keble,
1969 (I–G)

Johnston, C. E., Eton and New C.,
1899, 1900

Johnston, C. M., Shrewsbury and BNC,
1930–32

Jones, L. E., Eton and Ball., 1905, '06

Jordan, N. M., Latymer Upper and
Keble, 1979 (I–G)

Juel-Brockdorff, C. F., Svendborg,
Denmark, and Pemb., 1929

Kane, R. K., Harvard Univ. and Ball.,
1923

Kelly, F. H., Rugby and Univ., 1863, '64

Kelly, F. S., Eton and Ball., 1903

Kelly, M. A., Bassaleg GS and Regent's
Park, 1971 (I–G)

Keniston, K. H., Harvard Univ. and
Ball., 1952

Kennard, M. S., Radley and St Ed. H., 1965 (I–G), 1966–68

Kent, C. W., Private and BNC, 1891

Kent, J. de R., Sherborne and BNC, 1932

Kindersley, J. B., Clifton and Ex., 1914

Kindersley, R. S., Clifton and Ex., 1880–82

King, Walker, Westminster and Oriel, 1847 (H)

King, William, Durham and Mert., 1853 (H)

Kingsbury, H. T., Yale Univ. and Qu., 1927

Kirby, A. G., Eton and Magd., 1906–09

Kirke, M. A., Sherborne and Keble, 1936

Kirkpatrick, A. K., Durham Univ. and Oriel, 1982

Kitchin, A. E., Tonbridge and St Joh., 1908

Kittermaster, H. B., Shrewsbury and Ch.Ch., 1900

Knollys, C. C., Private and Magd., 1872, '73

Knox, R., Highgate and Ball., 1925

Komarakul-Na-Nagara, C., St Paul's and Magd., 1933

Lambert, W. F. A., Merchant Taylors' and Wadh., 1874

Lander, J. R. H., Shrewsbury and Ch.Ch., 1959

Lane, C. G., Westminster and Ch.Ch., 1858, '59, '59 (H)

Lane, E., Private and Ball., 1858, '59 (H)

Lascelles, J. H., Chr. Coll., NZ, and Ball., 1934

Lawless, Hon. V., (Lord Cloncurry), Eton and Ball., 1859

Lea, W., Rugby and BNC, 1841

Leckie, W. J. H., Edinburgh Academy and BNC, 1948 (O), '49

Lee, M. L. H., Shrewsbury and Worc., 1944 (W), 1945 (W)

Lee, S., Radley and Qu., 1839

Legge, H., Haileybury and Trin., 1893

Leigh, M. J., Eton and Keble, 1964, '65

Leigh-Wood, J., Eton and Keble, 1964

Lesley, R., Radley and Pemb., 1871, '72, president in '73 but did not row

Lewes, J. S., King's Sch., Paramatta, and Ch.Ch., 1936, president in '37 but did not row

Lewis, A. G. P., Eton and Univ., 1870

Lewis, G. B., Eton and Oriel, 1844 (H), '45 (H)

Lewis, H., Private and Pemb., 1845

Lindsay, A. T., Eton and Magd., 1959, '60, '60 (O)

Lips, D. L., Manchester Coll. and St Joh., 1979 (I–G)

Little, J. B., King Edward VI Sch., Norwich, and Ch.Ch., 1873

Littlejohn, C. W. B., Melbourne Univ. and New C., 1911, '12

Llewellyn, W. S., Eton and Ball., 1928

Long, A. de L., Winchester and New C., 1901, '03

Long, C. L. B., St Paul's and Oriel, 1982 (I–G)

Lonsdale, *see* Heywood-Lonsdale

Lonsdale, W. R. C., Monkton Combe and Keble, 1968 (I–G), '69, '70

Lothrop, F. B., Harvard Univ. and Trin., 1921

Lovett, N. J. B., St Edward's and Ch.Ch., 1967 (I–G)

Low, R. V., Winchester and Univ., 1930

Lowndes, R., Winchester and Ch.Ch., 1843 (H), '43 (T)

Lowry, R. S., St Edward's and Univ., 1943 (W)

Lucas, R. S. C., Eton and Magd., 1919 (P), '21

Lyon, E. H., Charterhouse and Hert., 1881–83

Maberly, S. E., Eton and Ch.Ch., 1839, '40

M'Clintock-Bunbury, J., Eton and BNC, 1871

Merriman, E. B., Winchester and Ex., 1861

Meyer, E. C., Canford and Univ., 1965 (I–G), '66

Meynell, G., Shrewsbury and BNC, 1840, '41

Michelmore, A. G., Melbourne Univ. and New C., 1977, '78

Migotti, W. H., Radley and Worc., 1932–34

Milburn, D., Hill Sch., USA, and Linc., 1902, '03

Milburn, J. G., Hill Sch., USA, and Linc., 1902

Miller, P. D., King's Sch., Canterbury, and St Cath., 1966 (I–G), '67

Milling, C. D., Radley and Mert., 1952

Milling, G., Radley and Mert., 1922

Millington-Drake, E. J. H. V., Eton and Magd., 1911

Mills, D. J., King's Sch., Canterbury, and St Ed. H., 1965

Milman, W. H., Westminster and Ch.Ch., 1844 (T), '45, '45 (H), '45 (T), '46, '46 (H), '48 (H)

Mirehouse, R. W. B., Eton and Univ., 1870

Miskin, S. F. A., St Paul's and Univ., 1957, '58

Mitchell, A. E., St Columba's and St Cath., 1982 (I–G)

Mitchison, A. M., Eton and Pemb., 1875, '76

Mitchison, R. S., Eton and Pemb., 1872, '73

Moncreiffe, P. D. E. M., Eton and Ch.Ch., 1972

Money-Coutts, C. J. A. N., Eton and Keble, 1975, '77

Monier-Williams, E. G., Winchester and Univ., 1903

Moon, E. G., Merchant Taylors' and Magd., 1847 (H)

Moore, G. B., Westminster and Ch.Ch., 1829

Moore, P. H., RFGS, Marlborough, and BNC, 1853 (H)

Moore, O. R., Eton and Ball., 1974 (I–G), '75 (I–G)

Moore, R. J., Tiffin and St Ed. H., 1977 (I–G), '78 (I–G), '79

Morahan, E. T. A., Qu. Univ., Belfast, and Keble, 1969 (I–G)

Moran, M. M., Brit. Columbia Univ. and Keble, 1977, '78

Morgan, H., Eton and Ch.Ch., 1844 (T)

Morland, M. Q., Radley and Linc., 1963–65

Morphett, H. C., Geelong GS and BNC, 1928, '29

Morris, G. E., Bedford and Oriel, 1973 (I–G), '74

Morris, S. R., Radley and St Ed. H., 1963, '65

Morrison, A., Eton and Ball., 1862, '63, president in '64 but did not row, '65

Morrison, G., Eton and Ball., 1859, '59 (H), '60, '61, president in '62 but did not row

Morrison, J. A., Eton and New C., 1893, '94

Morton Maskell, R. A., Bryanston and Keble, 1962, '63

Mosley, M. H., Shrewsbury and Trin., 1933

Mountain, J. G., Eton and Mert., 1840, '41

Mower-White, G. J., Rugby and BNC, 1923–25

Moynihan, C. B., Monmouth and Univ., 1975 (I–G), '77

Moysey, F. L., Westminster and Ch.Ch., 1836

Mulcahy, G. A., King's Sch., Worc., and Worc., 1969 (I–G)

Mulholland, Hon. A. J., Eton and Ball., 1877

Mullard, J. K., Radley and Keble, 1965 (I–G), '66, '67

Murison, F. W., Monkton Combe and Worc., 1980 (I–G)

Murray-Threipland, P. W., Eton and Ch.Ch., 1926, '28

Mynors, D. R. B., Eton and New C., 1935

Nairne, A. R., Radley and Univ., 1972 (I–G)

Neilson, D. A., Harrow and St Joh., 1869

Nevin, S. D., Westminster and Ch.Ch., 1971, '72 (I–G), '74

Newman, D. J., Westminster and Ch.Ch., 1975 (I–G), '76 (I–G)

Nicholls, H. G., Witwatersrand Univ., SA, and St Ed. H., 1966 (I–G)

Nicholson, A. W., Winchester and Magd., 1872–74

Nickalls, G., Eton and Magd., 1887–91

Nickalls, G. O., Eton and Magd., 1921–23

Nickalls, V., Eton and Magd., 1891–93

Nind, P. H., Eton and Ch.Ch., 1852, '52 (H), '53 (H), '54, '55 (H)

Nixon, W., Clapton GS and Worc., 1851 (H)

Noel, R. A., Oundle and Ch.Ch., 1948

Norsworthy, G., Winchester and Magd., 1860

Oldfield, S., Maidstone GS and Pemb., 1982 (I–G)

Oldham, J., Rugby and BNC, 1847 (H)

Ollivant, J. S., Eton and Worc., 1973

Orme, S. W., Shrewsbury and Ball., 1980 (I–G)

Ornsby, J. A., Doncaster and Linc., 1872, '73

Owen, R. H., Dulwich and Wadh., 1910

Pain, E. O. G., Sydney Univ. and Linc., 1954, '55

Paine, N., King's Sch., Canterbury, and Trin., 1956

Painter, A. W., Shrewsbury and Hert., 1967 (I–G), '68

Palgrave-Brown, Alastair, Shrewsbury and Qu., 1947, '49

Parish, C. R. W., Eton and Ch.Ch., 1969 (I–G), '70 (I–G), '71

Parker, A. P. (Dodds-), Private and Magd., 1888

Parker, H. R., Eton and BNC, 1887–89

Parson, J. C., Marlborough and Trin., 1864

Paterson, A. R., Loretto and Trin., 1881–84

Payne, D. R., Hampton GS and Ball., 1972–74

Payne, F. E. H., Cheltenham GS and St Joh., 1870–72

Peat, R. M., Sedbergh and Trin., 1907

Pechell, H. R. K., Eton and BNC, 1896–98

Pedder, J. E., Shrewsbury and Worc., 1922–24

Pelham, H., Haileybury and Magd., 1877, '78

Penfold, E. H., Maidstone and St Joh., 1845 (H), '45 (T), '46

Pennefather, J., Harrow and Ball., 1836

Petch, G., Durham and Linc., 1853 (H)

Philips, C. K., Eton and New C., 1895–98

Pike, J. R. P., Marlborough and Univ., 1975 (I–G)

Pilkington, M. C., Eton and Magd., 1893–95

Pinckney, R. A., Eton and Ex., 1881

Pinckney, W., Eton and Ex., 1854, '55 (H), president in '56 but did not row

Pitman, C. E., Eton and Ch.Ch., 1925, '26

Pitman, C. M., Eton and New C., 1892–95

Pitman, F. A. H., Eton and New C., 1912, '14

Pitman, R. O., Eton and New C., 1898, '99

Plunkett, S. G. H., Methodist Coll., Belfast, and Qu., 1974 (I–G), '75 (I–G), '76

Pocklington, D., Eton and BNC, 1864

Pocock, I. J. I., Eton and Mert., 1840

Polehampton, H. S., Eton and Pemb., 1846

Poole, A. R., Rugby and Trin., 1861, '62

Poole, R. A. J., Eton and BNC, 1931, '32

Poole, R. H. J., Durham and BNC, 1880, '81

Poole, W. M., Bedford Modern and Magd., 1891

Porritt, W. H., Wyggeston and Magd., 1920–22

Portman, L., Wellington and Univ., 1893, '94

Potts, S. G., CCC, Cambridge, and Magd., 1981 (I–G)

Powys, P. L., Eton and Ball., 1839

Poynter, G. N., St Edward's Sch. and Trin., 1944 (W)

Prescot, K., Macclesfield and BNC, 1852, '53 (H)

Prichard, P. C., Winchester and New C., 1966 (I–G), '67 (I–G), '68

Pritchard, T. E., Clifton and Ex., 1932

Purssell, A. J. R., Oundle and Oriel, 1946–48, '48 (O)

Puxley, E. L., Eton and BNC, 1883

Puxley, H. E. L., Eton and CCC, 1889, '90

Quenington, Viscount, Eton and Ch.Ch., 1972 (I–G)

Quick, H. M. C., Shrewsbury and Mert., 1952–54

Raikes, D. T., Radley and Mert., 1920–22

Raikes, R. D. J., Radley and Mert., 1954, '55

Raikes, R. M. T., Radley and Trin., 1946

Raikes, R. T., Radley and Mert., 1865, '66

Raikes, T. D., Radley and Trin., 1947, '49

Rankov, N. B., Bradford GS and CCC, 1974 (I–G), '75 (I–G), '78, '79, '80 (St Hugh's), '81, '82

Rathbone, W., Radley and Ch.Ch., 1926, '27

Reames, R. C. D., Monkton Combe and Keble, 1968 (I–G), '69 (I–G)

Rendel, D. D., Eton and St Cross, 1973 (I–G), '74

Renton, H. J., Eton and Magd., 1950, '51

Reynolds, P. J., Uppingham and St Ed. H., 1960, '60 (O), '61

Rich, W. G., Westminster and Ch.Ch., 1848 (H), '49i, '49ii, '50 (H), '51 (H)

Richards, E. V., Westminster and Ch.Ch., 1841

Richards, F. J., Eton and Mert., 1845

Richardson, D. J., Glyn GS and Mert., 1973 (I–G)

Ridsdale, S. O. B., Tonbridge and Wadh., 1861

Risley, R. W., Radley and Ex., 1857, '57 (H), '58, '59, '59 (H), '60

Rissik, S. A., Oundle and Oriel, 1919 (P)

Robarts, A. J., Eton and Ch.Ch., 1859, '59 (H), '60

Roberts, C. P., Marlborough and Trin., 1864

Roberts, G. Q., High Sch., Hobart, Tasmania, and Hert., 1883

Robertson, J. A., Eton and St Ed. H., 1978 (I–G)

Robertson, W., Geelong GS and Wadh., 1861

Robertson, W. St L., Geelong GS and Wadh., 1886

Robertson-Campbell, D. G., Edinburgh Academy and Magd., 1945 (W)

Robeson, F. E., Eton and Mert., 1892

Robinson, H. M., Harrow and New C., 1879

Rocke, A. B., Shrewsbury and Ch.Ch., 1856

Roff, P. A. V., Melbourne Univ. and New C., 1963

Rogers Jr, J. B., Yale Univ. and Ball., 1965 (I–G), '66

Rogers, W., Eton and Ball., 1840

Rooke, G. B., Radley and New C., 1943 (W)

Ross of Blandensburg, R. S., Radley and Ex., 1868

Rowbotham, J. G., Winchester and Hert., 1958, '59

Rowe, A. D., Eton and Trin., 1948, '49

Rowe, G. D., Marlborough and Univ., 1879, '80

Rowe, R. G., Eton and Univ., 1937

Rowe, R. P. P., Clifton and Magd., 1889–92

Rowley, C. P., Winchester and Magd., 1900

Royds, E., Rugby and BNC, 1840, '41, '43 (H), '43 (T)

Royds, F. C., Rugby and BNC, 1845, '46, '47 (H), '48 (H)

Rubin, R., Yale Univ. and Mert., 1958

Rutherford, D. C., Rugby and Magd., 1959, '60

Rutherford, M. S., Chigwell and Ex., 1980 (I–G)

Said, A., Peshawar Univ. and Pemb., 1957

Salmon, R. I., Durham and Ex., 1856

Saltmarsh, P. G., Shrewsbury and Keble, 1967–69

Sanders, N. W., Radley and Mert., 1952

Saunders, P. B., Eton and Wadh., 1970 (I–G)

Sawyier, D. R., Harvard Univ. and Ch.Ch., 1973, '74

Scarlett, J. Y., Eton and Ch.Ch., 1962

Schmidt, R. K., Fettes and Oriel, 1979 (I–G)

Schneider, H., Magd. Coll. Sch. and Trin., 1865

Sciortino, B. J., Shrewsbury and Univ., 1935, '36

Sears, R. D. M., Eton and Trin., 1979 (I–G)

Senhouse, H. P., Eton and Ch.Ch., 1865, '66

Serocold, C. P., Eton and New C., 1895

Sewell, J. O. B., (St Paul's, Concord), Harvard Univ. and BNC, 1961

Seymour, A. E., Charterhouse and Univ., 1864

Shadwell, A. T. W., Eton, (LMBC, Cam.) and Ball., 1842, '43 (H), '43 (T), '44 (T), '45 (H), '45 (T)

Shattock, A. G. C., Beaumont and Magd., 1943 (W)

Shaw, D. W., Shrewsbury and Keble, 1959, '60 (O)

Shaw, T. W., Shrewsbury and Ch.Ch., 1926–28

Shealy, A., Harvard Univ. and Univ., 1977, '78

Shepherd, S. J., Oundle and St Ed. H., 1978 (I–G)

Shepherd, R., Tonbridge and BNC, 1863

Sherratt, J. C. D., St Edward's and St Ed. H., 1961, '62

Sherwood, E. C., Magd. Coll. Sch. and Magd., 1896

Sherwood, W. E., Magd. Coll. Sch. and Ch.Ch., 1873, '74

Short, W. F., Winchester and New C., 1853 (H), '54, '55 (H)

Shortt, A. G., Private and Ch.Ch., 1884

Sinclair, J. S., Repton and Oriel, 1874

Skailes, D. D. S., Eton and Keble, 1962–64

Skelton, M. A., Canford and Keble, 1968 (I–G)

Slemeck, A. G., St Edward's Sch. and St Ed. H., 1939

Smith, A. J., Melbourne GS and Mert., 1951, '53

Smith, G. M. L., Winchester and BNC, 1931, '32

Smith, J. F. E., Eton and New C., 1951

Snow, R. Ebsworth, *see* Ebsworth-Snow

Soanes, C. J., King's Coll., London, and St Joh., 1846, '47 (H), '48 (H), '49i

Somers-Cocks, J. J. T., Westminster and BNC, 1840, '41

Somers-Smith, R. W., Eton and Mert., 1904, '05

Sorrell, G., St Paul's and Ch.Ch., 1955, '57, '58

Southwell, E. H. L., Eton and Magd., 1907, '08

Southwell, H. B., Charterhouse and Pemb., 1878–80

Spencer, D. C., Yale Univ. and Ch.Ch., 1963–65

Spottiswoode, W., Eton, Harrow and Ball., 1844 (T), '45 (H), '45 (T)

Spry, R. D. E., Westminster and Univ., 1965 (I–G), '66 (I–G)

Stanhope, Hon. R. P., Eton and Magd., 1908

Staniforth, T., Eton and Ch.Ch., 1829

Stayner, H. J., Somerset Coll., Bath, and St Joh., 1874, '77

Stearns, A. H., Bedford and Mert., 1957

Steel (-Maitland), A. H. D., Rugby and Ball., 1899

Steel, D. W., Eton and Keble, 1964

Stedall, L. P., Harrow and Mert., 1905, '06

Stephens, E., Blundell's and Ex., 1836

Steward, C. H., Rugby and Oriel, 1849i, '49ii, '50 (H)

Stewart, A. H., Eton and New Coll., 1888

Stewart, J. A. G. H., Harrow and Pemb., 1982 (I–G)

Stewart, J. S., Nottingham HS and Ch.Ch., 1967 (I–G)

Stewart, M. D., Canon Slade GS and New C., 1982 (I–G)

Stewart, R. R., Eton and Magd., 1937–39

Stewart, W. Burton, Loretto and BNC, 1894, '95

Stock, L., Felsted and Ex., 1884

Stocken, W. F., St Paul's and Ex., 1856

Stoddart, G. P. G., Winchester and Univ., 1974

Stokes, L. A. F., Winchester and New C., 1951, '52

Stopford, G. V., Radley and New C., 1929

Stretch, T. H. E., Radley and New C., 1894, '95

Strong, C. I., Harrow and Univ., 1859 (H), '60

Strong, C. M., Shrewsbury and Keble, 1962, '63

Sturrock, J. D., Winchester and Magd., 1936, '37

Sutcliffe, A. V., Shrewsbury and Trin., 1934, '35

Sutton, T. J., Oundle and St Cath., 1976 (I–G), '77 (I–G), '78

Swayze, T. S., Harvard Univ. and Wadh., 1960

Swift, J. B. H., Edward's Sch. and St Ed. H., 1969 (I–G)

Sykes, E. J., Eton and Worc., 1848 (H), '49i, '49ii, '50 (H), '57 (H)

Tahourdin, R., Shrewsbury and St Joh., 1869

Taylor, A. M., Radley and Univ., 1970 (I–G)

Taylor, P. W., Derby and Linc., 1884, '85

Tee, N. D. C., Emanuel and Ball., 1969, '70, '74, '75

Tennant, T. W., Eton and New C., 1962, '63 president but did not row

Tew, E. G., Shrewsbury and Magd., 1894

Thomas, G. G. T., *see* Trehearne

Thomas, M. L., Clifton and Jesus, 1952, '53

Thomson, C. E. L., Shrewsbury and Pemb., 1940 (W)

Thomson, D. G. C., Westminster and Keble, 1966 (I–G), '67 (I–G), '68

Thomson, G. I. F., Shrewsbury and Ball., 1934

Thomson, J. D. W., Eton and Univ., 1925–27

Thomson, W. S., Ruthin and Jesus, 1836

Thorley, J. T., St Paul's and Wadh., 1856, '57, '57 (H), '58

Thring, C. G., King's Sch., Canterbury, and Oriel, 1971 (I–G)

Tickler, J. E., Radley and New C., 1940 (W)

Tinné, C. E., Eton and Univ., 1911, '12

Tinné, D. E., Eton and Univ., 1929–31

Tinné, J. C., Eton and Univ., 1867–69, '69 (*v*. Harvard)

Tinné, N. D., Eton and Keble, 1962

Titherington, A. F., Charterhouse and Qu., 1887

Titherington, G. W., Radley and Qu., 1914

Todd, D. B., Hampton and Oriel, 1980 (I–G)

Tomkinson, C. W., Eton and Ball., 1899, 1900

Tomlin, E. E. D., Whitgift and Univ., 1935

Toogood, J. J., Harrow and Ball., 1829

Topolski, D., Westminster and New C., 1966 (I–G), '67, '68

Tottenham, C. R. W., Eton and Ch.Ch., 1864–68

Townsend, R. N., Crewkerne GS and Pemb., 1856

Trehearne, G. G. T., (previously Thomas), Eton and Ball., 1859

Tremayne, H. H., Eton and Ball., 1849i

Trippe, E. S., Yale Univ. and St Ed. H., 1965

Tuckett, P. D., Marlborough and Trin., 1890

Tuke, F. E., Eton and BNC, 1844 (H), '44 (T), '45

Tuke, P. G., Radley and Keble, 1965 (I–G), '66

Turner, C. G., Winchester and New C., 1951

Turner-Warwick, R. J., *see* Warwick

Tyser, A., Eton and Trin, 1940 (W)

Underhill, P. C., St Edward's Sch. and BNC, 1904

Unwin, W. S., Magd. Coll. Sch. and Magd., 1885, '86

Van Bergen, J. E., Radley and Trin., 1945 (W)

Vardey, G. E. G., St George's, Weybridge, and Ball., 1975 (I–G), '77

Venner, B. E. B. K., St Edward's and St Ed. H., 1956

Vine, E. V., Geelong GS and BNC, 1954–56

Wace, P. R., King's Sch., Canterbury, and BNC, 1923, '24

Waldron, F. A. L., Shrewsbury and Trin., 1938, '39

Walls, R. G., Rugby and BNC, 1839, '40

Walpole, H. S., Eton and Ball., 1858

Walter, S. J., Stoneyhurst Coll. and CCC, 1980 (I–G)

Ward, H. K., Sydney, Univ. and New C., 1913, '14

Warner, E. C. T., Eton and Ch.Ch., 1904

Warre, E., Eton and Ball., 1857, '57 (H), '58, '59 (H)

Warre, F. W., Eton and Ball., 1898, '99, president in 1900 but did not row, '01

Warwick, R. T. Turner, Bedales and Oriel, 1944 (W), '45 (W), '46

Waterhouse, M. J., Eton and Ball., 1930

Watson, I. A., Shrewsbury and Keble, 1955

Wauchope, D., Edinburgh Academy and Wadh., 1849i

Way, J. P., Somerset Coll., Bath, and BNC, 1874, '75

Wedderburn, A. H. M., Eton and Ball., 1912, '13

Wells, D. P., Stowe and Magd., 1955

Wells, H. B., Winchester and Magd., 1911–14

West, L. R., Eton and Ch.Ch., 1880, '81, '83

Westlake, R. G. A., Stowe and Ch.Ch., 1973

Wethered, F. O., Eton and Ch.Ch., 1885–87

Wharton, J. H. T. (RN Coll., Dartmouth), Magd. Coll. Sch. and Magd., 1879–81

Wheadon, R. A., Cranleigh and Ball., 1954

Whitechurch, W., Freiburg and Wadh., 1943 (W)

Whiting, N. E., Radley and Worc., 1927, '28

Whitworth-Jones, M. E., St Edward's Sch. and Trin., 1944 (W)

Wiggins, A. F. R., Eton and New C., 1912–14

Wiggins, A. J., Wallingford Sch. and Keble, 1976, '77, '79

Wilkinson, F., Trin. Coll., Melbourne, and BNC, 1891

Willan, F., Eton and Ex., 1866–69, '69 (*v.* Harvard)

Williams, J., Liverpool and Linc., 1874

Williams. S. G., Marlborough and CCC, 1887

Willis, C. A., Eton and Magd., 1903, president '04 but did not row

Willis, D. R. d'A., Radley and St Pet., 1971, '72

Wilmer, S. E., Yale Univ. and Ch.Ch., 1970

Wilson, F. M., Eton and Ch.Ch., 1844 (H), '44 (T), '45, '45 (H), '45 (T), '46 (H)

Wilson, J. M., St Edward's Sch. and Trin., 1953, '55

Wingfield, P., Radley and Keble, 1967 (I–G), '68 (I–G)

Winser, D. M. de R., Winchester and CCC, 1935–37

Winter, G. R., Eton and BNC, 1847 (H), '48 (H)

Wiseman, M. N., St Paul's and Ch.Ch., 1967 (I–G)

Wodehouse, J., Private and Ex., 1849ii

Wolfenden, J. K., Radley and St Ed. H., 1965 (I–G), '67 (I–G)

Wollaston, C. B., Ottery-St-Mary and Ex., 1841

Wood, J. W., Hampton and Pemb., 1978

Wood, S. R. C., Geelong GS and BNC, 1936

Wood, T., Louth GS and Pemb., 1865

Wood, W. H., Louth GS and Univ., 1857, '57 (H), '58

Wood, W. W., Eton and Univ., 1866, '67

Woodgate, W. B., Radley and BNC, 1862, '63

Woodhouse, S. H., Eton and Univ., 1869–71

Woodward, W. W., Shore Sch., NSW, and BNC, 1948, '48 (O)

Wordsworth, C., Harrow and Ch.Ch., 1829

Wormald, L. G., Eton and Magd., 1911–13

Wright, P. S. T., Hampton and Oriel, 1974 (I–G), '76 (I–G), '77

Wynne, O. S., Eton and Ch.Ch., 1862

Wynter, J. F., Worth and Ex., 1976 (I–G)

Yalouris, E., Harvard Univ. and Mert., 1972, '73

Yarborough, A. C., Eton and Linc., 1868, '69, '69 (*v.* Harvard)

Yonge, R. P., Univ. Coll. and Hosp. and New C., 1980 (I–G), '81, '82

Young, H. M., Westminster and Trin., 1938

Young, J. F., Harrow and CCC, 1860

Younger, J., Winchester and New C., 1901, '02

CAMBRIDGE

Abercrombie, J., Tonbridge and Caius, 1839

Addison, C. N. C., Roxburgh and Pemb., 1939

Adie, C. J. M., Fettes and 1 Trin., 1900

Adie, W. S., Lon. Int. Coll. and 1 Trin., 1895

Agar, C. T., Westminster and 3 Trin., 1893

Agnew, S., (Clapham GS), Edinburgh Univ. and 1 Trin., 1854

Alderson, F. C., Eton and 3 Trin., 1856

Aldous, N. M., St Joh., Leatherhead, and Selw., 1928

Allcard, R., Eton and 3 Trin., 1905

Allman-Ward, M. S., Oundle and Chr., 1946

Almond, H. H., Shrewsbury and LMBC, 1950, '51, '51 (*v.* Yale and Harvard)

Ambler, G. H., Shrewsbury and Clare, 1924–26

Anderson, W. H., Repton and 1 Trin., 1867–69

Arbuthnot, C. R. D., Eton and 1 & 3 Trin., 1976 (I–G), '77 (I–G)

Arbuthnot, R. W. M., Eton and 3 Trin., 1909–12

Archer, F. H., King's Sch., Canterbury, and CCC, 1862–65

Armstrong-Jones, A. C. R., Eton and Jesus, 1950

Armytage, C. N. L., Geelong GS and Jesus, 1880

Armytage, G. F., Geelong GS and Jesus, 1874

Arnold, F. M., Rugby and Caius, 1844 (T), '45, '45 (H)

Arthur, W. T., Witwatersrand, SA, and LMBC, 1950

Ashby, J. H., Harvard Univ. and 1 & 3 Trin., 1966

Ashton, M. H., Winchester and 1 & 3 Trin., 1971 (I–G)

Ashton, T. R., Monkton Combe and Chr., 1949

Askwith, T. G., Haileybury and Pet., 1932, '33

Askwith, W. M., Bedford and CCC, 1913

Atkin, P. W., Mill Hill and Jesus, 1881–83

Aylmer, J. A., Liverpool Coll. and 1 Trin., 1874, '75

Baart, L. W. J., Shrewsbury and Caius, 1979 (I–G), '80, '81

Bagshawe, W. L. G., Eton and 3 Trin., 1849i, '49ii

Bailey, J., Swanage and Jesus, 1978 (I–G), '80 (I–G)

Bailey, M. W., Beaumont and 1 & 3 Trin., 1945 (W)

Bailie, W. W., Private and Jesus, 1880

Baillieu, C. L., Radley and Jesus, 1970–73

Baines, A. D., Norwich Sch. and LMBC, 1978 (I–G)

Baker, G. H., Victoria Coll., Douglas, and Qu., 1886, '87

Baldry, A., Putney Coll. and 1 Trin., 1849ii

Balfour, R. A. L., Eton and 3 Trin., 1923

Barclay, C., Eton and 3 Trin., 1886, '87

Barclay, C. T., Eton and 3 Trin., 1887

Barker, T. W., Harrow and 1 Trin., 1878

Barnsley, M. J., Radley and Jesus, 1966 (I–G), '67 (I–G)

Bartlett, M. H., Radley and Pet., 1957

Barton, C. B. R., St Columba's, Dublin, and Jesus, 1948

Barton, W., Wellington, NZ, and LMBC, 1880

Bathurst, M. D., Merchant Taylors', Crosby, and Pemb., 1977, '78

Bayford, A. F., Kensington GS and Trin. H., 1829

Bayford, R. F., Eton and Trin. H., 1893

Baynes, H. G., Leighton Park and 1 Trin., 1906 (*v.* Harvard), '07

Baynes, M. G., Bryanston and Trin. H., 1954, '56

Beale, J. F., Harrow and 1 Trin., 1898

Beale, S. R., Marlborough and 1 Trin., 1903

Beckett, M. H., Bedford and Qu., 1963

Beebee, M. H. L., Rossall and LMBC, 1865

Beesly, R., Oundle and 1 Trin., 1927–29

Begg, F. C., Clifton and Trin. H., 1894, '95

Bell, A. S., Eton and Trin. H., 1895–98

Bell, C. B. P., Shrewsbury and Trin. H., 1888, '89

Bell, J. B., Geelong GS and Jesus, 1926, '27

Belousis, J. P., St Paul's and Qu., 1973 (I–G), '74 (I–G)

Benham, J. H. F., Fauconberge and Jesus, 1906, '06 (*v.* Harvard), '07

Benn, A., Cheltenham and Emm., 1857

Bennion, C. R., Radley and Fitz., 1970 (I–G), '71 (I–G)

Benson, C. W., Eton and 3 Trin., 1872, '73, '75

Bernstein, I., City of London Sch. and Emm., 1982

Bevan, L. V., Bedford and LMBC, 1926, '27

Bevan, M. V., Bedford and Dow., 1963, '64

Beveridge, J., St Paul's and Jesus, 1959–61

Bieber, W. A., Clifton and Trin. H., 1896, '97

Biker, A. D., Hastings and Trin. H., 1975 (I–G)

Billington, W. G., Loretto and Trin. H., 1940 (W)

Bircher, E. A. P., Radley and Chr., 1948–50

Bird, A. H. S., Haileybury and 1 Trin., 1879

Birdwood, J. G. B., Radley and Pemb., 1977 (I–G)

Biscoe, C. E., Tyndale *see* Tyndale Biscoe

Blake, H., Norwich and CCC, 1853 (H), '54, '55 (H)

Blake, J. S., Marlborough and CCC, 1860, '61

Bland, H. M., Eton and 3 Trin., 1894

Bliss, N. J., Barnard Castle and CCC, 1981 (I–G), '82

Bonsey, R. Y., Forest Sch. and LMBC, 1895, '96

Booth, G., Rugby and 1 Trin., 1849i, '49ii

Boret, H. O. C., Eton and 3 Trin., 1919 (P), '19 (AP), '20, '21

Born, J. R., Yale Univ. and 1 & 3 Trin., 1968 (I–G), '69 (I–G)

Borthwick, G., Uppingham and 1 Trin., 1864, '65

Bourke, J. U., St Columba's, Dublin, and 1 Trin., 1866, '67

Bowman, M. E., King James's Coll. and Churchill, 1982 (I–G)

Boyle, R. F. R. P., Bradfield and Trin. H., 1907, '08, '09 (O)

Braddon, J. V., Shrewsbury and Trin. H., 1891, '92

Bradley, M., Monkton Combe and Pemb., 1937

Bradley, N. C. A., Shrewsbury and Pemb., 1974, '75

Bradley, N. J., Monkton Combe and Pemb., 1934, president '35 but did not row

Bramwell, A., Rugby and 1 Trin., 1853 (H)

Brancker, P. W., Radley and Jesus, 1876

Brandt, H., Rugby and 1 Trin., 1851 (H), '52

Branson, G. A. H., Bedford and 1 Trin., 1893

Breare, R. R. A., Eton and Pemb., 1973 (I–G), '76

Brett, W. B., (Viscount Esher), Westminster and Caius, 1837 (L), '38 (L), '39

Brine, P. St J., St Edward's and LMBC, 1980 (I–G), '82

Bristow, T. R. M., Dulwich and Pemb., 1935

Bristowe, C. J., Repton and Trin. H., 1886, '87

Brocklebank, T. A., Eton and 3 Trin., 1929–31

Brooke, B. W. D., Winchester and 1 Trin., 1900, '01

Brookes, T. W., Private and 1 Trin., 1844 (T)

Brooksbank, E. C., Eton and Trin. H., 1881

Brooksby, I. A. B., Radley and LMBC, 1965 (I–G), '66

Brown, G. H., Shrewsbury and Trin. H., 1959, '60

Brown, H. G., Harrow and 1 Trin., 1898

Brown, J. A., Clifton and Caius, 1924–27

Bruce, J. N., St Paul's and Clare, 1954

Bruce, S. M., CEGS, Melbourne, and Trin. H., 1904

Buchanan, J. G., Private and 1 Trin., 1862

Buckle, C. K., Eastbourne and Magd., 1934

Buckmaster, A. C., Charterhouse and Clare, 1969 (I–G), '70

Budd, H. B., Yale Univ. and 1 & 3 Trin., 1962

Budd, R. H., Rugby and LMBC, 1837 (L)

Burch, A. J., Hathershaw and Qu., 1970 (I–G)

Burn, J. S., Harrow and 1 Trin., 1907, '08, '08 (O)

Burnand, C. F., Downside and 1 Trin., 1911

Burnet, N. G., Bedford and Clare, 1976 (I–G), '77

Burnford, D. W., St Paul's and Jesus, 1936

Burnham, A. B., Cornell Univ. and St Cath., 1965 (I–G)

Burrough, A., St Paul's and Jesus, 1937–39

Butcher, A. S. F., City of Lon. Sch. and Qu., 1947

Buxton, C. E. V., Eton and 3 Trin., 1913, '14, '19 (P), '19 (AP)

Buxton, M., Eton and 3 Trin., 1939

Buxton, M. V., Eton and 3 Trin., 1919 (P), '19 (AP)

Byrom, J. K., Denstone and Selw., 1943 (W)

Cadbury, G. A. H., Eton and King's, 1952

Cadwalader, G. A., Pennsylvania Univ. and LMBC, 1972

Calder, D. W. G., St Paul's and St Cath., 1961

Calvert, N. L., Geelong GS and Trin. H., 1899

Cameron, A., Dundee and Pemb., 1943 (W)

Campbell, A., Barrow GS and Selw., 1938

Campbell, J. A., Melbourne CEGS and Jesus, 1919 (P), '19 (AP), '20, '21

Campbell-Muir, D. E., Blairlodge and Trin. H., 1897

Candy, C. H., Cheltenham and Caius, 1873, '76

Capener, J. N., Sherborne and Trin. H., 1944 (W)

Carbonell, W. L. R., Shrewsbury and St Cath., 1953

Carpmael, P. N., Oundle and Jesus, 1930, '31

Carter, J. S., Eton and King's, 1903

Carter, M. W. J., Rossall and Pemb., 1965

Carter, S. W., Blundells and Emm., 1981 (I–G)

Carver, H. R., Eton and 3 Trin., 1925

Carver, O. A., Charterhouse and 1 Trin., 1908, '08 (O)

Carver, R. D., Eton and 1 & 3 Trin., 1958

Cashin, R. M., Harvard Univ. and 1 & 3 Trin., 1976

Challis, C. D. C., St Paul's and Selw., 1966 (I–G), '67

Chambers, J. G., Eton and 3 Trin., 1862, '63, president '65 but did not row

Champion, A., Northampton and Selw., 1940 (W)

Chapman, W. H., Eton and 3 Trin., 1899, '02, '03

Chaytor, H. J., Durham and Jesus, 1859, '59 (H), '60, '61

Cherry, B. N., Eton, Durham and Clare, 1860

Chewton, Viscount, Eton and 1 & 3 Trin., 1962, '63

Christian, M. W., Harvard Univ. and 1 & 3 Trin., 1961

Christie, A. N., The Leys and LMBC, 1973 (I–G), '75

Christie, D. C., Eton and Pemb., 1958, '59

Church, R. C. W., King's Sch., Canterbury, and 1 & 3 Trin., 1968

Church, W. E., Eton and 1 & 3 Trin., 1965

Churchill, F. E., Eton and 3 Trin., 1883–85

Clack, N. B. M., Wycliffe and LMBC, 1952

Clark, C. S., Bedford and Pemb., 1913, '14

Clark, M. J. S., Shrewsbury and Dow., 1980 (I–G), '81

Clarke, B. S., Giggleswick and LMBC, 1880

Clarke, R. J. S., Emanuel and St Cath., 1972

Clay, J. H., Eton and Pemb., 1974–76

Clayes, Q. Des., Radley and Clare, 1945 (W)

Clayre, I. F. C. S., Dean Close and Qu., 1957

Clegg, S. J., Shrewsbury and St Cath., 1977, '78, '79

Clissold, S. T., Eton and 3 Trin., 1846

Close, James, B., Wellington and 1 Trin., 1872–74

Close, John, B., Private and 1 Trin., 1871, '72

Close, W. B., Wellington and 1 Trin., 1875–77

Close-Brooks, A. B., Winchester and 1 Trin., 1906 (*v.* Harvard), '07

Cloves, W. P., Private and 1 Trin., 1844 (T), '45, '45 (H), '46

Cobbold, R. H., Shrewsbury and Pet., 1841, '42, '42 (H)

Cochrane, G. D., Eton and 3 Trin., 1906

Cochrane, H. B., Radley and Qu., 1944 (W)

Cockerell, S. P., Eton and 3 Trin., 1900

Coghill, E. J. N. T., Gordonstoun and Pemb., 1952

Coke, R. H., Westminster and Trin. H., 1885

Collard, J. M., Private and LMBC, 1867

Collet, T. D. A., Oundle and Pemb., 1922–24

Collier, A. J., Univ. Coll. Sch. and LMBC, 1961, '62

Collings, H. H., Eton and 3 Trin., 1859 (H), '61, '62

Collins, D. C., Wellington NZ and 1 Trin., 1912

Collins, J. B., Eton and 3 Trin., 1928–30

Collinson, S. P., Forest Sch. and Trin H., 1980 (I–G)

Collis, A. T. G., Shrewsbury and LMBC, 1965 (I–G)

Compston, G. D., Dulwich and Trin. H., 1909

Conze, P. H., Yale Univ. and 1 & 3 Trin., 1966

Cooke, A. V., King's Sch., Chester, and Jesus, 1963

Cooke, C. P., Geelong GS and Trin. H., 1910

Cooke-Yarborough, A. E., Eton and Caius, 1977, '78

Copeland, F. W. R., Radley and Clare, 1945 (W)

Corrie, J. R. la T., Winchester and 1 & 3 Trin., 1949

Coulton, B. T., Dulwich and Jesus, 1938

Courage, E., Harrow and 1 Trin., 1853 (H), '54

Coventry, M., King's Coll., London, and Trin. H., 1860, '61

Cowderoy, J. A. F., King's Sch., Canterbury, and Jesus, 1981 (I–G)

Cowie, H., King's Coll., Lon., and 1 Trin., 1851 (H)

Cowie, M. P., Cheltenham GS and Fitz., 1981

Cox, B. C., Harrow and Trin. H., 1901

Craggs, R. B. T., Shrewsbury and LMBC, 1926

Craig, K. N., Cheltenham and Pemb., 1922, '23

Cree, T. S., Geelong GS and Jesus, 1936, '37

Creed, F. H., Kingswood and Dow., 1968 (I–G)

Crick, J. L. M., Marlborough and LMBC, 1950

Croker, J. M., Private and Caius, 1841

Croker, W. R., Private and Caius, 1841

Cross, P. W., Cheadle Hulme and Dow., 1979

Crosse, C. H., Rugby and Caius, 1851 (H), '52

Crowden, J. G. P., Bedford and Pemb., 1951, '51 (*v* Yale and Harvard), '52

Cruttenden, D. L., The Leys and St Cath., 1969, '70

Cunningham, F. E., Eton and King's, 1867

Cutler, J. P., Tiffin and Sid. S., 1975 (I–G)

Dale, J. W., Tonbridge and LMBC, 1869, '70

Dalley, C. J., Winchester and Qu., 1968 (I–G), '69 (I–G), '70

Dalrymple, A. D., Eton and Dow., 1979 (I–G), '80, '81

Dannreuther, P. H., Radley and Pemb., 1972 (I–G)

Darroch, D., Harrow and 1 Trin., 1858, '58 (H), '59

Davey, C. J. T., Eton and Jesus, 1962, '64

Davies, C. M., Bryanston and Clare, 1954

Davies, J. M., Berkhamsted and Jesus, 1980 (I–G), '81 (I–G)

Davies, P. B., Tonbridge and 1 & 3 Trin., 1976

Davies, R., Hymer's Coll., Hull, and St Cath., 1910

Davies, R. N. E., Shrewsbury and St Cath., 1977 (I–G), '78, '79

Davies-Cooke, R. A., Eton and 3 Trin., 1929

Davis, G. L., St Peter's, York, and Clare, 1875–79

Davis, J. C., Eton and 3 Trin., 1854

Davis, R. D., Private and 1 Trin., 1879, '80

Dawkins, W. M. R., Westminster and 1 & 3 Trin., 1976 (I–G), '77 (I–G), '78

Daws, C. W., Winchester and 1 & 3 Trin., 1968 (I–G), '69

Day, D. I., Repton and LMBC, 1914

De Giles, P. A., Wellington and Qu., 1948

Delafield, P. G. R., St Edward's, and Jesus, 1966–68

Delahooke, M. G., Univ. Coll. Sch. and Jesus, 1956, '57

Denby, A. T., Radley and Magd., 1958

Denman, Hon. G., Repton and 1 Trin., 1841, '42, '42 (H)

Denman, Hon. L. W., Bt, Shrewsbury and Magd., 1841, '42, '42 (H)

Denny, J. P. M., Downside and Jesus, 1956

De Rancourt, F. G. G., Eton and 1 & 3 Trin., 1963

De Rutzen, A., Eton and 3 Trin., 1849i, '49ii

Dicker, G. C., Winchester and 1 Trin., 1875

Dingle, J. R., Chr. Hosp. and LMBC, 1952

Dixon, A. F. W., Monkton Combe and Chr., 1919 (P), '19 (AP), '20

Donaldson, M., Charterhouse and 1 Trin., 1906, '06 (*v.* Harvard)

Douglas, I. K. H., St Paul's and LMBC, 1943 (W)

Drake, J. A. C., Eton and Pemb., 1972 (I–G)

Drysdale, T., St Paul's and Jesus, 1902

Du Bois, P. M., Harvard Univ. and Emm., 1955

Duckworth, J. N., Lincoln and Jesus, 1934–36

Dudley Ward, W., Eton and 3 Trin., 1897, president '98 but did not row, '99, 1900

Duffield, A. S., Rugby and Trin. H., 1890

Duncan, R. P. B., Shrewsbury and St Cath., 1972 (I–G), '73, '74

Duncanson, E. F., Harrow and Emm., 1901

Duncanson, T. J. G., Harrow and Emm., 1895, '96

Eadie, D. S. M., Oundle and 1 Trin., 1938

Earl, D. F., Norwich and LMBC, 1966 (I–G), '67

Eddy, B. M., Carlisle GS and Pemb., 1953

Edgerley, W. T., Westminster and Pemb., 1977 (I–G)

Edwards-Moss, J., Eton and 3 Trin., 1902, '03

Egan, T. S., Rottingdean and Caius, 1836, '39, '40, '42 (H), '44 (T)

Eley, C. R. M., Eton and 3 Trin., 1924

Elgood, A. B., Bradfield and Pemb., 1974 (I–G)

Elin, G., Eton and 3 Trin., 1890–92

Elles, R. J., Marlborough and Trin. H., 1927, '29

Elliot-Smith, G. L., St Peter's, York, and LMBC, 1924, '25

Entwisle, T., Rugby and Trin., 1829

Escombe, E. J., Clifton and Trin. H., 1902

Estcourt, A. S., Marlborough and Trin. H., 1874

Etherington-Smith, R. B., Repton and 1 Trin., 1898–1900

Eyre, G. H., St Peter's, York, and CCC, 1884

Fairbairn, A. H., Rugby and 2 Trin., 1858, '58 (H), '60

Fairbairn, C., Geelong GS and Jesus, 1879

Fairbairn, G. E., Eton and Jesus, 1908, '11

Fairbairn, S., Geelong GS and Jesus, 1882, '83, '86, '87

Fairrh, E. H., Clapton GS and Trin. H., 1855 (H), '56

Fassnidge, N. W., Qu. Eliz. Sch., Crediton, and Pemb., 1969 (I–G), '70 (I–G)

Fell, J. A., Winchester and Pemb., 1965

Fellowes, J. C., Mannamead and 1 Trin., 1882

Fenn, J. C., Cheltenham and 1 Trin., 1877

Fernie, W. J., Malvern and Trin. H., 1896, '97

Finch, A. H., Eton and 3 Trin., 1894

Fischer, P. F., Beconsfield, Denmark and 1 & 3 Trin., 1943 (W)

Fisher, G. A., Winchester and Jesus, 1913

Fisher, G. H. C., Kingswood and 1 & 3 Trin., 1946, '47

Fisher, S. C., Clifton and Trin. H., 1970 (I–G), '71 (I–G)

Fison, E. T., Repton and CCC, 1880–92

Fitzgerald, R. U. P., Westminster and Trin. H., 1861, '62

Fleming, I. P., Merchant Taylors' and LMBC, 1975 (I–G)

Fletcher, C. M., Eton and 3 Trin., 1933

Fletcher, R., Sedbergh and LMBC, 1837 (L)

Flower, A. D., Bedford Mod. and Clare, 1886

Fogg-Elliot, C. T., Durham and Trin. H., 1891–94

Follett, J. S., Eton and 3 Trin., 1871

Foord, H. B., Rugby and 1 Trin., 1852

Forbes, A., Sedbergh and LMBC, 1866, '67

Formby, R., Repton and 1 Trin., 1851 (H)

Forster, G. B., St Peter's, York, and LMBC, 1853 (H)

Fortescue, H. J., Eton and Magd., 1866

Fox, F. W., Grove House Sch. and 1 Trin., 1883

Frame-Thomson, T., Eton and 3 Trin., 1933

Francklyn, B., Eton and 3 Trin., 1890–92

Fraser, J. W., Radley and Jesus, 1964, '65

Fraser, R. J., Radley and Jesus, 1961

Fremantle, Hon. J. W. H., Eton and 3 Trin., 1921, '22

Freshfield, E., Winchester and 1 Trin., 1853 (H)

Frisco, G. J., Dartmouth Coll., USA, and Pemb., 1982 (I–G)

Galton, R. C., Rugby and 1 Trin., 1854

Game, H. A., Harrow and 1 Trin., 1895, '96

Gardiner, M. I. M., St Paul's and Selw., 1968 (I–G)

Gardner, J. C., Rugby and Emm., 1888–90

Garfit, A., Private and 1 Trin., 1847 (H)

Garner, P. J., Bedford and King's, 1947

Garnett, K. G., St Paul's and 1 Trin., 1914

Garrod, D. C. H., Bootham and Trin. H., 1945 (W)

Garson, J. H., Malvern and Clare, 1944 (W)

Gaskell, T. K., Westminster and 3 Trin., 1861

Gibbon, J. H., Eton and 3 Trin., 1899, 1900

Giles, J. R., Winchester and Emm., 1958, '59

Gill, C. J., Oundle and Fitz., 1967 (I–G), '68

Gillies, H. D., Wanganui, NZ, and Caius, 1904

Gilmour, J. E., Eton and Trin. H., 1933

Gisbourne, T. M., Private and LMBC, 1847 (H)

Gleave, J. M. N., Uppingham and Dow., 1980 (I–G)

Gobbett, J. E.,St Paul's and St Cath., 1961

Goddard, G. E. G., Imp. Ser. Coll. and Jesus, 1924, '25

Goldie, C. J. D., Eton and 3 Trin., 1898, '99

Goldie, J. H. D., Eton and LMBC, 1869–72

Goldsmith, H. M., Sherborne and Jesus, 1906, '06 (*v.* Harvard), '07, '08 (O)

Goldsmith, J. H., Rossall and Jesus, 1912

Gordon, H. E., Twickenham and 1 Trin., 1869–71

Gordon, Hon. J. H., St Andrews Univ. and 1 Trin., 1867

Gorst, P. F., Brighton and LMBC, 1862

Gosse, J. G., St Peter's, Adelaide, and Trin. H., 1946

Gough, Sch. not recorded, 1 Trin., 1838 (L)

Graham, F. C., Private and 1 Trin., 1855 (H)

Graham, M. E. K., Wycliffe and LMBC, 1966

Granville, A. K. B., St Paul's and CCC, 1836, '37 (L)

Gray, A. H., Shrewsbury and Pemb., 1978 (I–G), '79

Gray, G., Bolton and Qu., 1931

Green, F. S., Shrewsbury and Caius, 1836, '37 (L)

Gridley, R. C. M. G., Eton and 3 Trin., 1881, '83, '84

Griffiths, W. R., Eton and 3 Trin., 1865–67

Gritten, M. R., RMA Sandhurst and Qu., 1976

Grylls, H. B., Rugby and 1 Trin., 1901–03

Guise, L. J., King Edward VI Sch., Stratford, and Magd., 1982 (I–G)

Gurdon, C., Haileybury and Jesus, 1876–79

Hadfield, D., Eton and King's, 1943 (W)

Haig, E. W., Eton and 3 Trin., 1884, '85

Haig, Thomas, P. *see* Thomas

Haig-Thomas, D., Eton and LMBC, 1930–32

Hale, J. R., Yale Univ. and 1 & 3 Trin., 1975 (I–G), '76 (I–G)

Hall, G. F., Tiffin and Dow., 1967 (I–G), '68, '69

Hall, J., Eton and Magd., 1858, '58 (H), '59, '59 (H), '60, '61

Hall, P. D., Berkhamsted and CCC, 1953

Hall-Craggs, J. F., Shrewsbury and LMBC, 1956

Hamilton-Russell, E. C., Eton and 3 Trin., 1926

Hannen, L., Radley and Trin. H., 1888, '89

Hardacre, W. K., Eton and Trin. H., 1885

Harkness, R., Eton and LMBC, 1845, '46, '47 (H)

Harkness, W., Eton and LMBC, 1845, '45 (H)

Harpum, R., RMA Sandhurst and Jesus, 1976

Harris, G. T., High Wycombe RGS and Jesus, 1955

Harris, M. J., Lymm. GS, and Emm., 1973 (I–G)

Harris, S. A., Desborough and Qu., 1982

Harrison, A. B. C., Geelong GS and 1 & 3 Trin., 1948

Hart, J. A., Hampton and Fitz., 1972

Hart, M. J., Hampton and Pet., 1971 (I–G), '72, '73

Hartley, P., Charterhouse and Trin. H., 1836

Hartley, P. H. G. H.-S., Eton and LMBC, 1919 (P), '19 (AP), '20–22

Havart, W. J., Rugby and LMBC, 1858, '58 (H)

Hawkins, E. C., Charterhouse and Caius, 1897, '98

Hawkins, W. W., St Peter's, York, and LMBC, 1864

Hawkshaw, J. C., Westminster and 3 Trin., 1863, '64

Hawley, E., Oakham and Sid. S., 1852, '53 (H)

Hawthorne, E. D., Westminster and 3 Trin., 1940 (W)

Heap, S. H., Eton and Jesus, 1923

Heard, C. D., Shrewsbury and LMBC, 1982

Heath, B. R., Eton and 1 Trin., 1829

Heathcote, S., Bath Coll. and 1 Trin., 1859 (H), '60

Hellyer, F. E., Winchester and 1 Trin., 1910, '11

Henderson, G., Radley and Dow., 1977 (I–G), '78, '79

Henderson, L. M., St Edward's and Selw., 1966, '67

Herbert, J. S., Eton and King's, 1924, '25

Hervey-Bathurst, J. F. S., Eton and 1 & 3 Trin., 1969 (I–G), '70, '71

Heyland, H. M., Wellington and Pemb., 1912

Heywood, B. C., Eton and 1 & 3 Trin., 1945 (W)

Heywood-Lonsdale, T. C., Eton and 1 & 3 Trin., 1959

Hibbert, P. J., Shrewsbury and LMBC, 1874, '75

Hill, C. G., Sherborne and 2 Trin., 1845, '45 (H), '46

Hill, D. K., Shrewsbury and Jesus, 1954, '55

Hinde, J. F. K., Malvern and Pemb., 1951, '51 (*v.* Yale and Harvard), '52

Hockin, T. E., Radley and Jesus, 1876–79

Hodgkin, A. J., Leighton Park and 1 Trin., 1922

Hodgson, W. C., Rugby and 1 Trin., 1849i, '49ii

Hoffman, M., Harvard Univ. and 1 & 3 Trin., 1961

Holcroft, J. C., Radley and Pemb., 1927, '28

Holden, C. J., Eton and 3 Trin., 1849i, '49ii, '51 (H)

Holdsworth, A. B. E., Charterhouse and 1 Trin., 1829

Holley, G. E. W., Michaelhouse, SA, and LMBC, 1940 (W)

Holley, H. H., Norwich GS and Trin. H., 1859 (H)

Holley, W. H., Private and Trin. H., 1857

Holme, A. P., Grange Sch., Sunderland, and 2 Trin., 1857

Holmes, P. W., Portora Royal Sch. and LMBC, 1960

Holroyd, G. F., Winchester and 1 Trin., 1846

Hope, T. B., Eton and Trin. H., 1895, '96

Hopkins, F. L., Uppingham and 1 Trin., 1845 (H)

Horner, J. N., St Paul's and Emm., 1972 (I–G)

Hornidge, E. S., Sherborne and Trin. H., 1909

Hornsby, N. J., Tonbridge and Trin. H., 1967–69

Horton, C. M., Eton and Dow., 1976 (I–G), '77, '78

Hoskyns, B. G., Haileybury and Jesus, 1877

Hoskyns, E., Haileybury and Jesus, 1873

Howell, B. H., Military Coll., USA, and Trin. H., 1897

Hughes, N. G., Winchester and Qu., 1970–72

Humphries, M. A. C., Eton and Dow., 1982 (I–G)

Hunt, A. G. L., Ipswich and LMBC, 1906

Hunt, P. L., Highgate and Cavendish, 1882, '83

Hunter, T. H., Harvard Univ. and Trin. H., 1937, '38

Hutchinson, A. M., Durham and Jesus, 1881, '82

Ingham, J. P., Westminster and 3 Trin., 1859 (H)

Inglis, D., Edinburgh Academy and 1 Trin., 1860

Ivory, B. G., Bedales and Pemb., 1922, '23

Jackson, B. J. R., Witwatersrand Univ., SA, and Clare, 1963

Jackson, F. C., Aldenham and LMBC, 1847 (H)

Jacobs, H. R., Winchester and Pemb., 1972 (I–G), '73, '74

James, N. W., Latymer Upper Sch. and Jesus, 1971, '72

Jamieson, E. A. O. A., Glenalmond and 1 Trin., 1901

Jelfs, A. N. de M., John Mason Sch., Abingdon, and Fitz., 1978, '79

Jenkins, N. S., Shrewsbury and LMBC, 1981 (I–G)

Jennens, D. M., Oundle and Clare, 1949–51, '51 (*v.* Yale and Harvard)

Jerwood, F. H., Oakham and Jesus, 1908, '08 (O)

Johnson, F. W., Eton and 3 Trin., 1851 (H), '52

Johnson, H. F., Eton and 3 Trin., 1854, '55 (H)

Johnson, M. W., Cheadle Hulme and Clare, 1978 (I–G)

Johnstone, B. C., Eton and 3 Trin., 1904–6, '06 (*v.* Harvard), '07

Johnstone, E. T. C., Shrewsbury and LMBC, 1960

Johnstone, R. T., Eton and Chr., 1919 (P), '19 (AP), '20

Jones, H. C., Shrewsbury and Magd., 1840

Jones, J. S. M., Shrewsbury and LMBC, 1952, '53

Jones, Ll. R., Durham and Jones, 1878, '82

Jones, W. J. H., Bedford and 2 Trin., 1849i

Jones, W. M., Westminster and Caius, 1836

Jones, H. R. Mansel-, Eton and 3 Trin., 1855 (H), '56

Keane, J. H., Rugby and 1 Trin., 1836, '37 (L)

Keen, M. F. A., Haileybury and LMBC, 1926

Keppel, G., Princeton Univ. and Trin. H., 1938

Kerr, G. C., Durham and 1 Trin., 1892, '93

Kerrison, R. O., Eton and 3 Trin., 1893, '94

Kerruish, S. G. I., Eton and Fitz., 1970 (I–G), '71 (I–G), '72

Kiely, J. R., Amherst, USA, and 1 & 3 Trin., 1964

King, J. M., Derby and LMBC, 1953

Kinglake, R. A., Eton and 3 Trin., 1863–66

King-Salter, J. P., Private and Trin. H., 1856

Kingsford, A. D., Uppingham and Pemb., 1934, '35

Kingsford, D. G., Uppingham and Pemb., 1935, '36

Kinsella, J. D., Bedford Modern and St Cath., 1982 (I–G)

Kitchin, D. J. T., Oundle and Fitz., 1975

Kitching, H. E., Uppingham and Trin. H., 1908, '08 (O), '09

Knight, A. R., Hampton and Clare, 1982

Lambert, E., Cheltenham and Pemb., 1881, '82

La Mothe, C. H., King William Coll. and LMBC, 1863

Landale, P., Hawthorne GS and Trin. H., 1887–89

Landale, W., Harrow and Trin. H., 1891, '92

Lang, I. M., Monkton Combe and Caius, 1947

Langridge, C., Sir Wm Borlase's and 1 & 3 Trin., 1973 (I–G), '74 (I–G), '75

Langton, T. B., Radley and Jesus, 1937, '38

Lapage, M. C., Monkton Combe and Selw., 1948

Laurie, A. W., Monkton Combe and Selw., 1940 (W)

Laurie, C. A., Eton and Selw., 1974 (I–G)

Laurie, J. H. C., Eton and Selw., 1980

Laurie, W. G. R. M., Monkton Combe and Selw., 1934–36

Law, F. W., St Paul's and LMBC, 1923

Lawes, C. B., Eton and 3 Trin., 1865

Lawes, W. R., Tonbridge and Pemb., 1966 (I–G), '67

Lawrence, A. L., Rugby and 1 Trin., 1904

Leadley, D. A. T., Bedford Modern and Emm., 1953

Lea-Wilson, K. L., Monkton Combe and Clare, 1940 (W)

Le Blanc-Smith, C. R., Eton and 3 Trin., 1910–12, president '13 but did not row

Lecky, J. M. S., Brit. Col. Univ. and Jesus, 1962, '64

Lecky-Browne, W. C., Radley and Jesus, 1873, '74

Legget, D. F., Radley and Trin. H., 1963, '64

Leggett, G. C. M., Portora Royal Sch. and St Cath., 1967, '68

Leng-Smith, C. C., The Leys and LMBC, 1976 (I–G)

Letchworth, T. E., Downside and Chr., 1927, '28

Lever, J. D., Westminster and 1 & 3 Trin., 1971 (I–G), '72 (I–G), '73

Lewis, G. M., Malvern and Pemb., 1936

Lewis, T. G. E., Eton and 3 Trin., 1893, '94

Lewis, T. W., King's Coll., Lon., and Caius, 1876, '77

Lewis-Lloyd, R., Eton and 3 Trin., and Magd., 1856–58, '58 (H), '59, '59 (H)

Lindsay, K. T., Liverpool Coll. and Jesus, 1948

Livingstone, P. C., Vancouver (also recorded as Private) and Jesus, 1914

Lloyd, C. B. M., Shore School, NSW, and LMBC, 1949–51, '51 (*v.* Yale and Harvard)

Lloyd, G. A., Eton and 3 Trin., 1899, 1900

Lloyd, L. S., Eton and 3 Trin., 1912

Lloyd, T. B., Shrewsbury and LMBC, 1846

Lockhart, W. S., King's Coll., Lon., and Chr., 1845, '45 (H)

Lomax, H. J., (Repton) (Harrow), Marlborough and 1 Trin., 1871

Longmore, W. S., Blundell's and Sid. S., 1851 (H), '52

Lonnon, M. P., Westminster and 3 Trin., 1935–37

Lord, E. W., Brisbane GS and Trin. H., 1891, '92

Lowe, C. M., Shrewsbury and Fitz., 1969 (I–G), '70

Lowe, W. H., Durham and Chr., 1868, '70, '71

Lubbock, H. H., Private and Caius, 1858

Ludford, G. S. S., Latymer Upper Sch. and Jesus, 1949

Luxton, L., Melbourne GS and Pemb., 1932

Maasland, J. H., St Kentigern, NZ, and Qu., 1963

McCagg, L. B., Harvard Univ. and Emm., 1953

M'Cormick, J., Liverpool and LMBC, 1856

McCowen, D. H. E., Cheltenham and Pemb., 1932

Macdonnell, P. L. P., U. Canada Coll. and Trin. H., 1946

McEwen, R. I. L., Eton and 3 Trin., 1920

McGarel Groves, H. M. J., Eton and 1 & 3 Trin., 1973 (I–G), '74 (I–G)

McKenna, R., King's Coll., Lon., and Trin. H., 1887

Macklin, D. D., Felstead and LMBC, 1951, '51 (*v.* Yale and Harvard)

Maclay, Hon. J. S., Winchester and 1 Trin., 1927

MacLellan, G. D. S., Rugby and Pemb., 1944 (W)

Macleod, A. L., Shrewsbury and LMBC, 1949, '50

Macleod, J., Bradford GS and LMBC, 1973 (I–G), '75

MacMichael, W. F., Ripon and Dow., 1868, '69

Macmillan, J. R. A., Eton and 1 & 3 Trin., 1953

Macnabb, J. A., Eton and 3 Trin., 1924

Macnaghten, E., Trin Coll., Dublin, and 1 Trin., 1852, '53 (H)

Maitland, G. M., Marlborough and 1 Trin., 1901

Major, P. G., RGS, Worc., and Fitz., 1966 (I–G), '67 (I–G)

Maltby, M. B., Bedford and Pemb., 1958, '59

Mann, G., Private and Caius, 1844 (T), '45, '45 (H)

Mansel-Jones, H. R., *see* Jones, H. R. M.

Manser, J. P., Westminster and Sid. S., 1976, '77

Marland, J. H., Radley and 1 & 3 Trin., 1972 (I–G)

Marshall, G. T., Bryanston and King's, 1952, '53

Marshall, M. J., Eton and Jesus, 1954

Mason, H. W., Clifton and Trin. H., 1936, '37

Masser, K. A., Shrewsbury and Trin. H., 1954–56

Massey, P. M. O., Oundle and LMBC, 1949, '50

Massey, W., Harrow and 1 Trin., 1840

Maugham, F. H., Dover and Trin. H., 1888, '89

Maule, W., Winchester and 1 Trin., 1847 (H)

Maxwell, D. L., Eton and Jesus, 1971, '72

Mays-Smith, A. A. M., Eton and 1 & 3 Trin., 1955, '56

Meadows, J. R., Yale and Jesus, 1957

Mellows, A. P., Monkton Combe and Clare, 1947, '48

Merivale, C., Harrow and LMBC, 1829

Meyrick, D. J. C., Eton and Trin. H., 1947, '48

Meyrick, F. C., Eton and Trin. H., 1883

Michell, R. G., Shrewsbury and Caius, 1928

Michell, W. G., Wellington and 1 Trin., 1875

Miller, H. J., Eton and 3 Trin., 1849ii

Milton, R. C., Harvard Univ. and Emm., 1957

Monks, R. A. G., Harvard Univ. and 1 & 3 Trin., 1955

Moore, C. W., Durham and Chr., 1881–84

Moore, D. P., Geelong GS and St Cath., 1965

Morland, J. T., Harrow and 1 Trin., 1858 (H), '59, '59 (H), '60

Morgan, R. H., Llandovery and Emm., 1863

Morris, P. E., Eton and Magd., 1980 (I–G), '82 (I–G)

Morrison, R. E., Eton and 3 Trin., 1923

Moulsdale, J. M., Shrewsbury and St Cath., 1977 (I–G)

Muirhead, A. R., Glenalmond and LMBC, 1955

Muir-Smith, M., Sir Wm Borlase's and Chr., 1964

Munding, R. H., Shrewsbury and St Cath., 1972 (I–G)

Munster, H., King's Coll., Lon., and 1 Trin., 1845, '45 (H)

Murdoch, G. F., Eton and LMBC, 1846, '47 (H)

Murtough, C. B., St Geo., Weybridge, and Fitz., 1968 (I–G), '69

Murray, D. W., Winchester and LMBC, 1979 (I–G)

Muttlebury, S. D., Eton and 3 Trin., 1886–90

Nadin, H. T., Leicester and Pemb., 1868

Nairne, S., Clapton GS and Emm., 1854

Napier, D. M. W., Eton and Magd., 1937

Napier, R. A., Winchester and LMBC, 1962

Neame, J. H., Lincoln HS, Portland, Oregon, and Trin. H., 1946

Neil, R. G., Greenock Coll. and Jesus, 1892

Nelson, R. H., Eton and 3 Trin., 1901–03

Nichols, J. P., Westminster and 3 Trin., 1868

Nicholson, C. A., Private and 1 Trin., 1847 (H)

Nicholson, M. A., Eton and King's, president 1947 but did not row

Nicholson, R. G., Shrewsbury and St Cath., 1961, '62

Nicholson, W. N., Charterhouse and 1 Trin., 1837 (L), '44 (T)

Nightingale, M. J. H., Tonbridge and Trin. H., 1956

Nissen, P. C. M., Eton and 1 & 3 Trin., 1945 (W)

Noble, J. W., Haileybury and Caius, 1891

Norman, T. P. A., Eton and 1 & 3 Trin., 1957

Norman-Butler, E. N., Eton and 3 Trin., 1929

Norris, W. A., Eton and 3 Trin., 1852

Northmore, T. W., Rossall and Qu., 1889, '90

Odhams, D. V. Lynch, Westminster and Jesus, 1949

Oldham, G. D. R., Eton and 1 & 3 Trin., 1971 (I–G)

Ollivant, L. A. E., Charterhouse and 1 Trin., 1893, '94

Orde, R. H. P., Richmond, Yorks, and 1 Trin., 1888, '89

Orford, J. R., Shrewsbury and King's, 1887

Overton, D. P., Bryanston and Pemb., 1970 (I–G)

Owen, J. R., Bedford and LMBC, 1959, '60

Page, A. S., Rossall and LMBC, 1851 (H)

Paget-Tomlinson, T. R., Aldenham and Trin. H., 1896

Paine, N. W., Eton and 3 Trin., 1894

Paley, G. A., Clapham GS and LMBC, 1858 (H), '59

Palmer, J. S., Eton and Pemb., 1979, '80, '81

Panter, M. F., Kingston GS and LMBC, 1979 (I–G), '80, '81

Paris, A., Cheam and CCC, 1838 (L), '39

Parker, G., Radley and 1 Trin., 1901

Parker, H., Tabor Academy and Trin. H., 1939

Parker, J., Shrewsbury and LMBC, 1960

Paton-Philip, J. S., Perse and LMBC, 1945 (W), '46

Payne, J. E., New Coll., Eastbourne, and Pet., 1899, 1900

Payne, K. M., Eton and 3 Trin., 1932, '34

Peabody, J. E., Private and 1 Trin., 1873

Peake, H., Eton and 3 Trin., 1919 (P), '19 (AP)

Pearson, A. D. B., Winchester and 1 Trin., 1921, '22

Pearson, E. M. G., King's Sch., Canterbury, and Jesus, 1982

Pearson (later Pearson-Pennant), P. P., Charterhouse and LMBC, 1855 (H), '57

Pearson, S. V., (Highgate), Manchester GS and Emm., 1898

Pellew, H. E., Eton and 3 Trin., 1849ii

Penney, A. G. W., Repton and Pemb., 1921

Pennington, D., Bath Coll. and Caius, 1896, '97

Penrose, C. T., Rugby and 1 Trin., 1837 (L), '38 (L), '39

Penrose, F. C., Winchester and Magd., 1840–42

Perfitt, R. J. L., KCS, Wimbledon, and Trin. H., 1937

Perkins, F. H. T., Shrewsbury and St Cath., 1974 (I–G)

Perrins, D. J. D., Dauntsey's and Jesus, 1946

Perrott, W. H. W., Private and 1 Trin., 1885

Phelps, E. L., Wimbledon and Sid. S., 1870, '71

Phillips, A. G., City of London Sch. and Jesus, 1979, '80, '81

Phillips, E. A., Shrewsbury and Jesus, 1875

Phillips, I. H., Winchester and 1 & 3 Trin., 1944 (W)

Phillpotts, G. J. O., St Paul's and Clare, 1970 (I–G), '71

Philp, B. M., Bryanston and Dow., 1982

Pigott, E. V., Marlborough and CCC, 1864, '65

Pike, L. G., Highgate and Caius, 1876–78

Pilkington, C. G. W., Winchester and 1 & 3 Trin., 1943 (W)

Pinckney, W. J., Rugby and 1 Trin., 1868

Pitchford, J. A., Tonbridge and Chr., 1957, '58

Pitman, F. I., Eton and 3 Trin., 1884–86

Pitt, G. H., Latymer Upper Sch. and Clare, 1977 (I–G), '79 (I–G)

Playford, H. B., St Paul's and Jesus, 1920–22

Pollock, A. B., Westminster and 3 Trin., 1842

Pollock, J. C., Eton and 3 Trin., 1842 (H)

Pooley, A. H., Charterhouse and 1 & 3 Trin., 1966 (I–G), '67 (I–G)

Potts, H. J., Wilton and 2 Trin., 1845 (H)

Powell, A. F. U., Tiffin and St Cath., 1974 (I–G), '75

Powell, C. S., St Paul's and Dow., 1967 (I–G), '68, '69

Powell, E. W., Eton and 3 Trin., 1906–08

Powell, J. H. C., Eton and 3 Trin., 1935

Powell, R. V., Eton and 3 Trin., 1904–06, '06 (*v.* Harvard)

Prest, E. H., Durham and Jesus, 1878–80

Price, S. R. M., Westminster and 1 & 3 Trin., 1960

Prideaux, W. A., Eton and 3 Trin., 1930, '31

Prior, R. D., Bedford and Qu., 1880

Proby, H., Cheam and 2 Trin., 1849i

Proffit, G. M. A., Lancaster RGS and Fitz., 1968 (I–G), '69 (I–G)

Prosser, N. D. K., Haileybury and Qu., 1980 (I–G)

Pumphrey, C. J., Winchester and Magd., 1957

Purcell, R. B. A., Shrewsbury and Pemb., 1965 (I–G)

Ramsay, D. A., Latymer Upper Sch. and St Cath., 1944 (W)

Randolph, E. S. L., Westminster and 3 Trin., 1870–72

Ranking, J. M., Cheltenham and Pemb., 1931, '32

Raven, J., Shrewsbury and Magd., 1844 (T)

Read, C. S., Radley and 1 Trin., 1872–74

Reddaway, J. H., Oundle and Fitz., 1967 (I–G), '68

Redfern, T. M., Shrewsbury and Fitz., 1969

Reeve, A. S., Brighton and Selw., 1930

Rennie, W. B., Giggleswick and Emm., 1898

Rhodes, H. E., Eton and Jesus, 1873–76

Rhodes, J. M., Kingston GS and LMBC, 1968 (I–G), '70 (I–G)

Richards, G. H., Rugby and 1 Trin., 1861, '62

Richardson, G. C., Winchester and Magd., 1947, '48

Richardson, J., Shrewsbury and 1 Trin., 1844 (T), '45

Rickett, H. R. N., Eton and 3 Trin., 1930–32

Rickett, P. D., Eton and 1 & 3 Trin., 1958

Ridley, J. H., Eton and Jesus, 1869, '70

Ridley, J. M., Eton and Jesus, 1840–42, '42 (H)

Ridley, L. E., Eastbourne and Jesus, 1913, '14

Ritchie, A. B., RN Coll., Dartmouth, and Trin. H., 1921

Ritchie, A. M., Private and 1 Trin., 1841

Ritchie, R. B., Geelong GS and CCC, 1958

Ritson, J. A., Rugby and 1 Trin., 1914

Roberts, C. H., St Paul's and Jesus, 1872

Roberts, C. P., St Paul's and Trin. H., 1982 (I–G)

Roberts, D. J., King's Sch., Chester, and St Cath., 1965, '66 (I–G)

Robertson, S. N. S., Radley and Fitz., 1970

Robinson, G. M., Repton and Chr., 1872

Robinson, P. J., Durham and LMBC, 1975

Robinson, W. J., Winchester and Caius, 1981 (I–G)

Robson, C. M., Kingston GS and Clare, 1969

Rockel, M. D., Chiswick Sch. and LMBC, 1978 (I–G)

Rodrigues, C. J., Univ. Coll. Sch. and Jesus, 1969 (I–G), '70, '71

Rogers, H. S., Dulwich and CCC, 1971 (I–G)

Rogers, N. S., Brentwood and Jesus, 1947

Roper, H., Blundell's and Sid. S., 1913

Rosher, J. B., Charterhouse and 1 Trin., 1909–11

Ross, Sir Charles, H. A. L., Bt, Eton and 3 Trin., 1894

Ross, R. C., King's Sch., Chester, and LMBC, 1977, '78, '79

Rossiter, T. W., Bryanston and Pemb., 1976 (I–G)

Routledge, T., Allhallow's and Emm., 1879

Rowe, J. M. T., St Paul's and Pemb., 1982 (I–G)

Rowlatt, J. F., Fettes and Trin. H., 1890, '91

Roxburgh, J. R., Edinburgh Coll. and Trin. H., 1888

Royds, J., Rugby and Chr., 1842, '42 (H)

Royds, N., Rugby and 1 Trin., 1858 (H), '59, '59 (H)

Rushton, J. A., Edinburgh Academy and Emm., 1869

Russell, J. A. L., Marlborough and Clare, 1956

Russell, J. P. A., Radley and LMBC, 1965 (I–G)

Sambell, W. A. T., Melbourne GS and Pemb., 1932–34

Sanders, B. G., Cambridge County Sch. and Chr., 1943 (W)

Sanders, T. R. B., Eton and 3 Trin., 1923

Sanderson, E., Lancaster GS and CCC, 1862

Sanderson, R. H., Harrow and 1 Trin., 1899, 1900

Sandford, H., Shrewsbury and LMBC, 1879–81

Sanford, C. B., Eton and Trin. H., 1939, 1940 (W)

Sanger, H., Dunstable and LMBC, 1904, '05

Saul, D. K., Becket Sch. and Jesus, 1975 (I–G)

Savill, J. L. L., Radley and Jesus, 1938, '39

Savory, W. B., Private and 1 Trin., 1905

Schreiber, H. W., Ipswich and Trin. H., 1855 (H)

Scott, B. G. A., St Paul's and Trin. H., 1903, '04, '06 (*v.* Harvard)

Scott, J. J., Radley and CCC, 1944 (W)

Searle, D. J., Radley and St Cath., 1975 (I–G), '76, '77

Seeley, E. A., *see* Szilagyi

Selwyn, G. A., Eton and LMBC, 1829

Selwyn, J. R., Eton and 3 Trin., 1864, '66

Sergel, C. J. S., Monkton Combe and Clare, 1931–33

Serjeantson, J. J., Rugby and 1 Trin., 1857

Shadwell, A. H., Eton and LMBC, 1838 (L), '39, '40

Shafto, C. D., Durham and Jesus, 1876, '77

Sharp, S. D., Sir Wm Borlase's and LMBC, 1967 (I–G)

Sharpley, R. F. A., Shrewsbury and LMBC, 1951, '51 (*v.* Yale and Harvard), '52

Shields, H. J. S., Loretto and Jesus, 1910

Shove, R. S., Uppingham and 1 Trin., 1912, '13

Simpson, A., Bedford and Qu., 1964

Simpson, J. H., Bedford and Pemb., 1920

Skinner, C. A., Durban HS, SA, and Jesus, 1910–12

Sladen, J. M., Harrow and Trin. H., 1890

Smith, A. L., Private and 1 Trin., 1857, '58, '58 (H), '59

Smith, C. T., Private and Caius, 1854

Smith, H. T., Eton and Magd., 1939

Smith, J. H., Winchester and Caius, 1974

Smith, M. V., Eton and Trin. H., 1904

Smith, N. H. K., Royal Belfast Acad. Inst. and LMBC, 1981 (I–G)

Smith, S. P., Repton and 1 Trin., 1882

Smith, W. F., Shrewsbury and 1 Trin., 1923, '25, '26

Smyly, W. C., Harrow and 1 Trin., 1862, '63

Smyth, W. W., Westminster and 2 Trin., 1838 (L), '39

Snow (subsequently Kynaston), H., Eton and LMBC, 1856, '57

Snow, W., Eton and LMBC, 1829

Solly, W. H., Harrow and 1 Trin., 1836

Spencer, E. A. A., Rossall and 2 Trin., 1870–72

Sprague, D. B., Durham and Emm., 1973 (I–G), '74

Spurrell, R. J., Ipswich and Trin. H., 1878

Stanbury, R. G., Shrewsbury and LMBC, 1964, '65

Stancliffe, J. C. G., Harrow and Pemb., 1954

Stanley, D. N., Sir Wm Borlase's and Fitz., 1974 (I–G)

Stanley, E. S., Eton and Jesus, 1836, '38 (L), '39

Stanning, J., Rugby and 1 Trin., 1863

Steavenson, D. F., King William Coll. and Trin. H., 1864–66

Stephens, L. E., Felsted and Trin. H., 1921, '22

Stephens, R. J., King's Coll. Sch., Wimbledon, and Emm., 1980 (I–G), '81, '82

Stephenson, N. H., Radley and CCC, 1981 (I–G), '82 (I–G)

Stephenson, S. V., King's Coll., Lon., and Caius, 1853 (H), president in '54 but did not row

Stewart, F. C., Harrow and Trin H., 1895

Still, J., Winchester and Caius, 1866–69

Stobart, A. B., RN Coll., Dartmouth, and Pemb., 1924

Strachan, J. F., Norwich and Trin. H., 1870

Straker, F., Harrow and Jesus, 1884

Stuart, D. C. R., Cheltenham and Trin. H., 1906, '06 (*v.* Harvard), '07, '08, '08 (O), '09

Sturge, D. P., Radley and LMBC, 1973

Suess, F. F. F., Hampton and Pet., 1975 (I–G)

Sulley, A. L., Denstone and Selw., 1928, '29

Sulley, J. S., Radley and Selw., 1958, '59

Sullivan, B. A., King's Sch., Chester, and Selw., 1971

Sullivan, T. J., Oundle and Clare, 1946

Summers, P. T., St Peter's, York, and CCC, 1970 (I–G), '71 (I–G)

Swann, A., Rugby and Trin. H., 1919 (P), '19 (AP), '20

Swann, S., Marlborough and Trin. H., 1883–85

Swann, S. E., Rugby and Trin. H., 1911–14

Swanston, A. W., Loretto and Jesus, 1898

Swanston, H. E., Loretto and Jesus, 1909

Swartwout, R. E., Middx, Concord, USA, and 1 Trin., 1930

Sweeney, M. A., Becket Sch. and LMBC, 1965, '66

Swithinbank, K. S., Oundle and Sid. S., 1975 (I–G), '76 (I–G)

Symonds, N. P., Hereford and LMBC, 1885, '86

Symonds, R. A., Bedford and LMBC, 1928

Symonds, R. H. H., Bedford and LMBC, 1931

Symonds-Tayler, R. H., Hereford and Trin. H., 1888, '89

Szilagyi (later Seeley), E. A., St Paul's and Jesus, 1935

Tanburn, J. W., Charterhouse and Jesus, 1954

Tarleton, W. H., Dedham and LMBC, 1861

Taylor, C. H. S., Rugby and Caius, 1905

Taylor, C. W. H., Eton and 3 Trin., 1901–03

Taylor, E. J. D., Bath Coll. and Caius, 1897

Taylor, S. B., Dr Pinckney's, Sheen, and 1 Trin., 1840

Tebay, M. D., KCS, Wimbledon, and 1 & 3 Trin., 1966, '67 (I–G)

Thomas, G. E. C., Shrewsbury and Jesus, 1946

Thomas, P. H., Eton and 3 Trin., 1902–05

Thomas, R. D., Hereford Cath. Sch. and LMBC, 1965 (I–G)

Thompson, R. J. M., Radley and Pemb., 1957

Thompson, W. T., Ruthin and Jesus, 1829

Thompson-McCausland, B. M. P., Eton and 1 & 3 Trin., 1959

Thomson, G. L., Univ. Coll. Sch. and Trin. H., 1909

Tollemache, J. N. L., Eton and 1 & 3 Trin., 1962

Tomkinson, H. R., Rugby and 1 Trin., 1853 (H)

Tourek, S. C., Dartmouth, USA, and 1 & 3 Trin., 1973, '75

Tower, F. E., Harrow and LMBC, 1842, '42 (H)

Tower, G. E., Eton and 3 Trin., 1913, '14

Tozer, R. E., Winchester and 1 & 3 Trin., 1965 (I–G)

Tozer, S. G. D., Winchester and 1 & 3 Trin., 1955

Tubbs, S. K., Shrewsbury and Caius, 1925–27

Tuckey, H. E., RFGS, Marlborough, and LMBC, 1851 (H), '52

Tumber, N. R., Winchester and Emm., 1966 (I–G)

Turnbull, J., Geelong GS and Clare, 1939

Turnbull, T., Shrewsbury and Magd., 1979 (I–G)

Turnbull, T. S., Private and Trin. H., 1873

Turnbull, W. M., Geelong GS and Clare, 1940 (W)

Turner, A. M., Cranleigh and CCC, 1938, '39

Tyndale Biscoe, C. E., Bradford and Jesus, 1884

Upcher, A. W., Private and 2 Trin., 1836

Uppleby, G. C., Shrewsbury and Magd., 1840

Uralli, S. S., Galatasay, Turkey, and 1 & 3 Trin., 1943 (W)

Utley, A. N., Shrewsbury and Jesus, 1965 (I–G)

Van der Byl, P. V. G., Diocesan Coll., Rondebosch, SA, and Pemb., 1911

Venables, H., Rugby and Jesus, 1844 (T)

Vernon, J. J., Radley and Trin. H., 1955

Vialls, C. M., Westminster and 3 Trin., 1840, '41, '42 (H)

Vincent, G. T., Harvard Univ. and Magd., 1968 (I–G)

Vincent, S., St Paul's and 1 Trin., 1847 (H)

Waddington, W. H., Rugby and 2 Trin., 1849i

Walker, D. J., Bootham and Clare, 1974

Waller, E. H. M., Highgate and CCC, 1893

Wallis, J. A. N., Bryanston and LMBC, 1953, '54

Walmsley, J., Uppingham and Trin. H., 1886

Walmsley, R., Fettes and Qu., 1962

Wansbrough, A. G., Eton and King's, 1925

Ward, M. G., Charterhouse and Qu., 1969 (I–G)

Ward, R. G., Charterhouse and Qu., 1965, '66

Ward, W. Dudley, *see* Dudley Ward

Wardle, D. B. J., Hereford and LMBC, 1945 (W)

Wardrop, J. E. G., Shrewsbury and Jesus, 1940 (W)

Warlow, W. M., Monmouth GS and Qu., 1880

Warner, T. D., CEGS, Melbourne, and Trin. H., 1868

Warren, C., Hammersmith and 2 Trin., 1829

Warriner, M. H., Harrow and 1 Trin., 1928–30

Wasbrough, C. H. S., Radley and Trin. H., 1902

Waterer, R. A., Radley and Sid. S., 1977, '78 (I–G), '79 (I–G)

Waters III, S. R., Pennsylvania Univ. and 1 & 3 Trin., 1971

Watkins-Ball, C. J., Witwatersrand Univ., SA, and Jesus, 1965 (I–G)

Watney, H., Rugby and LMBC, 1865–67

Watson, H. S., Manchester GS and Pemb., 1864

Watson, R. J. N., Berkhamsted and LMBC, 1976 (I–G)

Watson, S. V., Berkhamsted and Dow., 1978 (I–G)

Watson, W., Private and Jesus, 1842, '42 (H)

Watson-Taylor, J. A., Eton and Magd., 1878, '81

Wauchope, D. A., Repton and Trin. H., 1895

Webb, P. J., Monkton Combe and Qu., 1963

Webber, M. O'K., King's Sch., Canterbury, and Jesus, 1973

Wedd, E. P. W., Cheltenham and Caius, 1905

Wells, M. P., Aylesbury GS and Selw., 1975 (I–G), '76

Welsh, I. W., Shrewsbury and Qu., 1956

Weston, R. J., Dulwich and Selw., 1960, '61

Wharton, R., Eton and Magd., 1857, '58

Wheare, H. J. H., Magd. Sch. and Jesus, 1973 (I–G), '74

Wheeler, B. J. C., King's Sch., Canterbury, and Pemb., 1979 (I–G)

Wheeler, R. N., Clifton and Sid. S., 1933

Whitney, T. W., Dartmouth Coll., USA, and Jesus, 1980

Whitworth, M. D., Shrewsbury and LMBC, 1944 (W), '45 (W)

Wiggins, F. P. T., Univ. Coll. Sch. and LMBC, 1960

Wigglesworth, C. J., Bryanston and Jesus, 1980, '81

Wilder, E., Eton and Magd., 1846

Williams, E. G., Eton and 3 Trin., 1908, '08 (O), '09, '10

Williams, H., Marlborough and LMBC, 1855 (H), '56, '58, '59

Williams, M., Culford Sch. and Fitz., 1974 (I–G)

Williams, M. D., Oundle and Trin. H., 1972 (I–G), '73

Wilson, D. J., Melbourne GS and Clare, 1934

Wilson, G., Charterhouse and 1 Trin., 1885

Wilson, J. B., Giggleswick and Pemb., 1863

Wilson, J. H. T., Shrewsbury and Pemb, 1934–36

Winckless, R. N., Tiffin and Fitz., 1967–69

Windham, W. A. D., Bedford and Chr., 1947, '51, '51 (*v.* Yale and Harvard)

Wingfield, W., Rossall and 1 Trin., 1855 (H), '56

Winthrop-Smith, B. R., Eton and 3 Trin., 1905

Withers, P. N., St Peter's, York, and 1 & 3 Trin., 1977 (I–G), '78 (I–G)

Wolstenholme, E. P., Halifax and 1 Trin., 1846, '47 (H)

Wood, J. G., Private and Emm., 1868

Woodhouse, H., Manchester GS and Trin. H., 1881

Woodhouse, J. W., Shrewsbury and Selw., 1978 (I–G), '80

Wool-Lewis, C. E., Westminster and 3 Trin., 1929

Wooton, J. D., Malvern and Pet., 1979 (I–G)

Worlidge, E. J., Marlborough and LMBC, 1951, '51 (*v.* Yale and Harvard)

Wotherspoon, T. A., Shrewsbury and 1 & 3 Trin., 1943 (W), '44 (W)

Wray, J. C., King's Coll., Lon., and 2 Trin., 1849i, and Clare '49ii

Wright, J., Westminster and LMBC, 1854

Wylie, R. B. F., Shrewsbury and Clare, 1933

Yarrow, R. D., Durham and LMBC, 1966 (I–G), '67

Yatman, W. H., Winchester and Caius, 1838 (L), '39

Young, F. J., Leeds GS and Chr., 1869

Yuncken, T. F., Melbourne Univ. and Pemb., 1974

Bibliography

Boat Race histories (in order of publication)

W. F. MacMichael, *Oxford and Cambridge Boat Races*, Deighton Bell, 1870.

George G. T. Treherne and J. H. D. Goldie, *Record of the University Boat Race 1829–1888*, Bickers and Son (first published 1883 and updated).

Wadham, Peacock, *The Story of the Inter-University Boat Race*, Grant Richards, 1900.

C. M. Pitman, *The Record of the University Boat Race*, T. Fisher Unwin, 1909.

G. C. Drinkwater and T. R. B. Sanders, *The University Boat Race Official Centenary History* (commemorative edition has biographies of all blues to 1900), Cassell, 1929.

William Wimbledon Hill, *One Hundred Years of Boat Racing* (official centenary souvenir, 1829–1929), The Albion Publishing Co., 1929.

G. C. Drinkwater, *The Boat Race*, Blackie & Son, 1939.

Richard Burnell, *The Oxford and Cambridge Boat Race 1829–1953*, OUP, 1954.

Gordon Ross, *The Boat Race*, The Sportsman's Book Club, 1956.

Richard Burnell, *One Hundred and Fifty Years of the Oxford and Cambridge Boat Race* (an official history), Precision Press/Guinness, 1979; with supplement, 1980.

Mainly Oxford

'A. Don', *Lays of Modern Oxford*, A. Thomas Shrimpton & Son, 1887.

Max Beerbohm, *Zuleika Dobson*, Heinemann, 1911.

Boating Life at Oxford, James Hogg & Son, 1868.

Gilbert C. Bourne, *Memories of an Eton Wet-bob of the Seventies*, OUP, 1933.

Rev. Edward Bradley (Cuthbert Bede), *Adventures of Mr Verdant Green, An Oxford Freshman 1853–57)*, James Blackwood, 1900.

T. A. Cook, *The Sunlit Hours*, Nisbet, 1925.

Anne Clark, *The Real Alice*, Michael Joseph, 1981.

Charles Dickens Jr, *Dickens's Dictionary of the Thames*, Macmillan, 1885.

H. R. A. 'Jumbo' Edwards, *The Way of a Man with a Blade*, Routledge & Kegan Paul, 1963

Lewis R. Farnell, *An Oxonian Looks Back*, Martin Hopkinson, 1934.

A. P. Garland, *A Yank at Oxford*, Collins, 1938.

E. A. Greening Lambourn, *The Book of Oxford*, British Medical Association, 1936.

Thomas Hughes, *Tom Brown at Oxford*, Macmillan, 1861.

F. V. Morley, *River Thames from Source to Mouth*, Harper & Bros., 1926.

Beverley Nichols, *Oxford–London–Hollywood*, Jonathan Cape, 1931.

'Gully' G. O. Nickalls, *A Rainbow in the Sky*, Chatto & Windus, 1974.

Guy Nickalls, *Life's a Pudding*, Faber & Faber, 1939.

Mary Prior, *Fisher Row* (fishermen, bargemen and canal boatmen in Oxford 1500–1900), OUP, 1982.

Sir A. T. Quiller-Couch ('Q'), *Memories and Opinions*, CUP, 1944.

Rev. W. E. Sherwood, *Oxford Rowing*, OUP, 1900.

Ann Thwaite (ed.), *My Oxford*, Robson Books, 1977.

David Winser, 'The Boat Race Murder' (1942), from *Great Stories from the World of Sport*, vol. 2, Simon & Schuster, 1958.

W. B. Woodgate, *Reminiscences of an Old Sportsman*, Eveleigh Nash, 1909.

Mainly Cambridge

H. Armytage, *The Cam and Cambridge Rowing*, Spalding, c. 1886.

G. T. Atchison and G. C. Brown, *The History of Christ's College Boat Club*, Spalding, 1922.

Henry Bond, *A History of the Trinity Hall BC*, W. Heffer & Sons, 1930; additional volume updating to 1949 by J. Timothy Gann.

Frederick Brittain, *It's A Don's Life*, Heinemann, 1972.

F. Brittain, *A Short History of Jesus College*, Heffer, 1940.

F. Brittain and H. B. Playford, *The Jesus College BC*, W. Heffer & Sons, 1928.

James Douglas, *Rowing on the Cam*, Bird's Farm Publications, 1977.

Kenneth Duffield, *Savages and Kings*, Macdonald, 1945.

R. H. Forster, *Down by the River, A Rowing Man's Miscellany* (pieces from the *Eagle*), E. Johnson, Cambridge, 1901.

T. R. Glover, *Cambridge Retrospect*, CUP, 1943.

The Granta Rowing Centenary Number, 25 February 1927.

David Haig-Thomas, *I Leap Before I Look*, Putnam, 1936.

Ian Hay, *A Man's Man*, William Blackwood & Sons, 1912.

The History of the Lady Margaret BC, 1825–1926, The Johnian Society; vol. 2: *1926–1956*, The Johnian Society.

R. C. Lehmann, *Anni Fugaces*, Bodley Head, 1901.

R. C. Lehmann, *In Cambridge Courts*, Henry, *c.* 1896.

Shane Leslie, *The Cantab*, Chatto & Windus, 1926.

M. B. Maltby, *Pembroke College Cambridge BC*, R. Ackrill, 1981.

Magdalene BC, 1828–1928, Magdalene College Association, 1930.

F. A. Reeve, *Cambridge from the River*, Newton & Denny.

W. W. Rouse Ball, *A History of First Trinity BC*, Bowes & Bowes, 1908.

Louis T. Stanley, *The Cambridge Year*, Chatto & Windus, 1960.

Leslie Stephen, *Sketches from Cambridge*, OUP, 1932.

R. E. Swartwout, *Rhymes of the River*, Heffer, 1927.

Mainly Harvard and Yale

S. Crowther and A. Ruhl, *Rowing and Track Athletics*, Macmillan, 1905.

John DeGange, '100 Years of Yale–Harvard Rowing', *The New London Day* (serial), 1952.

Robert F. Herrick (ed.), *Red Top*, Harvard University Press, 1948.

Robert F. Kelley, *American Rowing*, G. P. Putnam's Sons, 1932.

Joseph J. Mathews, *George W. Smalley*, University of North Carolina Press, 1973.

Thomas C. Mendenhall, *Have Oar, Will Travel*, Yale Crew Association, 1956 (history of the Yale crew, 1956).

Ralph D. Paine, *The Stroke Oar*, Charles Scribner's Sons, 1911.

Waldron Kintzling Post, *Harvard Stories*, G. P. Putnam's Sons, 1908.

General

Martin Cobbett, *Sporting Notions*, Sands, 1908.

Martin Cobbett, *Wayfaring Notions*, Sands, 1906.

T. A. Cook, *Rowing at Henley*, OUP, 1919.

Christopher Dodd, *Henley Royal Regatta*, Stanley Paul, 1981.

R. C. Lehmann, *The Complete Oarsman*, Methuen, 1908.

R. C. Lehmann, *Rowing*, A. D. Innes (Isthmian Library), 1897.

R. C. Lehmann, *Sportsmen and Others*, G. Bell & Sons.

Thomas C. Mendenhall, *A Short History of American Rowing*, Charles River Books, 1981.

John Ed. Morgan MD, *University Oars*, Macmillan, 1873.

R. T. Rivington, *Punts and Punting*, R. T. Rivington, 1982.

A. T. W. Shadwell, *The Principles of Rowing and Steering*, Slatter & Rose, *c.* 1857.

Anthony Trollope (ed.), *British Sports and Pastimes*, Virtue, Spalding, *c.* 1868.

Caspar W. Whitney, *A Sporting Pilgrimage to Oxford, Cambridge and the Shires*, McIlvaine, 1895.

L. S. Wood and H. L. Burrows, *Sports and Pastimes in English Literature*, Nelson, 1925.

W. B. Woodgate, *Boating*, Longmans Green (Badminton Library), 1889.

Index